Published by the Arizona Daily Star,
a Lee Enterprises Newspaper,
Tucson, Arizona 2009

ISBN 10: 1-4392-5993-3

Cover photo illustration: David Sanders, 2009
Book design: Dylan McKinley

To Debby and my wonderful sons,
Ben, Jake and Ty.

**Coach makes his point:** "You're wrong," UA football coach John Mackovic tells Greg Hansen outside the locker room after a loss to Arizona State in 2002.

# Table of contents

# Acknowledgments

In the process of planning, producing and printing this book, Shannon Conner batted cleanup, played without error and pitched flawlessly in long relief. She won the Triple Crown.

Once she presented the idea of assembling this book, I only heard eight words: "I'm going to see that it gets done." I knew she would. In the newspaper business she is what the baseball writers call a clutch hitter.

Old Reliable.

Over the 14-month period required to complete this project, Shannon served as sports editor of the Daily Star (estimated average workweek: 60 hours), became pregnant and had a baby boy (Pre Conner Simonson) and did whatever necessary to help her husband, Scott, through his final year of law school.

I think she took a day of vacation once, too.

She was savvy enough to enlist the editing skills of former Star sports editor Mark Stewart, a pro among pros, whose diligence and intuition have set him apart from the day I met him in 1981. With Mark on the job, there would be no apprehension.

My youngest son, Tyler, was drafted as a troubleshooter. He did the heavy lifting and made sure the trains ran on time. Much like Shannon, Tyler was occupied elsewhere during this project, yet didn't let it chip away at the quality. Tyler completed degree requirements at the UA, worked four days a week in the sports department and was a selfless caregiver to his brother, Ben, disabled with a stroke.

The Lord truly smiled upon me the day Tyler was born, May 8, 1981, in Albany, Ore. Somewhere in heaven, his mother is smiling.

The Star's capable in-house team of Dylan McKinley, Mike Rice, Angela Pittenger and Jayne O'Sullivan were helpful and supportive in everything from design to archiving. Thank you so much.

I am forever indebted to many former editors who showed me the light, especially Star editor Bobbie Jo Buel. I'll never be able to repay Kurt McGregor, bless his soul, from my hometown paper in Logan, Utah. He gave me my first job and died, tragically, at 29 of Lou Gehrig's disease. Bob Chick, a gifted writer and terrific human being, got me through my Tampa Bay Buccaneers days with a minimum of damage.

John Buchner of the Albany Democrat-Herald, former editor and publisher, helped me more than he'll ever know.

Along the way, I have been blessed to work with (and learn from) many wonderful colleagues, especially those at the Star. I so enjoyed working with Chuck Kramer, Jack Magruder, Jim Elsleger, Jay Gonzales, Mike Downs, Jon Wilner, Javier Morales, Anthony Gimino, the Finley twins, Ryan and Pat, Glen Crevier, David Sanders, Bruce Pascoe, Bob Christ, James Bennett, Tom Heleba, Dave Ord, Myles Standish, Jeff Jackson, Dave Eubank and especially those who gave me a chance in Tucson, Sam Pollak and Steve Wilson.

When I was a kid, the first thing I did every morning was grab the Salt Lake Tribune from my driveway to read what sports columnist John Mooney wrote. After college, working at the rival newspaper in Salt Lake, I asked John if he ever thought of putting his columns into a book.

"You got a pair of scissors?" he asked with his typical biting wit. "Come to the office. I've got a whole pile of newspapers. You can make your own book."

Thank you to all the people who provided the scissors for this book.

# Foreword

*By Tyler Hansen*

I was sent to the principal's office only once in school, the most unlikely of fates for a play-by-the-rules twerp like me. I never lashed out, never caused my teachers any real distress. Sometimes, though, defending your family's honor supersedes good behavior, and — the way I saw it as an eighth-grader in 1994 — certain offenses must be met with vengeance.

So when some kid drew a mustache, devil horns and the word "DORK" in big, red letters on my dad's photo in the Arizona Daily Star, I picked a fight. It was more of a shouting match than anything, but I made sure the kid knew that Greg Hansen's son would not tolerate the family insults. I'm sure I even said something typical of a quick-witted teenager, a quip along the lines of, "YOUR dad is the dork!"

Being the son of the Arizona Daily Star's sports columnist sometimes provides interesting moments like that. Some people in Tucson recognize the Hansen name, and my brothers — Ben and Jake — and I often get quizzed about it. The conversation invariably goes something like this:

"Say, are you related to that sportswriter Hansen?" people ask.

"Yeah, he's our dad," we'll say.

"I read his stuff all the time. He usually doesn't know what the hell he's talking about, but I enjoy what he's done over the years."

Such is the premise for this book, a compilation of Greg Hansen's Arizona Daily Star columns from the past 27 years, works that countless readers have enjoyed and that stand as the definitive account of the modern era of Southern Arizona sports and sports people.

My dad would be the first to shoot down any suggestion that he holds the slightest place of importance in the Tucson sports community. In the early 1990s, a member of our old church asked if he would sign an autograph for the bishop's young son. My dad laughed uneasily at the idea for a few minutes before finally relenting and signing a copy of one of his columns. The word "celebrity" doesn't quite fit, but his impact on this town's athletic identity — however minor or significant — is certainly real.

Our family moved to Tucson from Oregon in the fall of 1981, a few months after I was born. My dad was contacted about an opening on the Star sports staff by his college friend Steve Wilson, who was then the assistant sports editor. Sports editor Sam Pollak initially assigned my dad to cover University of Arizona football and baseball, and then he took over the sports columnist job in August 1983. Since then, his views on everything from UA sports to the Super Bowl to World Wrestling Entertainment have stirred the passions of his most loyal readers and most vocal critics. Whenever there is news in the Tucson sports world, the thought that inevitably runs through the minds of thousands of people is, "I wonder what Hansen will have to say about this in the morning."

This may all sound like typical hyperbole coming from the guy's son, but he has a permanent place in the fabric of the local sports community. He was inducted into the Pima County Sports Hall of Fame in 2004, an honor given to those who have made a lasting contribution to and helped cultivate Southern Arizona's athletic progress. It's rare company: In a county of more than 1 million people, only 268 have been enshrined thus far. That day, he was inducted alongside UA basketball legend Steve Kerr. My dad had never been so cool, standing on the same stage as my childhood hero as they accepted identical awards. His dork status was officially gone.

Moments in the spotlight often have a way of making my dad somewhat uneasy, and his hall of fame induction that October was a good example. In the weeks leading up to the ceremony at the UA Student Union, he lamented having to give a speech in front of a big audience. I secretly wondered if anyone would heckle him on his walk to the stage. But the man who introduced him that day — Brad Tolson, a World War II-era baseball star at Tucson High School and Arizona — broke the ice perfectly with a wisecrack that sums up the hot-and-cold feeling some readers have toward newspaper columnists.

"I played baseball for Tucson High and the Wildcats about 35 years before Greg Hansen came to town," Tolson said. "I really can't decide whether I'm disappointed or fortunate to not have been critiqued by Greg."

My dad's start in the newspaper business was as far from hall-of-fame-worthy as possible. He was a junior cornerback on the varsity football team at Logan (Utah) High School when he broke his collarbone in practice. He had nothing to do but stand on the sidelines the rest of the year, so the sports editor at the Logan Herald Journal — who knew my dad was taking a journalism class — asked if he would be a correspondent for all Logan High football games. There was no money involved, but my dad got to see his name in print, and he did a fine enough job to be asked to work during the basketball and baseball seasons, too. My dad declined the offer at first, telling his editor, Gary Rawlings, that he was a member of both of those teams.

"That's OK," Rawlings said. "Your coaches tell me you're not one of the main players."

Hardly glorious, but sportswriting stuck. It was certainly easier than the get-your-hands-dirty work he did 10 hours a day at my grandpa's service station, pumping gas and fixing tires. There was another perk, too, even if it was somewhat less ethical: shameless self-promotion. A few years back, he found a shoe box filled with some of his 1960s game stories from the Herald Journal, and he noticed an embarrassing theme in all of them.

"There was always a paragraph right at the bottom, without fail, that said, 'Greg Hansen came off the bench to score three points,' or, 'Hansen got hit by a pitch in the sixth inning,'" he later confessed.

Luckily, his writing style evolved. His career took him from Salt Lake City, to Tampa, Fla., to Albany, Ore., and finally to Tucson. Along the way he has won about a dozen Sportswriter of the Year and Sports Columnist of the Year awards in the various states. He fielded offers over the years to leave Tucson and work in major, pro-sports markets in California and Ohio, among other places. But the Old Pueblo struck a chord early in his tenure at the Star, and he turned the task of chronicling the town's sports history into his life's work.

When he arrived in Tucson, he didn't recognize a single name in the local athletic community except that of then-UA men's basketball coach Fred Snowden. There was no foundation to work from, so he built it with what readers praise him for most: his meticulous research. He scoured the archives for clippings by esteemed Star sports editor and columnist Abe Chanin, who is the authority on UA and Tucson sports, 1920-1970 division. He soon gained a feel for the landscape and, since then, has traveled to every conceivable corner of Southern Arizona, writing about rodeo barrel racers in Marana, high school baseball coaches in St. David, men's softball players in Tumacacori — and on and on. Good stories are everywhere, and he has been willing to follow all leads, even if it meant driving to a Motel 6 in Gila Bend in January for a story on Dallas Cowboys fans.

My dad's is a career highlighted by covering icons like Lute Olson, Tiger Woods and Carl Lewis, but the columns that seem to resonate most with readers are the ones about the off-Broadway characters whose local stories leave a permanent mark. In October 1999, he wrote about a wide receiver at Sahuaro High School, Calvin Dacus, whose childhood was stained by a broken home, a slew of foster homes and a nightmarish military academy. Dacus' rise to self-sufficiency and football stardom — he still holds Arizona records for receptions in a season and career — was a tribute to his unyielding desire to make something of himself in the face of disadvantages. My dad's story about him hits you with emotion, a thud right to the chest in the first few paragraphs:

*When Calvin Dacus receives his college papers in a few months, he will fill it out like this: Mom: in jail. Dad: disappeared. Guardian: dead. Family: a sister in California. Address: unsure.*

I walked into the Star newsroom the day before the Dacus column was published, and copy editor Tom Heleba called me over to his desk.

"Your dad just wrote a classic," he told me. "It's one of the best stories I've ever read." (You can find it in Chapter three.)

It was strange hearing those words come from someone else. Growing up, I always considered my dad to be the best writer, much the same way a kid thinks his dad can beat up anyone, or his mom makes the world's best pancakes. I often thought my dad could do no wrong as a writer and — typical of a simple-minded youngster — believed that his opinion was gospel. After all, there it was every morning in black-and-white newsprint.

That skewed belief made for a peculiar situation for my brothers and me with regard to Arizona basketball when we were kids. We had season tickets at McKale Center beginning with the holiest-of-holy seasons, 1987-88, and cheered on Kerr, Sean Elliott and The Gumbies with as much fervor as anyone in town. Nevertheless, our dad had a prickly relationship with coach Lute Olson. My brothers and I weren't about to abandon our love for Lute's team, but family honor beckoned again, so we told our dad we were on his side. Then again, he was our dad — we didn't really have a choice.

If Arizona State hadn't been so inept against the UA in Lute's tenure, losing to the Wildcats 43 of 49 times, then maybe the coach wouldn't have viewed my dad as his biggest in-state rival. Their "feud" became a local news item once or twice over the years. Because Lute was widely hailed as "Saint Lute" — the most revered person in Tucson sports history — even my dad's slightest criticisms of the coach were viewed as blasphemy by a number of Wildcat fans. Lute, by most accounts, was untouchable. His teams achieved unprecedented success, with Final Four trips and Pac-10 titles and NBA draftees by the handful, so the fans' off-the-charts adoration of Lute was mostly warranted. It's the reason an entire chapter of this book is devoted to columns on him. No sports figure has had an impact on Tucson like he did, and the success of the UA basketball program undeniably raised my dad's profile.

Their paths to prominence — one of whose was decidedly more prominent than the other's — were coincidentally linked: My dad became the columnist about 90 days before Lute coached his first game with the Wildcats. In his tenure from 1983 to 2007, Lute coached the UA in 776 games, and my dad was on press row for at least 750 of them, including No. 1 and No. 776.

I love hearing my dad talk about Lute. His voice picks up a little each time, signaling the fact that, hey, this guy is Big Time. (Many of his best columns focus on Lute, so his amplified delivery in retelling a story is fitting.) My dad has an endless supply of anecdotes about being on the road with the venerable coach, each one offering a small glimpse into the "human" side of an immortalized icon. My favorite: While in Europe for the World Championships in 1986, my dad and the Tucson Citizen's Jack Rickard went to lunch with Lute and his Team USA assistant coaches at — of all places — a Wendy's in Paris. Lute, the man whose everlasting image is one of designer suits and perfectly coiffed hair, was walking while eating a cheeseburger when a glob of ketchup and mustard landed all over the front of his shirt. A few days later, Lute reassumed his usual image of excellence as he coached Elliott and a dozen other future NBA players to the gold medal, America's first since 1954, in a win over the favored Soviet Union with the Cold War serving as a backdrop.

No one tells a Lute Olson story like my dad, and that's precisely what led to their disputes over the years. My dad's contention is that Lute was unreasonably sensitive to any type of criticism for most of the 1990s, a decade that featured one national championship, two Final Four trips, five conference titles and 26 wins per season. It was also sprinkled with four first-round flameouts in the NCAA tournament. When my dad and others accurately reported that UA players Damon Stoudamire and Reggie Geary used the word "choke" to describe a loss to 15th-seeded Santa Clara in 1993, Lute kept it bookmarked. The Cats made the Final Four the next season, and in the post-game press conference after the Elite Eight win, the coach ripped the media for a half-hour for unjustifiably labeling his team "chokers."

The Olson-Hansen "saga" was at its peak in the early 1990s. My dad questioned Lute's saintly image on occasion with critiques that would make the intimidating coach seethe. One column in particular, in which my dad chided him for being unavailable to his players during a time of crisis in 1991, prompted a 1,180-word written response from Lute that ran on the Star's front page. His influence in this town was never more apparent. The newsroom was flooded with calls and letters from angry fans who wanted my dad's head on a platter, right next to his letter of resignation. Lute vowed to never speak to him again, and he didn't for many years, except begrudgingly when my dad had the gall to ask him questions in press conferences. In his 2006 autobiography, "Lute! The Seasons of My Life," the coach called it "an unpleasant situation for everybody."

Their relationship became amiable again in 2001, shortly after Lute's first wife, Bobbi, died of ovarian cancer. Even through the most

9

divisive times for the coach and columnist, she always treated my dad with respect. My entire perception of the rift with Lute changed in 1993 when my dad and I ran into Bobbi at a Safeway in the Foothills area. I stopped dead in my tracks as she walked toward us. I halfway expected her to ram her grocery cart into his knees. After all, how do you treat the man who calls your husband a "grouch" in the newspaper for all of Tucson to see?

Very politely, apparently.

Bobbi said hello and asked how we were, then went on her way. I was floored, and then I realized how petty sports "conflicts" can be. Was it ever really that big of a deal? Bobbi didn't seem to think so, and her actions taught me a new way to defend family honor: Stay above the fray.

Before she died on New Year's Day 2001, Bobbi orchestrated the resolution between Lute and my dad. She asked Lute to make amends with his media nemesis, and so he did.

One day, my dad's phone rang.

"Hello?" he answered.

"Please hold for Coach Olson," said Lute's longtime secretary, Monica Armenta.

Talk about your all-time out-of-left-field moments.

Lute invited my dad to come to his office for a talk, where they swept the bad feelings under the rug and agreed to start from scratch. They had a couple more bumpy moments in their time working alongside one another, but when the coach retired in October 2008, my dad reminisced about what it meant to cover the most successful figure in Tucson sports history, a man he once described in a column as "a cross between Cary Grant and John Wayne: Large. In Charge."

"You couldn't ask for a better person to write about," he told my brothers and me last winter. "He was intimidating. He was gruff. He was charming. His teams were relevant every week for a quarter-century. That's unheard of. Tucson had it so good for so long. There won't ever be anyone else like Lute."

Because of Lute's unparalleled success and lengthy tenure, my dad wrote about him more than probably any other two people combined, but that does not begin to define his career as the Star's most widely read columnist. His trademark, the thing people will best remember him for his Sunday Notebook. It's a column of dozens of items on Tucson-area sports, popularly referred to as "Sunday's short stuff" for many years. I can't begin to estimate the number of times people, even complete strangers, have told me how much they love reading my dad's Sunday notes column, that it's the first thing they do that morning and often the only article they read in the Sunday paper. (Sorry, colleagues.)

It is the primary source from which the community gets its sports news, and it's been that way for nearly three decades. The Sunday notes column is how former residents stay connected to Tucson, and it's the main outlet for people to have their stories/news/feats publicized. The most impressive thing is the networking system my dad has established to attain the mountains of information — all of it fresh and much of it of an "insider" nature — he prints on a weekly basis. When the UA decided to retire Sean Elliott's jersey number, the first place anyone heard about it was in Sunday's short stuff. When Mike Candrea was announced as America's Olympic softball coach, my dad broke the news in his notebook.

The idea of it sounds ludicrous for a writer from little ol' Tucson, but his expansive readership literally spans the globe. If some former high school distance runner wins a prominent race in Bangladesh, he'll get an e-mail about it the next day. It's unreal. His finger is on the pulse of everything.

The Sunday notes are wholly unique from all of his other columns. Although they offer the same adept, pertinent and witty commentary as his other works, they are often so time-specific that they lose some of their context after a while. That's why you won't find any examples of his notebook in this book.

The most enjoyment I get working and living alongside my dad the columnist comes from another one of his trademark items: the Top 100 Southern Arizona Sports Figures list. It runs on the last Sunday of December every year, a project so good that it feels like you found one more present hiding under the Christmas tree. The best part is that it's a yearlong challenge. I ask my dad every couple months, "Who's your No. 1 right now?" And then we'll rattle off 20 names that deserve to be near the top, only to reshuffle everything a few months later. The final list is only one man's opinion, done out of pure fun, but people take it to heart. I know of a few standout athletes who have made the list and include it on their résumés. "Ranked No. 34 on Greg Hansen's Top 100 list in 2002." Seriously.

No one — literally, no one — has done more than my dad to shed a glimmer of glory on the athletes and teams who call Tucson home. The Sunday Notebook and the Top 100 list are a major part of it, but he finds a way to make it happen on an almost-daily basis. Here's evidence: Last February — which is far and away the busiest sports month of the year in Southern Arizona — he had 26 bylines in 28 days. It wasn't all high-profile stuff, either. In that month, he wrote columns about high school football recruits; UA basketball; UA golf; UA football; Pima College football; horse racing; junior college hoops; spring training baseball; the

WGC-Accenture Match Play Championship golf event; and the Tucson rodeo. In all, he made references to 194 different athletes that month, the majority of them local.

For a couple years, the Star used to run a tagline at the end of his stories that read: Greg Hansen's column appears Tuesday, Thursday and Sunday, and whenever the spirit moves him. The spirit moved often. His byline has appeared in the Star an estimated 7,000 times since 1981; that's an average of about 250 per year, with research and interviews and travel taking up most of his "off" days.

His critics might contend that he has an ego that compels him to put his two cents in about everything. (And then those critics politely urge him to "move back to Utah!") I think he writes so frequently because he cares about the well-being of Tucson sports. Every time news hits that a franchise or tournament is leaving town for good, I can tell that it eats at him — and not because it leaves him with less to write about. (Hey, as long as Frank Busch and Candrea are coaching at the UA, there's always a story in town.) It's distressing because Tucson is his home. Writing a few columns a week probably makes him feel like he's giving back a tiny bit for all the memories it has provided him. I don't think I'm guilty of nepotism when I say that Tucson sports would be much less fun to follow without my dad's stories to accompany them.

For someone who is so gifted with words, though, my dad certainly lacks skill in other areas, namely with technology. It's a miracle that half of his columns were ever published because he has such a hard time using a computer. At least a dozen times he has called me in a panic because he was unable to find the file in which he saved his story. It took him a few months to learn how to properly use Microsoft Word. (Yes, Microsoft Word!) Worse, he still can't operate a DVD player. Nothing, however, is funnier than the text messages he sends. It's as if the award-winning writer, who can move people to tears with a few keystrokes, instantly becomes a caveman with a cell phone in his hand.

i in park lot. i no see u, — or — weather bad. hope rain soon.

It's a good thing his brain functions better with a keyboard, or else his coverage of the Match Play golf tournament would read something like: "Tiger make birdies. Tucson cheer loud!" I don't think I could defend my dad from the "dork" accusations if that were the case.

I spent a number of years gritting my teeth over the criticism tossed my dad's way. I used a stock response — "It's just one person's opinion" — but wondered why people got so worked up about his columns. It drove me crazy until I finally came to a realization in 2000. I was working on a freelance article for the UA's alumni magazine about the new Eddie Lynch Pavilion next to McKale Center. The research process took me to athletic director Jim Livengood's office, where I told his secretary that Tyler Hansen was there to conduct an interview.

"Are you Greg's son?" she asked.

I hesitated. I knew my dad had sharply criticized Livengood on occasion, so I was unsure how to answer. I asked her if being Greg Hansen's son was viewed as a good thing in that office.

"It depends on the day," she said with a wry smile.

That 10-second exchange helped ease years of mild frustration for me. I didn't feel the need to "defend" my dad any longer, because the reaction of his readers is what balances the whole equation. It's not enough to just read his opinions; they must be dissected and debunked and praised and ridiculed. People care so much because what he writes actually matters in some small way. He might never agree with that statement, but people keep reading the Star because they want to know what he thinks about certain topics. It either confirms their hopes or worries, or it verifies what they've known all along — that Hansen is a no-talent hack who should have retired years ago.

I'm proud to be my dad's son for all the obvious reasons. I can't separate my normal family experiences with him from my experiences reading his columns. I haven't lived under the same roof as him for 17 years, so waking up in the morning and reading his stories has been the equivalent of saying hello at the kitchen table. I can't imagine my daily life without it.

# Introduction

*By Greg Hansen*

In the summer of 1973, I drove from Utah to California to watch the New York Yankees play the Oakland A's. I was accompanied by Steve Wilson of the Salt Lake Tribune; when we weren't talking baseball, we talked sportswriting.

Both of us were eager to grow newspaper wings and fly away. We pledged to work together someday, preferably in New York or (and now I laugh at the dreaded thought) Los Angeles.

I got married and moved to Florida to cover the Tampa Bay Buccaneers. Steve became the assistant sports editor of the Arizona Daily Star and later held similar positions in Honolulu and Detroit. We kept in touch.

Steve phoned one August morning in 1981. I had been living in Oregon for three years and embraced the smaller-town environment.

"I've got a job for you covering Arizona football," he said. "It won't be easy; we just won a Pulitzer Prize revealing a scandal and corruption inside the Arizona athletic department; I hope you've got thick skin; you'll be the bad guy."

I flew to Tucson for an interview anyway. On the plane's approach to the airport I saw not green, but brown.

"I'd never live here," I told myself.

Daily Star sports editor Sam Pollak was waiting. We climbed into his rusted-out Pacer and began to talk.

"No air conditioning," he said. "But it's a short drive to the office. You'll be fine."

It was, what, 105 degrees? It wasn't fine. I had been living in the Willamette Valley of Oregon. My quality of life included fog, drizzle and moss on the sidewalks.

"No way am I going to live here," I repeated.

A few hours later, Pollak asked me how much I made as sports editor of a smaller daily in Oregon. It was $385 a week. My wife didn't work. Our three boys were 4, 2 and just out of the crib. I couldn't afford windshield wipers.

"I can get you $450 a week with a raise to $500 in three months," he said. "We'll pay for your moving expenses. We'll bump you to $550 after one year and you'll get a cost-of-living raise and two week's pay for a Christmas bonus. Call your wife. Talk it over."

I called; she began to cry. "We have to go," she said. "You know it, too. It's time."

I did not want to leave Oregon. I worked my own hours and knew the turf. Oregon State's basketball team was coming off a 26-2 season in which it was ranked No. 1 nationally. I couldn't imagine an assignment more enjoyable than sitting on press row at raucous Gill Coliseum watching the Beavers steamroll the Pac-10.

I wrote about fishing and liked it. Our city league softball team was a juggernaut, playing 60 games a season. It took 45 minutes to drive west to the coast and 30 minutes east to the Cascade Mountains. The Corvallis-Albany-Eugene area was paradise.

The last thing I wanted to do was move to a bigger city again. I tried that in Tampa and discovered, as an NFL beat writer, that I was a college-town guy.

"Tucson is the biggest college town in America," Pollak insisted. "The UA is the only game in town."

For a treasured friend who makes a living in the accuracy-accuracy-accuracy business, Sam was, for once, dreadfully wrong.

The joy of writing in Tucson has been its unpredictability, a daily freshness that goes outside the lines of McKale Center. The subjects have been endless.

In the late '80s, I got a phone call from Dr. Burt Strug, whose 13-year-old daughter had just returned from a gymnastics meet in Germany.

"I don't want to come across as a pushy Little League parent," he said. "But I think my daughter, Kerri, might be on the path to something big."

On a humid August evening in 1996, I stood next to Dr. Strug and his wife, Melanie, in a large, overcrowded tent outside the Georgia Dome. Little Kerri Strug had just become an international celebrity at the Atlanta Olympics.

"I remember the day you phoned to tell me about Kerri," I said in the crush of humanity. "I thought you might be a crackpot."

Dr. Strug sniffed away his tears. Kerri was wearing a gold medal around her neck.

One shining spring day in 1985, standing by the batting cage at Hi Corbett Field, 80-something Leo "The Lip" Durocher walked by. Out of nowhere he introduced himself.

"I'm Leo Durocher," he said.

I thought about all of the immortal baseball Durocher had witnessed: The Shot Heard 'Round the World. Ordering beers with his Yankee teammate Babe Ruth. Watching Willie Mays play his first big-league game.

I struggled to come up with something bright to say. I settled on "I've always thought you should be in the Hall of Fame."

"If I get elected to the Hall of Fame, it'll be long after I'm dead," he accurately predicted. "I've got too many enemies. They'll think of me differently when I'm dead."

Durocher died in 1991; he was elected into the Hall of Fame in 1994. But on that afternoon in 1985, in the sun at Hi Corbett Field, he talked until my notebook was overflowing with stories about the Babe and Willie Mays.

I asked if he had any regrets about his controversial career.

"I used the Lord's name in vain far too often," he said. "I've come to regret that." He gave me a solemn look, fixed his eyes on mine, and nodded his head. I was in the right place at the right time.

It wasn't a big story or a story that got any play outside Pima County. But it was my story, made in Tucson. Of such afternoons are a newspaper guy's career made.

I suppose I could've left a few times, to the Bay Area on a couple of occasions, to Cleveland, to New Orleans, and, sure, back home to Salt Lake City. I was all set to move to Seattle once, but I kept thinking of the sweat equity I had invested in Tucson.

This had become home. My kids all live here, and my wife's family lives here. I know where not to hit the ball — all of the trouble spots — at all of the golf courses. I'm not about to give up that advantage.

And, besides, I can't leave Tucson until I've crossed a few more items from my Bucket List.

I know what a privilege it is to play golf on New Year's Day and to watch Tiger Woods blitz the field at what used to be the Tucson Open. But I'd rather be at the Rose Bowl, for once, watching Arizona and not Arizona State.

I want to see Vern Friedli win another Big Game at Amphi. I want to be in the seats when Tucson's next Sean Elliott comes along. I want to see if Kenzie Fowler can go 40-0, a latter-day Jennie Finch, beating everybody in Oklahoma City.

I wish I had better recall of the Canyon del Oro High School baseball games I attended. Did I really see Ian Kinsler, Brian Anderson, Scott Hairston, Chris Duncan and Shelley Duncan — five future major leaguers — on the field at the same time?

I cherish that far more than any of the seven Super Bowls I have covered.

I was there, on duty, when the Diamondbacks won Game 7 of the 2001 World Series, beating the mighty Yankees. But I enjoyed it more in 1991 when the Toros won their first Pacific Coast League title, bottom of the ninth inning, every seat occupied, with Kenny Lofton racing around third base.

Lofton sprayed some champagne on my notebook that night. I think it was because he didn't like me. But that's OK. I liked him. I didn't have to pay to watch him help Arizona to the 1988 Final Four or for the Toros to win the '91 PCL title.

I'm in his debt.

A few years ago, at the induction ceremonies for the Pima County Sports Hall of Fame, I found myself choked up simply by reading the roster of inductees.

I began counting how many of the 250-plus Hall of Famers I knew, had interviewed and counted as friends. Gentleman Ed Updegraff, the most accomplished golfer in Tucson history. Rodeo star Sherry Cervi. Pima College baseball coach Rich Alday. Indy 500 star Roger McCluskey. UA distance running Olympian George Young. International gymnastic coach Yoichi Tomita.

For the first time, it hit me that I had been a small part of something very big.

Now when I'm in a plane on the approach to Tucson, I don't see the landscape as much as I see history.

Just before the wheels touch down, the plane flies over Sunnyside High School. I always think back to the chilly December night, 2001, when the undefeated Blue Devils were 90 seconds shy of reaching their first state championship game.

Star tailback Philo Sanchez, son of Blue Devils coach Richard Sanchez, had fumbled to put the game in doubt. Philo was sitting alone on the bench, tears streaking down his face.

Scottsdale Saguaro was driving for what would be the winning score. The tension was indescribable. Please, Lord, I said, don't let this all come down on Philo Sanchez.

On the play of the year, clock ticking to zero, Blue Devil safety Rafael Gallegos intercepted a pass in the end zone. Philo was off the hook; the Blue Devils would win the state title.

The coach and his son jumped into one another's arms, relieved and overjoyed, weeping, exhausted. It was almost poetry.

Driving home that night, hustling to beat deadline, I thought that someday I should put all of these happy memories into a book. And now I have.

# CHAPTER ONE

# Arizona football

## Tunnicliffe:
## 'Coach, they can't beat me'

*Sunday, November 13, 1983*

Wasn't this how it was supposed to be?

The goal posts coming down. Coaches embracing, tears of joy on their cheeks. Index fingers raised. Shouts of "We're No. 1!"

Even the security police were slapping hands and exchanging high-fives. Never mind that hordes of Arizona football fans wrestled $1,200 of goal posts to the ground and that CBS transmitted it to the country.

As brunches go, the UA and UCLA will get five stars for yesterday's before-noon performance at Arizona Stadium. High noon on the streets of Dodge couldn't have been more telling.

That Arizona won 27-24 will be little-noted and not long-remembered by the rest of the country.

But in this neck of the desert, Arizona's victory will likely be served to posterity as an entrée with conquests of USC, Notre Dame and Arizona State.

"Everything surrounding the game — UCLA's Rose Bowl hopes, the final home game for our seniors, national TV — made it special," UA receiver Jay Dobyns said. "I'm not going to forget it."

Did you think he would?

Dobyns caught an eight-yard touchdown pass from Tom Tunnicliffe with 1:01 remaining. Even a relatively simple 37-yard field-goal attempt by UCLA's John Lee on the last play of the game failed miserably.

But Lee proved that there's no such thing as an easy kick, unless, of course, you're watching it while eating a hot dog.

"The opera ain't over until the fat lady sings," Tunnicliffe said.

"You're damn right I thought he would miss it."

That attitude seemed to infuse the Wildcats as much as anything.

"Tunnicliffe came up to me after the game," said Arizona coach Larry Smith. "and he said, 'Coach, they can't beat me.'

"And he's right. I love it."

But this was not a game UCLA lost. It was beaten — and this is getting to be a cliché — by Tunnicliffe.

With 3:28 left, UCLA led 24-20. Arizona had the ball at its 31. Tunnicliffe took the field for what surely would be his last performance at Arizona Stadium.

Scrapbook time.

The next nine plays and 2:27 etched Tunnicliffe and the Class of '84 indelibly into the minds of Arizona boosters. These guys haven't been pretty or predictable. Just fun.

"I'm thrilled to death to go out like this," Tunnicliffe said. "I'd rather be undefeated, sure, but we didn't have that option.

"This," he said, smiling broadly, "will do."

If there is any consolation for the Bruins, it is that Tunnicliffe is a senior. In three starts against UCLA, he had a 2-0-1 record.

UCLA must look at Tunnicliffe in football the way Germany looks at the U.S. in wars. "Tunnicliffe beats Bruins" headlines are as almost as common as "Billy Martin fired."

Against everybody else in his career, Tunnicliffe has completed barely 51 percent of his passes. Against UCLA, he completed 62 percent. He has 55 career interceptions, almost 1½ per game. Against UCLA, he had one pass intercepted in 78 throws.

And that was only because he was blindsided and all by knocked out early in the fourth quarter yesterday.

Late in the game, CBS commentator Pat Haden put Tunnicliffe's performance into perspective. "Tunnicliffe is picking these people apart," Haden said. "I don't think I've seen any quarterback this year play any better than Tunnicliffe has today."

The winning drive, Tunnicliffe said, blotted out a month of frustration in which the UA was 0-3 and didn't win for 35 days. "I agree," he said. "The last drive made up for a lot of things."

"I don't have any harsh feelings toward UCLA. I'm not vindictive because they didn't ever recruit me. In fact, I used to be a UCLA fan and my sister, Tammy, graduated from UCLA last year."

Will UCLA be glad to see him go?

"I don't know," he said. "What do you think?"

Methinks it will.

But Arizona didn't just win a football game yesterday, or put a patch on a season that had begun to unravel.

For almost four hours, it went coast-to-coast with what amounts to a recruiting film. A highlights show.

Every time I peeked at the press box monitor, CBS was beaming the gorgeous Catalina Mountains back to Teaneck and Tuscaloosa. Haden all but made linebacker Ricky Hunley out to be a modern-day Dick Butkus.

The UA defense made a telling goal-line stand, the offense performed a high-wire act ... and did you get a load of all that blue sky?

The UA will frame this one and hang it on the wall.

"It was something special. It was a great feeling" Hunley said. "I don't know how it compares to our victories over Notre Dame and USC, but it's got to be great because everybody in the country had a chance to see us.

"... I think they liked what they saw."

EDITOR'S NOTE: Two weeks after beating UCLA, Tom Tunnicliffe capped his collegiate career with a win over Arizona State in Tempe. He left Arizona as its career leader in passing yards (7,618), touchdown passes (46), pass completions (574) and total offensive yards (7,336). All of those records stood for 25 years until Willie Tuitama broke them in 2008. Tunnicliffe works in real estate in Burbank, Calif.

JOY WOLF

Tom Tunnicliffe, who grew up a UCLA fan but was never recruited by the Bruins, had some of his best success against them, going 2-0-1 in three starts at the UA.

# In any language, UA was to win

*Sunday, November 24, 1985*

*TEMPE*

Sin ninguna duda — without any doubt.

That's what Max Zendejas said in Spanish. That's what Larry Smith said in English.

Arizona 16, Arizona State 13. Four in a row.

Without any doubt? Come on.

"I always look for the glory," said Zendejas. "I dreamed of having a chance to win the game. I knew I would do it." Sin ninguna duda.

"When we told the team at 5 o'clock that USC had upset UCLA, and Arizona State had a chance to go to the Rose Bowl," said Smith, "they stood up and cheered. They loved the pressure. That's what they wanted.

"I knew right then we were going to win. No doubt."

I call that blind faith. For 55 minutes last night at Sun Devil Stadium, Arizona State's chances of going to the Rose Bowl looked positively dreamy.

If Smith and Zendejas knew what was to come in the wild — and as close to inexplicable a finish as you'd ever see — they could've saved us all a lot of anxiety.

Zendejas and Smith, that unlikely combination, not only kept the Sun Devils out of the Rose Bowl for the second time in four seasons but broke Sun Devil hearts for the fourth consecutive year.

It might now be safe to say that all the misery has been wrung from this rivalry for the Wildcats. After years of being kicked around and treated like stepkids by ASU and Frank Kush, the UA has restored the glamour and sparkle to its football program in this state.

"I'm pretty sure ASU fans hate me by now," said Zendejas, who kicked a last-play-of-the-game field goal to win here two years ago, 17-15.

"Every time we've needed to beat ASU since I've been at Arizona, I've been able to come through. I'm glad to do it."

Late last night, when Sun Bowl president Sam Jenkins formally extended a bid to that game to the UA in the emotional UA locker room, Arizona's victory still seemed a little difficult to believe.

The UA's offense didn't look like it could score a touchdown if it played all night. The Sun Devils seemed totally in command, leading

13-3 with 21 minutes left.

"It looked bleak for a while," said UA nose guard Stan Mataele, "but the coaches keep telling us to find a way, find a way.

"And we found a way."

A few ways.

A fumbled punt by ASU's Anthony Parker was recovered for a Wildcat touchdown. Zendejas kicked a school-record-tying 57-yard field goal. And, most of all, Mataele recovered a fumble by ASU quarterback Jeff Van Raaphorst at the Sun Devil 20 with 3:10 remaining, on a hit by Dana Wells.

The game was then tied at 13. Zendejas, with Freon in his blood system, kicked a 32-yard field goal to win it.

"I was not nervous," he said. "I was looking forward to it."

Said Smith: "The name of the game is opportunities. We got 'em and we took advantage of 'em.

"That's how you win in this league."

Roses are red;

Sun Devils are blue;

The route to Pasadena;

Hasn't changed since '82.

Cruel, perhaps, but Smith said there is no space for sympathy in college football.

"No one felt sorry for us when we played under a cloud of NCAA probation for what amounts to six years," he said. "Well, tonight that cloud is totally gone. Our morale has never been better.

"I can't feel sorry for ASU, no matter what was riding on this game for them. When you think that way, you get your butt beat.

"I've been in that chair many times. You don't expect sympathy and you don't give it."

Smith knew precisely what the UA's victory meant, and it had nothing to do with the jubilation of beating ASU four straight games for the first time in 37 years.

"What it means," he said. "is that we finished in a tie for first place in the Pac-10. We had two losses, ASU had two losses, UCLA had two losses. It's the best finish in the history of the school.

"Sure, we aren't going to the Rose Bowl, but this is a damn good alternative."

Sin ninguna duda. Without any doubt.

# Smith's exit was short on tact, logic

*Thursday, January 15, 1987*

Somewhere over the Pacific Ocean yesterday, Dick Tomey went looking for Rainbows — the Hawaii Rainbows. To tell them goodbye.

"I'll probably cry like a baby," he said.

At a time when he doesn't have a mini-second to spare, Tomey is spending about 12 air hours just to tell Hawaii, his former institution, and the players he recruited something like "thanks for the memories."

That's class.

Thirteen days ago, when Larry Smith became a California dreamer, he went looking for rainbows too. The ones with pots of gold at the end. He did not say goodbye.

Smith has not contacted returning UA players by phone or via signing telegram. He did not hold a press conference locally to bid Tucson and the UA farewell. He did not say thanks for the memories or anything like that. It is a one-hour flight to Tucson from Los Angeles and Smith couldn't break away even for an afternoon.

His sterile departure stung — and puzzles — those in the UA athletic department, and, I presume, many of the 53,000 who showed up each Saturday at Arizona Stadium last fall.

If there was one thing Smith was consistent about in seven seasons at the UA, it was loyalty. It was his class.

He couldn't have made a more unexpected exit.

The most damning evidence is that Smith was attired in a "USC football" wardrobe at last week's Hula Bowl. His son, Corby, also wore Trojan football clothing. NBC commentators made a fuss out of it.

I find this newsworthy because four Arizona players — Stan Mataele, Byron Evans, David Adams and Jon Horton — were on Smith's team at the Hula Bowl. Combined, they had given 17 years to Smith in Tucson and then — bam! — as if overnight Smith one-upped them by wearing his Trojan outfit for the world to see.

Smith should've worn something neutral to the game, in respect to Evans, Adams and the guys. As a courtesy to the UA, he could've waited until next season to show his new colors on the sideline.

In Smith's defense, his work ethic and an eagerness to get started at USC may have overcome the public relations details he left unfinished. He begged off the Hula Bowl coaching job but was told by Trojan athletic director Mike McGee it would be best to honor the commitment. Like Tomey, Smith is pressed for time; in his first two days at USC he and his staff worked an estimated 32 hours.

"Things are so overwhelming here that when Larry gets in the door he has trouble getting away even for a drink of water," said Claire Snow, his new secretary at USC.

"We haven't given him any peace, and I've got his calendar even more loaded for the rest of the month."

But that doesn't explain all of Smith's erratic behavior, and the bruised feelings he has left in Tucson.

No football coach needs an excuse to go to USC, but Smith used one, and it was full of leaks.

"Had I had a five-year contract, I would not be sitting here," he said on the day he became the Trojans' coach. "... Had I signed a contract in September, there's no question I wouldn't be here."

You'll pardon Cedric Dempsey if he shakes his head.

"I don't understand that," said Dempsey, UA's director of athletics. "Larry knew there would be a five-year contract forthcoming. My interpretation was that there was no problem with the communication of it."

What also has gone unreported is that a series of UA boosters put together an annuity-type package for Smith last season that would've been worth roughly $500,000 at full maturity. Smith had just received the first $50,000 of it, or thereabouts, when he left Tucson without a trace.

But by now, most connected with the UA football program have rationalized the switch from Smith to Tomey. It is a good one. Smith was ready to leave, a fact that didn't escape most of his returning players. Quarterback Craig Bergman, for instance, said on Tuesday that the players could see Smith's departure coming.

In baseball terms, it was a good trade for both clubs.

Tomey will put some new energies into the UA; he'll restore some of the excitement that Smith's program lost merely through repetition. Otherwise, in many ways, especially in coaching style and strategy, Tomey and Smith are clones.

It's just that Tomey has a little more tact, and is a bit more polished, at his goodbyes.

# Former UA coach has 'no remorse, no regrets'

*Wednesday, November 11, 1987*

*LOS ANGELES*

He is accused of "abandoning" the UA, leaving it strapped to the tracks with the entire Pacific-10 Conference bearing down on it.

How do you plead, Larry Smith?

"Well," he said among a group of Los Angeles newsmen yesterday, "I have no remorse, no regrets.

"I think, in a way, it's a compliment that there were people upset when I left. ... You don't want to look like you're leading a parade when they're chasing you out of town.

"I know there'll always be people unhappy with me for the way I left Tucson. But, to me, you just move on and do the best you can."

Both parties are well aware of the bruised feelings that will accompany Arizona's game at USC Saturday.

"Coach Smith told us that ever since he left the UA, people have pointed to this week's game on their calendar," Trojan quarterback Rodney Peete said yesterday. "He caught everybody's attention real fast."

Even an offensive lineman, Trojan center John Katnik, emerged from the trenches long enough to catch up on the latest hate-gossip.

"Since coach Smith left Arizona, all we've heard is how bad his former players want to beat him," Katnik said yesterday. "I know I would. I'd wanna get some revenge, too.

"Coach Smith told us that every individual on the Arizona team will be thinking that way. This is really going to be an emotional game."

Smith did his best yesterday to defuse this angry little rivalry, but it didn't do any good. This one's gonna be painful for a while.

"I still get a few negative letters from Tucson," Smith said. "The one that sticks out came last February after Arizona slaughtered USC in basketball. Some guy cut the headline out of the newspaper and sent it to me. And then he wrote, 'This is what's going to happen to you in November.'"

This volatile subplot has even aroused some Los Angeles newsmen, who usually don't raise an eyebrow at USC unless Notre Dame or UCLA is involved.

Mal Florence, who has been covering USC for the Los Angeles Times for more than 20 years, said: "I talked to (UA safety) Chuck Cecil last night, and he said he felt a sense of abandonment. Does he have any basis to say that, Larry?"

And Smith, who was never one for ducking the hard questions, met it head on.

"I'm sure Chuck's exactly right," he said. "When I left I understood how they felt — that I left them for someone else. I think they somewhat understand why I left, but Chuck's feelings are exactly right."

Smith has difficulty believing someone — anyone — would hold his move to USC against him. How could he not go to USC? He did not leave the UA in tatters. He elevated every detail of the program, from academics to a Top 10 ranking.

"The best way for me to understand how the people in Tucson felt was to remember how I felt when one of my assistants took a job at another school," Smith said. "I might not want them to leave, but in the end it was their decision. They did what was best for them, not what was best for Larry Smith.

"There are some people who think there is no greater utopia than being in Tucson, Arizona. And then there are those who feel the opposite — that they've got to get out of Tucson as quick as they can.

"Look I wasn't trying to get out of Tucson in any way, shape or form, and I didn't have to.

"... As far as I'm concerned, from the people I know in Tucson, it's been an amiable separation. I'll always feel comfortable going back there."

But let's get one thing straight. For all the misguided people who believe Smith left the UA without a thought, he bled a little Wildcat red and blue yesterday.

There was no mistaking the nostalgia that ran through Smith's mind as he gave what was supposed to be a routine scouting assignment of the Wildcats.

"Art Greathouse is a big-time back," he said.

"Derek (Hill) is as big a threat as Notre Dame's Timmy Brown. ...

"Dana Wells, of the teams we've played, is the best nose guard we've seen. ...

"Arizona has the best kicking game in the conference. We show our kids films of their kicking game and tell them that's how it's done. ...

"They've got the best offensive skill people of anybody we've played. ...

"The biggest mistake anybody can make is to underestimate Arizona. You may think I'm making a mountain out of a molehill, but let me assure you, we have tremendous respect for those kids. ..."

It was about then that Tom Kelly, the longtime Voice of the Trojans, leaned to a reporter and said, "You keep listening to this guy, and he makes you think he's still the coach at Arizona."

And, maybe, part of him still is.

EDITOR'S NOTE: Three days after this column was published, USC beat Arizona 12-10, and Larry Smith's inaugural Trojans team went on to win the Pac-10 and play in the Rose Bowl. Smith coached six seasons at USC, posting a 44-25-3 in his tenure and going 1-2 in the Rose Bowl. He was fired after the 1992 season. Smith then coached Missouri from 1994 to 2000, where he led the Tigers to two bowl games and a 33-46-1 record in seven seasons. For more on Larry Smith, turn to Chapter 7.

Arizona's Doug Pfaff celebrates a first-half field goal in a 1989 game against Oklahoma. His game-winner in the last minute kicked off a bigger celebration.

# UA football program is reawakened by win

*Sunday, September 17, 1989*

By the fourth quarter last night, Arizona was out of ammo. Hanging on.

A tie would be nice.

The Wildcats had milked three points from their new offense, the multiple-backpedal, and were moving at a glacial clip.

Their best play was an Oklahoma fumble.

Could they win with defense? A safety? A blocked kick?

No. They couldn't. They didn't.

They won on guts. On character.

Arizona manufactured the best 37-yard drive in school history — Ronald Veal, Mario Hampton and some hard running behind Glenn Parker and John Brandon — and then Doug Pfaff came through when he had to. Presto. The Wildcats draped a wicked 6-3 defeat on the Boomer Sooners.

Figured by the new math of college football, Arizona is now unbeaten. The Stanford and Texas Tech games don't really count.

The Wildcats started over last night and all of their goals are back in place.

"When it got to the fourth quarter, it was just a matter of hanging on," said UA safety Jeff Hammerschmidt. "If we could hold 'em, if we could keep 'em at 3, hey, it was our dang season on the line.

"They didn't have a chance."

Yes, Beano Cook picked the Wildcats to win. Who else? No one. OK, Cedric Dempsey did, too, but what's he going to say — Sooners by eight?

No.

The Wildcats have been out of the Big Shock business since Larry Smith left town; except for the annual victory over Arizona State, the UA hadn't beaten anyone who was someone since it toppled No. 3 SMU in 1985.

The fans have even forgotten how to tear down a goal post. Celebrations have been short at Arizona Stadium for a few years.

But when it was over last night, Dick Tomey, who is customarily as emotional as a monk, threw his arms around his son, Richie, danced

31

the Texas two-step to midfield and tried to rub his goose bumps down.

Big victory.

"It's not fair to compare this one with other wins," Tomey said. "We had some incredible wins at Hawaii."

Against whom? Wyoming?

"This is obviously this team's best win," he said, "but it demeans other (victories) to say this one is the best."

But Oklahoma was ranked No. 6. And Arizona still had the emotional bruises to show for last week's 24-14 humiliation at Texas Tech. And, well, if the Wildcats had lost last night, a 3-8 finish would not have been an outrageous projection.

What must please Tomey most is that his club found a way to win on a night it: (a) couldn't pass; (b) held auditions at quarterback; and (c) gave up some serious second-half yardage.

Hammerschmidt wasn't fooled.

"It was the fumbles," he said. "Oklahoma has a history of fumbles. They pound it at you, pound it at you and pound it at you, and sooner or later you expect them to fumble.

"We bent, bent and bent ... but we didn't break. And then they'd fumble."

As much as Pfaff's field goal, and Larry Mac Duff's run defense, and Tomey's fourth-and-one call at the 50-yard line with 3:30 remaining led to the victory, OU's two second-half fumbles made the difference.

The first one touched down at Arizona's 24 with 15:17 remaining.

Cost? Probably three points, minimum.

The second Sooner fumble found a blue Arizona jersey at the UA 15 with 12:10 left.

Cost? At least three more points. Bottom line: the ball game.

"The fumbles were the breaks we needed," said Parker, the UA's offensive line leader. "When we got the ball back (with 5:17 left), I put my head down and went to work. I didn't worry about the clock or what yard line we were on.

"And we weren't thinking field goal. That would've been selling ourselves short. We were thinking touchdown."

After 37 yards and 5:14, Arizona was at the OU 22. Parker's plan was abbreviated.

"I looked at the clock and saw seven seconds and realized we wouldn't be able to get the touchdown," he said, smiling. "On the field goal, someone knocked me down and just about amputated my left knee. I was on the ground and couldn't see it, so I judged from the crowd's reaction.

"The roar of the crowd made the pain in my knee go right away. It was a good general anesthesia."

It also served as a quick fix for the Wildcats.

"We had some unfinished business out there," said Veal. "… We had to win, that was the bottom line. This was the turning point of the season."

Of particular encouragement for Arizona was the return of its big-play defense. Quaint it ain't. Anthony Smith and Chris Singleton, Ken Hakes and Richard Holt bored in on OU's running game with indelicate effect.

What Texas Tech game?

"In the fourth quarter, the motivational aspects came into play," said Mac Duff, an OU grad who is the UA's defensive coordinator. "We had said we wanted to have a chance going into the fourth quarter … have a chance to win the dang ballgame."

"Their guys sensed it and their play reflected it. It wasn't anything tricky or fancy, it was just a win."

And the reawakening of a football program.

ARIZONA DAILY STAR 1992

From top, UA "Desert Swarm" defenders Jimmie Hopkins, Tedy Bruschi and
Jim Hoffman leave Washington QB Mark Brunell smothered in a 1992 upset.

# Patient Cats grind their way to win over No. 1

*Sunday, November 8, 1992*

The day came up perfect: blue sky, bright sun, a crispness in the air. The ideal college football day.

"I told (UA director of athletics) Cedric Dempsey there's no time, no place, nowhere in the world that's better than being here," Arizona senior Heath Bray said, his voice rising with each word.

And Heath Bray said that after the game, which should tell you all you need to know about the Pac-10 Game of the Year, which, in Tucson, became the Game of the Decade/Century/Lifetime, depending on how long you have been frustrated by the UA's somewhat empty football history.

As the Washington players and coaches waited silently to board their buses, linebacker Jamal Fountaine looked at several reporters and said: "To me, they're No.1 now."

He meant the Wildcats.

Arizona 16, Washington 3.

Really.

After all these years, Arizona is no longer just "The Opponent" in these big games.

"I don't think it was an upset," UA coach Dick Tomey said. "We expected to win. I don't think a team can upset five teams in a row."

It was dark last night, 6 o'clock, by the time a computer operator hit the switch and erased "Wildcats 16, Huskies 3" from the giant scoreboard at empty Arizona Stadium. I don't think anyone will forget.

And I don't know what happened to the goalposts. They were down and gone before the clock hit zero. And I don't know how long it took UA defensive coordinator Larry Mac Duff to rub down his goose bumps. He ran from the field, dodging a mob of fans, drenched from a celebratory shower of ice water.

"Now this was fun," Mac Duff said.

Who would know better? The last two times Mac Duff sent his defense out to play the Huskies he lost 54-0 and 54-10. Fun indeed.

The men in suits from the Fiesta, Rose and Cotton bowls jostled to get through the door into the crowded Arizona locker room and schmooze with players and coaches they had never heard of a couple of

35

weeks ago.

"I admit, sometimes I do get amazed," Arizona nose guard Rob Waldrop said. "I've never been part of anything like this in my life."

If you sat on your sofa and watched this game, or even if you were sitting in the sun at the 40-yard line, it didn't take you long to recognize the trend. For five weeks it's been the same thing.

Arizona's offense is so stolid it looks like it has gum stuck to its shoe. The Wildcats can't pass. Can't run. Can't call in sick.

And then Josh Miller comes in and punts and suddenly the Huskies are so far from the end zone that they need a 29-cent stamp to get there.

Tick, tick, tick.

The clock winds down, the Huskies don't threaten to score any more than Miami or Stanford or UCLA did, and before you know it, someone fumbles and Steve McLaughlin is setting up for a field goal.

Tick, tick, tick.

You wonder if Arizona is ever going to get a first down and how long can the Wildcat defense contain Napoleon Kaufman, and where has all the time gone? It's the fourth quarter. Arizona leads 9-3.

Hey, you say to yourself, they planned it this way. Duane Akina, the UA's offensive coordinator, becomes a genius. Who needs flash? Discipline and patience work. Don't make any mistakes and you can win with defense and the kicking game.

"This is my first trip down this road," said Akina, who learned the business, ironically, in five years under Husky coach Don James as a player/coach in the '70s. "Coach James is one of the best things to ever happen to me. He taught me discipline and patience and gave me structure."

In effect, James taught Akina how to beat the Huskies.

"My blood is all over Husky Stadium," Akina said. "They really got after us the last two years ... but we know what our strengths are. We're not BYU. We felt that as long as we remained patient we could eventually break them with our running game and wear them down."

And isn't that what happened? Arizona was superior physically to a program that has put on a Pac-10 clinic about wearing people down.

For 5½ years, Tomey has been hardened by criticism that his teams don't pass enough. Yet in the last six weeks Washington won precisely because it didn't need to pass. The Huskies averaged 24 passes per game in that six-week stretch. Don James must've been aghast when he saw yesterday's statistics — the Huskies, who couldn't run, attempted 42 passes.

Said Tomey, "They threw the ball 42 times, which is tremendously out of character for them."

The character of the Pac-10 is now as different as it has ever been. It's almost mid-November and Arizona and Washington State are as likely to get to the Rose Bowl as the powerhouses in Los Angeles and Seattle.

The worst news Arizona can hear today is that (a) it has been installed as a favorite against USC on Saturday, and (b) it leaps ahead of the Trojans and Huskies in the polls.

This is a club that operates best as an underdog.

"It's a mad dash for the Rose Bowl," said Arizona senior corner-back Keshon Johnson. "It's a matter of whose defense allows the most points and now it appears that we are the stingiest defense in the country, not Washington."

Long after the game ended, Tomey sat on a folding chair in the corner of basement room at the stadium. A horde of reporters from coast-to-coast, the kind of people who usually don't come to Tucson unless it has something to do with basketball, carried on as if they had just discovered the mother lode. To them, this is a fresh and romantic story.

The Other Guy beats the odds.

Was this the finest moment of Tomey's career? How does it feel to be discovered after 15 years?

"Well, it beats anything we've had lately," he said, typically understated.

He said he would go home, have dinner, watch a tape of the game, meet a few recruits and avoid any breast-beating.

"I like to stay home," he said.

But he did give his rare captive audience something to take home to tell their readers.

"This team now has beaten Washington in three of five games. It has beaten UCLA three out of four, and USC two in a row. At some point, the Arizona program needed to get some credit for what it's been."

And, perhaps, for where it's going.

Dick Tomey flashes a wide smile in the final seconds of Arizona's 1994 Fiesta Bowl win over Miami, called "the biggest win Arizona has ever had."

DAVID SANDERS

# Tomey hits recruiting trail 'while the iron's hot'

*Sunday, January 2, 1994*

*TEMPE*

A few minutes past 3 o'clock yesterday afternoon, Dick Tomey looked at his watch and wondered if he had enough time to stand in the middle of the Wildcat locker room and soak it all in a little longer.

It was the first time he fidgeted all day.

He had a 4:45 p.m. flight to Dallas and, besides, it was suddenly 1994, wasn't it? His mind was in future tense; Tomey knows precisely where he wants to be on the first day of 1995, and it's not Sun Devil Stadium.

So he condensed any celebration to a few handshakes and hugs in the locker room, grabbed a suitcase and got a ride to the airport.

Tomey will be in Dallas, New Orleans and Honolulu in the next six days, and he didn't pack his golf clubs. "Recruiting," he said. "You've got to strike while the iron's hot."

And so on the day Arizona celebrated the greatest victory in Wildcat football and a history-making 10-win season, its head coach left town before the final statistics were printed.

The moral of the story is that the UA enjoyed the taste of its 29-0 rout over Miami so much that it couldn't wait to start work on the only thing that could one-up it — the Rose Bowl in '95.

"It's the biggest win Arizona has ever had," said Wildcat offensive line coach Jim Young, an expert in perspective who piloted the UA to two 9-2 seasons in the '70s. "To beat a team of that stature, and to beat them the way we did. ... they just don't get shut out."

But they did this time. Had a man just in from Mars decided to watch his first football game yesterday, the Fiesta Bowl, he would've learned one thing: They master race wore the navy-blue shirts.

"We destroyed 'em," said UA senior linebacker Brant Boyer, who then shook his head at the mere idea of dominating, actually intimidating, the NCAA's most successful football program of the last decade. "I thought we'd win, sure, but not like this."

Consider that any Wildcat victory over Miami yesterday would've been classified as the most monumental in school history. Any score. Any way. But let's be straight: The final score was not indicative of the difference between the teams yesterday. It could've been 45-0. I mean, it felt like it was a 45-0 game.

"We expected to play well," Tomey said, deadpan. "I can't say I'm surprised."

But that's just Tomey. His theme in '93 was that Arizona no longer "upset" opponents, that his club had developed so thoroughly that whenever it beat USC or Washington, he was offended to see people arch their eyebrows.

"People in the West know that we can play," he said, almost defiantly. "Now the other people with questions about us, those people who usually don't get to see us play, should know."

The cynics howled that Miami didn't want to be at the little old Fiesta Bowl playing a 16th-ranked team. The Hurricanes are used to better theater — they've played in the Orange, Sugar and Cotton bowls with national title implications the last three seasons.

This was the runner-up bowl for Miami.

If that's true, if the Canes lacked motivation, that was their miscalculation. And I don't know how valid that theory is anyway. Miami is used to being the second biggest target in college football (trailing only Notre Dame). If Miami football stands for anything, it is that every week the Canes have to be prepared for their opponent's best shot. They had a month to get squared away and emotionally ready for Arizona — if only to avoid a blow to their shiny reputation.

"We wanted to play so bad," said Boyer. "It wasn't just Miami, though, but that was part of it. But we have so much fun playing together we couldn't wait to play, no matter who it would've been."

Miami was in the wrong place at the wrong time. The Wildcat coaches had been successful in convincing their troops that this was the stage that Arizona had been trying to get on for a century.

Arizona's Desert Swarm had never been better. They came from every direction. Shawn Jarrett from his mysterious "X" position. Rob Waldrop up the middle. Tedy Bruschi from the corners. Sean Harris from everywhere.

In the third quarter I put on the headphones and listened to Kevin Harlan's analysis of the game on the Mutual radio network. It was probably typical of the reaction from a nationwide audience. "It's kind of hard for the ear to accept, Arizona 22-0," said Harlan. "I'm shocked."

It was a day of redemption for the Wildcat offense, maligned so frequently that you'd swear offensive coordinator Duane Akina's middle name is anemic. And sophomore quarterback Dan White wasn't smokin' the way he did in Wildcat victories over USC and Arizona State. He was, simply, adequate.

What worked best, aside from Chuck Levy's 68-yard bolt that will suffice as his official farewell to college football and get him drafted a whole lot earlier by the NFL than he would've before the Fiesta Bowl, was the UA offensive line.

Hicham El-Mashtoub, Warner Smith, Joe Smigiel, Rod Lewis, Mu Tagoai and Eric Johnson owned the line of scrimmage. Arizona averaged 5.1 yards per run and gave White sufficient time to find Troy Dickey and Terry Vaughn for game-turning gains.

"You know, Miami had the best defense we faced all year," Akina insisted after the game. "Their defensive numbers were as good or better than our defense's. That's what impressed me. We hit some runs and throws against a very good outfit."

Arizona gained 409 yards, which means that once it began the Pac-10 season, and those break-in games against UTEP, Illinois and Pacific were history, the Wildcats averaged 376 yards per game.

Those are figures almost unprecedented in Arizona offense in the Tomey years. Desert Swarm has a working, effective partner in this business.

The offensive line coaches, Young and Charlie Dickey, put the month of preparation work to good use. "We felt we understood their defense," said Young. "We knew what they were going to do and we had close to a month to work on the blocking. And the thing that impressed me was that we intimidated them, not with any crap and a lot of words, but with our performance on the field."

When next we see the Wildcats, at Camp Cochise in August, it's inevitable that they will be favored to get to the Rose Bowl. The cast returns nearly intact, although minus four key elements — Levy, Waldrop, Dickey and Boyer. Otherwise, this group will be expected to be bigger, tougher and faster.

The Wildcats will have a big-time rep.

"Hey, the expectations were high this year," said Tomey. "And we didn't flinch from them."

They just met them.

# Three plays cost Cats Rose Bowl streak

*Tuesday, December 27, 1994*

*PASADENA, Calif.*

Dear Dad:

Sorry about Christmas, but things haven't been the same over the holidays since Arizona started coming to the Rose Bowl three years ago. You know what they say about bowl games: If you haven't played in the Rose Bowl, you're just practicing.

I hoped to call last night and ask what you're planning for New Year's, but the boss sent me to do a piece on Tedy Bruschi, who had been invited to L.A. to whip up a little something in the back room at Spago.

The people back in Tucson are convinced that this three-peat in the Rose Bowl is the most important thing since, gosh, getting here for the first time, in '92. Bruschi came over in early December to do a little hype work for the Tournament of Roses people — you know how possessive they are with their MVP alumni — and the next thing you know, Mr. Personality's tossing back tequila with some Hollywood type. The talk gets around to Italian food and, well, now Bruschi's dealing pasta at Spago.

It's all connections, you know. Play in a few Rose Bowls and you've got 'em.

I know I promised that the next time Arizona won the Pac-10, I'd get you some tickets. You'd assume that after a couple of these things, Wildcat fans would get a little jaded, maybe stay home and see some hoops for a change. How soon they forget. I saw some guy in a red sweater down in the lobby offering his season tickets at McKale — right behind Lute, he said — and a wad of bills, for two Rose Bowl tickets.

The guy just laughed. "That'd be like leaving Cindy Crawford for Rosie O'Donnell," he said. It's also another way of saying I couldn't get any tickets again this year, Dad. I can't get over how Dick Tomey has handled the fame. You oughta see this guy. In '92, after Jey Phillips intercepted that halfback-to-QB pass in the end zone to beat USC, I thought Tomey was just numb or something. That happens after you win six consecutive games, five as an underdog, and get to the Rose Bowl after a 1-2-1 start.

42

But when an ABC cameraman asked Tomey to "look alive" at a lavish Rose Parade dinner the other night, Tomey yawned. Excited? Not quite; he looks like his vital signs are being stolen. Look for him on TV. He makes BYU's great stone face, LaVell Edwards, come off as Soupy Sales.

I remember coming over here last year when the whole damn state of Wisconsin showed up, 98 percent of them without tickets. While they worried about hotel rooms and directions to Disneyland, Tomey distributed 85 copies of the '93 loss to UCLA just to remind the Wildcats how close they had come to playing for the national championship.

Just getting to the Rose Bowl no longer counts, Dad. You've got to win it. Hah, I remember when a week in El Paso at the Hancock Bowl was big stuff for Arizona.

Yesterday, I had lunch with Larry Mac Duff, the old Wildcat defensive coordinator, the architect of Desert Swarm, who has just finished his first year as the head coach at San Diego State. As usual, Mac Duff took no credit for his part in Arizona's three-peat.

"People keep writing about Desert Swarm," he said, "but the most important play of '93 was a tackle by an offensive player. Remember when Terry Vaughn had that pass slip through his hands in the final three minutes at Cal, and it was intercepted? Well, Arizona's back in the Rose Bowl because he had the presence of mind to turn around and tackle Cal's Eric Zomalt.

"You know," Mac Duff said, shaking his head, "I don't think I'd have gotten the San Diego State job unless we had beaten Cal that day and returned to the Rose Bowl. If you look at the film, Zomalt had nothing but clear sailing into the end zone after the interception. One slip, one play — you never know what it means in this crazy game."

The pressure this year was greater than the others, Dad. There was the Sports Illustrated cover thing and that harrowing victory in Oregon. Tomey couldn't get anyone to take the Ducks seriously — not until Oregon reached the UA 27 late in the game, trailing 9-3. That's when Mike Scurlock made that marvelous defensive play, stripping an Oregon receiver of the ball on a fourth-and-five play.

Maybe you read how Rich Brooks got fined by the Pac-10, tearing into the zebras, claiming it was pass interference. But those calls can go either way. One way, and Oregon's a legitimate threat for, who knows, maybe even the Rose Bowl. The other way, and Arizona's in Pasadena for a third year in succession.

It could drive Mother Teresa to drink.

If three plays go the other way, it could've meant empty seats. Deficit spending. Recruiting woes. It'd be just like Utah State. (Whoops, sorry Dad).

There never would've been enough money for Ced Dempsey to build the new (appropriately titled) Cedric Dempsey Football Center, adjacent to McKale, before he left to take charge of the NCAA. The Wildcats would've never been able to recruit those '93 Best in the West all-stars — Keyshawn Johnson probably would've ended up at USC, instead of catching all those passes to beat the Trojans; Sabino's Corey Hill might've gone to Stanford; the expansion of Arizona Stadium to 66,000 seats — and 12 straight sellouts — would've been just an empty dream.

Three plays.

I mean, use your imagination. If Jey Phillips doesn't break up that pass at 'SC; if Terry Vaughn's tipped-pass is returned for a Cal TD; if Oregon makes one more completion in that fourth-quarter drive, the Wildcats might be playing in, dread the thought, the Freedom Bowl.

Nothing against Disneyland, but I'd rather spend my Christmas vacations with the family.

I remember how it was a few years ago, when Arizona used to break the hearts of its fans every November. The Cats would get everybody up on their tiptoes, expecting a kiss — and then turn into a toad. The joke about Arizona football was, anything would've been preferable to another November collapse. It was like a Charlie Brown whiff.

Three plays changed a lot of things.

The reason I haven't had much free time on this visit to Pasadena is that we've had to chase down all those rumors about Tomey interviewing for the jobs with the Eagles/Sooners/Rams.

But last night, just before I finished my "Forget the Rose Bowl, Arizona's goal should be to win the national championship" story, I bumped into Tomey in the lobby. I asked him if he had done all that he could do at Arizona. Was he ready for a new challenge?

"If I have only one game left to coach," he said, "I will coach it at the Rose Bowl."

Some things never change, Dad.

# Wildcats make best of worst-case scenarios

*Sunday, October 4, 1998*

*SEATTLE*

Unbeaten. Unbelievable.

A worst-case scenario isn't necessarily Arizona's Trung Canidate fumbling on the first play of the game, or the Wildcats missing an extra point, a short field goal, or finding themselves down to their fifth receiver, fourth cornerback and eighth defensive back.

A worst-case scenario is Ortege Jenkins running toward the goal-line, 12 seconds remaining, out of timeouts, his path blocked by several Washington tacklers. The only way he could score would be a somer-sault, vaulting over whomever was in his path, hoping he landed in the end zone instead of the hospital.

Anything less than the most perfect vault since Kerri Strug would mean one of the most agonizing Arizona losses of the decade.

So, naturally, Jenkins lands on his feet in the end zone, and the Wildcats are 5-0. Unbeaten. Unbelievable.

It might not become the most legendary play in school history — the regular season has seven games to go — but for the next six days it will be replayed on Tucson TV more than a Jim Click commercial.

On a night the Wildcats had every reason to lose, they won one of the most significant games of their 21 seasons in the Pac-10. They beat the Huskies 31-28 when Jenkins drove them 80 yards in the final 2:52. Whatever it took, he did. He even caught a pass.

I wonder if he'll get a cut of the 10,000 extra tickets that will now be sold for Saturday's game at Arizona Stadium against 3-0 UCLA?

For the first 57 minutes last night, the UA played with a cloud over its head.

The week began to unravel at a little summit meeting on the UA practice field Tuesday afternoon between UA coach Dick Tomey and Bill Morgan, the school's director of compliance. (Which is a nice way of saying Morgan is the poor soul assigned to sit in the NCAA's neck-deep red tape and find periodic reasons to breathe.)

Morgan approached Tomey, a grim look on his face, explaining that the UA's franchise player, Chris McAlister, accepted two loans, totaling $24,800, from a Texas bank over the summer and the school had some explaining to do. As educated people do, the UA decided to phone the NCAA with the details.

This could not be good. The NCAA enforcement division and its catalog of committees has the history of a hanging judge. A bunch of Roy Beans. The last time it went easy on anybody — gave someone the benefit of the doubt — was, well, a better way of putting it is that Damon Stoudamire was robbed of the chance to play his final game at McKale Center because his father once took a free plane ride.

Tomey and Morgan walked quickly from the practice field to a phone hanging on a wall near McKale. Tomey talked at length, his manner animated. Anyone watching knew it couldn't have been good news.

He probably wasn't phoning ESPN's Lee Corso saying, "Hey, we're going to beat Washington to go 5-0."

Instead, you could imagine Tomey picturing his replacement cornerbacks, their heads on a swivel, looking waywardly at Washington touchdown passes all night. That's an apt description of how the Huskies took a 28-24 lead with 2:52 remaining.

Everybody's open.

There was no appeal for McAlister. There was an appeal for his teammates and at a time when things looked most hopeless. Whatever pain there was from a neck injury to cornerback Lee Gayles, or the injured groin muscle that forced the team's top receiver, Jeremy McDaniel, from the game, or an inexplicable 13 penalties were overcome in The Drive. Unbeaten. Unbelievable.

It should have a nickname, shouldn't it?

The gain here, from an Arizona perspective, is that it won a Meaningful Game, one that could have lasted longer than a few days of good feeling, such as it usually is in a victory over ASU. Now the Wildcats get to play in one of those Game of the Year scenarios that they haven't experienced since 1994. UA gets to fill the stadium, and it gets to tell football stories on the countdown to basketball practice.

All because Jenkins could improvise when it seemed most unlikely.

One game in Seattle isn't going to make Arizona's season. That will be determined in the weeks to come against Oregon and UCLA and Arizona State. But one play in Seattle reversed what would've been a devastating defeat.

Unbeaten. Unbelievable.

# Arizona earns its best season against big, strong Nebraska

*Thursday, December 31, 1998*

*SAN DIEGO*

With 10 minutes remaining, Nanci Kincaid sat on an empty equipment locker behind her husband's bench, searching for the words to console Arizona's football coach.

What do you say to a man who for 22 years has scratched and sweated and dreamed of being in a position to beat one of the game's ranking giants, the defending national champions, a chance that has come Dick Tomey's way once this lifetime?

"I wanted to cheer him up," she would say after the game. "I was preparing for that."

With 10 minutes to play, the Holiday Bowl had already been a classic. Nebraska led 20-16, and the Cornhuskers were everything Arizona thought they would be.

They were bigger, faster and stronger than anyone the Wildcats had played all year. They were fundamentally sound, almost clinical. They didn't miss a tackle. They played expertly on special teams. They had a fire that made you think it was the Orange Bowl and they were playing Florida State for the national championship.

An Arizona football team had never won a game like this. For that matter, an Arizona football team had never been in a game like this.

"I've been on teams (at UCLA and Kansas) that beat Nebraska before," Tomey said. "But it was nothing like this."

Nothing like this is right.

Arizona not only had what it took to drive 68 yards and take a 23-20 lead — seizing the moment like no UA team in 100 years — it had the moxie to stop two final Cornhusker possessions and therefore make 1998 the greatest year in school history.

What does it mean? Said Tomey: "It means we have 12 victories and no one in the country has more."

It means that the Wildcats will finish the season ranked in the top four or five and sell almost all the tickets they can print for the 1999 home season. The respect is priceless.

"This catapults our whole university," said tailback Trung Canidate, a tough guy on the toughest night, finding a way to rush for

47

101 yards. "This gives us respect all over the nation."

Opportunity was not lost. The school that for so many years had to say "could've" or "should've" left Qualcomm Stadium last night with just one word.

Did.

Everything fell the UA's way. UCLA's loss to Miami took the Wildcats out of the Rose Bowl, which created some temporary angst, but when the big picture came into view it became clear that Arizona had a much greater opportunity at the Holiday Bowl.

Beating Nebraska in 1998 is like beating John Wooden's UCLA basketball teams in the '60s and '70s.

It wasn't easy.

UA defensive coordinator Rich Ellerson had a month to install a new system that he hoped would slow down Nebraska's smothering option offense. The result was better than even Ellerson could have expected. The Huskers rushed 34 times for 87 yards, their worst total of the season. That forced Nebraska to do what it didn't want to do: pass 28 times.

"We warmed up to the option," Tomey said. "That was way below their total."

Offensive coordinator Dino Babers had his game plan scuttled early in the first quarter. The team's franchise receiver, Jeremy McDaniel, injured his hip and didn't return.

It took three quarters and a ton of patience before Babers and quarterback Keith Smith found a way to move the ball effectively. Mostly it was the improvisational excellence of Smith, who ran three times for 36 yards in the winning drive. Smith's 15-yard touchdown pass to Brad Brennan to open the fourth quarter was, in a word, perfect.

The only place the ball could have gone without being intercepted or deflected was at Brennan's fingertips. The ball got there and he made the catch of his life.

"It's just sick," said Brennan. "I grew up watching Nebraska and all you'd hear is how great they are. And here we are, beating them with a fourth-quarter comeback. We begged for respect all year. We won't have to beg anymore."

At halftime, trailing 13-9, the first time the Wildcats trailed at half this season, Tomey did some of his best work. He studied the statistics sheet and threw it down. Arizona had zero yards rushing at half.

It was the motivation Tomey was searching for.

"He was pretty inspirational," Canidate said. "He wrote on the blackboard that our goal was to win the fourth quarter and to run the ball, and we've got to protect the passer. That's the way it happened."

Smith was superb. Without McDaniel, he improvised. Hitting Dennis Northcutt in the UA's deadly short-passing game. He saw running space and took it. "We knew we had to score on that last drive," he said. "The offensive line knew it. We all knew it. That was so fun."

During the trophy presentation after the game, Smith accepted the trophy for Most Outstanding Player, walked down a few steps and was greeted by quarterback Ortege Jenkins.

Jenkins was crying.

They embraced for about 30 seconds, reveling in the greatest moment of their football careers, the snapshot of all snapshots in Arizona's 12-1 season. Two unselfish young men, sharing the moment.

When they broke apart, Smith, too, was crying.

"I don't know what this means yet," he said. "But it's something sweet, something real damn sweet."

DAVID SANDERS

UA running back Trung Canidate gives head coach Dick Tomey an impromptu shower after the Cats rallied late to beat Nebraska in the 1998 Holiday Bowl.

# UA '29-'59: slow-track trips, fast-track growth

*Friday, October 15, 1999*

In order to properly appreciate tomorrow's Centennial Football game at Arizona Stadium, I went back — way back — to UA anniversary teams in 1929, 1939, 1949 and 1959.

What I found in my time travel was as amusing as it was engrossing. I discovered 50 ways UA football has changed.

**The 1929 season**

1. Sophomore tackle Laurence W. Bever Jr. reports for practice out of shape. The Star writes that he "resembles a middle-aged Papago Indian."

2. For the opener, a 24-man traveling squad leaves Tucson via train at 9 p.m. on a Thursday for a Friday night game against Occidental in the Rose Bowl. They arrive at noon on game day.

3. UA beats Occidental 16-7 in the first night game ever played at the Rose Bowl. At halftime, a fireworks display spells out "Welcome Arzona." The "i" doesn't ignite.

4. In the game story, The Associated Press refers to UA coach J.F. McKale as "Fred."

5. UA halfback Frank Sancet (later the school's baseball coach) makes a tackle so hard against Occidental that McKale tells the Star "that's the way football should sound."

6. Hayzel Daniels, the 1926 Arizona high school Player of the Year at Tucson High School, is allowed to play on the UA freshman team, but not the varsity. It will be another 20 years before a black player appears in a UA varsity football uniform.

7. A day after beating Occidental, McKale takes his team to the USC-UCLA game. The Bruins win 76-0. (A year earlier the Trojans beat Arizona 78-6.)

8. About 500 people pay $2.25 each for reserved seats on the 50-yard line for the first game played at UA's new on-campus football stadium. Cost to build the facility: $16,000.

9. School officials, coaches and community leaders have a "Pajama Parade" downtown a day before the opening of the football stadium.

10. On Oct. 12, about 8,000 fans squeeze into the 7,300-seat sta-

dium in the first game played at the new stadium, a 35-0 victory over Caltech. Because of a 3:30 p.m. start, the final four minutes of the game are played in virtual darkness.

11. Cal Tech gains 19 total yards in the game, a school record for defense.

12. The Star reports that the stadium puts UA football "in fast company" and questions whether it should continue to play the New Mexico State Aggies and Arizona State.

13. UA's biggest player, Gus Seidel, weighs 192 pounds.

14. UA beats Arizona State 26-0, meaning it has outscored ASU 225-3 at that point of the 20th century.

**The 1939 season**

15. UA returns from its previous game, a 13-6 loss at Marquette, on a Tuesday afternoon. By train.

16. Coach Miles Casteel takes the team immediately from the train — abbreviating a welcome-home serenade by the school band at the Southern Pacific terminal — to the practice field.

17. Marquette and Arizona combine for 27 punts in that game.

18. UA's next game, against Centenary, sells out, 11,000 strong. Yes. In Tucson. After a loss.

19. Wildcat home games are played at Varsity Stadium.

20. Arizona State is not on the schedule.

21. Centenary's best running back is named Weenie Bynum.

22. Helen Casteel, wife of UA's head coach, has a Tuesday evening radio program on KVOA titled "Punt Formation."

23. Arizona's heaviest player is Jack Dungan. He weighs 204 pounds.

24. A college football game requires just four referees (there are seven today).

25. There are no black players on UA's roster.

26. UA has its first "Hail Mary" in history when John Black completes a 60-yard pass to Hank Stanton with 29 seconds remaining to beat Centenary 7-0.

27. In the first paragraph of the next day's newspaper account of the Black-to-Stanton pass, the words "galvanized," "frenzied," "scintillating" and "courageous" are used.

28. The writer further states the '39 UA-Centenary game "would live forever in UA annals."

29. There is no "Bear Down, Arizona" song. Not for another 12 years.

**The 1949 season**

30. UA's best player, halfback Eddie Wolgast, is known as

"Ounces." He weighs 155 pounds.

31. Arizona has football ticket outlets in Winkelman, Superior, Hayden, Globe and Benson.

32. All-conference end Max Spilsbury is the UA heavyweight boxing champion and the top point scorer on the UA rodeo team.

33. UA has one black player, Fred Batiste.

34. Arizona wears gold helmets. True.

35. Tackle Larry Howard, at 225 pounds, is UA's biggest player.

36. The Wildcat roster has 12 players from Tucson and only nine from California.

37. No UA player has a jersey number above 89, or below 10.

38. The UA marching band has no females.

39. The full-page ad on the inside front cover of the UA-Utah game program is for Phillip Morris cigarettes. Its slogan: "You'll be glad tomorrow that you smoked today."

40. Sancet is the head freshman football coach.

41. A column in the Star reports that Michigan State "can't beat the Wildcats as badly in Tucson as it did a year earlier (61-7) in East Lansing, Mich." Final score: MSU 75, Arizona 0.

## The 1959 season

42. The homecoming dance, the alumni dance, the letterman's breakfast and the Towncats boosters luncheon are all held at the Pioneer Hotel downtown.

43. UA breaks its season attendance record with a 19,189 average.

44. There are only 48 players on the varsity roster.

45. Guard Steve Kerr (the other guard Steve Kerr) lists his hometown as "Cut & Shoot, Texas" in the game program. It is later changed to Conroe, Texas.

46. UA's biggest player is tackle Harold Tomlin, at 218 pounds.

47. All home games start at 8 p.m.

48. Utah beats Arizona 54-6 in Salt Lake City on a day in which winds of 84 mph are clocked at the stadium.

49. Preseason practice doesn't begin until Aug. 28, and the first game isn't until Sept. 19.

50. After a tiny crowd of 6,000 watches UA and West Texas State in a Border Conference game in Canyon, Texas, Star columnist Abe Chanin writes that Arizona should get out of the league. "It isn't an impossibility that someday Arizona will be playing in the same league as USC, UCLA, Stanford and Cal. Just watch Arizona athletics grow."

# It was painful for good man to step aside

*Saturday, November 25, 2000*

So many of Dick Tomey's boys came home yesterday to stand on the sideline with their old coach again.

Ty Parten. Chuck Cecil. Jimmy Sprotte. Everywhere the coach looked, he was surrounded by 14 years of success. Paul Stamer. Chuck Osborne. Heath Bray. Joe Tofflemire.

This is the way it had been for 164 games. If you have Wildcat blood, you are family. Marc Lunsford came back yesterday. Rip Scherer. Mike Flores.

Even when Tomey left the field for the final time as Arizona's coach, he was escorted by one of his old linemen, Val Bichekas. Bichekas escorted Tomey off the field when the Wildcats beat Miami in the 1994 Fiesta Bowl. Now, in the tough times, he didn't turn away.

Bichekas helped Tomey down a set of stairs, turned back toward the quiet stadium and pounded a fist into his hand. "Dammit!" he said aloud. "Damn it all to hell."

Yes.

Bichekas knew. So did the 54,297 who saw the Sun Devils beat the Wildcats 30-17 at Arizona Stadium and thousands upon thousands of others who watched or listened to the final game of the Dick Tomey era.

It was time for a good man to go.

It isn't that he can't coach college football at the highest level. It isn't that he can't win at the highest level of the game. It's that we shouted too long and too often for his head.

We wanted him out. We got it.

We simply wore him down.

Those who cried for Tomey to leave should have been in the room beneath Arizona Stadium when he told his players that he was leaving. They should be forced to see what it is they wrought, and then try to live with themselves.

They would have seen ex-Wildcat fullback Kelvin Eafon, his eligibility exhausted two seasons ago, sitting on a table, dabbing a towel at his eyes.

"He gave us all a chance. He made us feel like part of his family," Eafon said between sobs. "He didn't let anybody down. We let him

53

down."

They would have seen Tomey's only son, Rich, appalled as he regarded a mob of cameramen and reporters circling his father, probing for a sound bite.

To Tomey's credit, for the first time, he didn't give them more than a few seconds of what is the rest of his life. He is 62 years old. He has better things to do than let us see him suffer.

They should have seen sophomore receiver Bobby Wade embrace his coach and cry like a baby.

And they should have seen Tomey simultaneously hug two of his former coaches, Scherer and Flores. Tears everywhere. Or perhaps they should have been forced to watch as two of his assistant coaches, Charlie Dickey and Dino Babers, walked slowly from the locker room, their faces covered with hurt.

College football is a lot of things, but it shouldn't be about seeing grown men cry.

Tucson never did take Dick Tomey to its soul and welcome him. In his good years we appreciated those victories over USC and UCLA, and we let down our guard and admitted that he was "OK" whenever he beat the Sun Devils.

But mostly we kept him at arm's length, critical that he didn't have a quarterback with an NFL arm, or that he couldn't kick down the door to the Rose Bowl just once.

We too often measured him against Lute Olson and for every one of us who did so, shame on us.

Dick Tomey is about much more than Rose Bowls. How many coaches are so thoroughly liked — loved, perhaps? — by his former players as Dick Tomey? Whatever the number, it is a small one.

In the 14 years he coached the Wildcats, he had a better record than Stanford, Cal, Oregon, Oregon State, Washington State, Arizona State and UCLA. Let's see if the next coach can do that.

In the end, Tomey made it easy on his boss, Jim Livengood, by simply walking away. He left with the same quiet dignity he displayed for 14 years. When he decided to quit, he told his family, he told his team and then he told us. As always, his priorities are in order.

The measure of a football coach isn't always beating Arizona State.

Eight or nine years ago, I came across a former UA football player near the school library. Earl Johnson was a reserve tackle from Washington, D.C., with no immediate family and no real life plan.

He had quit the team a year earlier, and nobody missed him. I didn't even know he had quit the team until I saw him on campus that day.

"Earl," I said, "where have you been?"

"Oh, just going to school," he said.

"What about football?"

"I went in to coach Tomey last year and told him I was quitting the team and leaving school, maybe moving to Las Vegas. He told me that it was OK to quit football, but that he wouldn't let me quit school. He left me on scholarship and here I am, trying to graduate."

Earl Johnson is one of Dick Tomey's boys.

He didn't get to the Rose Bowl, either. He went way beyond that.

May we all remember that when Arizona's new coach loses his first few games and we cry for something better.

We just let better get away.

John Mackovic shouts at Larry Mac Duff, his defensive coordinator, in a game against UCLA on Nov. 9, 2002 — 10 months before Mackovic was fired.

JAMES S. WOOD

# UA missed opportunity to start fresh

*Thursday, November 14, 2002*

This is what I saw when I walked up a tunnel to the visitor's locker room at Husky Stadium on Oct. 12 in Seattle:

Rather than address his team and staff after a 32-28 loss to Washington, UA football coach John Mackovic chose to scold junior safety Clay Hardt in a public corridor.

"I don't know if I'll let you back on my team," Mackovic said.

"Coach, I work my butt off for you," Hardt said, loudly. "I'm never going to quit."

"I'll decide if you quit or not," Mackovic said.

The conversation lasted five minutes, maybe longer. It was such an awkward scene that I moved 10 or 20 yards down the tunnel to get out of earshot. Mackovic did not talk to his team after the game. After reducing Hardt to tears, he went to a media interview room and spoke calmly about the day's events.

Since that day, I've talked to a dozen Arizona players, assistant coaches and support personnel about the incident in the tunnel. One bizarre story led to another: a tirade after a loss at Wisconsin; the threat to fire coaches in a Monday team meeting; the humiliating criticism of tight end Justin Levasseur on the sidelines against UCLA.

The story was always the same: I'll give you the details, but you didn't get this from me.

No one dared to stand up to John Mackovic.

Wednesday, Levasseur's father, Michael, told me: "Being in that program, Justin has been made to feel worthless, like he's a bad human being."

So, now, the difficulty facing Mackovic, 59, who is 8-13 as Arizona's head coach, isn't about wins and losses. It is about behavior and civility.

Tuesday night, I stood on the steps outside the UA administration building and counted 41 players walking through the front door and into a large classroom, where they were greeted by UA president Peter Likins.

They were not there to discuss curriculum for spring semester. Wednesday, with his job and reputation at stake, Mackovic wept and said, "I'm terribly sorry for this turmoil and unrest."

His boss, athletic director Jim Livengood, pledged allegiance to

Mackovic and said of the UA's football constituency, "We're quick to condemn and less quick to embrace."

Once Mackovic dabbed away his tears and embraced his boss, a cleansing scene recorded by a dozen television cameras, you couldn't help but regain faith in the human spirit.

Arizona will give Mackovic a second chance, not much different from the second chance Indiana gave churlish basketball coach Bob Knight a few years ago.

It was so warm and fuzzy you would have thought the Wildcats had at long last punched their Rose Bowl ticket.

But as Indiana learned with Knight, once the TV lights fade and life goes on, the problems usually remain.

What happens the next time Mackovic calls someone an SOB? Will that constitute a firing offense?

"Sometimes," said Mackovic, "what looks like an obstacle turns into an opportunity."

It says here that the UA got this one backward.

The UA kept the obstacle and let the opportunity slip. With a perfect opportunity to refresh the Arizona football program, to hire Mike Riley, a former Pac-10 and NFL head coach, or Ricky Hunley, the former UA All-America linebacker, or someone who hasn't compromised his standing with (a) the Tucson community, (b) UA football players, and (c) recruitable high school seniors, the Wildcats swung and missed.

Mackovic's career is almost certainly in ruins, and as a result, so is the Arizona football program.

The irreparable damage done by a player insurrection begs this question: How can Mackovic earn the respect of his players, now and in the future?

How will he command authority in a game that insists the head coach rise above pettiness, exhibiting fairness, toughness and compassion? In his UA career, Mackovic has mostly defaulted in those areas.

Would the mother and father of a 17-year-old high school prospect send their son to Arizona with the knowledge that Mackovic said, "I'm sorrowful for my actions and inactions?"

Livengood produced the administrative equivalent of a shell game Wednesday. He turned an awful situation into a love-fest. He's good at that. But in the end, the Wildcat football program is in worse shape today than it was Wednesday.

Where does the UA go to recruit new players? Where does it go to hire capable assistant coaches if Mackovic elects to clean house? Who would come here now?

In most seasons, even bad seasons, Arizona can sell hope and the future. What can it sell now, contrition?

The bill for hiring John Mackovic has come due and it goes far beyond his $800,000-a-year salary.

EDITOR'S NOTE: Arizona won its next game after the player revolt against John Mackovic, but the Wildcats lost the season finale at home to Arizona State. Mackovic was fired Sept. 28, 2003, five games into the season after four straight losses — by a combined margin of 179-40 — left the UA with a 1-4 record. Defensive coordinator Mike Hankwitz took over as interim coach, and the Wildcats finished the year 2-10, the most losses in school history. Mackovic has not coached in the college game since his ouster at Arizona, but he was named head coach of the United States national team in 2006. In 2007, he led the U.S. to the championship of the six-nation American Football World Cup by beating tournament host Japan. Mackovic lives in Palm Springs, Calif. He writes an occasional column for the city's newspaper, The Desert Sun.

Receiver Mike Thomas beats a UCLA defender to the end zone in Arizona's stunning 52-14 win over the seventh-ranked, unbeaten Bruins in 2005.

BENJIE SANDERS

# Wildcats rout undefeated UCLA: ALL RIGHT!

*Sunday, November 6, 2005*

Picture your best day of the year: The mail includes a notice from the IRS, detailing the $4,286 you have overpaid. The office phones with news that you have been recommended for a promotion, a raise and a Christmas bonus.

You meet your cardiologist at the golf course. He slaps you on the back and says "Mr. Stoops, the X-rays all came back negative. You don't have high blood pressure or a heart problem, after all. It was just some bad pizza."

Or, if you're an Arizona football player, the best day of the year is beating undefeated UCLA 52-14 the way the long-suffering Wildcats did Saturday.

The UA won the running game, the passing game and the kicking game by playing a perfect game.

"Everything we tried to do, we did," said freshman quarterback Willie Tuitama, who required a full five minutes to work his way off the field, stacked up by thousands of celebrating fans. "I'm sort of shocked. It's crazy."

How crazy? Junior receiver and kick returner Syndric Steptoe emerged from the UA locker room carrying two footballs.

"One was a game ball that coach (Mike) Stoops gave me," he said. "The other is the ball I caught on the punt and returned for a touchdown."

Two game balls, one player. That hardly fits the profile of an Arizona football program that has struggled since 1998 without a winning season.

In scope and magnitude, Saturday's game will surely be judged among the three most meaningful Wildcat home victories (not including Arizona State games) since the UA joined the Pac-10 in 1978. But rarely has any UA football victory been more resounding and unexpected at the same time.

One, plainly, was a 16-3 victory over No. 1 Washington in 1992, a November game that triggered the Desert Swarm era.

The other, in 1980, bears a close resemblance to Saturday's epic performance. Struggling under first-year coach Larry Smith, the 2-4

61

Wildcats of '80 started true freshman quarterback Tom Tunnicliffe against No. 2 UCLA, winning 23-17.

By coincidence, Smith was in the press box Saturday, having spent a homecoming weekend with members of that silver anniversary team.

"That game ignited our younger guys, sort of launching us for all the success we had the next few years," he said. "I see the same thing here now. Tuitama has a magic about him that has touched the whole program and has now touched everybody in the stadium."

Tuitama has won both of his collegiate starts. That borders on the absurd when you consider that Arizona last won two games in succession in September 2002, and not in the Pac-10 since October 2000.

When Wildcat coaches activated Tuitama in the first half of the Oregon game three weeks ago, the unstated goal was to give him some break-in time so that next September Tuitama might have enough game savvy to help the Wildcats avoid another dreadful season.

Deploying Tuitama was one way of writing off this season. And, besides, what did the UA have left to lose?

And then — boom — Arizona scores 52 points against the nation's seventh-ranked team.

"It has just kind of snowballed," said UA offensive coordinator Mike Canales, whose play-calling and strategy on Saturday was as superb as in last week's upset victory at Oregon State. "You could see it starting to happen, the whole atmosphere had changed. It has been contagious. It's amazing what one man can do."

The Wildcats drew 55,775 for Saturday's game, and if they can sell about 53,000 tickets for the home finale against Washington, they will establish a season attendance record. That's just nuts. This is a city so hungry for a football winner that people are turning out in unprecedented numbers.

Until Saturday, most of the ticket buyers were attracted by a sense of hope. Now the gloves are off. Why can't Arizona win out, beat Washington and ASU? Ladies and gentlemen, start your expectations.

"The program is now going uphill, in the right direction," said linebacker Spencer Larsen, who has been in the program since 2001. "Back in the olden days, it felt like we were standing still."

After showering and returning to his street clothes, Tuitama walked onto a concourse adjacent to the UA locker room. Several hundred fans remained, some shouting his name. The 18-year-old quarterback was instantly surrounded by a score of media people.

Three weeks earlier, in the same space, Arizona had lost its fifth consecutive game. There were no fans and no happy chants. It was football as Tucson had painfully come to know it.

But on Saturday night, the kid quarterback soaked it in. He has come so far, so fast. Everything has changed.

"I guess I wish I had played all year," he said, softly. "But I had to wait until my time was called."

For Tuitama and the Wildcats, the time is now.

Minutes after he lifted coach Mike Stoops off the ground in celebration, the UA's Ronnie Palmer hoists the 2008 Las Vegas Bowl championship trophy.

# UA finally finds light at end of tunnel

*Sunday, December 21, 2008*

*LAS VEGAS*

By sundown Saturday, more than 15,000 Wildcat fans had over-come the numbing traffic, parked in the mud near Sam Boyd Stadium and dusted off their rarely used winter gear.

In this chilly, unfamiliar and faraway place, they had arrived.

A lot of them blew their Christmas budgets, drove through snow-storms, waited for the Mike Stoops-to-Iowa State fiasco to play out and, finally, celebrated Arizona's return to football relevance.

But their journey couldn't touch the difficulty encountered by the Wildcats, who have spent the last decade lost in a football wilderness.

"We've been in some dark places," UA coach Mike Stoops said 24 hours before kickoff.

On Saturday night, the lights came on. Arizona thumped BYU 31-21. Almost instantly, the chill went away.

"It's a good day to be a Wildcat," said Ricky Hunley, the school's greatest player. "It took a long time."

Beating a third-place Mountain West Conference team, even BYU, isn't going to shake up college football. But the Wildcats and their fans were overjoyed, celebrating amid a spray of confetti. It is one of the best arguments yet for not having a playoff system in college football.

"We're winners," said senior safety Nate Ness. "We're going out winners."

Unlike previous Pac-10 visitors to the Las Vegas Bowl, the Wildcats liked everything about it. They couldn't wait to get here. They enjoyed a snowstorm. They won a dance contest and a battle of the bands, and they loved their posh, all-suites hotel.

But they enjoyed most the opportunity to play the Cougars on a national stage, whip 'em, and walk away from a season with something more than their self-respect. This time they went home with a cham-pionship trophy.

Plenty of shelf space available at McKale Center.

The perfect symbolism to a decade of bad football played out in the final three minutes. After closing to within 10 points, the Cougars recovered on onside kick. In an instant, a doomsday scenario — an unthinkable shocking collapse — manifested itself.

But when kicker Mitch Payne's field goal attempt caromed off the crossbar, no good, it was as if to balance 10 years of bad bounces for Arizona football.

"We've gone through so much for so long, and this is a reward for sticking it out," quarterback Willie Tuitama said. "And this is just the beginning; Arizona is going to keep winning."

Saturday's game was an expected measurement of Arizona football. Against perhaps the nation's top mid-major program, the Wildcats would play BYU in Game 3 of a three-game series that began in Tucson in the fall of 2006.

Arizona won in Tucson on a last-second kick, 16-13. The Cougars won in Utah 20-7, dominating Sonny Dykes' new spread offense in its 2007 debut. But that was 23 games ago. The offense Dykes and Tuitama put on the field Saturday has been refined, tested and corrected.

When the Cougar defense chose to take out UA tight end Rob Gronkowski and limit Arizona's running game, it essentially dared Dykes and Tuitama to beat them passing to his co-stars. And they were resourceful enough to do it.

"We knew we had a faster offense than them," fullback Chris Gronkowski said. "We used our speed to spread the field."

Tuitama's final half in a Wildcat uniform was among his best. He hit on 10 of 12 passes in the second half, two of them for touchdowns. To cap his career, he sprinted — that's no misprint, either — 6 yards for the clinching touchdown.

Imagine that.

Tuitama completed 13 passes to his secondary targets, Delashaun Dean, Terrell Turner and Chris Gronkowski, rather than try to force passes to Rob Gronkowski or Mike Thomas, both of whom were BYU's primary defensive targets.

The Arizona offense no longer splashes. It swims.

In the final two minutes, with the clock ticking toward happiness and Mike Stoops fidgeting with his red-colored copy of the defensive game plan, he was thoughtful enough to call a timeout and order a final pass to Thomas. More winning symbolism. The pass allowed Thomas to become the Pac-10's career receiving leader.

After the record pass was delivered, senior linebacker Ronnie Palmer picked up Stoops and embraced him. When he returned Stoops to the turf, junior defensive lineman Donald Horton did the same thing. It was a hug-fest at a school that for so long went without a hug.

On the day Stoops was hired, Nov. 29, 2003, he boldly said, "I always felt you could win anywhere."

At the time, Tucson was, gulp, "anywhere." Now it is somewhere.

"There's no way the average Joe can understand the trials and tribulations we've gone through in five years," Stoops said Friday. "It's very taxing and wears on you and your family. Getting to this point is the payoff for five years."

Along the way, the Wildcats learned enough about winning to move into a class with the best teams in school history.

In its 31 seasons of Pac-10 football, Arizona has won eight or more games only in 1985, 1986, 1989, 1993, 1994 and 1998. It seemed like it took forever to add 2008 to the list.

"This is just the start," said Ness, who repeated himself twice more. "This is just the start. This is just the start."

In the context of Arizona football, you can repeat it until it becomes an echo.

# CHAPTER TWO

# Golf in Tucson

## Early years of Tucson Open provided special moments

*Monday, October 21, 1985*

The Tucson Open, by any name, turns 40 this week. Forget the jokes about life beginning at 40, or that it took Tucson 39 years to get it right.

Pro golf in Tucson has been right for 39 years.

No matter how long I examined the archives and studied the first 39 years of the Tucson Open, one thought kept coming back to me — the best tournament might have been the first one.

I give full due to Cactus Johnny Miller, his four championships and the round of 61 he shot to win in 1975.

On a clear day you can probably still hear the cheers of Arnie's Army echoing through the Catalinas — even though it has been 18 years since Mr. Palmer strode victoriously from the 72nd hole of the 1967 tournament.

Lee Trevino's consecutive championships in '69 and '70 were unforgettable, as were the successive victories by Jimmy Demaret in '46 and '47. The old-timers still talk about the all-purple outfit Demaret wore for the final round of the '47 tournament — and of the 10-over-par 14 he shot on the No. 18 hole at El Rio in 1952. That's one record that will never fall: five out-of-bounds shots by one pro, one hole, one year, one round.

If you backed some of Tucson's veteran golf observers into a corner and asked for a vote on their favorite tournament, Lloyd Mangrum's 1951 victory would surely get mention.

"There used to be a big Calcutta event and a big-stakes craps game before every tournament," said Paul Bohardt, 68, a retired Tucson chief of police who played as an amateur in the first Tucson Open.

"Well, in 1951, Mangrum won the big money in both the Calcutta and at craps. And then he won the tournament. Since he had won the Tucson

Open in 1949, he was really getting to like this town.

"But I still remember Mangrum walking from the practice tee one day during the '51 tournament when a young woman approached him and asked if he wanted to buy a $1 raffle ticket for a new Plymouth. He flipped her a dollar and walked away.

"Wouldn't you know it? Damned if Mangrum didn't win the new car, too. Talk about a good tournament."

But the precedent for good golf tournaments had been set six years before, when the late Leo Diegel, then the pro at El Rio, convinced PGA Commissioner Fred Corcoran that Tucson was big enough to support a pro tournament.

"Leo was always talking about a pro tournament and he was putting in a word to the pros about Tucson," said Roy Drachman, a prominent Tucson businessman who was among those active in getting the PGA to town.

"I really thought it was a pipe dream, though. I didn't think it would happen. The persistence of Diegel was the big factor."

So was the financial collapse of the El Paso Open, which had to withdraw from the tour in 1945. Tucson was ready, insofar as 65 businessmen put up $100 each to underwrite the tournament. A $5,000 purse was offered, and that was good enough for the PGA, which inserted Tucson into El Paso's spot and made it the third stop on the tour in January 1945.

All the leading names of golf hit town.

Sam Snead, Byron Nelson, George Zaharias and his wife, Babe Didrikson. Former New York Yankee outfielder Sam Byrd. The Mangrum brothers, Ray and Lloyd. Harold "Jug" McSpaden, who, with Nelson, made up the "Gold Dust Twins."

Season tickets were $4.80, a day pass was $1.29, and the golfers were benevolent enough to donate a 25-cent penalty to the war effort every time they hit a ball into a sand trap. The Red Cross collected $40 in penalties during the pro-am alone.

Snead shot a 66 in a practice round at El Rio and then was taken to Davis-Monthan Air Force Base, where he entered a long-drive contest on a runway. His drives measured 350, 352, 311 and 365 yards. Snead collected $100 in war bonds.

A day later, Jan. 19, 1945, the first official round of professional golf was played in Tucson. The leading headline in a local newspaper: "Yanks Report Reds 250 Miles from Berlin." Ginger Rogers was starring in "Tender Comrade" at the Fox Theatre downtown. Price of admission: 30 cents. Smoot-Harmer Realty advertised a six-room, three-bedroom house on five acres for $9,500.

Joe Zarhardt, a Philadelphian, broke the El Rio course record, shooting a 65 to lead the first round. Tucsonan Cliff Hadley, one of 10 local amateurs to earn a berth in the tournament, shot a 92, despite making an eagle-3 by chipping in on the ninth hole. Byron Nelson's drive on the No. 1 hole, 321 yards, won the long-drive contest and $100 in war bonds.

After the second day of play, in which Jug McSpaden led Snead by two strokes, Commissioner Corcoran announced that the Tucson Open had officially been added to the 1946 tour calendar. "And hopefully beyond that," said Corcoran.

Two rounds, 36 holes, were played on the third day. Snead faltered when his drives at holes Nos. 2, 3, 4 and 6 hit trees. "Just like a dog!" Snead yelled.

Ray Mangrum rallied to shoot 64-66 and defeated Nelson by a stroke, 268 to 269, and won the $1,000 championship check. Tournament Chairman Hi Corbett announced that the first Tucson Open had made a $300 profit and the money would be put toward improving the 1946 tournament.

"The tournaments in the '40s and '50s weren't as publicized as they are now," said Bohardt, who played in six of them. "And now they have million-dollar purses, bigger crowds and the players are bigger and stronger.

"But the first tournament in '45, and those soon thereafter, seemed to be just as glamorous. Maybe more so. There was more intimate contact between the players and the gallery. I still go as a spectator every year, but I liked it more the way it was back then."

ELIZABETH MANGELSDORF

Southern Arizona's first try at match play golf was a failure. When Jim Thorpe, right, won the title in 1985, interest in the event — and hot dogs — was minimal.

# Fans outnumber cacti — barely

*Sunday, October 27, 1985*

ABC's skycams panned the Tucson valley yesterday morning and showed America a few saguaros, a couple of tall buildings, a mountain-top and several golf fans.

You could have taken a nap on the 15th green at Randolph North Golf Course. It was like a late-September Braves-Giants game at Candlestick in which the TV cameraman pulls back and you get a picture of 58,000 empty seats and a few beer vendors.

Where were you? If you slept in, the third day of the Seiko Tucson Match Play tournament — Breakfast on Broadway and Alvernon — you missed it. ABC was off the air by noon, and an estimated crowd of 4,500 had the run of the place.

Geez, Joe Garagiola used to attract 4,500 people to the first tee block at this tournament. In the rain. To watch Scatman Crothers hit a duck hook.

And do you want to know where to get a good deal on a few gross of stale hot dog buns? The hot-dogs-cooked-to-hot-dogs-sold ratio was probably 25-1.

And, if you've forgotten, the final two rounds of the Match Play Championship are to be played today.

Don't be fooled by the semifinalist pairings — Jim Thorpe against Mac O'Grady, and Jack Renner vs. Bob Tway. The PGA adheres to truth-in-advertising.

This is still professional golf, and today's winner gets $150,000. Trust me.

I've got a plan that might double the size of the gallery: Invite the kin of semifinalists Thorpe and O'Grady. Thorpe is one of 12 children. O'Grady has four brothers, an older sister and a twin sister.

In any scenario, the PGA couldn't have handpicked a more intriguing match than Thorpe-O'Grady.

You can't get Thorpe to stop talking, and you can't get O'Grady to start. Thorpe's a former college football player (Morgan State), and O'Grady has had the grand slam of occupations — dishwasher, mortician, cook, factory grinder.

Unlike Tway and Renner, two soft-spoken, blend-into-the-landscape guys, Thorpe and O'Grady seem capable of turning the game into a contact sport.

73

When O'Grady walked from the ninth green Thursday morning, having been told by Bob Eastwood to tap in a gimme putt, O'Grady bristled. "If he's gonna do that," he said, audibly, "I'm gonna kick his ass."

O'Grady not only booted Eastwood out of the tournament, he got rid of Jay Haas, Larry Rinker and Tom "Go Royals" Watson, who didn't seem too upset at the thought of being able to get back to Kansas City in time for Game 6 of the World Series.

Thorpe, built like a pulling guard, kidded his first-round opponent, Tony Sills, by saying, "If I don't win I'm gonna break your head."

Sills went home shortly thereafter, head intact.

The most obvious casualty was Thorpe, who was missing a front tooth after yesterday's quarterfinal victory over Mark Wiebe.

"My (capped) tooth fell out during the round," Thorpe said. "I'm going to the dentist this afternoon."

Thorpe sounded more afraid of the dentist's chair than he did of O'Grady.

"I'm gonna win tomorrow," he said. "Believe me."

What O'Grady believes is anyone's guess.

He hasn't granted an interview this year, an attitude that can be traced to an April 1984 article by Sports Illustrated's Steve Wulf. O'Grady said the magazine made him out to be a "freak show."

Why? Well, the magazine not only detailed O'Grady's two-month existence in a 10x4x5-foot storage cabinet, it published a picture of his former "residence."

After O'Grady made a dramatic par putt on the 18th green yesterday, eliminating Watson, he dodged three TV crews and jogged to the dressing room.

"No interviews," he said. "I'll send a representative to the press room."

When O'Grady's representative reached the press room, a PGA official told him to take a hike. O'Grady stiffed the news media at the Byron Nelson Classic in midsummer, a tournament he led after three rounds. He said he would grant an interview only when he won a tournament, and only to get his story straight.

It's not exactly the same type of anticipation that might exist if say, Steve Carlton or Greta Garbo agreed to talk, but, well, it has been a slow week, what with the top 12 money winners in this tournament eliminated in preliminary rounds. Could today be that magic day?

Look at it this way: Even if nothing much happens, you should be able to get a good parking space.

# Clock is ticking to find LPGA sponsor

*Thursday, July 15, 2004*

Across the last five years, the LPGA Tour has lost title sponsors Ping, Oldsmobile, Subaru, Hyundai, Sara Lee, Mobile, ShopRite, ALL-TEL, AFLAC, AIG and a half-dozen other groups, big letters and small ones.

Cup Noodles, for instance. And Yoplait.

The last two to secede from women's pro golf were Tucson newly-weds Welch's and Fry's, whose union didn't fully last two years. On July 1, they became ex-sponsors of our leadoff spot on the LPGA Tour, leaving a desperate need for the Tucson Parks Foundation to raise close to $2 million.

In comparison, the LPGA Tour continues upright, in remarkably good health. It hopes to add a tournament in Mexico City next spring and is aggressively pursuing expansion in San Diego and Los Angeles, as well as the Southwest, perhaps Albuquerque or El Paso.

That's because when Electrolux and Japan Airlines leave the golf sponsorship business, the LPGA (and its tour members) have been successful in adding Giant Eagle (an online grocery), Hammond Hotels and Franklin American Mortgage, to name a few.

One thing is clear: The LPGA, currently in the most prosperous stage of its history, won't fold up and go away if the Parks Foundation cannot locate a title sponsor by late September.

This has become a way of life in Tucson golf. Our LPGA tournament has gone through sponsors — Circle K, Ping, the Arizona Mining Association, Welch's, Fry's — at a frightening pace. That's not odd in pro golf. Ten years ago, LPGA title sponsors included McCall's, Safeco, J.C. Penney, Sprint and Chrysler-Plymouth, now long gone from women's golf.

In the fall of 2002, Sue Brooks of Tucson's Marathon Marketing put together a deadline sponsorship with Fry's to keep our tournament afloat. She knows how it goes.

"The minute I heard Welch's pulled out, I started all over," Brooks said Wednesday. "We've got a real, real short window to put something together, but I've got some good prospects. If you put it on a hot-warm-cold scale, I'd say we're pretty warm."

Brooks has assistance from MVP, a national sports marketing group that is part of a corporate kingdom. It includes GEICO, Quizno's,

Thomasville and Olympus cameras, to name a few. Further, the Tucson Parks Foundation has employed retired Tucson IBM executive Jim Kasel to pursue a title sponsor and assume other management duties.

"I think our prospects of getting a sponsor by the LPGA's (September) deadline is greater than 50 percent," said Stan Turley, a Tucson soils engineer consultant who is a member of the Parks Foundation board of directors. "We aren't dead."

Who's potentially available to write a seven-figure check?

How about Audi, which aggressively stepped forward to sponsor former UA standout Lorena Ochoa? How about Home Depot, now in every Tucson neighborhood? And wouldn't it be a timely fit for Chase, which absorbed Bank One, to introduce itself to Southern Arizona by rescuing our golf tournament? Target, perhaps?

Someone. Anyone.

Welch's paid about $800,000 last year; Fry's was responsible for close to $600,000. Tucson's purse, $800,000, has been the lowest on the LPGA Tour, a full $200,000 under commissioner Ty Votaw's stated minimum.

Given its empty calendar in January and February, the LPGA can't easily dismiss Tucson. It needs more tournaments, even minimum-purse events. For that reason, the Parks Foundation has been blessed with the LPGA's assistance in locating potential sponsors.

"I've been with the tournament for eight years and we've successfully gone through some trials and tribulations," said Tucson contractor Tommy Roof. "This isn't the first time we've had a serious sponsorship challenge. We've been a good partner for the LPGA. They are willing to work with us."

Tucson's history as a pro sports host is abysmal. It has lost the Cleveland Indians, USA Baseball and the Insight.com Bowl, all in the last 11 years. It hasn't been willing to support a handful of minorleague hockey teams. And the latest casualty might be the Arizona Heat women's pro fastpitch team. The Heat's owner relinquished control to the league this week.

The PGA and LPGA tours have been exceptions. They have appeal and staying power, a rare combination in a relatively small sports market of 900,000 people.

It would be a shame to lose our spot on the women's tour, just as it begins to develop some steady intrigue, from Annika Sorenstam to Grace Park to Michelle Wie.

"Tucson and Arizona don't have the available corporate presence to step in; there are very few prospects here," said Brooks. "That's why we're going national in our search. We're going to shake bigger trees."

Meanwhile, the clock is ticking. Sorenstam is obligated, per LPGA rules, to play in our tournament next year, her first stop in Tucson since 2002. It would be a shame if she couldn't get a game here.

# Tucson's golf coup comes at no charge

*Monday, February 27, 2006*

*CARLSBAD, Calif.*

Parking was no problem. Many of the up-close spaces remained vacant Sunday afternoon. Ticket lines? None. Souvenir shop? Inventory was taken off the shelves and packed by 1 p.m.

The La Costa Resort and Spa is a lovely place with an idyllic sea breeze, Spanish-mission architecture, a setting so timeless you almost expect to see Bing Crosby and Bob Hope kibitzing on the 18th green.

The PGA Tour would be nuts not to want a world-class golf tournament here.

But at the WGC-Accenture Match Play Championship last week — Tiger Woods in the house! — the galleries never swelled to more than about 8,500. The galleries didn't swell at all.

By Sunday afternoon, you could almost count the house one-by-one, perhaps 2,000 fans, as 2005 Chrysler Classic of Tucson champion Geoff Ogilvy completed a dazzling week — six winning matches — beating Davis Love III 3 and 2.

Ogilvy laughed when asked which of the two tournaments was more difficult.

"Probably Tucson, because on the last five holes there are five guys that can beat you," he said. "Now I can go back to Tucson to defend next year. It's kind of ironic, isn't it? This has probably never happened before."

When Ogilvy, an Australian, won in Tucson last year, an estimated gallery of 30,000 watched the final round at Tucson National. On Sunday's 16th hole, when Ogilvy closed out Love, there were probably 500 people near the green.

"When we move to Tucson next year," said James Murphy, chief marketing and communications officer for Accenture, "we expect to have much larger crowds than we've had here."

Wade Dunagan, project manager of the Gallery Golf Club, smiled as Murphy talked.

When the Gallery played host to part of the first two rounds of the 2001 Chrysler Classic of Tucson — and remember, it was early January and snowed during Round 2 — Dunagan's initial plan was to convoy interested Tucson golf fans in three, 12-seat vans.

"By the end of that first day, we had five city buses," Dunagan remembers. "We had between 12,500 to 15,000 people out there."

The sporting earth had to move for Tucson to acquire one of golf's leading events. (1) The PGA Tour first had to give its blessing. (2) The sponsoring Accenture group had to agree. (3) The tour's management arm had to approve the venue. (4) And the enduring, capable Tucson Conquistadores had to be accommodated.

"We had umpteen meetings with all those people," said Russ Perlich, a Conquistador and PGA Tour board member most involved in bringing all groups together. "What it came down to was that Tucson is a community that can embrace the Match Play Championships. The Accenture people want the warm-and-fuzzies. Southern California couldn't provide that. We can."

The trigger for this transaction was supplied, innocently enough, by Tiger Woods. During one of the maddening rain delays at La Costa, Woods mentioned that it wasn't raining in Tucson, a quote that got exceptional length when published in the Los Angeles Times.

"It had a pretty big effect," said Perlich, who, since 2001, has flown to PGA Tour headquarters in Florida four or five times a year in an attempt to help broker this Tucson-wins transaction. "At first, the Accenture people came to Tucson with lukewarm results. Over time, they found we had what they wanted."

The Conquistadores and the Gallery scored heavily in this deal, so much so that it's in the we-can't-believe-our-good-fortune category.

The Gallery is expected to pay something in the $500,000 to $750,000 range to play host to the Match Play Championships. The typical PGA Tour host fee is 37 percent of the purse (or about $3 million in this case). How's that for a discount? When the Match Play purse rises to $8 million next year, the Tour and Accenture will pay almost all of it.

The attendant exposure should launch the Gallery into the stratosphere of elite-level golf facilities. It already has 367 members for two courses. It could double that by its relationship with a world-class golf event.

The Conquistadores will be given the entire ticket inventory. They will distribute all tickets and keep all the profit for their charities, the First Tee program and their foundation. More importantly, they will be able to retain their identity with pro golf.

They no longer will operate the tournament, but their charitable profits are expected to increase. Crazy.

The Dove Mountain development, part of Tucsonan Dave Mehl's tony 6,200-acre property, will become Southern Arizona's Scottsdale, a community that will next include a Jack Nicklaus-designed course scheduled to play host to the Match Play event beginning in 2009.

"We expect to break ground perhaps in August," said Mehl, who has twice met with Nicklaus at the Gallery in recent months.

Accenture, which posted a 2005 net profit of $15.5 billion and has more than 125,000 employees worldwide, uses the WGC event as a corporate celebration. Championship golf is merely part of it. It plans to lodge its CEOs and CFOs at the new Ritz-Carlton Hotel at Dove Mountain when/if that project is completed, possibly by 2008.

"Accenture is eager to have the event look, feel and sound like a global event," said Perlich. "This community can do that."

Given Tucson's spirit and ability to create a festival atmosphere for the La Fiesta de los Vaqueros, it shouldn't be difficult to summon similar energy for a golf tournament involving Woods, Ernie Els and Vijay Singh.

For a city of Tucson's size, this is as good as it gets in pro sports.

Moving to Tucson as day-to-day director of the event will be Mike Garten, who has operated in the same capacity at La Costa for eight years.

"Last week, we had maybe 7,500 to 10,000 people here on Friday, our top day," Garten said. "Everything I've been told is that Tucson will double that."

Match Play is a front-loaded event that supplies its best viewership on Wednesdays, Thursdays and Fridays. Unless Woods, John Daly or Phil Mickelson is involved on the weekend, it becomes more of a TV event.

The key word here is event. We now have one of the best, and we didn't have to pay a cent of public money or sell our soul to get it.

# Tucson crowd earns its stripes

*Thursday, February 22, 2007*

The Golf Channel's live broadcast of our little golf tournament began Wednesday precisely at noon. Tiger Woods was on the first tee at 12:02 p.m.

What a coincidence.

The first thing on camera was flesh. Those sunburned people who squeezed into maybe 350 first-tee seats couldn't have identified Bradley Dredge or Niclas Fasth in a police lineup. But they all shared the same information: Tiger was due at 12:02.

Ladies and gentlemen, we have liftoff.

When ABC/ESPN went on the air at the La Costa Resort and Spa for last year's WGC-Accenture Match Play Championship — any day, any time — you wondered if you had tuned to the South African Sunshine Tour by mistake.

"It was pretty shocking to see nobody in the crowd, and I mean virtually nobody," said Russ Perlich, the Conquistador most responsible for selling the PGA Tour and Accenture decision-makers on a move to Tucson. "I remember telling everybody that when the cameras came here, they would see a crowd at the first tee."

A crowd at the first tee? Did he get a look at the 15-deep lines at the 15th-hole concession tent?

We came, we saw, we liked it.

It doesn't matter how many people come through the gates at The Gallery Golf Club, South Course. The $50,000 Super Suites (that's about $70,000 with full catering) and the $30,000 Chalets sold out last fall.

The demand was such that the glitzy Mirage Hotel — yes, the same one on the Las Vegas Strip — agreed to buy a stake in the Global Aircraft Solutions Chalet on the agreement that it could send some big shots (such as Gene Simmons) out for a few days.

This is indeed a sun-KISSed event.

The TV people and the tour people and the Accenture people are happy. If nothing else, we made it look like a big event. Almost unimaginably, the final sanction came from Tiger himself.

After winning his first-round match Wednesday, Tiger walked stoically into the pressroom and said: "There's atmosphere out here... Today you could hear roars across the way."

If Tiger is satisfied, it's a go.

Dissenting opinions came quickly, however. The San Diego Union-Tribune, jilted when this tournament left La Costa, has been critical of the tournament's location. We expected that. The Los Angeles Times doesn't like the personality of the place. The Associated Press golf writer Doug Ferguson, a mightily respected voice in the industry, wrote "what are we doing here?"

Good question. The answer: The best we can.

We are under the microscope, an interloper in the Big Game business, trying to prove ourselves as we go.

The biggest sin of the Gallery's South Course is that it isn't entirely walkable. Unlike traditional golf courses that route their holes so that Nos. 9 and 18 return to the clubhouse, the Gallery South seems to stretch halfway to Picacho Peak before turning back to the clubhouse. The most distant point from the clubhouse is the No. 7 green.

You can get lost out there with the Border Patrol.

The PGA Tour's management group was quick to fix many of the early quirks. It installed an internal shuttle service between the No. 12 and No. 18 holes that takes 30 minutes off everyone's foray into the faraway desert. And it installed four extra porta-potties on the front nine, which probably could use 14 more.

Give them time. These Guys Are Good. Isn't that what it says on the TV ads? The same goes for the tour's management crew. These guys aren't running their first golf tournament.

In the meantime, the brackets weren't blown to smithereens Wednesday by J.J. Henry or Richard Green. We've got our Valpo (16th-seeded Shaun Micheel) and our Gonzaga (the 15th-seeded Dredge) and our homeboys, Jim Furyk and Rory Sabbatini, survived challenging first-round matches.

More importantly, Tiger Woods, Phil Mickelson, Vijay Singh and Sergio Garcia are still on the board. It's not unlike NBC's game show "Deal or No Deal." That splendid foursome represents $1 million, $750,000, $500,000 and $300,000 on the big board.

If you don't watch NBC, let's just say that Duke, North Carolina, Kansas and Arizona are still in the hunt.

But the intrigue is that you never know about match play. It's as fickle as an August thundercloud.

The only certainty is that The Golf Channel's live broadcast today begins at high noon. Tiger's tee time? What a coincidence: noon.

Don't be late.

# Tiger caps amazing week: World's finest golfer belonged to us for 7 glorious days — and he'll be back

*Monday, February 25, 2008*

Except for a Wednesday night appearance for the Accenture people at Starr Pass, Tiger Woods' week in Tucson was spent almost exclusively on the golf course and in his hotel room at the Westin La Paloma.

Someone reported seeing him buy a bottle of water at 7-Eleven. Another described the way he was quietly escorted through the back entrance of a Foothills restaurant, unseen by other diners.

By his choice, Woods twice awoke at 3:45 a.m., for early tee-times. True to his desire for privacy, the only thing he disclosed about his time away from The Gallery Golf Club was that he watched ESPN's "SportsCenter" a few times. And a few more times.

He wasn't here to ride in the Rodeo Parade.

But over seven days at The Gallery Golf Club's South Course, we got what we thought would never be possible. We got Tiger Woods playing nine rounds of golf (seven of them counted) on our turf.

For 27 hours, the WGC-Accenture Match Play Championship was televised to every corner of America and they saw, as a backdrop to Woods' captivating run to victory, every imaginable shade of desert green and blue.

It was a weeklong postcard from Tucson with a Tiger Woods stamp.

Seven days. No rain.

Seven days. Tiger Woods at his best.

It's still difficult to absorb this sudden change of fortune. It was only a few years ago that the Tucson Open was being won by Gabriel Hjertstedt and Garrett Willis.

Ticket sales were down 5 percent this year, but the buses ran on time, access to and from Dove Mountain Boulevard was superb and, from Monday through Sunday, about 90,000 people were treated to a golf spectacle of such drama — Tiger rallies to beat J.B. Holmes! Tiger goes overtime to stun Aaron Baddeley! — that it was ridiculous.

The week's only real pain came when one of Tiger's few errant shots smacked into the head of a marshal, drawing blood but not controversy.

Ticket sales were down, in part, because the novelty had vanished, and because first-year access and mobility to and from the course created some bad feelings in 2007. And, sure, because it costs $60 for a cheap ticket and because you've got to walk a few miles to get up close to Tiger or any golfer you recognize.

And let's not forget that The Gallery Golf Club isn't close to anything except Eloy.

Many who preferred the tranquility and closeness of the former venue, Tucson National, and its relatively easy access, much cheaper ticket prices and anonymous golfers, did not return. Hey, it was on TV, right?

But it would be stubborn and totally silly for Tucson and Marana and Southern Arizona not to grasp this event and hold it with a death grip. In a decade in which we have lost the LPGA Tour, a college football bowl game, a Pacific Coast League franchise and a spring training tenant, the PGA Tour is only thing that saves us from being Fresno.

There were a few bumps Sunday, none greater than the brevity of the Woods-Stewart Cink championship match. Woods was so superior that he closed out Cink on the 11th hole about 2:40 p.m.

Ideally, the match would have run all 18 holes through 4 p.m., which would have given NBC a full four hours of coverage. In the absence of golf, a one-hour infomercial appeared on KVOA, Tucson's NBC affiliate. Worse, all of the afternoon Federation Cup and Championship Club patrons lining the 12th hole, perhaps 5,000 of them, did not get a glimpse of real golf.

Those who weren't in their reserved (and very expensive) spots along the 12th hole when Woods and Cink played their morning round (about 10:45) were limited to the consolation match between Henrik Stenson and Justin Leonard.

But that's the inherent risk with the final rounds of any match play event. It is a front-loaded event that overflows with action Wednesday through Friday. You take your chances on the weekend, especially when someone like Tiger is capable of closing out any mere human golfer at the earliest moment possible.

In Tucson's first foray as a PGA Tour match play site, 1984-86, fans planted on the back nine were guaranteed activity when officials made the tournament a stroke-play, head-to-head event. But Jim Thorpe, bless his soul, beat Scott Simpson, 67 to 71. Tucson golf fans went home miffed that they had never heard of Jim Thorpe or Scott

Simpson.

This is better. Phil Mickelson and Ernie Els exited early. Given the caliber of those remaining, who even noticed?

As those at the 12th hole Sunday sadly began to realize Woods would win his match at the 11th (or even 10th hole), PGA Tour Commissioner Tim Finchem and a brigade of people from Accenture, the Conquistadores and NBC hustled down crowded cement walkways in an attempt to get to the trophy presentation on time.

Just as they arrived, Tiger birdied again to win the championship. He accepted a trophy, held a press conference and bolted for the airport.

See ya next year, Tiger. Aren't those the five best words of the week?

A.E. ARAIZA

Tiger Woods' weeklong run to victory in the 2008 WGC-Accenture Match Play Championship was a picturesque postcard of Tucson broadcast to the nation.

# All you could want — and golf, too

*Tuesday, February 24, 2009*

The rough at the Ritz-Carlton Golf Club, Dove Mountain is a dark shade of green. It looks like it has been steam-cleaned and sprayed, perhaps to kill the scorpions. It is 3 inches deep, and while it's not a good place to hit a golf ball, it would be a nice place to take a nap.

But you do not care about the rough at the Ritz. You don't care about the Stimpmeter readings or that the jumbo greens all look like random piles of rocks, buried and covered with field turf. It's not your job to worry about three-putting them or to remind Jim Furyk that they break toward Sombrero Peak.

To the guy buying the $45 daily-fee badge, the first test of any good golf tournament is "Where do I park?" It is followed by "How much is the beer?" and "I hope Nick O'Hern doesn't beat Tiger again this year."

You do not go to the WGC-Accenture Match Play Championship curious to see Sergio Garcia's club selection from 172 yards. You go because you want to get outside, work on your winter tan lines and look at all the people who aren't at work today.

It's the Rodeo Parade without street sweepers.

You go because on the day you go back to work, you want to tell everybody that you stood 6 feet from Phil Mickelson — "he wore all black and it was dead hot, 88 degrees," you say — and that you saw someone in the gallery with a biceps tattoo that said "LIFE, LOVE, LUTE."

"How's he gonna get that off?" you ask.

To the average guy riding the shuttle on Dove Mountain Boulevard this week, golf is secondary. There is no emotional attachment to golfers the way there is on an NFL weekend or when the Cubs play anybody.

It's the same concept that fills the spring training bleachers at Tucson Electric Park when the Dodgers play the Diamondbacks. If the Dodgers bring their utility infielders and Triple-A pitchers, it's still baseball, day-game baseball, on a Tuesday, and you're not in a workplace cubicle worried about getting laid off.

It can't strictly be about the golf because the world's 64 leading golfers are at the Ritz, which has limited space and access, but nobody in authority has threatened to cap ticket sales. If it was purely about the golf, you couldn't get a ticket.

Therefore, to those who plan to attend Match Play III Marana, The Return of Tiger, the best advice is this: If you've paid $750 for a ticket to the Canyon Club, and Saturday's semifinals include Rod Pampling, Richard Sterne, Alvaro Quiros and some guy named Soren, try to remember how much fun it was on Wednesday and Thursday. Try to remember that it didn't (can't possibly) rain and that you got to see Tiger's historic comeback and that Tiger doesn't play in Los Angeles or New York and hasn't hit a golf ball in Phoenix this century.

And, besides, the walk won't kill you.

The happy news from Monday's practice sessions at the Ritz is that the new course passed the logistics tests. Isn't that what matters most?

There is but one uphill climb that tests your oxygen supply. It is the final 100 yards at the 18th green. The rest of Jack Nicklaus' new desert beauty is wide, walkable and wonderful.

The Ritz is not a spectator-challenging facility the way The Gallery Golf Club, South Course was. The main entry is actually a main entry. The nearby practice area is a buzz of activity through which each golfer must pass. It's up-close stuff, just like at the U.S. Open or the Masters.

It's as though the Ritz was truly designed to route spectators to favorable viewing positions.

Life as a golf fan at The Gallery was scattered and often remote. Sometimes you couldn't get there from here.

But the Ritz has quick-exit areas at No. 9 and No. 13. You don't have to commit to a full day's hike into the Sonoran unknown. If you take kids, you won't have to worry about phoning the Bureau of Missing Persons.

And know this: The party is already in session. At 11 a.m. Monday, about 500 people, railbirds, stood on the deck at the Walter Hagen Club, which lines the 13th fairway. Not a single golfer had passed their way. The beer flowed anyway. Monday morning.

Someone in the Hagen Club pointed to a golfer on the 13th tee. He was soon identified as Henrik Stenson, 2007 Match Play champ.

"Henrik!" someone shouted. "You the man!"

Game on.

# CHAPTER THREE

# High school figures

## Catalina's Kellner
## continues tradition

*Wednesday, April 3, 1985*

*"Kellner Pitches Catalina Past Sahuaro"* — Headline, March 23, 1985
*"Kellner Strikes Out 27!"* — Headline, May 17, 1942

Kellner? Now there's a name that brings back some memories. Best baseball family ever to come out of these parts. You don't think he could be any kin to Alex and Walt, do you?

You remember the Kellners. Alex, the second of Pop Kellner's three sons — the one named after Grover Alexander — signed a professional contract when he was 16.

He's the one who missed Amphitheater's 1941 graduation ceremony because he was on the road with the Tucson Cowboys. Yep, that Alex Kellner; signed a pro contract when he was 16 — still in high school — and won 14 games against grown-ups in the old Arizona-Texas League that season.

He's still sharp as a tack, too. I talked to him yesterday and he hadn't forgotten a detail.

"Amphi finally had to mail me my diploma," he said. "Yep. That was quite a year."

The 27-strikeout game?

"Sure I remember," he said. "It was against the Southern Pacific team in the old Tucson semipro league. It was a 12-inning game. You didn't think I struck out all 27 batters in a nine-inning game did you?"

Well, Alex Kellner did win 20 games for the Philadelphia A's in 1949, and 101 in his 11-year major-league career. You know how easy it is to exaggerate a few statistics over the years.

Besides, the Kellners aren't just another family.

Remember Walt, the youngest of Pop Kellner's three sons? Pop named him after Walter Johnson, the Big Train, and Walt didn't miss by much.

He pitched for the UA in the late '40s and eventually joined Alex in Philadelphia, shortly before the Athletics moved to Kansas City.

Well, Walt spent parts of two seasons in the bigs and eventually grew weary of trips to the minors. He returned to Tucson to raise a family.

And that's making a long story short.

Anyway, Walt's oldest son, Joey, perpetuated the Kellner name and kept up his part of the family's baseball legacy. He was one of Yavapai's leading pitchers when the Roughriders won the 1978 national junior college championship.

So maybe there is something special about the Kellner name.

I mean, when Joey played for the UA in 1980, the Wildcats won the NCAA championship and Kellner didn't exactly pale next to the Terry Franconas and Ed Vosbergs. Joey was 3-0 with five saves for Arizona that year.

Now we've got Frank Kellner, who inspired the headline at the top of this story. Frank, a senior at Catalina High School, not only batted .374 as a junior shortstop, he also won four games for the Trojans.

The story I get this year is that Frank might be the best pitcher in the city.

Which, I suppose, figures. Good genes are good genes.

"Baseball has always been the most popular sport in our family," said John Kellner Jr., the eldest of John Kellner Sr.'s three sons. "My father was really the one that got it all started."

Pop Kellner was a right-hander in the old Copper State semipro league in Arizona and set a pretty tough standard.

Maybe you'll want to look it up, just to make sure I'm not fibbing a bit, but when Randolph Park, now Hi Corbett Field, was dedicated about 60 years ago, Pop Kellner pitched a no-hitter in the first game there.

Go ahead, look it up. Fact.

So you can imagine how proud he was of his boys. Why, Alex pitched four no-hitters for Amphi and never had a bad game. He lost twice as a senior. One of the defeats was in a game against Bisbee in which he struck out 17 and pitched a two-hitter. What happened? His teammates committed seven errors.

"I couldn't strike 'em all out," he says now, laughing.

Anyway, you can imagine how the Kellners feel about Frank. He not only can pitch and play shortstop, but he also was the starting point guard for Catalina's basketball team, which finished second in the Class AAA state tournament last month.

"Frank's got that something special," Alex Kellner said. "I think he's got the ability to play college ball or beyond that because he's got more than just the ability.

"One thing I really like about him is that he's not like the other guys. He's not happy just to be on the team. He wants to be the best player on the team.

"That's the way I was. That's the way Walt was. We didn't just want to play, we wanted to be the best.

"And Frank's got a lot of that in him, too."

Yep. Sounds like kin to me.

EDITOR'S NOTE: After graduating from Catalina High School, Frank Kellner played two years at Pima College and two at Louisiana Tech before a professional career. He spent eight seasons in the minor leagues, including parts of four with the Triple-A Tucson Toros between 1990 and 1997. His dad, Walt, passed away in 2006, and uncle Alex died in 1996.

BENJIE SANDERS

Frank Kellner, right, followed in father Walt's footsteps as a professional baseball player who fostered his abilities while growing up in Tucson.

DAVID SANDERS

Legendary Sahuaro High boys basketball coach Dick McConnell stalks the sidelines in 1995 during his 500th victory. He went on to win 274 more.

# McConnell doesn't coach stars, he coaches winners

*Wednesday, January 18, 1995*

In the beginning, Dick McConnell wasn't aiming high, he was merely scatter-shooting.

When he went to the post office in Linn, Kan., and dropped a few résumés into the mailbox in 1960, the real issue wasn't whether he would get a job. The issue was whether he would take it.

One letter went to Benson. Another to McNary. A third to Tombstone. Oh, yes, a young coach can get buried there if he's not awfully good. It's usually a good way to get a start on a career in insurance.

"I got a phone call from a guy in Tombstone, who told me I could have the job if I wanted it," McConnell says. "At the time my team in Kansas was 18-6, and we had reached the state quarterfinal. I had every player coming back."

But when you're 30 you do some crazy things. You do not resist that first impulse to stay home and take it slowly. You take a chance. You tell yourself that if anyone can get noticed coaching basketball in Tombstone, you're the one.

Besides, McConnell had spent a year at Narka High School in Kansas — enrollment 27 — and if you can make it there, you can make it anywhere. "I coached every sport," he says. "I was the chaperon at every dance. I loved it there, but I thought I had better go to a bigger school."

Tombstone?

"I took the job," McConnell says, "having never seen the place."

As the years go by, winning season upon winning season, the mental image of Sahuaro High School basketball is that Dick McConnell always has the players. Yes, that's how he wins all those games, isn't it? He has the guns.

And then one day you make a list, and it isn't anywhere near what you thought it would be.

His best players have gone on to Bucknell, Eastern Kentucky, NAU, Seattle, San Diego, Utah, Texas A&M. One of his former players went to Arizona and rode the bench. Another went to ASU and couldn't make it. That's about it.

There have been no real stars in Dick McConnell's 25 years at Sahuaro, not in the sense of a Fat Lever or Jermaine Watts or Sean Elliott. When McConnell earned his 400th career victory, in 1989, his best player was Marc Barcelo, who was a baseball player staying in shape over the winter. It has been a no-star school, a basketball program that, simply, wins all the time.

It must be a coach's school.

McConnell has turned out more coaches than anything else. Ten of his former players or assistants have become head coaches, from Gary Lewis and Jim Ferguson to Brian Peabody, Buddy Doolen and Jim Flannery. McConnell's son, Rick, has won more than 300 games at Mesa Dobson.

He has produced a lineage of coaches that doesn't quit.

So naturally, when McConnell earned his 500th career win, a 67-49 victory over Desert View last night, he seemed uncomfortable looking into the TV lenses, talking about himself. "I just enjoy the game and all that comes with it," he says. "I get a kick out of seeing someone like (Desert View coach) Raul Hodgers turn his program around. I'll tell you who the people are who don't get enough credit — my assistants."

Bob Vielledent, who, with Rick Gary, sits on the bench with McConnell these days, puts McConnell's ego in perspective.

"I've been around him for all these years, and I've never heard him say that he grew up with (North Carolina coach) Dean Smith, playing on the same high school team, growing up as neighborhood buddies. He never brings it up. Never drops a name.

"One day I answered the phone, and it was a guy who said he was Dean Smith, calling for Dick McConnell. I said, 'Right, and I'm Don Shula,' and hung up. A week later Dick gets a letter from Dean Smith asking him why he couldn't get through on the phone."

Getting through: 500 career victories, 22 state tournament appearances, seven trips to the Arizona high school "Final Four."

This is how you hired a high school basketball coach in the Tucson Unified School District in 1967: You went to the district office and asked how many people had applied for the boys basketball coaching job at Sahuaro, a new school scheduled to open in the fall of '68.

Hank Egbert, who was to be Sahuaro's first principal, was told there were 126 applications.

Now, 27 years later, Egbert understands what he did when he settled on McConnell, who had left Tombstone after one season and spent the next eight years as a junior varsity coach at Rincon.

"That was a phenomenal bit of luck," he says with a laugh. "Do you know that when I hired Dick McConnell I also hired (baseball coach) Hal Eustice and (football coach) Howard Breinig? I'm very proud of what transpired with that original coaching staff at Sahuaro. Ha, ha, ha. How do you beat those three?"

Eustice became something of a local legend in high school baseball before his death four years ago, and Breinig, originally hired as Sahuaro's wrestling coach, won state titles in two sports.

But it is McConnell who has persevered, winning state championships in 1970 and 1982, making him second to the late B.C. Doolen as the winningest coach in Tucson prep history. How good is that? This good: McConnell was selected to the Arizona Coaches Hall of Fame 11 years ago, when he was only 53 years old.

That's like having your jersey retired while you're still playing.

"Dick turned out to be a wonderful coach," Egbert says. "Never, not even for a second, did I regret hiring him. He was a remarkable communicator, not only with students, but the faculty loved him, and the administrators enjoyed him. He's a people person. I mean the kids just worshipped him."

What Dick McConnell really wanted to be was a shortstop.

After starring at Topeka High School and at Washburn University in Kansas, he played six years of semipro baseball, some of it with the barnstorming Casa Grande Cotton Kings while stationed at Davis-Monthan Air Force Base in the '50s.

He developed a kinship with Lee Carey, a legendary baseball player from Tucson High School, and it was Carey who did his best to arrange a coaching job in Arizona. "I wanted to play baseball. That was my motivating force," McConnell says. "So Lee kept me informed on the coaching jobs. If not for Lee, I'd probably still be in Kansas."

After a year in Tombstone, McConnell applied for a job in Eloy. That's a normal progression, isn't it? Tombstone to Eloy. But on the same day the Eloy job came through, McConnell got a call from Rincon High School. Would he like to join the Rangers staff?

Would he? Is tomorrow too late?

"I think the only time I worried about getting a job was when I was at Rincon," McConnell says of his eight-year stint as an assistant under Dick King. "I didn't think I'd ever get (a head coaching position)."

That accounts for his late start on the road to 500. Had he not spent the 1960-68 seasons as a junior varsity coach, McConnell might

95

be working on 600 victories now, challenging Doolen's state record of 643.

But who's counting? He's on a season-to-season clock, driven by his love for the game, not by a count of victories.

"I'm not in this for 500 or whatever the number might be," he says. "I've been very lucky; this has been my life. For me to get all the recognition doesn't seem fair."

Sahuaro started 0-6 in its first season, 1968-69, and struggled to a 5-15 record. The newspaper headline after the school's first victory, over Amphi in January 1969, said Cougars stun Amphi. That was about the last time Sahuaro stunned anybody.

A year later, in the fastest building job imaginable, Sahuaro won the state championship. Elapsed time to get to the top: two years.

"Now we have some tradition," McConnell said after the game. "Now we're on the map."

Now you can multiply that by 500.

EDITOR'S NOTE: Dick McConnell's Sahuaro teams won back-to-back state championships in 2000 and 2001, giving him four career titles, and he broke the state's all-time record for wins on Dec. 28, 2001. McConnell retired as Sahuaro's coach on Oct. 16, 2007, following 39 seasons at the east side school. His 774 victories in Arizona are 111 more than any other coach in state history. He sells real estate in Tucson with his wife, Clarine.

# Amphi falls short only on scoreboard

*Saturday, December 13, 1997*

*TEMPE*

Vern Friedli walked into the Amphi huddle with 3:30 remaining in the 1997 football season, fourth down, ball at the Mesa Mountain View 39-yard line, protecting a three-point lead.

The call was his. Punt and try to hold on. Or go for it, 1 yard, if that. It was more like 30 inches.

In almost 40 years in the coaching business, starting at Sunnyside Junior High School when the parents of Antrel Bates and Jesse Quintana were still in grade school, Friedli has made thousands of calls. Some of them helped win a state championship in 1979. Others helped make him the winningest coach in the history of high school football in Tucson, and No. 2 in Arizona.

But none was bigger than this one would be.

"He asked us what we wanted to run and everyone said '22,' let's give it to our main guy," Quintana, the Panthers' 5-foot-10-inch quarterback, said.

Amphi's main guy is Bates, a 2,000-yard rusher and the fourth most prolific rusher in the history of high school football in this state. His reaction? "I love that play, '22 smash.' Give it to me. I'll get the yard."

Friedli went into the huddle with a Plan B, which was to punt. That's the safe way out, isn't it? Punt, play defense, hope for the best, kill the clock.

But that's not Amphi football.

Amphi football is 42 guys on the roster for the 5A state championship game against Mesa Mountain View, which suited up 85.

Amphi football is two players on the roster 6-2, the tallest Panthers on the field, against a Mountain View team with 15 players 6-2 or taller.

Amphi football is a student body of 1,980 students against a Mountain View population of 3,968.

If Amphi had punted I would have fainted. The Panthers always go for the pin, never lay up. Amphi football is all about opportunity.

The Panthers could beat Mountain View if they could make 36 inches. They would lose if they didn't. The vote in the huddle was quick and unanimous.

97

"Everybody wanted to go," Bates said.

But "22 smash" didn't get 36 inches it got 25, maybe 30. It took Mountain View a few plays to score and win the state championship 28-24 in a game for the ages.

Funny, but I could swear that the Panthers really won. Forget what the scoreboard said. I can't remember a game in which the team that didn't get the biggest trophy seemed to win more than Amphi did last night.

"I'm sure we're winners at heart," said Quintana, the most astute observation of the evening. "That happens, though. That's life."

Most of this year, and in many of past years, I have watched from afar as the Panthers bucked it up and went headfirst into the almost unwinnable battle that is 5A football. Half the players. Half the resources. There was always a painful exit at year's end, almost always against one of the monolithic Mesa schools, which, like Mountain View, suit up more cheerleaders than the Panthers suit up ballplayers.

Friedli is 61, and it has been 18 years since a Tucson team — his — last won a 5A title. Isn't that enough time to bang your head against a wall, fruitlessly waging a war on the teams-that-can't-be-beaten?

I have sat down at this word processor many times determined to write what I felt: Please, Amphi, move to 4A and win another state title for the old coach before he steps away.

Maybe now we have figured him out. He likes this challenge, it drives him and he is not going to give an inch until he gets it done.

And now, for the first time, I think that someday Amphi is going to win it all, and that Friedli won't have to watch the final 3:30 tick agonizingly off the clock, knowing that he must wait another 12 months.

As he stood in the middle of his courageous team after last night's game, tears falling freely, the old coach began to apologize for calling that fourth-down run. No one was buying that. The Panthers played the game the way they all wanted to play it, ears back, hearts pumping.

"What a crew," he said. "They're just a raggy-taggy bunch of kids. You don't let this game take away from the season. Nobody has tested (Mountain View) like we did. My admiration for these kids is immeasurable."

Someone asked Friedli if he was considering retiring, giving up on his battle to beat 'em all, any size, anytime, which stopped him short.

"End it now?" he asked. "Hell, no. We've still got this Phoenix thing to deal with."

This year the Panthers were five inches and 3½ minutes short of

defeating the "Phoenix thing."
Now it's just getting interesting.

EDITOR'S NOTE: Vern Friedli entered his 34th season as Amphi's head coach in 2009, fresh off his 26th state playoff appearance at the school. In 2008, he won the 309th game of his illustrious, 43-year career to set the state record. He is still the last Tucson-area coach to lead his team to the 5A state championship, and Amphi's field was renamed in his honor — Friedli Field — in 2001. In 2008, the University of Arizona Foundation established the Vernon F. Friedli Scholarship Endowment in the College of Education.

Amphi High School coach Vern Friedli remains the face of high school football in Southern Arizona after 43 years. He led Amphi to the 1979 state title.

JIM DAVIS

AARON J. LATHAM

At Sahuaro High School in the '90s, Calvin Dacus overcame a rough upbringing to become an honor student and the most prolific receiver in state history.

# Hard knocks won't keep this receiver down

*Thursday, October 21, 1999*

Calvin Dacus is possibly the best receiver to play high school football in Tucson the last 10 years, maybe the last 25 years.

Wherever he belongs, it's a short list: Eric Drage. John Mistler. Brian Poli-Dixon. Jay Dobyns. Steve Martin.

Drage went to BYU and broke records. Mistler went to the NFL. Dobyns was the guts of Arizona's passing game in the early '80s. Poli-Dixon helped UCLA to the Rose Bowl. Martin left ASU to sign a pro baseball contract.

All of those former schoolboy greats had one more thing in common: Their parents signed their scholarship papers and saw them off to college.

When Calvin Dacus receives his college papers in a few months, he will fill it out like this: Mom: in jail. Dad: disappeared. Guardian: dead. Family: a sister in California. Address: unsure.

"You talk about a kid who has overcome problems to make a man of himself, that's Calvin," Sahuaro coach Nemer Hassey says. "Most kids in his situation drop out of school and find trouble. Calvin has overcome all of it."

Dacus has caught 115 passes from Sahuaro QB Reggie Robertson during the last two seasons, including 76 as a junior and 15 in the state 4A quarterfinals against Agua Fria. Only one player in Tucson history, Mistler, a Sahuaro star 24 years ago, caught more balls (81) in a season.

And yet when UA's football office phoned this week to offer Dacus two tickets for Saturday's game against Oregon (as permitted by NCAA rules), he told them he would be working his regular shift at a local skating rink and would get to the game when he could.

"I need that job," he says. "During the football season I can't work on weekdays because of practice and schoolwork, so on the weekends I can't cut back. NAU has wanted me to come up and watch them play, but I haven't been able to go. I need the money."

This isn't a sob story. It could be, but Dacus has made sure it isn't.

Dacus lives in a group home near Sahuaro with nine other boys ranging in age from 10 to 17. It is a foster-kids program sponsored by United Parcel Service that has served as Dacus' home for three years.

He gets room and board and a robust allowance of $10.25 every two weeks.

Before that he went through hell.

His mother has been in and out of jail since he was a toddler. "She hasn't been able to stay off drugs long enough to be a mother, so she gave me and my sister, Sandy, to our grandmother," he says. "My grandma was 80, though, and in poor health. That didn't last very long."

Dacus bumped around in foster homes beginning at age 5, when his grandmother died. The state sent him to the all-boys Colorado Boarding School in Evergreen, Colo., until he reached the age limit of 12.

"I went there considered a troubled kid," he says. "They told me I was depressed and needed to work through my feelings. I enjoyed it. It was a great time. Someday I'd like to move back to Colorado and work for the Fish & Game department."

He was sent back to Tucson when he was 13 and given two options: another foster home or the St. John's Military Academy in Salina, Kan. He'd had his fill of foster homes. He chose Kansas.

It was not his best decision.

"It was the worst experience I've ever had," he says. "We'd be up at 4:30 every morning, marching, cleaning, doing schoolwork, and then marching and cleaning again before we went to bed. We got to leave one week a year, at Christmas, and one week in the summer. I couldn't wait to get out of there."

When Dacus would return to Tucson for his week's leave from military school he would be escorted by a surrogate father who had befriended him years earlier. That relationship ended a few years ago when, Dacus says, his father-figure was put in jail.

"I haven't seen him for a year or two," he says. "It's just one thing after another. Since then I've been on my own, in the group home, being monitored by a caseworker."

After two years at the military academy, Dacus requested to return to Tucson and enroll in high school, first at Palo Verde, then at Sahuaro, where he has thrived.

Dacus went out for football and was elevated to the varsity during his sophomore season. His grade-point average was 3.5 ("my goal is never to have more than two B's," he says), he became a high-scoring sprinter and hurdler for the Cougars track team, and he kept his nose clean away from school, earning the trust of his social worker and his group-home supervisors.

His friends say he doesn't drink or smoke. His coach says, "I wish all of our kids were such positive examples." His one known vice: He celebrates when he scores a touchdown. His teammates call him "Dances in the End Zone."

There are no signs of self-pity.

"People say I've had it bad, and maybe I have," he says. "But the foster-home program has given me a lot of benefits. I've learned to be independent and stand on my own. Sometimes when I see my team-mates' parents pick them up after a game — or when we have functions at school that brings out the moms and dads — I'll wish I had a family. But I can deal with it."

Dacus has saved almost $2,000 while working part time the last 18 months. He says he's saving it, not to buy a car, but to have it available when he goes to college. He hasn't been offered a football scholarship yet, but New Mexico State and NAU continue to show interest, and by the time the Cougars finish the season — possibly in the 4A state championship game, or close to it — recruiting interest seems likely to increase.

Calvin Dacus has been a champion with or without football.

"When I came to Sahuaro I hesitated to tell people, even my team-mates, that I lived in a group home," he says. "There seemed to be a negative thing to that. But now everybody knows, and it's fine. I think I've shown that you can grow up without parents and make something of yourself."

Indeed.

EDITOR'S NOTE: Calvin Dacus broke Arizona's Class 4A state records for receptions in a season (100) and a career (176) later in the 1999 season. The records still stand. He signed a letter of intent to play for Northern Arizona University, but he suffered a knee injury early in his freshman year in 2000 and returned to Tucson. He currently works as a banker in the Old Pueblo.

Between 2006 to 2007, Jeff Scurran turned Santa Rita High's football team from a winless squad with academic woes into a championship-caliber group.

# Scurran walks the walk: Coach backs up big talk — 0-10 Eagles in '06 are 11-1 state semifinalists

*Wednesday, November 28, 2007*

On Thanksgiving morning, Jeff Scurran pulled a gold Santa Rita Eagles T-shirt over his head, zipped up a green Santa Rita windbreaker and chose green shorts and green-highlighted shoes.

He was out of the house by 9 and on the high school football field by 9:30. It all seemed so familiar: Thanksgiving workouts. Playoff football. Jeff Scurran. And yet it all looked so odd.

At Sabino High School, Scurran wore purple when he won three state championships. At Pima Community College, where he built a team from scratch and had it in the Top 10 almost overnight, Scurran wore blue.

Now green has become the color of success. Scurran's Eagles are 11-1 and playing in the state 4A-II semifinals Friday.

"If you're not playing after Thanksgiving, you haven't had a good year," he said. "We always play after Thanksgiving."

So there it is, the famous Scurran ego. Isn't that why he has so many detractors? Isn't that why so many were so reluctant to acknowledge his success at Sabino? Isn't that why the administration at Pima did not sob when he left, and in fact pushed him to the door?

Let's get one thing straight: Santa Rita finished 0-10 last year, so this is not just some guy getting lucky.

This is a remarkable 60-year-old football coach who so believes in himself — "you know me, I'm not going to fail," he said in typical Scurranese — that he pursued the Santa Rita vacancy even though he knew at least 20 players (it turned out to be 28) were in academic peril.

"When we were interviewing candidates for our football coaching job, we heard that Jeff wasn't serious about coaching here, that maybe it was a ploy to have other schools learn that he was available," said Jim Ferguson, a Santa Rita counselor and boys basketball coach who served on the search committee.

Why would Scurran want to take on a tradition-poor and numbers-challenged football program at Santa Rita when there was a vacancy at affluent Catalina Foothills High School? Didn't he know that the Eagles were coming off a winless season and that roughly 80 percent of the probable roster was not likely to be academically eligible?

"Jeff had a terrific interview," Ferguson remembers. "He didn't go on and on about himself. He kind of downplayed his achievements. He was so positive; he seemed to genuinely appreciate the opportunity to coach here and work with a new set of kids. After we hired him, I thought if we won five games it would be a great year."

Five wins? The Eagles blew past No. 5 in early October. It is a story of such unexpected success that you can get lost in the imagination of it.

"This is a once-in-a-lifetime thing," said Scurran, who then corrected himself. "No, if you go back to the Sabino years, it's No. 2. Or, maybe I should make that three. I've got to count Pima."

He paused to chuckle. Before he stopped counting his "once-in-a-lifetime things" he was at No. 5 and rolling.

That is Scurran. But so is his commitment to detail, preparation and discipline. He talks a big game. He walks a bigger one.

"The first time I watched films of last year's team I went, 'Oh, boy, what have we gotten ourselves into?'" said Kevin Amidan, Santa Rita's line coach, who played for Scurran both at Sabino and PCC. "I personally haven't seen anything like this, and, remember, I was at Pima when we started from scratch."

Scratch is a word Scurran uses all the time. It is a word that applies to Santa Rita football.

"At the beginning, all these kids could do was scratch and claw," he said. "That's how we got here: scratching and clawing. If we let up for a minute, we're done."

The scratching began in early summer when 28 Santa Rita football players were not academically eligible to compete. The only way they could remain part of the team was to attend summer school without getting an F. Beyond that was mandatory attendance at a four-days-a-week tutoring session taught by Amidan, a UA grad who is a Santa Rita special-education teacher.

Only then would they get to the football stuff. And this was summer vacation. By the time two-a-days began in August, it was almost a relief.

"The commitment we asked of the kids was pretty intense," Amidan said. "They would go to summer school until 1, go to lunch, then study with me until 3. After that, they'd go into the weight room until 5.

"We rode 'em. We monitored each of them every week. Somehow we got it done. All 28 of those kids are eligible. They did everything we've asked."

What were the odds?

Santa Rita has 42 players on its varsity roster. To coach them, Scurran surrounded himself with many of his Sabino and Pima College associates such as Amidan, Manny and Santos Olague and Brad Wood. Old success equals new success. Scurran raised more than $15,000 to redo the school's weight room, buy new uniforms, both for practice and games, and put a shine on an oft-moribund program.

In the process, he did a makeover on the Eagles' self-image.

"The kids look nice, and they feel good about themselves," said Ferguson. "They feel they are part of something that is good, something that makes them proud.

"When Jeff took over, there were a number of kids I looked at and said 'no way.' They weren't motivated. And now they're out there on an 11-1 football team. It's not just for football but for their own growth. It's phenomenal."

And it is also true. Santa Rita is 11-1. You can look it up.

EDITOR'S NOTE: The 2007 Santa Rita Eagles lost 35-7 in the state semifinals to Cottonwood Mingus. The following season, Scurran led the Eagles to their second straight region championship, and they advanced to the state championship game for the first time in school history. They lost 30-26 to Scottsdale Notre Dame when their fourth-quarter rally fell short in the final seconds.

# CHAPTER FOUR

# Baseball in Tucson

## Kindall and Brock are leagues apart

*Saturday, June 11, 1983*

Late in 1971, several weeks after Jerry Kindall was appointed base-ball coach at the University of Arizona, he offered Jim Brock a position as the UA's full-time assistant.

Brock, then coach at Mesa Community College, declined. Shortly thereafter, he became coach at Arizona State.

In the years since, Brock and Kindall both have coached two national championship teams. That's where the similarities end, a fact that has never been more obvious than on ESPN's recent telecasts of the College World Series.

When Brock is on the air for an interview — when the camera pans ASU's dugout — you get the impression he's putting you on. Or pulling a big con.

He always tries to get a laugh and usually does.

When Kindall is wired for sound — he is one of ESPN's commen-tators — he describes the action as a biology professor might explain the dissection of a frog. Cold, hard facts.

That isn't to say that Kindall doesn't editorialize.

When James Madison was beaten, 12-0, in a first-round game against Texas, Kindall sympathized with the Dukes. "The score isn't a true indication of James Madison's ability," he said. "I'm sure they're a much better club than we saw tonight."

Brock, interviewed on ESPN later (although not by Kindall), said "if you don't belong here, it becomes obvious in a hurry."

Although ASU and UA are only about 100 miles apart as the crow flies, their baseball coaches are as similar as Broadway and Mayberry R.F.D.

Brock looks like something floating over the Rose Parade. Kindall

109

looks as if he runs marathons.

Kindall looks as if he just put a pitchfork down. Brock looks as if he just put a beer down.

Kindall's idea of a great movie is probably "The Sound of Music." Brock's is "Patton."

A year ago, for example, I asked both to comment on the prowess of former Sahuaro High School shortstop Sammy Khalifa, who was to become the No. 1 draft pick of the Pittsburgh Pirates.

Brock's reply: "Two years from now, there will be absolutely nothing he can't do. He's one in a million at a premium position. He's going to be a very wealthy young man."

Kindall: "He's a fine young man and a good student, too."

Kindall recruits players you'd want your daughter to marry. Brock's teams take no prisoners.

On the subject of the 1983 NCAA regional playoffs, to which ASU subsequently was invited, Brock said, "If we're not in it, there had better be an investigation."

Said Kindall, "I'm sure the (NCAA) selection committee will input all the necessary information and make the appropriate selection."

Get the picture?

Kindall would say a mediocre club is "well-balanced." Brock might say it's a bunch of stiffs.

Kindall's idea of a good hairdo is a crew cut. Brock wears his hair over his ears.

Brock is on the cover of ASU's 1983 baseball yearbook. Kindall shares the cover of the UA guide with five players.

Kindall and Brock have had run-ins before but not many.

In 1981, for example, Brock publicly criticized UA fans after beating Arizona, 23-11, at Wildcat Field.

"I've always thought Jerry was embarrassed by that kind of activity and genuinely concerned about it," Brock said. "After this, I no longer believe that."

Kindall said: "I am not going to let him provoke me. No comment. Let it die."

I mean, these guys can't even enjoy a good fight.

Assigned to broadcast Wednesday's Stanford-Michigan game with play-by-play man Jim Simpson, Kindall probably even had his patience tested.

Simpson was woefully unprepared. He twice misidentified Stanford's base coaches as those from Michigan. He consistently misidentified players and mispronounced their names. Once Simpson said a batter had walked, forcing in the tying run. The count was 1-2.

It was as bad or maybe worse than the infamous series of errors Curt Gowdy made while announcing an NCAA basketball game involving Kansas and UCLA in 1978.

Kindall probably should have ducked out the back door between innings. I don't know how he did it, but Kindall politely and without embarrassing Simpson corrected each error.

As a result, the broadcast went more smoothly than it had a right to.

I have a feeling that had Brock been in the same broadcast booth, he would have strangled Simpson or put the microphone in his mouth.

Kindall's favorite coaches are probably Bud Grant and Tom Landry. Brock's are probably Billy Martin and John Madden.

When Kindall refers to good players, he calls them "bell cows" and "standouts" and "marvelous young men." Brock calls them "studs."

It's a fascinating contrast: Kindall and Brock. I just hope that ESPN realizes that Kindall interviewing Brock would be good for the ratings.

I can hear it now.

Kindall: Will your club steal a lot?

Brock: Yes, so lock your lockers.

Kindall: What do you think of your bench?

Brock: It's the best bench in the league. But the players sitting on it aren't much good.

Kindall: Your starting pitcher tonight has an arm like The Goose, doesn't he?

Brock: Right. It's got five fingers, an elbow and a biceps. Unfortunately, it's attached to a guy who throws like a goose.

Kindall: Good luck tonight, Jim.

Brock: Bet you wish you were playing here, too, huh Jer?

Stay tuned.

EDITOR'S NOTE: Read more on Jerry Kindall later in the chapter.

Max Patkin, lovingly called The Clown Prince of Baseball, performs his act during a visit to Hi Corbett Field in June 1977.

# Clowning around at Hi Corbett Field

*Monday, July 8, 1985*

Guess who's coming to Hi Corbett Field tomorrow night? I'll give you three clues about the good news.

1. When you look at him, you wonder if someone in heaven's assembly room got the instructions wrong.

2. They say he's "all ears," and it doesn't have a thing to do with hearing.

3. He looks as if he sleeps on a broomstick in a cornfield.

Step right up, folks. Appearing on the Tucson midway, or at least the third-base line for perhaps the last time in a 40-year career, is the Clown Prince of Baseball, Max Patkin.

He's the man the San Diego Chicken said "makes me look like an amateur." He's Meadowlark Lemon going solo, Meadowlark Lemon getting water thrown in his face. And dirt, too.

Max Patkin is what the Phillie Phanatic and assorted feathered-and-furry creatures of America's ballparks, Chief Noc-a-homa, the Ooh-Aah Man and Disney's cartoonists have been trying to duplicate for years. But couldn't. Can't.

He was a baseball comic before being a baseball comic was cool.

Max Patkin has played Tucson four times and there seems to be reason to believe tomorrow night's show might be his curtain call here. He's 65, coming off the first serious physical aliment — off-season back surgery — of his four-decade career.

He can't continue his role as the funny bone of baseball forever.

"But I still run good, and I still get laughs," he said before embarking on his 72-city tour of 1985. "Sometimes I have to stop and catch my breath, but I can still make faces, and I've still got good body movement."

The term "good" in this case is inadequate.

Remember Wild Bill Hagy, the rage of the '83 World Series, who would stand on the Baltimore dugout and contort his body as if to spell "O-r-i-o-l-e-s?" Well, Patkin, is 6 feet 3 inches and 190 pounds, and 25 percent of it is neck. Most of the rest is arms and legs.

It would be nothing for him to stand on the Toro dugout and spell out "xylophone" with his eyes closed.

I first caught Max Patkin's act when I was 13. I couldn't wait to see him again. He was funny just standing still, and I remember someone saying he looked like a man with a permanent case of hiccups.

Well, it has been almost 20 years since I saw Max Patkin perform in a minor-league ballpark in Salt Lake City, and since then he hasn't stopped to turn back his odometer. He's done more than 3,500 shows — almost all of them in minor-league parks — and he has traveled more than 5 million miles.

Now he belongs to frequent-flier clubs. In the old days, they called it barnstorming. But he made his $300 a night — now it's almost 10 times that — and usually quadruples or quintuples attendance.

Patkin performed in McCook, Neb., when Phil Niekro was a 21-year-old beginner. He shared the field with Pete Rose in Macon, Ga., 22 years before Rose got his 4,000th hit.

But Patkin's best story is about the day in 1942 when he pitched to Joe DiMaggio.

A star was born — and it wasn't Joltin' Joe.

Patkin's service team, a Navy outfit stationed in Honolulu, met DiMaggio's Air Corps team. First time up, Patkin, a Class D pitcher in the Cleveland system, struck out DiMaggio. Next time, DiMaggio hit a long home run.

Legend has it that Patkin, then 22, feigned outrage. He threw his glove to the mound, twisted his hat sideways and began to chase DiMaggio around the bases.

The closer Patkin got to DiMaggio — imitating DiMaggio's long-striding, gliding style — the louder the crowd howled. When the two reached home plate, the dugouts emptied.

"They were waiting for me!" Patkin said. "They congratulated me, not DiMaggio. I had just ad-libbed it, but 10,000 Navy guys loved it."

It was natural.

"When I was coaching on the base lines in the minors, I was a goof, nothing really serious," Patkin said. "It helped having a homely face and being loose and lanky.

"I was the Ray Bolger of baseball. I guess I looked funny and people laughed."

Patkin's pitching career ended soon after World War II. In 1946, Cleveland Indians owner Bill Veeck sent Patkin to Wilkes-Barre, Pa., another Class D city, and told him to work not on his curveball but on his comic routine.

Patkin took the numeral off his uniform and replaced it with a skinny question mark. When he tore his uniform pants, he just patched them, making sure the colors didn't match.

His waist was 36, so he bought size 44. He put his size 14 cleats on his size 11 feet. When he rolled in the dirt near first base, or took a nap on third base, he made sure not to brush himself off.

"My uniform is grotesque," he said. "It's the worst-looking uniform you ever saw, but the more grotesque the uniform, the better the act."

So step right this way. The best act in baseball returns to Tucson tomorrow night. Catch it while you can.

EDITOR'S NOTE: Max Patkin continued his act as baseball's Clown Prince until 1993, estimating that he made more than 4,000 appearances at ballparks across the country — without ever breaking a scheduled commitment. He died in 1999.

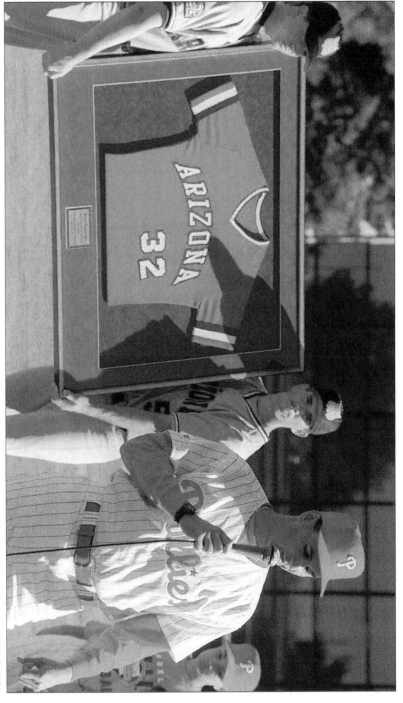

Former Arizona baseball star Terry Francona speaks to the crowd at Sancet Field on the day his jersey number was re-tired by the school in 1997.

JAMES S. WOOD

# Tucsonan Francona seeks a trade — to anywhere

*Wednesday, January 29, 1986*

The origin and roots of a big-league rumor:

A baseball writer in Montreal wrote that Terry Francona was so peeved at the Expos that he would be ecstatic even to be traded to the Indians.

He'd even agree to live in Cleveland. In January.

An astute baseball writer in Toronto interpreted this to mean that no baseball is the equivalent of baseball in Cleveland. So he wrote that Francona would boycott spring training and stay in Tucson until the Expos traded him.

The rumor eventually trickled across the border. In Detroit, a newsman wrote that Francona would retire if not traded. And then some dummy in Tucson perpetuated the tale.

"Everywhere I went," Francona was saying the other day, "people would go 'Gee, why are you retiring already? You're only 26.' They'd read what I was asking for ($350,000 a year) and I'm sure they thought I was a spoiled brat.

"It sure has been embarrassing."

The whole truth: Reports of Francona's retirement have been greatly exaggerated. "I've been complaining but I'll never quit."

The sad truth: The Expos have been trying to trade Francona for a year.

"We're still attempting to accommodate Terry," Montreal general manager Murray Cook said yesterday. "Yes, we've had offers for Terry, but we're not going to give him away. We're confident we'll be able to work something out soon."

But the Expos and Francona are in sync on at least one thing: Francona is not in their plans in 1986 and thereafter.

"They have no plans for me to play," said Francona.

"We expect Andres Galarraga to be our first baseman," said Cook.

Understandably, Francona would like to start over. In 4½ years with Montreal he has had, in no particular order, two major knee surgeries, more than 230 days on the disabled list, a career .290 batting average in 951 at-bats and no steady job.

"I'd love to get out of Montreal real bad," Francona said. "To

117

where? I have no preference. Anywhere. All I asked of Murray is that he did not bury me, but that's kind of what happened."

In November, the Expos promised they'd trade Francona, who was the 1980 NCAA Player of the Year while leading the University of Arizona to the College World Series championship.

"They said there was no question they'd trade me," said Francona. "They'd take the best deal they could get. I asked them if I could go play winter ball and they said no on the basis that if I got hurt, it would foul up my trade value."

The origin of Francona's de-emphasis in Montreal can be traced to September 1984. That's when Cook was hired as the Expos' GM. Until then, Francona had a career batting average of .300 and seemed to have the capacity to someday challenge for a National League batting championship.

"Murray brought in a lot of new people and a lot of new ideas into the organization," said Francona. "One of his philosophies is that a first baseman has to hit a lot of home runs."

Francona hit two home runs last season, seven in his major-league career.

That's one every 136 at-bats. Galarraga, a 6-foot-3-inch, 210-pound rookie from Venezuela, hit 27 home runs in Class AA a year ago. And although Galarraga batted just .187 with two homers in 75 at-bats with the Expos last season, the first base job is his to lose.

Doug Frobel, obtained from Pittsburgh last season, hit 75 homers his last three minor-league seasons and will be Galarraga's backup. Frobel hit 12 homers for the Pirates in 1984.

"It doesn't matter what I do in spring training," Francona said. "I can't win the job in Montreal. I understand that they've got to give Galarraga a chance. Figured it was coming, but it's still difficult to accept.

"I mean, I'm only 26. I'm not over the hill."

The last two months have been periods of high anxiety for Francona.

"During the baseball meetings last month, every time the phone rang, I got excited, hoping it was news of a trade," he said. "And then last week my wife (Jacquie) answered the phone and I heard her say, 'Hi, Murray.' I knew it had to be about the trade."

No such luck.

"It was just the usual B.S.," Francona said. "Murray just wanted to know how I was doing and said he was working on the trade. I told him that I hope they're not too greedy."

EDITOR'S NOTE: Terry Francona was released by the Montreal Expos on April 1, 1986, and he signed as a free agent with the Chicago Cubs one month later. He played in parts of 10 seasons in the major leagues before retiring in 1990. Francona was back in the majors as manager of the Philadelphia Phillies from 1997 to 2000, and he has served as the skipper for the Boston Red Sox since 2004, winning the World Series in his first year and again in 2007.

The Tucson Toros' Kenny Lofton gets help from the fans as he parades the Pacific Coast League championship trophy around Hi Corbett Field in 1991.

# Strictly baseball at Hi Corbett

*Saturday, September 14, 1991*

Tucson's definition of minor-league baseball forever changed last night, and not just because Toros GM Mike Feder said he might've sold 30,000 tickets if the stadium could've accommodated the crowd.

As it was, Hi Corbett Field ran out of beer and hot dogs in the fifth inning.

This was baseball as good as it gets. A very special night.

Wearing their adrenal glands on their sleeves, 8,919 Tucsonans crammed into the old ballpark, and if you could freeze the moment and put it in a time capsule, the message for posterity would be:

Tucson was a hell of a baseball town.

The anticipation was great, but the Toros' 4-3 victory in the PCL championship game matched it. Exceeded it.

It was the Game for the Ages in a city that for 23 years identified its pro baseball franchise by failure.

"Sweep! Sweep! Sweep!" bellowed Kenny Lofton as he stood in a shower of champagne in the Toros locker room. Someone asked Lofton a question and he didn't even hear it. His eyes were bigger, wider, than second base.

"Yes! Yes! Yes!" he yelled. He danced. He hugged everyone. He was the MVP and how fitting is that?

The post-game party on the field wasn't a mob of Boston fans carrying Jim Lonborg in a sea of bodies in the 1967 pennant winner. And it wasn't Pittsburghers flooding the field to get a touch of Bill Mazeroski in 1960. But now Tucsonans have their own magic memory of baseball.

Commemorative T-shirts went on sale immediately following the game and lines were 20-deep at 11 p.m.

"I've only been on this team for a week or two," said outfielder Joe Mikulik, whose single in the ninth inning gave Tucson its first pro baseball title since 1953. "But you could tell right away there was something special about these guys.

"I don't know what it's like in the (major leagues), but if it's better than this . . . wow."

By the time the 10 o'clock news had come and gone, the Toros and Cannons were tied in the ninth. If you weren't among the 8,918 at Hi Corbett — nobody left early — your only source for the final score should have been KTKT (990-AM). In an unprecedented move, some of the local TV stations squeezed the climax of the game into their newscasts.

KTKT's ratings must've gone off the charts. As a result of all the nouveau interest in the Toros, they have had a priceless image face-lift.

The Toros used to be as recreational as summer vacation.

Hiking, swimming, arts, crafts and six or so innings at Hi Corbett Field on, your choice, 7-Eleven Night, 50-cent Beer Night or Free Slurpee Night.

You used to go to the park to cheer for Max Patkin to eat some dirt, to see The Chicken goose an umpire, to see a fat lady win a cheap watch.

But there was never much of an urgency to see the home team win.

Alas, it has occurred to Tucsonans in the last two weeks that, while winning isn't everything in the Pacific Coast League, it is something.

The Toros returned from Calgary on Wednesday, down 2-0 in the best-of-five series. They were basically an underestimated, overlooked and disrespected ballclub. And why not?

The Cannons were the PCL's team-of-the-moment, which happens a lot in the minor leagues. The bulk — but not the heart — of the Toros starting lineup that swept through late May and June in the best six weeks of baseball in Tucson's 23-year PCL history had long since departed for Houston.

Andy Mota and Andujar Cedeño are now the Houston Astros' middle infield of the future. Jose Tolentino is batting in excess of .300 in the National League. Ryan Bowen is in the Astros' rotation. The Toros are using reinforcements at catcher, first base, in the bullpen, everywhere.

But there was never a compromise on the field.

The subplot of the Toros' championship was the most sweet of all. It was smiling Kenny Lofton (most likely) ending his active athletic association with Tucson as a champion. He'll be an Astro by the weekend and the sky's the limit.

In his final two basketball seasons at Arizona, Lofton played on two teams ranked No. 1 in the nation. But each season was bittersweet, and each ended with Lofton in tears in the Wildcat locker room.

They are vivid scenes that won't soon fade from Tucson's consciousness.

No one deserved to go out a winner more than he.

So justice was served last night when Lofton was named the MVP of the championship series and figured prominently not only in the fifth-inning comeback, but in the deciding scenario in the ninth.

Yes, as Tucson baseball fans now understand, good things come to those who wait.

JIM DAVIS

Members of the Cleveland Indians play in the franchise's final spring training game at Hi Corbett Field in 1992, ending a 46-year stay in Tucson.

# All things must pass: Time runs out on Tribe tenure at Hi Corbett

*Wednesday, April 1, 1992*

It's 9 a.m., and Hi Corbett Field is a place aching for a ball game. All 7,609 tickets have been sold, and the Chicago Cubs are scheduled to arrive via bus in an hour.

The clock is ticking on the Cleveland Indians' 46-year-old spring training relationship with Tucson. Just 6 hours and 27 minutes remain.

**9:10 a.m.** Bob Feller arrives at the ballpark for the last time. It's the same place Feller reported for work March 9, 1947, the day the Indians played their inaugural spring training game in Tucson. He is asked if he remembers pitching that day. "I don't think I did," he says, accurately. Bob Lemon opened for the Indians against the New York Giants that day in 1947. Feller's only activity was in a wheelbarrow race around the bases, being pushed by teammate Al Gettek. (They lost to Whitey Lockman and Buddy Blattner of the Giants.)

**10 a.m.** Twenty or 30 fans greet the Cubs' bus from Phoenix. Most-asked question: Did the Cubs bring any starters? Did they bring Ryno or even Shawon Dunston? Bad omen: Cubs manager Jim Lefebvre doesn't even make the trip; he sends coach Tom Treblehorn instead. No one asks who will play for the Indians.

**10:02 a.m.** Ryne Sandberg is the last Cub off the bus. He receives his first ovation of the day.

**10:35 a.m.** The last parking space in the auxiliary lot west of the ballpark is gone. By noon, every parking place in a half-mile radius will be gone.

**10:40 a.m.** About 500 people stand outside the locked gates at Hi Corbett Field, almost all of them holding tickets to the first-come, first-served bleacher seats on either foul line. The gates are opened about 20 minutes earlier than normal to disperse the crowd. Many of them walk fast or run to pick the choicest seats.

**11:05 a.m.** Cubs catcher Joe Girardi stops Cleveland pitcher Jack Armstrong for a brief chat near the Cubs dugout. "We've got chicken soup for lunch," says Girardi with a laugh. "All that way in a bus for chicken soup." Armstrong smiles. "We've got vegetable soup," he says.

**11:15 a.m.** Feller stands on the third base concourse for the first of about five nostalgic interviews. "I hated Tucson at first," he says. "We'd have scorpions in the clubhouse, things like that. I'd never been to any-place like this. But I made so many friends here over the years, I would-n't trade Tucson for anything."

**11:25 a.m.** Larry Sluder, a souvenir vendor for the Uptown Optimist Club, says Cleveland's departure has spurred sales this year. "We've sold about three times as many (souvenirs) as we expected to," he says. "People are trying to get them before they leave town."

**11:35 a.m.** Stuart Start of KAMP, a cable-TV sports-talk program in Tucson, waits by the batting cage in hopes of getting a brief inter-view with Sandberg. But every time someone approaches for an auto-graph or an interview, Ryno barks, consistently, "Gotta hit."

**11:45 a.m.** Former Baltimore shortstop Mark Belanger, now an executive in the Major League Players Association, greets Hall of Fame outfielder Billy Williams of the Cubs next to the batting cage. "We were 10 years ahead of our time," says Williams. "If we were playing now, we wouldn't need to work when we retired."

**12:10 p.m.** Former Cincinnati Reds pitcher Pat Darcy, a Tucsonan who was influential in the successful recruitment of the Colorado Rockies to Hi Corbett Field, eats a hot dog in the pressroom.

"Toughest pitcher I ever batted against was Steve Carlton," Darcy says, smiling. "He'd throw that big curveball behind my head and bend it over the plate. All I wanted to do against him was take three quick hacks and get back to the dugout as fast as I could."

**1:05 p.m.** Indians equipment manager Cy Buynak, in his 31st spring training in Tucson, throws out the first pitch in the last game. "I wonder if he'll get it to the plate?" asks someone in the press box. Buynak's smooth, overhand delivery is down the pipe to catcher Sandy Alomar. "Hey, Cy could make this team," says the same press box joke-ster.

**1:16 p.m.** Former UA pitcher Lance Dickson faces former UA out-fielder Kenny Lofton, Cleveland's leadoff batter. Forty-six years ago, Jim Hegan was Cleveland's leadoff batter in the first spring training game at Hi Corbett. (The pitcher: Bob Carpenter.) Lofton singles to center.

**1:42 p.m.** Lute Olson, wearing a sky-blue sport coat and sun-glasses, takes a seat behind home plate.

**1:43 p.m.** Lute Olson signs his first autograph.

**2:03 p.m.** Cleveland catcher Sandy Alomar hits a monster three-run home run over the scoreboard in left. The Tribe leads 5-1, and Dickson's ERA goes to 6.63.

**2:23 p.m.** Cleveland's Paul Sorrento homers deep over the right-field wall. Dickson's ERA soars to 7.47 in five starts; he is removed from the game and informed that Frank Castillo and Shawn Boskie have won the Cubs' No. 4 and No. 5 starters' jobs. Dickson is headed to Class AAA Iowa.

**2:54 p.m.** Executives of the Colorado Rockies are introduced, sitting behind the third base dugout. That draws more applause than the announcement asking that those in the sellout crowd thank the Indians for their long stay in Tucson. (Thank goodness for the Rockies; if the Indians were leaving Tucson shut out of spring training, there would have been boos.)

**3:17 p.m.** Sandberg singles to center, triggering the day's loudest ovation. (We know where this town's priorities are.)

**3:25 p.m.** Lute Olson is still signing autographs.

**3:27 p.m.** Chicago's Rey Sanchez grounds out against Cleveland's Dennis Boucher to end the 484th game the Indians have played in Tucson.

**3:34 p.m.** Sandberg, the game's highest-paid ($29 million contract) player, declines an interview in the Cubs' locker room. "Gotta catch the bus," he says, toting a briefcase with him as he leaves.

Times change.

Forty-six years ago, on March 8, 1947, Feller, who was then baseball's highest paid player ($90,000 a year) celebrated Cleveland's first game in Tucson racing around the infield at Hi Corbett Field in a wheelbarrow.

Someone asked Sandberg if he would ever do something like that.

"A wheelbarrow?" he asked, arching his eyebrows. "Are you kidding?"

**3:50 p.m.** Colorado Rockies souvenirs are still going fast at the vendor tables outside Hi Corbett Field.

127

# Pima's Marc Barcelo pitches himself into spotlight

*Friday, May 29, 1992*

The switchboard operator at the Horizon Hills Motel in Grand Junction, Colo., wanted to know if the call was meant for Mr. Barcelo the baseball player, or Mr. Barcelo the father of the baseball player.

"Wait a minute," said the caller. "How do you know he's a baseball player?"

"You're not the first one to call," she said. "Everyone wants to talk to the baseball players from Arizona."

Word gets out.

On Wednesday night at Suplizio Stadium, "the baseball players from Arizona" won their fourth consecutive game at the Junior College World Series and Marc Barcelo — the pitcher, not the father — drew all manner of attention to himself.

He won his second start in five days on a night he probably shouldn't have even picked up a baseball. His season might've ended early in Saturday's opening victory, against Wallace State of Georgia.

But this is someone who understands that the extraordinary is expected of Pima Community College's lead pitcher in the JC World Series, the way Gil Heredia did it in '85 when he won his first two starts and pitched the Aztecs into the national championship game.

"I got hit on the foot by a line drive in the first inning of Saturday's game," Barcelo was saying yesterday. "It forced me to change my delivery and pitching motion, and the result was that I pulled or strained a deltoid muscle in my right (pitching) arm. It hurt like hell."

After a 40-minute rain delay in Saturday's opener, Barcelo thought his 1992 baseball season had ended. His ankle was sore. His arm throbbed. "We won (10-4), but it didn't go as well as it sounded."

Somehow Barcelo pitched a complete game, extending his season record to 11-4 and buying coach Roger Werbylo some precious time at a tournament in which pitching staffs are customarily thin in numbers and time.

And how far could Pima expect to go in the World Series if its No.1 pitcher was gone? George Arias can't hit a grand slam every other at-bat.

There were several reasons that Barcelo, a former all-city basketball player from Sahuaro High School — "I was just average in base-ball," he says now — might have turned into a spectator and watched Wednesday's winners bracket game against Essex County of Maryland from the bench.

The major-league draft is next week. Why let the scouts see him pitch hurt and ineffectively? And he has signed a letter of intent to play at Arizona State next year. What if he blows his arm out in the Juco Series, irreparably damaging his career as a Sun Devil and beyond?

But three hours before game time Wednesday, Aztec pitching coach Len Anderson said Barcelo would pitch. "He can't wait," Anderson said. "He's ready."

Barcelo's reasoning? "The season was on the line," he said. "You just do the best you can."

What Marc Barcelo proved in a 6-3 victory over Essex College is that he's the kind of player who has a gift for stepping into the fire and not getting burned. He looked at it as an opportunity to succeed, not as a chance to fail.

If he doesn't pitch, Pima probably doesn't win. But this time Barcelo sensed his obligation was greater than the average player's.

"I wasn't sure I could pitch (Wednesday), and I admit that my arm was bothering me when I warmed up," he said. "But this was probably my last chance to pitch for Pima, and it meant a lot to me.

"So I said to hell with it and pitched through the pain."

And Barcelo didn't just show up; he pitched a three-hitter through seven innings.

"Around the sixth inning my arm started hurting pretty bad," he said, "but I had enough adrenaline to put it out of my mind."

Barcelo is a large part of a tapestry of unforgettable stories at Pima this season. The club lost seven of nine players from last year's team, which was ranked No.3 in the nation before departing in the regional playoffs. It limped home in fourth place in the ACCAC this year. Its .400-hitting shortstop was killed in an automobile accident.

"No way we figured to be here," Barcelo said with a laugh. "No way."

One more improbable story — Barcelo, injured, pitching Pima into the championship rounds of the 1992 JC World Series — just adds to the mystique.

"Obviously, we're ecstatic about being in this position," he said. "But it's not like we sit around talking about how it all came together. I mean, it just happened. Once we beat Phoenix College in the first round of the playoffs, things kept rolling.

"Sometimes I can't believe we're here."

The Aztecs could win the national championship tonight, and if they do, it will have to be without Barcelo. He understands that he has pushed his aching right arm to its limit.

"It bothers me a lot knowing I won't be out there," he said. "But the way our season has gone I think we're going to find a way to win the whole thing no matter who plays."

EDITOR'S NOTE: Marc Barcelo was the Pac-10 Player of the Year in 1993 while helping Arizona State reach the College World Series. That same summer he was drafted by the Minnesota Twins in the first round of the Major League Baseball draft. He pitched five seasons in the minors, reaching the Triple-A level before arm injuries scuttled his career in 1997. Now, Barcelo is the golf pro at the famed Doral Resort Golf Course, the Blue Monster, site of the WGC-CA Championship event.

During the 1993 season, Arizona walk-on Tod Brown went from feeling "unwanted" to being a postseason star and one of the team's top pitchers.

# Wildcats lifted by an unlikely hero

*Thursday, June 3, 1993*

Out of the ashes of another punishing 61-game baseball season, Arizona's four-month march to Omaha came down to the will of one man whose presence in this crisis was almost unimaginable.

Tod Brown.

No scholarship. No real fastball. No rhyme or reason why the UA's baseball season would come down to this walk-on from Sabino High School, a pitcher who has never known what it was like to struggle with celebrity on a team of celebrities.

The Wildcats would go as far as Tod Brown could take them.

"Considering where I came from, the fact that I wasn't even recruited out of high school, no one would've believed this, nobody, not even my best friend," Brown was saying yesterday.

But it was true. Arizona desperately wanted two more innings out of an arm that had already given it 10⅔ innings Monday, an aching left arm that, Brown says, "was washed up" in the fourth inning.

And here he was in the eighth, six outs from the College World Series. "I had been dreaming about going to Omaha since I was 10," Brown says. "But my arm was dead, I was exhausted, and my legs were cramping."

Six outs to Omaha.

There was, essentially, no one else ready or rested enough to get Oklahoma State out. "No matter how tired I was," Brown says, "I was going to keep going until they took me out."

In his first two appearances in the NCAA Regional in Stillwater, Okla., Brown had saved two Arizona victories. He had twice pitched 2⅔ innings, and no one had scored.

Given three hours to rest between an afternoon victory over OSU on Monday, the Wildcat pitching staff was spent. Jerry Kindall would have to start a freshman, Ben White, in the championship game against the Cowboys. Who else was left? If White couldn't make it, who could relieve?

"Before the game, (pitching coach Gil Lopez) asked me if I could go again, and I said yes, but to tell you the truth, I could probably go, maybe, two innings," Brown recollects. "Gil just said OK, we'll use you late in the game. If comes down to a crunch."

The crunch came much earlier than feared. It came in the first inning. Oklahoma State scored five times. No one was out. Lopez had already used two pitchers, and frankly, there was no one else but Tod Brown. It had been barely three hours since he last pitched, and he didn't exactly feel like Sandy Koufax in the bullpen.

Yet it was his game and nobody else's. Imagine that.

Yes, there are still nine to a side in baseball, all the time, and one-against-nine is much more unfair when it is a well-worn Tod Brown vs. Oklahoma State than it is when it's Roger Clemens against the Yankees. But on Monday in Stillwater, Okla., it was the power of one, Tod Brown, that would ultimately make the difference.

How long could he last?

He closed down OSU in the first without further damage. He shut them out in the second, third, fourth, fifth, sixth . . . and by then his teammates had scored 10 times. The drama grew. How much heart did he have? Brown's off-speed pitches kept getting the Cowboys out. A double-play grounder here. A deep fly caught on the warning track there.

By the eighth inning, the MVP trophy of the NCAA Midwest Regional was all but zipped away in Brown's travel bag.

"Tod reached the point of human limitation," Kindall would say after the game. "He went beyond it."

Indeed, the baseball world takes some unexpected twists.

A year ago in the NCAA Regionals in Tucson, Brown was summoned from the Arizona bullpen and ordered to walk a Hawaii batter on four pitches. That done, he was removed from the game at once, not trusted to pitch to even one live hitter. Brown was as angry as he was embarrassed as he stalked off the mound that day. It was his only appearance in the postseason, and it mirrored his career at Arizona.

It was a pretty strong hint that he was unappreciated.

"I don't know if I felt unwanted," he says now. "But, well, yes, I guess I was. I felt like it had been, a rough road, and I didn't know what to do next. I'd lie in bed wondering what to do — maybe try a junior college or maybe transfer somewhere else.

"But deep down inside I knew I could contribute if I just kept pushing. I really couldn't understand why I couldn't help the team. I didn't want to transfer because I was established in school and because I had established a group of friends. I just decided to keep working hard and something good would happen."

Something good: a team-high six victories in 1993.

Something better: a team-high eight saves.

Something best: a school-record 35 appearances.

Something to dream about: a starring role in the NCAA tournament.

Much of Brown's improvement came from his diligence in the off-season. He moved to Ohio and pitched in a collegiate league, going 6-0 and setting a conference record with a 1.20 ERA. He realized that, at his level, he could pitch successfully even though his top fastball was clocked at a mortal 82 mph. Control and savvy can get a lot of batters out in any league.

It got him on the NCAA all-regional team.

It would be nice to report that Brown got those final six outs in Oklahoma and that he lugged his team on his back all the way to Omaha. But he never got out of the eighth inning. Neither did the UA, which lost 11-10.

"It's going to eat me alive for the rest of my life," Brown says, unaware that time will help him get over the sense of disappointment; unaware that, in time, he will savor what he accomplished in 1993 much more than what got away.

"I haven't slept very well," he says.

Yesterday, Brown went to McKale Center to meet with his coaches and talk about 1994. His goal is to get out of the bullpen and crack the starting rotation. He will pitch in the Cape Cod League this summer and, who knows, if that doesn't work, he's only five saves shy of Joe Estes' UA career record.

When Brown took a seat in Kindall's office yesterday, there was one more thing on his mind. Would it be possible, now, to be put on scholarship? Isn't that the right thing to do? "I've never received one dime from the university," he says. "I thought I maybe deserved one."

And Kindall agreed.

There would be a successful finish to the season after all.

EDITOR'S NOTE: Tod Brown pitched two seasons of independent-league baseball in the mid-1990s in Minnesota and North Dakota. He later was a teacher at Sabino High School and a volunteer assistant coach at the UA before serving as the pitching coach at Bowling Green State from 2000 to 2007. Brown now lives in Fargo, N.D., where he has been the head coach at North Dakota State since 2008.

SERGEY SHAYEVICH

Joe Mikulik attained legendary status as a Tucson Toro in the early 1990s, when he had the game-winning hits to clinch the PCL titles in '91 and '93.

# Toros' hero brings magic to ballpark

*Wednesday, September 15, 1993*

Summer is over, and it is time for Joe Mikulik to go home.

He tells those of us in Tucson that home is Asheville, N.C., where he played Class A ball in 1985 and met his wife.

But I think by now we have started to wonder if Joe Mikulik is really flesh and blood at all. We wonder if he has full-time residency on planet Earth. Maybe he is just a character on loan from some fairy-tale land, a man who leaves Hi Corbett Field at night and strolls unwatched into a cornfield.

Poof, he's gone.

Every town has its local baseball legend, a mystical figure who comes and goes and leaves in his wake a series of unexplained, almost magical events. Roy Hobbs. Moonlight Graham. Joe Hardy.

Sure, that's fiction, stuff in the movies. But you wonder about Joe Mikulik. Is he for real?

He not only helped the Toros win their only two PCL championships but at the same time is possibly the most-liked Toro who has ever played here.

Unlike too many ballplayers, Mikulik is loyal to more than just the highest bidder. If there's a movie, Tom Hanks gets the part.

We first heard about Joe Mikulik during the Toros' 1991 PCL Championship series. The circumstances were unusual. He got in town two days before the playoffs began, on Sept. 1. He had spent the season in Mississippi Class AA ball. He could've walked in from a cornfield for all we knew.

Predictably, Mikulik went 0 for 9, the Toros lost the first two games of a best-of-five series, and he was benched.

But then, strangely, Mikulik was back in the lineup in the championship game, batting second, of all places. Try to explain that.

He doubled and scored the tying run in the fifth inning. No one expected that. And that's the way it stayed until the ninth when — in the most dramatic baseball game ever played in this town — he singled to right, scoring the winning run.

The story got better yet. Before he went to bat, he had scrawled never surrender on his wrist bands. "That's my motto," he said. Reporters couldn't write it down fast enough. Never surrender? Priceless.

137

Yesterday I dug out an old champagne-soaked notebook from the 1991 championship series, looking for clues. "There is no ecstasy like winning," Mikulik said that night. "Nothing else feels as good."

Summer was over, Mikulik disappeared, and I thought we had seen the last of him.

He was demoted to Class AA a year later, hit just .262 and, at 28, his career appeared to be over. No longer do Class AAA franchises provide a last hurrah for aging ballplayers whose skills are deserting them. What is wanted today are young men, who, like championship race-horses, become stronger and faster with each new season.

Summoned again to Tucson in 1992, Mikulik batted a meek .248. But at least he got his 1,000th career minor-league hit. It would be a nice, sentimental reminder of a good minor-league ballplayer. "I'd trade them all for one hit in the majors," he said.

But you've got to get to the majors before you can get a hit there.

Mikulik reappeared in the lives of Tucson baseball fans in mid-August, when he hit a three-run homer to beat first-place Albuquerque. The Toros won the next 14. The pennant race was over and Mikulik got it started.

Didn't Roy Hobbs do this once?

Then, almost magically, a fan walked up to Mikulik the day before the PCL championship series began and said he had a gift. It was Mikulik's bat used in the 1991 championship game. Just like that. The fan kept the bat for two years, having grabbed it while Mikulik and the '91 Toros were spraying champagne and dancing wildly on the field.

Mikulik put the bat in the Toros' bat rack. "Just for luck," he said.

In the first inning of Monday's championship game, Mikulik was stationed in left field when a Portland batter hit a sacrifice fly to right. The throw went to third base as the run scored. Yet, somehow, Mikulik was standing behind third base, backing up the throw.

You've got to be Carl Lewis to get from left field to back up third base on a sacrifice fly. Then, once the play ended, Mikulik turned and sprinted, I mean flew, back to left field.

What's he doing backing up third base, anyway? That's a play for the pitcher. But those who follow the Tucson Toros have come to understand that Mikulik plays by a different book. He plays in-your-face baseball, inning by inning. As an extra, he batted .300 again.

Several members of the Portland bullpen, who witnessed Mikulik's hustle, gave him the raised-eyebrows look and kidded among themselves. "What's with this guy?" they laughed, loud enough for some nearby fans to hear.

They would laugh no more.

Mikulik's sacrifice fly gave Tucson a 3-2 lead in the fourth. His two-run triple in the sixth clinched it. The lucky bat was in the rack. Tucson was a champion again.

The first chill breeze of September blew across the ballpark late Monday night, about the time the Toros burst from the dugout and ran toward left field. Mikulik met the mob halfway and they danced and hugged and felt the same ecstasy that Mikulik talked about two years ago.

"It's unbelievable how things work out," he would say.

It would be nice to say that Mikulik walked off into the corn patch, his mission complete, everybody happy. But that's just in movies.

Mikulik knows neither fame nor fortune in baseball. When the Houston Astros added several Toros to the major-league roster yesterday, Mikulik, who will be 30 next month, was not among them. His baseball clock is ticking. What does he have to do to get that one hit?

If baseball had a heart, Mikulik would be in Houston today. The Astros are hopelessly out of the race, and yet they can't make room for Joe Mikulik for three weeks. If the Astros had any sense, they would put Mikulik on the roster just to let his enthusiasm rub off on those millionaire ballplayers who have been corrupted by fame and fortune.

Instead, the Astros looked the other way. It makes you ill.

In the next year or two, Mikulik is probably going to be laid off with no compensation and, as is the case in minor-league baseball, no pension plan. And no big-league hit either.

If he is lucky, if we are lucky, he will someday be a coach or manager for the Toros. Pro baseball is a long and hard endurance test, and in the end, Joe Mikulik thinks he will win.

He won't surrender.

EDITOR'S NOTE: Joe Mikulik only played 13 more games in his professional career, doing so with the Toros in 1994, before turning to a managerial career. That is where he found a new niche. The 2009 season was his 12th as a minor-league skipper, and he's spent the last 10 with the Asheville Tourists in the Single-A South Atlantic League. Mikulik is the winningest manager in South Atlantic history and was selected to the league's hall of fame in June 2009.

JOE VITTI

Jerry Kindall's place in UA baseball lore is etched in stone after his wildly successful tenure as coach, one that included three NCAA championships.

# Lifetime achievement: Wildcats honor former baseball coach

*Sunday, January 25, 2004*

If winning a bunch of championships were the only requisite to naming a ballpark after a coach, every Pac-10 school would have a cumbersome, hyphenated campus directory.

At USC, it would be the Los Angeles Coliseum at Howard Jones-John McKay-John Robinson Field. At Washington, the basketball arena would be Bank of America Arena at Hec Edmundson Pavilion-Marv Harshman Court. At Oregon, the hallowed track stadium would be Bill Bowerman-Bill Dellinger Track at Bill Hayward Field.

There's got to be more than winning to motivate a school to put a name on the bricks. There's got to be more to remember than Arizona 10, Florida State 2, College World Series championship game, 1986.

When the UA announced it would name its baseball facility after Jerry Kindall this weekend, more than 340 former ballplayers, coaches, staff members and friends of the Arizona baseball program phoned or wrote to say they would be here. Terry Francona, manager of the Boston Red Sox, paid his own expenses. So did his first base coach, Brad Mills.

It was not the winning with Kindall. It was not the national championships of 1976, 1980 and 1986. It was not the coach. It was the man.

"What Coach taught me," Francona said, "was how he expected us to treat the game and how he expected us to treat other people. I can see why my parents wanted to send me here. Under Coach, I learned the right way to grow up."

The UA henceforth will play baseball at Jerry Kindall Field at Frank Sancet Stadium, a dual honor to a pair of men who coached the Wildcats to 1,691 victories and 13 appearances at the College World Series.

Tucsonan Bud Grainger, a retired bank executive and NCAA umpire who worked scores of games for the two coaches, attended the weekend ceremonies. He was, by profession, an adversary of Kindall and Sancet.

"They didn't see it that way," he said. "Both men coached to win, with such intensity, boy, they never let up. I made dozens of calls that they didn't like. Some of those calls must have cost them a ballgame or

141

two, in their opinion. But they never treated me with anything less than respect. And you know what, over all those years, I never threw either of them out of a ballgame."

Kindall is 68. He could still be coaching, had he decided to do so. He is fit and sharp, a man who almost always finds the best in others.

Saturday, he spent most of his dedication speech talking about his former coaches and players, his family and his faith. He rarely resorted to "I" or "me." He said, typical of his modesty, the university was bestowing this honor on "an unworthy person."

The first time I met Kindall, more than 20 years ago, I sat in his office and asked him about his major-league career and about his successes at the UA.

He didn't talk about any of that stuff.

"I'd like to stress that I haven't built anything here," he said. "I'm simply trying to maintain what Coach Sancet and Coach Pop McKale established. I hope I don't mess it up."

At the time, he had won two national titles in five years, the first in any sport in UA history.

The legacy of Kindall's 24-year Arizona coaching career is best defined by a two-year period, 1980-81, in which the Wildcat baseball program turned out what surely must be an unprecedented roster of baseball luminaries.

That period produced the following players who went on to become pro, college and high school managers, coaches and scouts: Francona, Mills, Ed Vosberg, Craig Lefferts, Johnny Moses, Clark Crist, Scott Stanley, Jim Bagnall, Wes Clements, Chuck Hoyack, Dave Landrith, Jeff Morris, Alan Regier and Pat Roessler.

That's just two of 24 years. And that's just part of the list. Talk about a man having an impact in the lives of those he touched.

Kindall's baseball family tree is among the most impressive in the history of the sport.

He coached the 1986 World Series championship team while dealing with unimaginable pain. His first wife, Georgia, was dying of Lou Gehrig's disease. And yet he took a team no one predicted to be a title contender — a team that did not win the Pac-10 title — to the NCAA championship.

Georgia died a year later. Kindall somehow coached the Wildcats to another NCAA tournament.

Kindall has written numerous books on baseball. You can buy any of a half-dozen Kindall-produced baseball instructional videos on the

Internet. He can tell you everything you need to know about executing the double play and how to win a baseball game.

But when his name went on the wall Saturday at Arizona's baseball stadium, it was not because of the baseball. It was because of the man.

EDITOR'S NOTE: Jerry Kindall lives in Tucson and can be seen occasionally at Arizona baseball home games. He is employed by Crystal Cruises as part of the entertainment package, where he gives speeches as a "special interest lecturer" on baseball. He also serves as a senior adviser for USA Baseball.

MAMTA POPAT

Jerry Kindall waves to a gathering of hundreds of admirers during a January 2004 ceremony in which the UA renamed its baseball facility in his honor.

Spring training scenes like this one in February 2009 will soon be mere memories due to the desire of Major League Baseball teams to leave Tucson for the Phoenix area.

BENJIE SANDERS

# 'Heading north' not nice words in Tucson

*Thursday, March 27, 2008*

Wednesday morning at Hi Corbett Field, an 18-wheeler from Fort Worth Freight Lines carefully maneuvered into a small space behind the right field wall.

A dozen men commenced the laborious task of moving the Colorado Rockies' weightlifting equipment from underneath two makeshift pavilions.

"Heading north," said Kent Thorpe, one of those doing the heavy lifting. "All the way to Coors Field."

Alas, in Tucson, the two sorriest words of spring training are heading north.

At least they did not mean north to Phoenix. Not yet.

You would have never suspected spring training 2008 was in its last day at Hi Corbett Field.

Behind the right field wall at the old ballpark, another world, one that is mostly off limits and unknown to the casual spring training fan, was in full whirl.

About 150 Rockies' minor-league ballplayers, coaches, scouts, umpires, trainers and attendant baseball personnel had just begun playing three intrasquad games with Class A, Class AA and Class AAA teams. Two additional fields on the Reid Park Annex were being used for infield and bunting practice.

"A lot of us are here until June," said Rockies minor-league coach Anthony Sanders, a former big-league outfielder from Tucson who played high school ball at Santa Rita. "There's stuff happening out here every day."

It made you wonder: In the limited baseball facilities of Hi Corbett Field, where do they all go to take a shower?

As the minor-leaguers played through the lunch hour, 8,643 fans — the largest gathering of the spring at Hi Corbett — were processed through the turnstiles. It was, officially or otherwise, "Save Spring Training Day," the first public effort by community leaders to manifest interest in keeping the Rockies here.

Before the first pitch, Tucson activist/broadcaster Dave Sitton stood behind home plate with a microphone and exhorted those in attendance to recognize the perilous future of spring training baseball here.

"It's not going to be a committee of six that makes this happen," he said. Flanking Sitton, executives from the Diamondbacks and Rockies politely applauded his words.

The "saving" has quietly begun.

At first glance, the Rockies' spring attendance average of 4,928, which ranks 13th of 16 National League teams and dead last of the 12 Cactus League clubs, appears to be an indignity to the defending National League champs, and a signal that Tucson does not care much.

But it is not attendance as much as it is amenities and convenience that drive spring training decisions.

The Rockies can legally leave Tucson if the White Sox's inevitable move to Glendale is not accompanied by a suitable replacement team. What appears to be of great importance is an upgrade of the facilities at Hi Corbett.

How much of an upgrade? Probably $25 million, minimum. Gulp. You know how that plays in the political arena.

Realistically, the long-term use and viability of Hi Corbett Field is not a good buy. There is no chance to spin off that $25 million with private investment, commercial development or residential expansion.

The Hi Corbett area is built out. You cannot even squeeze in another parking space.

Barring an 11th-hour campaign to build a ballpark downtown — that ship sailed about 15 years ago and shipwrecked on Ajo Way — it would make more sense for the business leaders in space-available Marana or Oro Valley to spend $25 million on a spring training facility.

Not happenin'.

So it spins on the remake of Hi Corbett.

To their credit, the Rockies have not alienated Southern Arizonans by publicly criticizing local entertainment options, the weather, financial opportunities or by expressing Phoenix-envy.

They have said they would like a more modern ballpark. And they have a good case.

Here is a comparison: After 16 years, the Cleveland Indians played their final game in Winter Haven, Fla., on Wednesday. They are moving to the Phoenix suburb of Goodyear and will transition into a 42,000-square foot clubhouse.

That is about double the size of the Rockies' cramped clubhouse.

The Indians' new complex will include a permanent weight room;

the Rockies' is actually outdoors, protected from the weather only by some hastily installed plastic wrap.

In Goodyear, the Indians will have indoor hydrotherapy chambers, video training rooms, two offices for team psychologists, conference rooms for coaches and even a room specially equipped for a "cultural coordinator," in which Latin and Asian players will be able to acclimate themselves to language and cultural barriers.

It will be a year-round site for Cleveland's minor-league operations, instructional league endeavors and a medical rehabilitation center for the entire franchise.

The Rockies have none of the above in Tucson.

Such is the price of living in the Big City as it relates to spring training and 21st century baseball.

By comparison, Pima County officials last week indicated they are "very seriously" looking at a Chicago proposal to replace the White Sox with (please, don't laugh) a youth baseball tournament.

Given that mentality, those 18-wheelers heading north today are apt to return to Hi Corbett Field someday to move the Colorado Rockies to Phoenix.

EDITOR'S NOTE: The White Sox played in their Glendale facility in spring 2009. By spring 2011, the Rockies and the Diamondbacks will enjoy spring training at a joint facility near Scottsdale built and maintained by the Salt River Indian Community.

KELLY PRESNELL

Trent Oeltjen is the last Tucson Sidewinders player to leave the field following the Triple-A franchise's final game in the Old Pueblo in September 2008.

# Tucson baseball touched lives, made a difference

*Tuesday, September 2, 2008*

In 1969, a few days before the Tucson Toros' inaugural Pacific Coast League game, a cheapie scoreboard costing $7,557 was installed at Hi Corbett Field.

Even then, in the start-up phase, standards for minor-league baseball here were curiously low. Rather than have "Toros" or "Tucson" on the scoreboard, it said simply "Home" and "Visitor."

For the next 40 years, minor-league baseball in Tucson was treated with a similar indifference.

But it doesn't mean that four decades of minor-league baseball didn't touch lives and make a difference.

A few months before that 1969 opener, 24-year-old Rincon High grad Russ Gill recently out of the Navy and working the front desk at the Los Angeles Biltmore, registered a Tucson guest.

The men had become acquainted during 1960s spring training at Hi Corbett Field. Gill had done odd jobs and worked as a batboy for the Cleveland Indians. His hotel guest, Abe Chanin, had written about the Indians for this newspaper.

"This was a total chance meeting," Gill says now. "Abe told me Tucson was getting a PCL baseball team. He said he would call the owner and see if they needed any help.

"Fifteen minutes later — I'm not kidding, 15 minutes! — Abe came downstairs and said 'you're hired.' I packed my old VW and drove to Tucson the next day."

His life changed forever.

For the grand sum of $85 a week, Russ Gill became the Toros' first assistant general manager. He sold his first ad for $125 to Bargain Furniture Center. When the uniforms arrived a few days before opening night, he drove downtown and gave one of those old "T" caps to the mayor. The photograph was in all the papers.

Gill was so absorbed by the opportunity of Class AAA baseball in Tucson that he moved into the Toros' clubhouse.

"I lived there all season," he said, laughing. "I bought a 2-inch pad and slept on it for months. I was fascinated by the ballpark at night, when everyone had gone home and it was quiet. I'd look out across the

149

outfield grass and was taken by the silence. There was nothing but moonlight in the ballpark. That might have been the best summer of my life."

Gill went on to work for minor-league clubs in Wichita and Oklahoma City and by the late '70s created a national marketing business for all of minor-league baseball. He has since been in the marketing and promotional business, working mostly with Hollywood celebrities and for charities.

He remains so connected in baseball that he successfully acquired 36 primo tickets at July's All-Star Game in Yankee Stadium.

"Those tickets cost $53,000," he says, chuckling. "I got them for Kellogg's, the grocery people. They were entertaining clients. That's the way my life has gone. Baseball has become my family. I trace it all back to that first year with the Toros."

The Toros and the Sidewinders have had seven owners, 22 managers, about 950 players and they played more than 5,600 games. They won PCL titles in 1991, 1993 and 2006 and have drawn about 9.2 million fans.

Yet their announced move to Reno, Nev., next spring generated no local protest of substance, no real resistance.

Forty years. Just like that. Gone.

"Tucson should always have Class AAA baseball," says Jimmy Johnson, a Rincon High School grad who managed the Toros in 1980-82 and again in 1985. "It's not the most successful franchise, but it established a good tradition that got lost when they moved from Hi Corbett Field over to Tucson Electric Park.

"Once the move took place, it became harder to get to a game. It lost its intimacy. It isn't as friendly over at TEP. It's sad, just sad. A lot of people put years of sweat and love into that franchise."

Johnson, now part of the Colorado Rockies instructional staff, made his mark as the Toros manager the way Gill launched his career by selling ballpark ads for $125.

They are the winners.

The losers are those who won't be able to take their kids to watch the Three Stooges clown around in the grandstands, as they did in 1969, or watch as John Wayne walks through the gates from a filming session at Old Tucson, taking a seat in the Toros' dugout.

The losers are those of future generations who won't see the next Max Patkin, baseball's Clown Prince, in the third base coaching box, or the next Famous Chicken holding up an eye chart for an umpire to read.

On a dramatic September night in 1991, former UA basketball star Kenny Lofton raced home with the championship run, two outs, bottom of the ninth, as the Toros won their first PCL title.

Many in the overflow crowd of 8,919 rushed the field and didn't go home until the last drop of champagne was spilled. It was the signature moment in Tucson's 40 years of Pacific Coast League baseball.

On Monday night at TEP, after the last out in the last game, the Sidewinders shot off fireworks. It wasn't a celebration. It was, rather, a signal of transition. The home team has become the visitors.

# CHAPTER FIVE

# Miscellany

## Trip to Spain means hurry up and be 'wait-listed'

*Friday, July 4, 1986*

*MALAGA, Spain*

A world traveler I am not. I am more like the character Kathleen Turner played in "Romancing the Stone." That is, someone who gets on a bus for the big city and instead is up to his elbows in crocodiles and quick-sand.

Yesterday, the U.S. World Championship basketball team went from Lyon, France, to the south coast of Spain, and feel free to make liberal use of the word "day."

Lewis and Clark found the Pacific Ocean faster than we got to Malaga. There was no time for basketball.

Dear Diary:

**7:15 a.m.** The sound of a ringing telephone in France must have been adapted from a ship lost somewhere in the fog. Only louder.

When I got a wake-up call, I was so frightened by the phone my whole life — the not-so nice part — flashed before my eyes. Beach invasions are more subtle.

Syracuse's Rony Seikaly was awakened by a hotel charge of 540 francs for telephone use. That's roughly $90.

"They had me calling Ohio, Florida — everywhere," said Seikaly.

An interpreter finally pared Seikaly's bill to 75 francs — about $14.

**10:30 a.m.** A long-delayed bus trip finally leaves Hotel Mercure in Lyon and gets a police escort to the airport. Coach Lute Olson poses for photographs wearing an Indiana Hoosiers shirt. Olson's luggage has been lost for six days.

Upon check-in at the airport, I am instructed there has been a mistake. I am "wait-listed," which sounds harmless enough.

Olson, his staff, 12 players and assorted team doctors and administrators board a plane for Madrid, Spain, while I am left behind, one of six on the wait list.

"Usually," said the Air France official, "one or two of you will make it, but this plane is full. Sorry."

I hastily arrange a backup flight, one that won't leave until the next day. My baggage is already on a plane for Madrid.

Now, I don't mind being left behind in Pocatello, Idaho, but when it's somewhere in the middle of France, the adventurer in me isn't brought out. Nobody speaks English. I'm a goner.

**12: 14 p.m.** Tom McGrath, the team's escort from the sponsoring ABAUSA, pleads my case to an Air France official. The plane is loaded and ready to leave at 12:20.

"You are a lucky man," says the woman at the counter. "This is the last ticket."

For the first time, I do not complain about getting the middle seat.

**12:22 p.m.** I have celebrated my good fortune for two minutes. Then I realize I'm "wait-listed" again at the Madrid airport. This is the same airport where a bomb exploded last week, injuring 13 people.

But at least I'll have company. Six others in the U.S. traveling party have been "wait-listed," including the Tucson Citizen's Jack Rickard. Misery loves company.

**1:55 p.m.** At the Madrid airport, the Israeli national basketball team is gathered in the same Iberia ticket counter as I am. Last week's bomb was exploded at the Israeli terminal.

I am number seven on the wait list for a 4:15 p.m. flight to Malaga. I am told I can get a flight the next day at 4:15 p.m. I decide not to wait for the flight or for the Israelis to leave.

I inform Rickard I'm taking a cab to the train station and to hold my hotel reservation in Malaga. About that time, a man, apparently suffering from infirmities of age, is wheeled into the ticket line.

"That man must have been wait-listed once," said Rickard, who is number six in the line. He has no room to laugh.

But again, unexpectedly, McGrath comes to the rescue. The interpreter from the World Championship organizing committee pulls a few strings and attempts to get seven more seats on a soldout flight to Malaga. It works.

"We bribed the Iberia people with promises of free dinners and later flights," says the interpreter, a woman named Rosa.

I promised to buy McGrath dinner.

**4:30 p.m.** Our flight is delayed by two hours. "This is not one of my better days," says Arizona guard Steve Kerr. "I once had an 18-hour flight from Cairo (Egypt) to Los Angeles, and it was easier than this one."

**6:15 p.m.** Olson emerges from a Spanish cafeteria $22 richer. He won the money in a game of gin (cards) against assistant coach Jerry Pimm and others.

While the players groan about the long delay and get in another line to board the plane, Olson just laughs. "What delay are you guys talking about?"

**9 p.m.** We are informed that journalists may not be permitted in Hotel Melia Torremolinos for security reasons.

I have already reserved a room, but after going two for two, I expect the worst. I am due for a bad break. At Malaga, we are greeted in festival atmosphere. TV cameras, reporters, interpreters, autograph seekers.

A team bus gets a police export, and, not only that, a police helicopter escort. At the hotel, there are more than 25 armed policemen, including some on the roof and some on each floor.

Security is so tight, says McGrath, that journalists won't even be allowed to stay here. The rest of the town is booked solid, says our interpreter.

I worry about my job security.

**9:40 p.m.** The hotel manager greets me ceremoniously in the lobby. I wonder if he has me mixed up with someone else.

"American journalist," he says. "We have been waiting for you."

In my room are a bouquet of flowers and a huge bowl of fruit. Can it be — journalists from America are considered something special in Spain?

**10:20 p.m.** Tired, but not grouchy, I confront my last problem. Press credentials. Last week, I was informed it was too late. May 15 was the deadline.

Rickard and I are introduced to the World Championship press chief.

"Come in my office first thing in the morning," he says, "and let's get you processed."

**11:30 p.m.** Against all odds, I have batted a thousand. Five for five. I honestly expected to be driving a small rental car tonight from France to the west coast of Spain. With no hotel room waiting. Instead, I am in a luxury hotel, that would go for more than $150 a night in Tucson, for $45 a night.

It is a block from a Mediterranean beach. Tomorrow must surely be the Fourth of July.

# 7-year-old finds never isn't forever

*Thursday, December 22, 1988*

Tyler's bottom lip quivered slightly, and tears welled in his eyes.
"There'll be no football, Tyler," the doctor said. "Never."

Basketball? No. One stray elbow in the wrong place is too much to chance.

Never.

Baseball? Not this year. Maybe when you're older you can play a little softball.

Tears were trickling down Ty's cheeks. His heart had just been repaired but suddenly it felt broken again.

No baseball? How could that be? He had always been the best player on his team, even when he was 5. When the 8- and 9-year-olds on the block played street ball, Ty always held his own. One year soon, someday, he would hit one over the fence and race around the bases at Arthur Pack Park as if he had conquered the world.

Just like his brother. Just like his favorite player, Mark McGwire.

No, said the doctor. Never.

The doctor prescribed golf and tennis. Swimming would be good.

By now Ty was crying the way 7-year-olds cry when their heart burns for something they can't have.

No basketball? Then why had his dad built him one of those adjustable backboards and lowered it to 7 feet just so he could hit a three-pointer? Why had he fallen in love with Steve Kerr and Sean Elliott if he wouldn't be allowed to "be them" in the afternoon game on the driveway?

Never.

Tuesday night, two months after he had been released from the pediatric intensive care unit at University Medical Center, Tyler took his seat in the nosebleed section of McKale Center to watch the Wildcats play Washington.

"I want to give Joe Turner a high-five," Tyler said. "Do you think he'll remember me?"

Joe Turner had visited Tyler in the hospital two months ago. Armed with autographs, photos and a mile-wide smile, Joe Turner had made Ty's last night in the hospital a memorable one.

A 7-inch vertical scar dissects Ty's chest, but the pain and most of his fears are gone. He is no longer held together by stitches and staples,

156

but by a monumental badge of energy.

Never?

He wants a new bat for Christmas. "A 27," he says. And when his mom and dad aren't watching, Ty plops his recording of "Wild About the Cats" into his tape player and turns the sound to "highest" and buries a few three-pointers on the driveway.

No, the doctor said. Never.

On Tuesday night, Ty saw exactly what "never" might be.

"Never" was No. 40 in purple for the Washington Huskies, sophomore center Todd Lautenbach. Two years ago this month, Lautenbach was carted into Room 5260 at University Hospital in Seattle, his chestbone held together by a series of stitches and staples.

The scar on Lautenbach's chest runs vertically. Maybe 8 inches long. Like Tyler, Lautenbach takes daily medication to regulate his heartbeat for a condition that causes an irregular beat.

Doctors had once said Lautenbach might never play basketball again.

"They had hoped to fix my (heart condition) with laser surgery," Lautenbach said. "The doctors hadn't originally planned to have open-heart surgery.

"In high school I had been playing and getting away with it. My heart would just start beating fast. It would drain my energy so I would have to slow down. We had been treating it with medication. I thought it would go away."

Ty has a word, an unpleasant word, for what happened to Lautenbach and for what happened to him.

"They slashed him, too?" Ty asked, looking down at No. 40. "How come he can play basketball? The doctor said I couldn't."

Never?

Well, Tuesday night Lautenbach scored 21 points. More than Sean Elliott. More than anyone on the court. He played more minutes, 26, than anyone in the game. Afterward, as he was toweling off from a shower, Lautenbach sat on a bench and accepted congratulations from his teammates. No one for Washington had played better than No. 40, the man with the 8-inch scar on his chest.

Never?

For Tyler, this was the end of never.

# Dreaming is part of baseball

*Thursday, April 27, 1989*

The distance from home plate to the outfield fence at Arthur Pack Field No. 3 is almost 225 feet. For a boy of 12, it had always been too far.

Every weekend morning for the last six weeks, without fail, Ben has tapped his father on the shoulder long before he wanted to get out of bed.

Ben's request always seemed urgent.

"Dad, can we go have batting practice?" he'd ask. "I know I can hit one out."

If the dream of a 12-year-old is to hit a baseball over a faraway fence, it is a dream he shares with his father. With many fathers. And with many 12-year-olds.

But the fence has always been too far for Ben. Too far for his father.

"Dad," he used to say when he was 9, playing his first season in the major league category of Tucson's Little League organization, "when will I be big enough to hit it out?"

I never did tell him what I really thought.

"By the time you're 12," I'd say, "you'll be hitting 'em out all the time. Maybe when you're 11."

But when Ben was 11, he had to take batting practice at second base to hit one out. The better players on his team, most of them a head taller, would clear the fence once or twice a week.

"When Dad? When?"

What I would tell Ben was that every time I go to the ballpark today — in an old man's softball league and in an adult baseball league that has resurrected the dreams of childhood — I feel much the same way he does.

It's like being 12 again. I can share his anxiety. I want to know "when," too.

I still dream that someday, some way, a pitch will find my "wheel-house," as they say on TV. I will crank one out, trot slowly around the bases and realize a dream that has lingered for a quarter-century.

A home run. Over the fence. Out of the park.

But no. It's too late. Never. Never have. Never will.

If there is a baseball curse, it is to go oh-for-a-lifetime. Homerless. Singles hitters, father and son.

This year Ben is, at long last, among the tallest players on his team. But our batting practice excursions would always end in frustration.

"How close did that one come, Dad?" he'd ask as a fly ball landed 15 feet shy of the chain-link fence.

"It hit the fence on two bounces," I'd say. "You're getting closer."

The sense of urgency goes unspoken. Next year, at the next level, the boys will play on a high school field. If not this year, it may be never.

On game day, invariably, someone would get a pitch in his "wheelhouse" and hit one into the desert, with the ball bounding toward the distant golf course. And every time someone hit a home run, the other 24 boys on the field and in the dugouts would look at the slugger with unspeakable envy.

"When, Dad? When?"

I am convinced that every 10-, 11- and 12-year-old who plays baseball in this town, in any town, goes to bed at night with a similar vision: Hitting one out, waiting to be greeted at home plate by 12 awed teammates.

The dialogue in Little League dugouts isn't very complicated. A boy named Dwayne Compton in the Thornydale district has already cleared the scoreboard with several notable blasts.

Whenever Dwayne Compton comes to bat, the dugout dialogue begins. "He's already hit six out," the young voices say. "Six. Geez."

It is six more homers than most of the boys will ever hit.

Last Saturday, Ben got a pitch in his wheelhouse, driving it far and deep to left field. I jumped to my feet and yelled, the first time I can ever remember yelling at one of Ben's games.

"Go! Get out. Get out!"

The ball hit several feet short of the fence and bounced over. Ground-rule double.

The dugout came alive. No one on Ben's team had even bounced one over this year. I looked out at second base, saw Ben's joy, and felt as if I had done it myself. I took a seat, tears welling in my eyes, overcome by the sense of his accomplishment.

Ben's team lost that day 15-3, but on the way home his countenance was not unlike his team had won 50-3. He was on the brink and he knew it.

"Dad," he asked, not really needing an answer, "now do you think I'll hit one over?"

On Tuesday night, for the first time, I could not attend Ben's game. My team had a game and, predictably, I had neither hit one out nor sent an outfielder to the warning track in pursuit of a long fly ball.

When I got home, about 10, the light was on in Ben's room. As I got out of the car, the garage door opened and Ben and his brothers, in their skivvies, came running to meet me.

"Dad, Dad, you won't believe it!" said Jake, breathlessly. "Ben hit a home run. It went way over the fence!"

I looked at Ben, standing tall, holding a baseball in his hand. His coach had scrawled, "April 25, 1989 — Home run" across the white hide.

"Dad," Ben said. "I hit one out. I finally did it."

And in a way, I guess I finally did it, too.

**THORNYDALE LITTLE LEAGUE '88**

Ben Hansen's home run in 1989 was his first and last, but he was an all-star catcher in his remaining youth baseball years. He still lives in Tucson.

160

# Hopefully, Lewis will learn that life is option No. 1

*Thursday, May 6, 1993*

My son Tyler turns 12 on Saturday, and when I asked him what he wanted for his birthday, he didn't have a long list.

"A Seattle Mariners hat," he said, "and a box of baseball cards."

That's it?

"Yep."

There was no mention of Nintendo, a new bike or anything else. A Mariners cap and some baseball cards. I didn't know what to think. Is it so wrong to have a son who is a Mariners fan? Didn't I feel the same way about Mickey Mantle as he feels about Ken Griffey Jr.?

Sometimes when Ty tells me about his dreams, I find it hard to believe that five years ago he had heart surgery to correct a condition similar to the one that killed former Loyola Marymount basketball star Hank Gathers. The scar that runs vertically down Tyler's chest seems to fade and become a little smaller with each year. Those awful memories of the days and nights in intensive care are not as vivid.

But the scar is a reminder that a heart can be a health problem no less cruel than the cancer that killed Jim Valvano last week.

Last week Reggie Lewis of the Boston Celtics collapsed during Game 1 of the Celtics-Charlotte playoff series. He lost consciousness and, in a horrifying sequence of events, was twice allowed to return to the game before he was taken to a hospital. It was Russian roulette, and all the cable highlight shows have played and replayed Lewis' frightening collapse until the tape was worn thin.

Unlike Gathers, Reggie Lewis and my son Ty got to the hospital in time.

A panel of 12 cardiologists and electrophysiologists familiar with the Gathers case determined after three days of tests that Lewis is suffering from cardiomyopathy, a condition that can cause dangerous irregular heartbeats. It is the same condition Ty has.

"It's the ultimate severity," said Dr. Arnold Scheller, the Celtics' team physician. "We were all lucky. Reggie was lucky primarily."

I'm certain that Reggie Lewis does not attach the word "luck" to anything that has happened to him in the last week. He is 28 years old, and his pro basketball career is effectively over. In 1992, he was an NBA

161

All-Star. Today he is alive. Maybe Lewis doesn't know it yet, but alive is a better deal.

Over the weekend, Lewis abruptly left the hospital in Boston and changed doctors, apparently to get a second opinion. And who can blame him? Who else can really understand his competitive desire?

Lewis makes about $2 million a year playing for the Celtics, and he was entering the prime of his career. If his performance had continued to progress as it had the last three seasons, it was likely that someday Lewis' number would be retired in the rafters at Boston Garden, next to those of Larry Bird and Bill Russell and Bob Cousy.

But now these appear to be false hopes.

Now Reggie Lewis is going to have to be satisfied with being alive. It's not a bad option.

My son Ty still wants to be a basketball player when he grows up, and he has even figured out the routing: Straight through Tortolita Junior High School to the UA and, if Sean Elliott can last that long, into the San Antonio Spurs' lineup alongside No. 32.

It's a healthy dream, and I wouldn't want it any other way. Someday Ty will discover what his body and mind will allow him to do best.

Ty knows that medical science is capable of performing some marvelous works. He followed Kevin Singleton's war against leukemia closely, and he knows that Kevin Singleton is possibly on the brink of getting into the National Football League.

What Ty learned from his heart surgery is the same thing we hope that Reggie Lewis will ultimately learn from his premature exit from the NBA: There is more to life than the Celtics-Charlotte playoff series.

The scar on Ty's chest hasn't held him back. He plays basketball with abandon, mostly with older and bigger boys, and he can hold his own. The doctors have told him that he can run and jump and play but not to expect to have as much endurance or stamina as the other kids. When he gets winded he knows he is to take a break.

Ty has had to grow up faster than most 12-year-old boys. And that's OK, too. He has learned not what his limitations are, but what he can overcome and what he can accomplish. He has learned that life is a pretty nice alternative.

We can pray that Reggie Lewis will, too.

EDITOR'S NOTE: On July 27, 1993, Reggie Lewis collapsed while shooting baskets at the Brandeis University gymnasium in Waltham, Mass. He was pronounced dead at a nearby hospital 2½ hours later.

**THORNYDALE LITTLE LEAGUE '88**

Tyler Hansen was a sports reporter for the Arizona Daily Star from 1996 to 2009. He now teaches journalism at Tucson High School.

# Yanks' No. 7 will always be a hero

*Friday, June 9, 1995*

Every so often I dig through a box of nostalgia until I find the manila envelope. I run my fingers across the name and the return address, and every time I'm spellbound.

M. Mantle
Dallas, Texas

It is his handwriting. With his home address. Do you know what it's like to go to your mailbox expecting the water bill, and you pull out a manila envelope and recognize Mickey Mantle's handwriting?

"Dear Greg," it says on the 8 x 11 color photograph inside, written in felt-tip pen across the Yankee pinstripes. "Thank you for the story in the Daily Star — Mickey Mantle."

It was like news from some ancient oracle.

I have never been an autograph nut, never chased after entertainers to get a closer look, never really been swayed by the cult of celebrity.

But Mickey Mantle moved me like no one else. When I was 16, I persuaded my dad to drive 1,000 miles to Anaheim, Calif., so I could see Mickey Mantle for the first time. By then, 1967, Mantle was a broken-down first baseman who had been caught in the Yankees' decline and fall. He got one single in three games, ran with a disturbing limp, but, oh, Lord, every time he turned his back to the field and I saw that blue '7' on his back, all the old memories came back. It was as if you were looking at someone descended from the gods.

Mickey Mantle was imperial in a way no baseball player may ever be again. He was baseball's flag-bearer at a time when money wasn't the issue and loyalty was. He was the Rock of Gibraltar, a stabilizer, an American hero. But if I was going to someday play center field for the Yankees — and of that I was certain — there was no way I could let Teddy Ricks continue to strike me out. How are you going to get to Yankee Stadium if Teddy Ricks fries your nerves?

And, oh, how I loved him.

I stepped into the batter's box, intimidated to the fullest extent of fear. I was 9 years old and had never faced anything as frightening as a Teddy Ricks fastball.

And so I squeezed the bat and pretended that Mickey Mantle was sitting in the bleachers behind home plate. Courage comes in many forms, but for me on that afternoon in 1960, it came in the form of Mickey Mantle.

I copied his stance, move for move. I began switch-hitting when I was 7. No team I ever played on was allowed to issue jersey No. 7 to anyone but me. No glove I ever wore was anything but a Rawlings, Mickey Mantle model. I know his life story better than he does.

I smacked Teddy Ricks' pitch into the gap, raced to third and looked into the bleachers at my imaginary friend. To this day I know that it was the thought of Mickey Mantle that helped me hit a triple off Teddy Ricks, the most fearsome pitcher in the Logan (Utah) Little League.

After that, in times of crisis, I always had Mickey on my side.

In the dentist's chair, when Dr. Allen pulled out his steely tools, I closed my eyes and imagined that Mickey was pulling Barney Schultz's knuckleball into the right field stands, bottom of the ninth, to win Game 3 of the '64 World Series. It never failed. When I couldn't bring myself to pick up the phone and ask Janet Thompson to the prom, I'd think of Mickey. He wouldn't be afraid of girls, and neither would I. Mickey Mantle will never know it, but whenever I had a crisis, he helped me through.

Years later, yes, I heard about the booze. One weekend in 1975, I drove four hours with some friends to Vernal, Utah, of all places, where Mantle was making an appearance at some sort of charity auction. We got there after the auction concluded, and asked Mantle's whereabouts.

"He's over in the bar," someone said. "And he ain't feeling no pain."

My friends went to see Mantle and Moose Skowron, his old Yankee teammate. They stood in the bar and stared at the legend. I stayed in the parking lot. My image of Mickey was unalterable.

"He was smashed," they told me later. "You don't want to see him."

Mickey Mantle didn't need marketing. He was Michael Jordan without McDonald's and Nike.

He was handsome, powerful, magnetic, almost mythic. His base-ball lineage could be traced to Ruth, Gehrig and DiMaggio. He came along when there was much less competition for our attention and affection, and I think we all felt, in some way, that we knew him.

Most of us who grew up with Mickey are in our 40s now, and

many of us don't like baseball the way we used to, worn down by strikes, free agency and the game's anti-ambassadors such as Barry Bonds. The irony is that Mantle, as a role model, may have struck out more thoroughly than any of the modern players.

He is alive today only because he has someone else's liver. He is living on borrowed time, and there are those angry detractors who claim that Mantle, because of his celebrity, got a liver transplant when it should have gone to someone else. Someone younger, preferably someone who didn't betray his own body.

But that's not really the point. The message from Mickey Mantle today and tomorrow is that we can learn from his mistakes.

"I can't do my career over, and I can't get back the seasons I may have lost," Mantle wrote in his most recent book, "All My Octobers." "I do worry about the young people who have looked up to me. And I appeal to them: The best time not to do drugs or alcohol is the first time."

This is a hard road, the hardest road Mickey Mantle has ever taken. But now, for the first time, he is showing us the way.

EDITOR'S NOTE: Mickey Mantle died of liver cancer on Aug. 13, 1995, a mere 66 days after he received a liver transplant. He still holds career records for most home runs (18), RBIs (40) and runs (42) in World Series games.

Primetime, all 1,600 raging pounds of him, made his way to Tucson in 2001 for an all-star rodeo event. He was the reigning Bull of the Year at the time.

DAVID SANDERS

# 'It ain't easy being me': Primetime bucks big trend by speaking his mind

*Friday, May 18, 2001*

*COOLIDGE*

Primetime is standing in a corral with his game face on. He looks in my direction as if to say, "Don't even think about it, sonny."

It's as if he knows I'm here to get a story on the rankest bull in the territory, a raging, snorting, sumbuck whose occupation it is to stomp on pro cowboys from here to Helena.

Primetime gives no interviews. He gives you a piece of his mind. Such as:

"People say the way to make me buck is to tease me, starve me, stab me with one of those damn electric sticks, but those people don't know a bull from a brick. The first thing I expect to hear when I get to Tucson on Saturday is, 'Hey, flea-brain, what a waste of good hamburger.' That stuff rolls off my gray brahma-hide. Give me 25 pounds of hay a day, 15 pounds of grain, and I'll kick my back legs 12 feet high, spin until I get dizzy. Quality in, quality out. That's my credo.

"My boss, Skip Beeler, has a picture in the big house, showin' me a full four feet off the ground. That's 1,600 pounds comin' down hard. Do you realize the pounding these hooves take? I go out 20 times a year — spinning and kicking — and it takes a toll. What, I'm 5 already, which has gotta be 30 in human years. Most bulls are back in the pasture, at stud, by the time they're 8. So you gotta make hay — that's a pun — while you can. You're in your prime at 6. I hear all this talk about Viper and Bodacious and Straitjacket. They get the TV time and go to Cheyenne and Calgary, but that's just reputation, a bunch of bull. I was the Bull of the Year in 2000, Turquoise Circuit. No one's spent eight seconds on my backside since March 1999. That's almost 60 rodeos. That's like DiMaggio and 56 straight, ain't it?

"It ain't easy being me. I'm in these disgustingly filthy pens at a different rodeo every week. That's stress, babe. Other bulls invadin' my space. People poking at me. Do you know what it's like to spend 12 hours in a trailer all the way to Bakersfield? And now we've got night rodeos, clowns from hell to breakfast calling themselves 'bullfighters.' Fighters? Don't make me laugh. They're clowns. This bull-riding stuff is a one-way street. We run, they scatter. But the cowboys get all the fame. We get grain. We get BRANDED. How would you like a big '672' across your backside?

"I've got pride, you know. I was bred to buck, that's what I hear 'em say. Very few of us in the herd, maybe two of every 100, have the instincts to make it to the National Finals in Vegas. I'm one of the two. My life isn't about milk or meat. My life is about breeding and bucking. That may sound a little crass, but that's the business.

"I've already produced 12 calves, 12 little Primetimes, all trying to get to the big leagues like pops. One of the livestock contractors in Texas is offering $80,000, but my boss Skip ain't parting with me, no way. I heard him tell that Texan most bulls are worth 64 cents a pound, but when it comes to Primetime, there is no price. I had to laugh. He said, 'Please don't make me an offer, because if I turn it down, the bull gods will get me, and Primetime will get sick or something.' Well, I ain't about to get sick. I've got a good 10 years left to do some serious breeding. I'm never gonna get up to 2,000 pounds and get sloppy like some offensive lineman. Once you lose your speed, you're back on the ranch, swattin' flies all day, watching everybody else getting all prettied up for the weekend rodeos.

"One thing I'd like the fans to know is that we're misunderstood. People think we're nothin' but dumb old lumps of beef. We're athletes the same way Michael Jordan and Secretariat were athletes. Skip took me up to a mountain pasture near Prescott so I could develop my footwork. Nature takes over when you're stepping on rocks all day. You learn how to move. I could squish a rattler with one hoof, no problem, but I usually run until I meet barbed-wire when I see something that slithers. You spend a few months in open range and you're as nimble as a ballerina.

"You can't sit on your scrapbook in this business. There's always the next Mr. Somebody coming along, the son of Viper or Red Rock. Worse, the cowboys are getting smarter. They're on the computer, giving scouting reports on all of us. There's a Web site now. Blah, blah, blah. Says I'm a kicker and I'm welly, whatever that means. Some of those cowboys make 20 phone calls a week, searching for a piece of information that might let 'em hang on for another fraction of a second. The scouting report on me is that I'm vertical. Hoo, baby, am I vertical! Skip says that you only need to ride me for four seconds, not eight, because I spend half the time in the air, doing nothin'. Right, Skip. That's like doing nothin' on the Wild Mouse ride. Four seconds of terror doesn't translate to four seconds of idle time.

"My brother, Double Shot, is coming down to Tucson with me for Saturday's pro bull-ridin' event. It's kinda like Jose Canseco and his brother, Ozzie. We look almost identical, but I'm the one who was born with the talent. My bro doesn't have the mentality it takes to get the 24s from the judges, which is like Mary Lou Retton getting a 9.9 at the Olympics. I get 24'd a lot. That's what they call it. Best score for a bull is 25. After a few years, you outsmart the cowboys. I set 'em up. They think I'm going high, but then I get into a spin and the next thing they know I'm trying to take a bite out of their head. Let's see Viper do that. He's got one move — a hellacious spin to the right — I can go both ways.

"You gotta want to buck, babe. You've got to be thinking of the future, those 160 acres of alfalfa just waiting for you, all the cows making eyes at you. You treat Skip right, he'll treat you right. Personally, I didn't like it when Skip's wife named me Primetime. I mean, didn't some football dude already have that name? It's like my idol, 777. He was so good they didn't give him a name. Everybody knows big old 777. But at least I've been able to make a name for myself. Skip says I'm 'spac-taculer.' I'm coming down to Tucson and I ain't taking prisoners, if you get my drift. Donnie Gay's gonna be there, and the crowd's gonna cheer and holler, and old Donnie Gay's gonna be smilin' and actin' like he could take me for the full 8 with no problem.

"I remember Donnie Gay. He's the best bull-rider I ever knew, but I also know what he wrote on Skip's big old photograph of me that sits in the house. 'Reminds me of why I quit.' That's what Donnie wrote across the picture. Took him about 8 seconds. I reckon that's the longest I ever let anyone stay on me."

JIM DAVIS

Jennie Finch pieced together one of the most spectacular seasons in UA sports history when she went 32-0 and led the Cats to the NCAA title in 2001.

# Finch takes place among Wildcats' big-game pitchers

*Tuesday, May 29, 2001*

Regardless of what the statistics say — and they say that Jennie Finch was 32-0 this season — she was really 3-0.

Arizona and UCLA were so superior to the college softball field this season, combining to win 127 of 137 games, that nothing seemed to matter except Arizona vs. UCLA, 1 vs. 1A, or vice versa, teams with multiple stars, the Yankees and Dodgers of their sport.

Finch routinely won 29 games against the field, the same way Arizona pitching legends Susie Parra and Nancy Evans dominated the wannabes over the last decade. But as Evans and Parra proved by beating the Bruins in national championship games, if you don't beat UCLA, the others don't count.

Finch counts.

She was 3-0 against UCLA this year; the Bruins were 62-3 against everyone else.

Finch shut them out 4-0 at Easton Field in Los Angeles. She shut them out 4-0 at Hillenbrand Stadium in Tucson. She shut them out 1-0 Monday at ASA Hall of Fame Stadium in Oklahoma City.

This was not unfamiliar turf to the 6-foot right-hander from Orange County, Calif. With Finch in a leading role, her ASA summer teams won national championships when she was 12, 14 and 18.

As with Parra and Evans, Finch has become the epitome of the Big Game Pitcher.

The kicker to all of this is that Finch seemed destined to fit seamlessly into the Bruins' pantheon of pitching superstars, from Lisa Fernandez to Debbie Doom to Tanya Harding to Amanda Freed.

After all, Finch grew up in UCLA's backyard, and spent hours at the Bruins' Easton Stadium, in the Bruins dugout, a batgirl, a Bruin-to-be.

Instead she was a Bruin-beater-to-be.

In three appearances against UCLA this season, across 21 innings, Finch didn't allow a run. She struck out 25. Against everyone else, UCLA had a team batting average of .344. Against Jennie Finch, the Bruins hit .158.

If you throw in Finch's batting numbers — a .323 average with 11

173

home runs and 57 RBIs — she might've had the single best season by an athlete in college sports this year.

Male or female. Any sport.

The final test to Finch's season came in the fire of Monday's sixth inning. Arizona led 1-0, the Bruins had a runner at second, one out. UCLA's two best hitters awaited: former Salpointe Catholic first baseman Tairia Mims (.379 with 17 home runs) and Olympic gold medalist Stacey Nuveman (.445 with 19 home runs).

UA coach Mike Candrea didn't want to pitch to Nuveman — he could purposely walk her if Mims didn't reach base — which meant that Finch absolutely had to get Mims out.

In a classic 12-pitch at-bat, in which Mims fouled off six pitches and ran the count full at 3-2, Finch ultimately got Mims on a harmless foul pop-up.

Nuveman was intentionally walked, and Finch fought her way out of the most important inning of the season.

How impressive is this: Mims and Nuveman went a combined 0 for 13 against Finch this season.

Of such performances are national championships made.

There is much, much more to Candrea's sixth NCAA title team than Jennie Finch. Speedy, savvy slap-hitters Lauren Bauer and Nicole Giordano were the best 1-2 connection at the top of anyone's batting order. Power-hitting third baseman Toni Mascarenas pulled the Wildcats back from the edge of trouble in three straight World Series victories. Senior pitcher Becky Lemke was on top of her game when she absolutely had to be, in Sunday's semifinal shutout over Stanford.

And senior catcher Lindsey Collins, who used to bat against Finch when the two were high school rivals in Orange County, rocketed the winning home run on Monday, the 40th of her Wildcat career, a trip around the bases that she'll never forget. How many of the 20 home runs hit by freshman outfielder Mackenzie Vandergeest helped Finch win?

But in the end it was Finch against the Bruins, the way it used to be Parra and Evans against the Bruins.

On Nov. 13, 1997, when Candrea received Finch's letter-of-intent form in the mail, beating Washington in a struggle for the nation's most-coveted high school softball player, the UA coach was typically understated.

"Jennie was definitely our first priority," he said that day. "We feel she's the type of player who can come in and make an impact."

In the perspective of UA softball, impacts are measured by national championships.

EDITOR'S NOTE: Jennie Finch was named the NCAA Player of the Year for her 2001 campaign, and she won the award again as a senior in 2002. She has been a member of the United States national team since 2001 and won an Olympic gold medal at the Athens Games in 2004. Four years later, she and the American team earned silver in Beijing in 2008. In between her duties with Team USA, Finch plays for the Chicago Bandits of the National Pro Fastpitch league.

Showing a flair for prophecy upon taking over the Pima College softball team in 2001, Stacy Iveson said she envisioned the Aztecs as national contenders.

# Iveson's career move appears risky

*Saturday, August 4, 2001*

In chronological order, Stacy Iveson has been: a high school baseball player; an All-Pac-10 softball catcher; a third-grade teacher; head
coach of a Salpointe Catholic state championship softball team; and
the pitching coach for the NCAA's best team and best pitcher, Arizona's
Jennie Finch.

Success doesn't follow Stacy Iveson, it rides shotgun. Wouldn't
you hire her?

Now, at 33, Iveson undertakes not just the biggest challenge of her
life, but two of them. She is a first-time mom, cuddling 4-week-old
Jared Thomas Iveson — "we're calling him J.T.," she says — at the same
time she has (gulp) agreed to become the head coach of the Pima
College softball team.

"We've got nine players, total," she says, followed by a muffled
scream and a chuckle. "I've never bitten off anything like this."

Pima College has an accomplished history in baseball, tennis and
several other sports. But the Aztecs have struggled in softball forever,
one coach followed by another, stringing together eight straight losing
seasons.

Why would someone leave the nation's No. 1 softball program —
Finch has another year remaining at the UA, for crying out loud, and
the nation's leading high school pitcher, Marissa Marzan of Fresno,
Calif., will be a Wildcat freshman this season — to take a program with
a shoestring budget of $35,000 a year?

Iveson doesn't flinch.

"I absolutely think we can become (a national contender)," she
says. "I've always scratched my head and wondered why Pima hasn't
been (better). I see potential."

The work begins now. With a reed-thin roster of six returning
players and three incoming recruits (added by former coach Bill
Moten), Iveson will stage an all-comers tryout camp today at 9 a.m. at
the PCC field — what there is of it. The outfield fence is in disrepair
and about 40 feet too far from home plate. The dugouts are spartan and
unprotected from the playing field.

If that's not daunting enough, Pima plays in a league opposite the
nation's No. 1 junior college team, Central Arizona, which annually
siphons off the leading high school players from Tucson, and then uses

them to clobber the Aztecs.

"People say that those who believe in fate and destiny are corny, but I disagree," says Iveson, a Catalina High product who was a catcher on UA coach Mike Candrea's first four Arizona teams (1986-89). "I've had too many positive experiences to think that this can't be done. When I went to Salpointe, they had won two games the year before I got there; a few years later, we were state champs. My feeling with the Pima job was, hey, let's do it."

Iveson, who played as Stacy Engle, her maiden name, while at Catalina and the UA, will use Candrea as a model for reconstruction. When the two began their UA careers in 1986, the Wildcats were not as good as Candrea's old school, Central Arizona.

"We had to play on the old Giddings Field, and wait until P.E. classes were over until we could take batting practice," Iveson remembers. "Coach Candrea would drag the infield by himself. People on campus would ask me what I did, and when I told them we played softball, they acted surprised, like they didn't know we had a team."

The same questions will be asked of Iveson at Pima. Do the Aztecs really play softball?

They do now.

Iveson planned to leave the UA staff at the completion of the 2001 national championship season and become head coach at the new Ironwood Ridge High School in northwest Tucson. She wants to be a stay-at-home mom, which meant she couldn't commit to a recruiting schedule, to five-day road trips and to another Pac-10 season. But when Moten left the PCC job, she reconsidered and decided not to take the Ironwood Ridge position.

"My husband, Tom, is a schoolteacher and we can take turns with J.T.," says Iveson. "When he gets home from school, I'll go to practice at Pima. It's going to take a lot of work and coordination, but we'll get it done.

"I'm convinced we can make Pima a top program. There are so many outstanding players in Tucson who leave town; my plan is to give them a reason to stay home."

Getting started won't be easy. The 2001-02 schedule and a thin, three-woman recruiting class was complete before Iveson was hired. Her first act was to hire Ted Farhat, formerly an assistant at Salpointe, to help her acquire and evaluate local players.

Now there's nothing left but to roll up some sleeves and begin — at the bottom.

"I'm realistic. I know how difficult this will be," she says. "Coach Candrea thinks Pima will be a good place for me. I do, too."

EDITOR'S NOTE: Stacy Iveson coached Pima College to the conference playoffs in 2002, her first season, and then led the Aztecs to the NJCAA national championship in 2004 and 2006. Following the program's fifth straight 50-plus-win season in '07, Iveson left Pima to start the softball program at Yavapai College in Prescott. She won the conference title in her first season with Yavapai and the national championship in her second. Iveson also coached the Arizona Heat of the National Pro Fastpitch league in '05 and '06.

# Normalcy will return; memories will remain

*Sunday, September 16, 2001*

On a winter morning in 1965, my mom sat on the side of my bed and told me she had some bad news.

Her eyes were red, her nose sniffling. She looked at me for what seemed forever, unable to find the words.

I remember looking at the clock. It was just after 6, more than an hour before I would normally get out of bed. What could be so wrong?

The night before, I had gone, as I always did, to Utah State's basketball game at the old Nelson Fieldhouse. The Aggies had the nation's leading scorer that season, Wayne Estes, a giant of a young man from Anaconda, Mont., a first-team All-American who had taken USU to consecutive appearances in the NCAA tournament.

He was to my hometown of Logan, Utah, what Sean Elliott was to Tucson 12 years ago.

On that Monday night in February, Estes played the most remarkable game of his career. He scored 48 points, a school record, and his last basket gave him 2,001 points, making him one of the few collegians to reach that level at that time.

I remained in the fieldhouse after the game, sitting in a row of bleachers near the radio announcer. It got me close enough so that I could hear what Estes was saying about his record-setting game.

In my world, Wayne Estes was bigger than life.

And now my mom was trying to tell me the horrible news: Wayne Estes had been killed, electrocuted by a wire severed from a utility pole. On his way home from the game, Estes stopped at the site of an automobile accident. In the darkness, the wire dangled unseen, hanging 6 feet 5 inches off the ground.

Estes was 6-6. He reached up to brush it away. In the days immediately after his death, the rural college town of 25,000 was engulfed by a grief I could not comprehend. That week's games were canceled. A memorial service at the fieldhouse, capacity 6,000, was full an hour before it began. More than 2,000 people stood outside in a snowstorm.

The Aggies eventually resumed action and played a handful of meaningless games to complete the season. Estes' parents, Joe and Helen, drove to Logan for one of those, at which time their son's jersey was retired. I remember trying not to cry, afraid that my macho buddies would see.

It was no use. My little hometown carried that pain for years. I continue to think about it often.

On the 25th anniversary of Estes' death, in 1990, an editor at The Sporting News phoned and asked if I would write a story about the tragedy. I said it would be fine.

I phoned directory assistance for Anaconda, Mont., and asked for Joseph Estes. I assumed, wrongly, that Estes' parents might be dead. It took me a day or two to decide whether to make the call, but I ultimately gave in and punched in the numbers.

Helen Estes answered. I identified myself, asked a few questions but was stopped when she began to cry.

After 25 years, the wound remained open.

"He would only be 46 now," Helen Estes said. "He had his whole life left to live. He would be a father and a husband. I pray about him every day."

I have thought back to Joe and Helen Estes this week, and to their son, my childhood hero. It gave me a reference point for what to tell those in my family about the horror of the World Trade Center: This will be with us forever.

This time, my mom didn't wake me up with bad news. This time, she phoned. Her longtime golf partner, Mary Wahlstrom, and Mary's daughter, Carolyn, were among those killed on the first plane to explode into the World Trade Center. The Wahlstroms lived in our neighborhood; Carolyn and her brother, Phil, were my high school friends. I had gone to scores of church activities with all of Mary Wahlstrom's children.

In varying degrees, this tragedy touches all of us.

Part of the way we recover is by getting back to our national lifestyle, sports included. As difficult as it was in 1965, Wayne Estes' teammates, and those who loved him from afar, went back to school, back to basketball, a few days after he was buried.

We must now go back, but we will never forget.

Powered by a 1,200-horsepower engine, "Shocker" plows into and over a row of cars during the Tournament of Destruction demolition derby in 2002.

# Monster Mania: It's crude, loud, extremely dusty but captivating

*Saturday, June 15, 2002*

In yet another glimpse into the decline of civilization, about 1,500 people paid $10 a ticket Friday night to watch the Tournament of Destruction at the Tucson Rodeo Grounds.

It began with the temperature about 100 degrees, dust as thick as fog, led by Demolition Derby car No. 4,100 — equipped with a large Confederate flag, police lights and a flame-thrower mounted on its hood.

"Let's hear it for the Demo Derby beauty parade," said the public address announcer, who, in lieu of a performer, tape or music, sang the national anthem himself.

It wasn't ballroom dancing.

A man sitting in the front row, wearing a "Progressive Roofing" T-shirt, had bright yellow plugs in each ear.

"Why don't you sit in the back row and take out the earplugs?" I said, fishing for a quote.

"What's it to you, dumb a-?" he replied.

No, it wasn't the Ice Capades.

According to the crowd's reaction, the night's highlight came when Pat Gerber of Bakersfield, Calif., revved up the 1,200-horsepower Monster Truck engine in "Shocker" and fractured neighborhood noise ordinance laws from South Tucson to Oro Valley.

Gerber has spent well into six figures on Shocker (and its elaborate travel trailer) and in doing so, created a 3-D body that comes off as a cross between a San Diego Chargers helmet and something out of "Batman."

Really cool stuff.

"How tall are those tires?" I asked.

"Sixty-six inches," he said. About as tall as Will Bynum, for instance.

"How much do they cost?"

"About $1,800."

"Each?"

"Each."

Friday's show — Pickup Trucks on Steroids — will be repeated tonight. Same place. Same time. Same car-crushing, ear-splitting, behavioral deficits.

America's obsession for entertainment has created far more than a Friday night of Monster Truck racing/Demolition Derby/Motocross Madness in Tucson. What's the attraction? Well, what's the attraction of the Westminster Kennel Club Dog Show?

In a culture that insists upon, and supports, more than 100 cable TV channels, the Tournament of Destruction is simply another channel. It's no different than several thousand fans lounging on a beachfront somewhere in California as Miss Budweiser, a superboat, soars across the lake at 105 mph, nothing but a blur to the human eye.

It's better than staying home and playing pinochle.

In the 1960s, we had bumper cars and a wrestler wearing a mask matched against a bear. Monster Truck racing has become our bear-wrestling of the 21st century.

True story: In 2001, 17 of the 20 largest crowds for sports events in this country involved racing (car or truck) of some sort.

Not baseball or football.

The Learning Channel, a distinguished cable-TV outlet, has regular features of "Daredevils" and "Junkyard Wars," which are all about car and truck racing.

ESPN2 would go out of business without car racing.

The History Channel, which is educational if nothing else, features car and truck racing in its regular programming of "Modern Marvels" and "The Secret World of Modern Trucks."

I confess: As entertainment goes, it's a step up from the Insight.com Bowl.

Out at the Tucson Rodeo Grounds on Friday, there were no secrets. Moms and dads broke away from the ballfields to bring their kids to watch motocross daredevils soaring over dirt mounds at ridiculous speeds, side-by-side with other riders. The audience demographic wasn't any different than at a Little League game.

It was, frankly, captivating.

It was hot and dusty, and the guy next to me blew enough cigarette smoke to give me stage 5, secondhand cancer.

But there's something about watching "Kongo Kong," an 11,000-pound Monster Truck, put some serious tread over the hood of an old Buick that you can't get anywhere else, except maybe the "Jerry Springer Show."

It makes baseball come off as a spelling bee.

Rillito Raectrack has been a historic horse-racing site for jockeys like Terry Gard since 1943, but the sport's future in Tucson has been on the ropes for years.

# Rillito pulls in 'every walk of life'

*Wednesday, February 19, 2003*

The line to place a bet on Sunday's sixth race at Rillito Racetrack is 10-deep. There are 18 such lines in the grandstand area.

There are four more lines on the mezzanine level, each one a dozen people in length. Two more in the clubhouse. Two more on the east end of the track. Plus, there are two automated betting machines, which are used almost exclusively by the so-called sophisticated bettors, the possessive, suspicious types who do not want anybody to overhear their valued selections.

It is two minutes to post, which means, if you are aching to bet $4 on Real Dancer, you might not make it. You might be forced to keep your $4. Hurry, guys, hurry.

Out in the parking lot on the 60-acre plot of ground (purchased for a mere $6,000 in 1943), the valet section is full. Space for about 1,000 more vehicles is overflowing.

I laugh, thinking back to how many times I've heard people say horse racing in Tucson is dead.

"This is a pretty rocking operation," says Tim Kelly, vice president of the Pima County Horsemen's Association. "What's odd is that I believe there remain a lot of people in Tucson who don't know the track is running."

Over last weekend, Tucsonans bet about $200,000 on 18 races at Rillito Racetrack. In the seven-weekend season, concluding March 2, attendance at the grand old track will reach close to 50,000.

Who are these people?

Before the sixth race on Sunday, I was standing near the finish line when a rumpled older man, decidedly underdressed, muscled in next to me and created space where there had been none. He was smoking a cigarette, wearing a T-shirt that read: I'M RETIRED. THIS IS AS DRESSED UP AS I GET.

"A typical crowd out here is what you see anywhere in Tucson," says Jim Collins, track handicapper and volunteer marketing specialist. "Every walk of life."

I see people wearing NASCAR T-shirts, and I see people (attorney Burt Kinerk, for instance) dressed in golf gear. You see $300 cowboy hats, and I see well-worn, sweat-stained UA caps. Overall, Wrangler jeans rule. Style: tight and tighter. Beer flows.

If Pima County is 25 percent Hispanic, a weekend at Rillito Racetrack is double that. You hear as much Spanish as English. Four guys standing near me on Sunday spent 20 minutes talking about bowling.

Not a word about Luke Walton's ankle.

Horse racing in Tucson began in the late 1930s — the Moltacqua Turf Club at Sabino Canyon — on property that now houses the Tack Room restaurant. It has three times ceased operation for several years, each time for political reasons more than finances.

There is no pretense. This is neither Turf Paradise (Phoenix) nor Ruidoso Downs (Ruidoso, N.M.). This is a neighborhood operation in need of some paint and polish. About 90 percent of the horses, jockeys, trainers and owners are from Southern Arizona. After the Rillito season is complete, most of those will journey to the Arizona County Fair circuit, which begins in Duncan, and goes straight through into May with two-week meets in Safford, Douglas, Sonoita and Kingman.

It is an off-Hollywood production, if ever there were one.

Nobody is getting rich, so it must be a labor of love, right?

"We're a nonprofit organization," says Kelly, whose father, Moss Kelly, was the track's mutuel manager a half-century ago, a job that has been handed down in the family. "If we make $12,000 a month, it all goes back into operations and for purses. I'm constantly amazed at what it takes to keep (Rillito) going. For example, we have to pay $70 an hour every morning to have an ambulance on site for the exercise riders. The vet bills. The cost of feed. The expense of moving manure. The operational expenses are never-ending."

There are no Secretariats at Rillito Racetrack, and no one expects there to be.

Collins, who holds free handicapping seminars each Saturday and Sunday at noon, usually with classes of 75 to 100 people — "I picked all nine races successfully on Sunday," he says when prodded — has a favorite. Who doesn't?

He likes Littlefield.

Littlefield is 11 years old, ancient in horse racing terms, but still athletic enough to finish second in Saturday's eighth race.

"He's a tough old pro," Collins says. "He runs only in county fairs, but he's as tough as they come." And that is a working description of Rillito Racetrack, survivor of six decades matched against Tucson's high sports season: the PGA Tour; UA basketball; spring training baseball; and La Fiesta de los Vaqueros.

Many, if not most, of the owners, trainers and jockeys at Rillito are locals, distinguished horsemen such as trainer Eddie Tellez, owner Jose Badilla and jockey Fernando Gamez. Many stable their horses on their own property — "a series of Ma and Pop operations," according to Kelly — rather than bunk in any of the 475 stalls at Rillito. That saves money and makes the Rillito season possible.

On Sunday, as the betting lines swelled, Kelly stood back and watched. "Dismayed," he says. He extended post time four or five minutes several times to accommodate each line of bettors.

"I marvel at how many people stood in lines, with the clock ticking, intent on placing their bets," he says. "But if we had another 1,500 people there, if we had crowds of 5,000 or so, I don't know if we could handle it. The facility works better for 3,500 to 3,800 people."

Key word: works.

After all these years, Rillito Racetrack still works.

EDITOR'S NOTE: In August 2006, the Pima County Board of Supervisors announced plans to convert Rillito Racetrack from a horse-racing facility into an 18-field soccer complex. Voter approval for races at the oval track ends Dec. 31, 2009, meaning local politicians will then be legally free to do whatever they would like with Rillito Racetrack. The last race of the 2009 season was run Feb. 22, likely the last one ever to be run at the historic track.

# Proper reverence: Playing 18 holes at Augusta ranks as a lifetime thrill

*Wednesday, April 13, 2005*

I am standing on the 12th tee at Augusta National, the Hogan Bridge to my left, Rae's Creek reflecting in my eyes, Amen Corner at hand.

Hallelujah!

My caddie, Freddie, outfitted in all-white Masters coveralls, hands me a 6-iron and nods.

"Go straight at it," he says.

I place a never-hit Titleist Pro V1x (No. 7) on a tee. I step back and take in the moment. This cannot be happening. I am playing Augusta National, with a caddie, and I have been awake since 3 a.m. thinking about the magnitude of it.

But I have not fully lost my instincts. I stoop down, retrieve my No. 7 Titleist and slip it into my pocket. I walk over to Freddie and tell him I am changing balls, clutching an older Nike.

"Don't want to lose my No. 7 in Rae's Creek," I tell Freddie.

"How many times y'all going to play here?" he asks.

"Once," I say.

"Then don't play scared," he suggests.

How is it you're supposed to play Augusta National?

Awed, certainly.

But you do not pop out of the press center, winning lottery ticket (No. 743) in hand, and charge into Monday's morning-after-the-Masters media invitational — yes, the detail-oriented Augusta National people actually deliver invitations to 32 winners of the annual media lottery — firing at the pins Tiger Woods played 12 hours earlier.

You show proper reverence.

I am playing with a sports anchor from Charlotte, another TV guy from Greenville, S.C., and a writer from Orlando. At Amen Corner, they are posing by some azaleas, stacking up play, a sacrilege on this turf. This is not a good day to anger the golf gods, so I do not bring a camera.

All three of my partners plop their tee shots into Rae's Creek. Let's see them take a picture of that. I stay dry, but three-putt the uber-fast green, a speed that will be trouble all morning.

190

Once you win the media lottery, you are forbidden to enter again for seven years. That's fair; everyone should get a chance. The only rules are that you tip your caddie sufficiently ($100 is suggested) and do not do anything stupid, like asking where you can find the beer cart.

There is one negative: You are not allowed to practice at the range adjacent to Magnolia Lane before (the 7:37 a.m.) tee time; it is closed. And the putting green is rendered useless, having been the stage for Sunday's green jacket ceremony. It has been poked full of holes by the legs of many folding chairs.

So you stand at the No. 10 tee — we started on the second nine — cold, stiff, your heart rate at 210 beats per minute.

My nerves finally begin to simmer at No. 13. I am already 5 over par, and at that rate, I'll shoot a 102.

"I'm not this bad," I tell Freddie.

"Slow down," he says. "You won't have a chance to come back and do it over."

I stand 185 yards from the No. 13 green — Rae's Creek continues here — and elect a 9-wood (hey, Vijay Singh carries one, so why not?) There is not mere trouble near No. 13. There is the potential for a golf cataclysm. If you goof up here, you get a 10 or 12, shoot 100, and ruin your day.

My unexpectedly nutted 9-wood shot touches down in the middle of the green, takes one short hop and dies. I have a 15-foot birdie putt at one of Augusta's signature holes.

Freddie looks at me in near-shock.

I can die happy now.

I par Nos. 13, 14 and 15. It occurs to me that this is the sports high-light of my life. Three straight pars on the back nine at Augusta National. I am tempted to pull out my cell phone and call somebody — can you believe what I'm doing? — but then I recall my photo-snapping partners, all of whom are en route to 100-plus.

I do not tempt the golf gods. I pull out a 5-iron at the knee-bend-ing beautiful 16th hole, site of Tiger's last-Swoosh-drops miracle shot 13 hours earlier. The bleachers are empty now, but the echoes are still in the trees.

My tee shot hits the green, 50 feet right of an impossibly tucked left pin.

Freddie stands on a slope, 10 yards right of my projected putting line.

"Right here," he says.

"What?"

"Right here," he says.

So I putt in a direction somewhere toward Nebraska. It reaches the top of the slope and begins a Tiger-trickle toward the cup, picks up speed and almost goes in. I make a 4-foot comebacker for a par.

"Kiss me, Freddie," I say.

Rather than a smooch, he hands me my driver. The course will strike back. I return to earth when my drive at 17 hits the trees. Double-bogey. Augusta National resumes control.

Two hours later, I reluctantly walk, slowly, to the No. 9 tee. One hole remains. Where did the time go? My partners are out of film, and in 15 minutes, I'll be stepping out of the four most cherished hours of sports in a lifetime.

At the green, I linger, taking plenty of time to align a 6-footer for par. Make it for 89. Miss it for 90.

"Inside left edge," says Freddie. "Downhill. Very fast."

It rolls in.

Freddie takes my clubs to a breezeway near Butler Cabin and says goodbye. I walk alone, down Magnolia Lane, my feet not hitting the ground.

Talk about hitting the lottery.

## Hansen vs. the best

Greg Hansen parred holes 13, 14 and 15 at Augusta. Here's how he compares to the best rounds by three top players in this year's Masters:

**Greg Hansen**
- Hole 13, Par 5: 5
- Hole 14, Par 4: 4
- Hole 15, Par 5: 5
**Total:** 14, even par

**Vijay Singh**
- Hole 13, Par 5: 4
- Hole 14, Par 4: 3
- Hole 15, Par 5: 5
**Total:** 12, 2 under, 1st rd.

**Tiger Woods**
- Hole 13, Par 5: 5
- Hole 14, Par 4: 4
- Hole 15, Par 5: 4
**Total:** 13, 1 under, 4th rd.

**Phil Mickelson**
- Hole 13, Par 5: 4
- Hole 14, Par 4: 4
- Hole 15, Par 5: 4
**Total:** 12, 2 under, 3rd rd.

# WWE SmackDown at Tucson Convention Center

*Wednesday, June 22, 2005*

They came by the thousands, filling every seat at the Tucson Convention Center, wearing T-shirts that read:

Misfit

The Animal

101 Proof

Of the capacity crowd Tuesday night, estimated at 8,000, about two of every five people carried hand-scrawled signs.

One read: Undertaker — You're a Dead Man.

Another: This Means War.

One lady, about 60, wore a black T-shirt with an oversized skull on the front. Each sleeve was adorned with three more skulls. The back said, simply, "Vengeance '03."

It was loud, it was outrageous, it was WWE's SmackDown. Can't remember when I've been more entertained.

Pro wrestling is no longer Bobo Brazil, fat and sloppy, building a reputation mostly by rumor in backwater towns of America. It is no more civil than in the days of Haystack Calhoun, but the 21st century WWE is slick and theatrical, almost weekly the nation's highest-rated cable TV programming.

If you watch the taped version of Tuesday's events at the TCC — it airs Thursday at 7 p.m. (KTTU, Channel 18) — you will be one of about 5 million in the audience. The demographic of Tuesday's capacity crowd was decidedly under-25, many young parents with children. They knew the WWE stars the way a 47-year-old, remote-control couch potato knows the lineup of the '84 Chicago Cubs.

Proof that Americana has a niche audience for everything.

For 2½ hours, SmackDown produced the usual array of kicking, gouging, punching and elbowing. But the most captivating scene of the night involved an enormous, fearsome man named Mark Calaway, aka the Undertaker, star of all things WWE.

He didn't so much as throw a punch.

The Undertaker, good guy, is an indestructible company man, as big in the wrestling community as Kenny Chesney is in the music business. (Both live comfortably in Nashville).

At 43, the Undertaker, 6 feet 10 inches, 350 pounds, is the biggest face of SmackDown's impressive list of stars. He has a presence equal to that of uber-stars JBL and Big Show, a celebrity ranking with pro wrestling's past luminaries such as Hulk Hogan, Jesse Ventura and Andre the Giant.

One of the great unknowns of a live WWE show is that there is no announced lineup. You never know who's going to walk out on stage. The Undertaker in Tucson? Oh, Lordy!

After five energizing preliminaries Tuesday, including top-shelf stars Scotty Hotty, Booker T and Orlando Jordan, emerging personality Randy Orton, in suit coat, stood at middle ring denigrating the great Undertaker.

"My reputation has been made by killing legends," Orton boasted. "The Undertaker will bow to my greatness."

Predictably, in a din matched in this town only by one of those memorable comebacks from a Lute Olson team, the ring was filled with smoke. Poof. The Undertaker appeared out of nowhere.

Orton made a beeline for safety in the locker room. The Undertaker, accompanied by his haunting funereal music, postured in the ring for 10 minutes, flexing and grimacing. The crowd went nuts.

It was awesome, man.

As for the wrestling itself, much has changed. These guys are athletic — XXXL gymnasts — whose bodies absorb so much punishment that it's a wonder they can "compete" about 100 times annually. No more beer bellies.

Predictably, each match follows a decades-old script. The good guy gets off to a dominant start, putting his poor opponent, battered and bruised, in a near-pin situation. But each time, the underdog rallies, finding a strength to put The Hero in a headlock, a near-pin situation, gouging and kicking and flailing.

Ultimately, our Hero gets off the canvas, wins, and spends five minutes in the ring, flexing muscles, promising mayhem to any who dare to oppose him.

Tuesday night, a sellout crowd spent up to $40 a ticket to roar its approval.

You say it's all fake?

Who cares?

DAVID SANDERS

Few events offer the spectacle and theater of WWE's SmackDown, which rolled Orlando Jordan, arm raised, and his act through Tucson in 2005.

# Successful career of UA swim coach had humble beginning

*Thursday, April 3, 2008*

In the stillness of her suburban Northern Virginia home, careful not to awaken her husband and two children, Crissy Ahmann Perham sat at her computer until almost 2 a.m., gathering results of the NCAA men's swimming championships.

"For three nights in a row, while everyone else slept, I would raise a quiet fist in the dark," says the Arizona Wildcats' first female Olympic gold medal swimmer.

The final fist pump saluted the UA's second national championship in eight days.

A week earlier, wearing her old UA letterman's jacket, Perham traveled to Columbus, Ohio, to watch her alma mater win its first NCAA women's swimming championship. Predictably, her old coach and mentor, Frank Busch, insisted she sit not in the bleachers, but walk the deck with the UA staff.

"Being on the deck and being so warmly included when they won the championship was one of the best gifts I could have ever received," says Perham, who won NCAA titles in the 100 butterfly in 1991 and 1992, the first titles for a UA female swimmer.

Busch's 19-year journey to the national championship began when Perham, then a free-spirited Wildcat sophomore, was a promising young butterfly specialist from Benson High School.

The long Road to the Top began with a humble first step.

In the final hiring transaction of former UA associate athletic director Mary Roby's remarkable career — she also hired Mike Candrea and Rocky LaRose — Roby hired Busch, then at the University of Cincinnati, from a stack of "80 to 100 applications."

"I retired after hiring Frank," Roby says now, chuckling. "I went to (former athletic director) Cedric Dempsey and said, 'This is who I would like to have. He is very impressive.' My instincts were very strong about Frank. Ced said, 'Fine. OK. Frank is the epitome of what a coach should be.'"

Perham was the first name of an international scope Busch produced at Arizona. At the 1992 Barcelona Olympics, she won a gold medal on the 400 medley relay team and subsequently earned a silver in the 100 butterfly.

The timing was perfect. By '92, Arizona had become a top-10 program in both men's and women's swimming. Perham and Busch poured the foundation; it was appropriate that they were together when Arizona broke through and won its first NCAA title.

The Perham-Busch relationship defines the impact Busch has had — continues to have — with his swimmers. They call him "Frank," not coach. But it's more like "Father" than Frank.

Perham's admiration for her former coach is typical of the testimonials Busch draws from every segment of the Tucson swimming community.

"I still call Frank regularly to talk shop," says Perham, who coaches a youth-group swim program in Virginia. "I ask for parenting advice, which I desperately need. Frank and his wife, Patty, are the godparents of my son, Alex.

" Frank is the reason I made the Olympic team. He and I did not get off to a good start, and it could have ended before it began. I was looking into transferring. But I believe that Frank was put there for many reasons, and one of them was to be an influence in my life: as a student, as a swimmer, as a coach and as a parent. He and Patty are the living examples of the kind of people my husband, Charlie, and I strive to be."

Busch would not want you to know this, but on Wednesday morning, he was hand-writing notes to the more than 100 people who have e-mailed him this week. So typical. He took parts of two days off and Wednesday afternoon began full-scale training for the Beijing Olympics, an event that could include more than 20 of his swimmers, past and present.

Do not expect a change; it's not about Frank. What will he most remember from two national titles in two weeks?

"I'll remember the looks of joy on the faces of our staff and our swimmers," he said.

Do you know that rather than insist on a suite in his team's hotel, as so many coaches do — as almost all Big Time coaches do — that Busch still shares a room with his valued assistant coach Rick DeMont?

" Frank does it the right way," said Roric Fink, head coach of the Tucson Ford Dealers club team, a national champion coach himself. "He doesn't chop corners, and he doesn't use loopholes. He's so respected in swimming. He treats people the right way."

Upon returning from the women's championship meet in Ohio,

Busch had 22 hours to do some laundry, re-pack and fly to Washington for the men's meet. He did not get time, he says, "to savor" the women's title.

Early this week, he finally turned on a DVD and watched his women's team win its historic title. He saw all those happy faces, and all of those tears, including his own.

After 19 years, he is on top. Let the savoring begin.

# Job with Dad hard, dirty, priceless

*Sunday, June 15, 2008*

The small advertisement in The Sporting News said "three weeks of intensive baseball instruction." I was 15. The only words that could possibly have piqued more interest were, "Mickey Mantle has invited you to suit up at Yankee Stadium."

My high school teammate mailed $180 to the Bo Belcher Baseball Camp in Chandler, Okla., and would soon embark to that faraway baseball heaven for some intensive training. He asked if I would join him.

I didn't have 10 cents. My dad? No. He said the house payment was $120 and to be sure he could cover it each month, my mom had taken a job checking groceries at Safeway.

The next morning, before sunrise, my dad tapped me on the shoulder and instructed me to get dressed and accompany him to Jack's Tire and Oil. He said it was time I had a job and that being late for my first day of work was not permissible.

And so for the next month, I learned how to work 10-hour days, fix tires, pump gas, lube cars and, in general, understand that I did not want to work at a gas station for a living — especially not for $1.10 an hour.

On Saturdays, I got off at noon and immediately began to dread the coming of Monday. I thought my dad must not like me. Up at 6 a.m., home at 6 p.m. That was no way to be 15 in the Age of Aquarius.

At the end of my first month in America's work force, my dad handed me an envelope with a check for $217.

"When you get back from the baseball camp," he said, smiling as he saw the surprise engulf my face, "I'll see if I can get your old job back."

No boy ever had a better summer than I had in 1967. I played baseball all day and all night — doubleheaders every Sunday! — in the celestial glory of Chandler, Okla. Later, when an interminable Greyhound bus trip finally ended, delivering me home late on a Sunday night, my dad was waiting.

"Gotta be to work at 6," he said. "You want to buy a car, don't you?"

My dad didn't go to college, but he raised five kids and set a standard for responsibility that you couldn't learn in the Ivy League.

He didn't play baseball as a kid, although he loved Yogi, Mickey and the Yankees and passed it on to me. He once separated his shoulder sliding into second base in a church softball game. His face turned yellow with pain. My mom drove him to the hospital where they popped his

199

shoulder back into place.

He was back at Jack's Tire and Oil at 6 the next morning, grinding it out. He was thinking about covering that $120 mortgage payment.

He wanted me to enjoy baseball, but to also learn there was a time and a place for it. He was old-school and then some. His way of saying he loved me was to show up at a ballgame, wearing his grease-stained work uniform with "Nellie" printed in script above the pocket. I knew he didn't leave the gas station unless it was for something very important.

When I hit a bloop double to win the 1962 Little League championship game, a walk-off job, he sprinted out to second base, lifted me to his shoulders and carried me back to the dugout. It was the only time I ever saw tears in his eyes.

As he got older, moving past 40, he found a new joy — grandkids. Through them he learned how to hug and laugh and lighten up. He would whisper, "I love you" when he thought no one else was listening.

He knew what it was to get a hole-in-one, bowl a 250 game, and I can't possibly thank him enough for the memories of those wonderful autumn afternoons, walking through the Wasatch Mountains, pretending to hunt pheasants.

He was fussy to the extreme about our yard — Better Homes and Gardens should have put him on payroll — but when he came home from work and saw six neighborhood kids wearing out the grass, playing all-day Wiffle ball, his attitude was that he wasn't raising grass, he was raising kids.

In the summer of '71, on break from school and working full-time shifts at the gas station, I was introduced to a man from the local newspaper. He asked if I wanted to fill in at the newspaper while people were on vacation.

I told him my dad didn't have anyone to replace me. It was the busy time of the year for gas and tires and delivering fuel oil to the farm accounts.

A day later, the man from the newspaper phoned.

"Your dad saw me at the gas station and gave me a call," he said. "You're starting Monday in the sports department."

My dad had punched my ticket out of the gas station.

In February, he phoned to say he was going in for "a little back surgery" but would be fine and not to worry. He said to get him a ticket and he would come to Tucson to watch Tiger Woods at next year's golf tournament.

He died the next day. I never did tell him how much I loved him.

Bernell Hansen, holding grandsons Ben, left, and Jake in Oregon in 1980, loved the Yankees, pretending to hunt pheasants and — mostly — his family.

# CHAPTER SIX

# Olympics

## A far cry from failure

*Wednesday, April 3, 1985*

*LOS ANGELES*

Dear Mom:

Sorry I haven't written, but if you think this is overdue, you should see my laundry.

I've been here 18 days and I can safely say I've seen no sign of the Official Detergent of the '84 Summer Games.

But Mom, I wish you could've been here. I don't think I can adequately tell you how I feel and what I saw.

Remember when I graduated from school? You got all emotional and wouldn't stop hugging me and all I wanted was to get to the party? You said it was a special moment and you just didn't want it to end.

I didn't really understand how you felt then, Mom, but I do now.

I know it was just a big track meet and the Soviets didn't come, but, Mom, I've never seen so many grown men cry.

Every now and then I got so absorbed, so swept up in the crest of emotions that I almost felt guilty. I've never had so many good feelings for so long. I had to buy some sunglasses, Mom. And not because it was too sunny.

You might have read about controversy in the papers. Some judges were capricious, some athletes wore jealousy on their sleeves, and some cynics said they were afraid the country would overdose on patriotism.

That's baloney, Mom. Those people must've covered the Olympics from a hotel room.

Remember how it used to feel the week before Christmas? Everybody seemed friendlier. There was something special about every day. If you heard a song on the radio, you'd sing along. I remember the year you even sent mean old Mr. Colston a Christmas card.

That's the way it was, Mom. Every day seemed like Christmas Eve.

Maybe this sounds a bit melodramatic, but I tried to make a list of my 10 favorite moments of the Summer Games and almost none of them are sprints, spikes or overhand rights.

If you've ever been to USC and the area around the Coliseum, you know that it's not exactly Oz. It's just down the street from Watts, where there were riots and all hell broke loose 19 years ago.

A week ago Friday, I was on a broken-down old school bus with some other journalists heading toward the Coliseum. But traffic was blocked; the 20-kilometer walk was in progress on the main thorough-fares. The bus was forced to take back streets. It was "Starsky and Hutch" territory. Every time the bus stopped, I got a little antsy.

Anyway, Mom, I'm looking out the window expecting to see some signs of anger; some unrest. After all, the Olympics trod on these peo-ple. Jammed their streets. Took their parking places. In general, made it all inconvenient as hell. (Sorry about the French, Mom.)
Was I wrong.

Our buses were easily identified because they are marked with a series of Olympic stars. The people knew we were attached, in some way, to the Games.

We were at a stop sign in a beaten-down tenement area. A burly man was sitting on the hood of his car, about six feet from my window. He had a portable TV set and was watching the Olympics. I looked at the man hesitantly. He looked at me, smiled widely and gave a thumbs-up sign.

"Allll-right," he said.

That was better than a Carl Lewis jump or a Mary Lou Retton smile, Mom.

Several minutes later, we turned the corner into another rough neighborhood. An elderly black woman was sitting on a folding chair in the middle of the front lawn. She was holding one of those small American flags that have been so prevalent.

Well, as we drove by, she stood up and waved that flag at us. I kept looking at her as the bus pulled away. She didn't stop waving that flag until we were out of sight.

Maybe it loses something in the translation, Mom — maybe you had to be there — but that's when I knew the Olympics are no sports festival. I knew then that the Olympics are more than the separation of winners from losers.

Sure, Mom, I'm a sucker for a good time, but take my word for it.

I saw the King of Sweden out here, Tom Selleck, Muhammad Ali, Barbra Streisand, you name 'em. I was there when the American men's gymnastics team won its gold medal. I could almost reach out and touch the tears on Peter Vidmar's cheek.

Nice stuff, but I'd rather store the memory of Gabriela Andersen-Schiess zig-zagging for the finish line, refusing to quit.

I gained a new respect for the dedication and singleness of purpose of water polo players, volleyball players, swimmers and divers.

I came away suitably impressed by the way our guests represented their countries. Sebastian Coe, Koji Gushiken, Maricica Puica ... I hope John McEnroe took notes.

But mostly I'll remember the '84 Games for the contented feeling of well-being it brought to the people here.

The second night I was here, our hotel bus drove through Inglewood at 1 a.m. Inglewood might remind you a lot of "Hill Street Blues", Mom. It's best not to stay out after dark.

The crowds in Inglewood were enormous, maybe 10 to 12 deep. Never-ending. They cheered our bus with the Olympic stars at every stop. Loudly.

They were waiting for the Olympic Torch relay, which was two hours behind schedule. Most of 'em didn't get home until 3 in the morning. They were still happy. And where did they get all those flags?

I'll never forget it.

I was going to splurge tonight, Mom, celebrate a bit, take a cab to the hotel and forgo the 90-minute bus ride that has given me a new appreciation for Tucson's traffic system. Get some sleep for a change.

But on second thought, I'll take the bus. I don't want this to end any sooner than it has to.

Kerri Strug — shown here at age 12 in 1990 — began her rise to fame in Tucson. Her early advice from Olympic coach Bela Karolyi: Don't be "a scaredy puppy."

# Olympic sacrifice: Gymnast Kerri Strug is committed to goal

*Friday, June 14, 1991*

Kerri Strug is not quite 14 years old, not quite 75 pounds, not quite 5 feet tall, not quite Mary Lou Retton. But no one can say Kerri Strug is not quite tough enough.

"She's the baby of the family. She's just teeny," her mother, Melanie Strug says. "It's very, very difficult to have her living a thousand miles from home. Neither my husband nor myself wanted her to move away when she was 13, but it was her decision."

Tough? Yes. Tough.

In January, Kerri Strug moved from Tucson to Houston to train under the world's most omnipotent gymnastics coach, the indomitable Bela Karolyi, whose credits include Olympic gold medalists/media darlings Mary Lou Retton and Nadia Comaneci. Karolyi is a gruff and outspoken bear of a man, a Romanian immigrant who had these words of welcome for Kerri Strug:

"If you're a timid, scaredy-type performer, a scaredy puppy dog, you cannot do this."

Kerri Strug can do this.

At the U.S. Women's Gymnastics Championships last weekend in Cincinnati, her first meet against senior/elite competition, Strug became the sport's youngest national champion ever, winning the vault competition with a near-perfect 9.825. She was third overall, and in an instant became the leading lady of gymnastics, America's premier hope for the 1992 Summer Olympics.

"She used to be a little scaredy girl, running away when you look at her," Karolyi says in his best Romanian/American mix. "Now she smiles big for the audience."

As a reward for five months of labor in Karolyi's Olympic Gymnastic workshop in north Houston, Kerri Strug got to return to Tucson for two days this week. She was on the first flight out yesterday morning and back in the famous gym on Barnwood Drive by midafternoon.

Sometimes homesickness prevails. Sometimes not.

"I get through it," she says, handling the first of what is sure to be a legion of interviews in the months and years to come. "We usually get

207

Sundays off and my mother calls me every night and comes to visit me every two or three weeks. I'm doing OK."

This is not a scared little girl.

In her winning vault competition Sunday, Kerri almost flawlessly executed a maneuver that Karolyi calls "the Yurchenko layout." Basically, Kerri approaches the vault horse blind. "I do a back hand-spring onto the horse without looking," she says. "You finish with a layout flip and a full twist."

It's more difficult than anything Olga Korbut or Nadia or Mary Lou ever did. Also, more dangerous. No scaredy puppy dog can do it. "I'm just learning to do it," says Kerri, the national champion. "A lot of people do it ... but not very well."

She has also learned modesty.

Dr. Burt and Melanie Strug (he's a Texan, she's from Chicago) moved to Tucson from Houston 14 years ago, a few months before Kerri was born. Burt is a heart surgeon. Melanie grew up admiring ballet legend Margot Fonteyn, and that became the family link to gymnastics.

The Strugs' oldest daughter, Lisa, 22, was on the UCLA gymnastics team for three years. Her career was halted a year ago by a broken arm. Their son, Kevin, 19, competed in gymnastics under Tucsonan Yoichi Tomita, who, with Karolyi, was a member of the U.S. Gymnastics coaching staff in the 1984 Summer Olympics. Kevin is now a cheerleader at American University in Washington, D.C.

"We didn't push Kerri at all," says Melanie. "She followed the lead of her brother and sister. She was always tumbling all over the house. It came to her naturally."

It soon became inevitable that Kerri would have to intensify her training program if she wanted to keep her place among America's prominent gymnasts. That meant she had to make a difficult break with University of Arizona gymnastics coach Jim Gault, who had been her personal coach for four years. It meant that she would have to leave home. An "A" student at Green Fields Country Day School, Kerri would also have to leave her social friends.

These were not easy decisions.

"Mr. Gault did a wonderful job, but in all honesty his first commitment has to be with the university," Melanie says. "If Kerri wants to make the World Championships and the Olympics, she needed a full-time coach. When she got to be the No. 1 junior in the United States last year, Bela Karolyi expressed an interest and we flew to Houston and examined the situation."

The Strugs liked what they saw.

Bela Karolyi has more than 1,000 students enrolled at his Houston gymnastics ranch, but he and his wife, Marta, only give full-time personal instruction to five handpicked girls. Mary Lou Retton went through the same process. Karolyi hires independent choreographers, dance instructors, specialists.

The cost for instruction, room and board, private school, phone bill, airfares is staggering. Karolyi doesn't come cheap. "Fortunately," says Melanie, "my husband makes a very nice living. It's not as much a financial burden on us as it would be on another family."

Kerri lives with a surrogate family in Houston, as arranged by Karolyi. The Houston family has two children, ages 10 and 12, and Kerri goes to a school on a special schedule from 11 a.m. to 2:30 p.m. daily.

Her twice-daily workouts, always intense, never easy, go from 8 to 10:30 a.m., and after school from 4 to 8 p.m., sometimes until 9. It takes time to perfect those blind vaults.

"Bela has a track record," says Melanie. "No one has the track record he has. He expects total perfection and total commitment and he gets it. They work on everything: heads, hands, smile, absolutely no stone is left unturned. You pay the price. Kerri misses out on a lot of things, and we miss her a lot. But Nadia and Mary Lou have been in and out of the gym a lot and Kerri has been able to meet a lot of new friends. It's been a wonderful experience for her."

Kerri is winning the battle with homesickness. An aunt lives nearby in Houston, and on some weekends she is able to go to the mall or to a movie and blend into the crowd. For a few hours she can be just another 4-foot-7-inch, 70-pound ninth-grader. A year from now, at the Summer Olympics, she may be much more than that.

"This is the first step," says Karolyi. "You bet on your life Kerri Strug be much hungrier next time."

With her gold medal from the 1996 Atlanta Games in tow, Kerri Strug returned to Tucson for a ceremony at Hi Corbett Field and received a hero's welcome.

# Kerri Strug: An American sports hero

*Wednesday, July 24, 1996*

*"I don't think TV or the newspapers could write a drama like this one."* — Burt Strug

*ATLANTA*

As it turns out, the biggest story of the 1996 Olympics has been written by a 4-foot-7-inch, 88-pound champion with a heart the size of Alaska.

She is Kerri Strug, our Kerri Strug, an Olympic moment for a lifetime. She is a Dream Team unto herself, the best role model in or out of the '96 Olympics.

When she was driven to a large press center outside the Georgia Dome late last night, her left ankle elevated against the front seat to combat swelling, Kerri was still dressed in her Olympic uniform.

It was more than three hours after she had been wheeled out of the arena on a stretcher, a gold medal around her neck, wondering how the world ever got so crazy.

Even now, and probably not for a long time, Kerri Strug will not understand what she accomplished last night. She became the story of the '96 Olympics, leaving a legacy that will be recounted over and over and over. As long as she lives, and even after that, her story will be told.

This is a story for the ages. This is Kirk Gibson, limping to the plate, hitting a game-winning homer in the World Series. This is Willis Reed, fighting through the pain, inspiring the Knicks to the world championship.

It matters not if you are 6-11 or 4-7. The pain is the same. What matters is the courage.

"After my first vault," Kerri said, "I heard a snap in my foot and I was scared. I couldn't walk normal. But the other girls on the team were saying, 'Come on, you can do it. Shake it off.' I couldn't tell them, 'No, you're wrong, you don't understand. Something's wrong.' It was for the gold."

So Kerri Strug, not yet 19, said a little prayer. "I said, 'Please God, let me get through this.' I was in shock at first and it seemed like a nightmare for a few seconds." But she had been working for a gold medal for more than half of her young life. It was one vault away.

"When she got hurt, we were very obviously upset," said her

211

father, Burt Strug, a heart surgeon who knows a thing or two about suspense.

"But without Kerri Strug, there would be no gold medal."

Even the hard-boiled, cynical columnists from New York and Detroit and Chicago crowded into the sauna-like interview rooms outside the Georgia Dome — battling deadline — to hear what Kerri had to say last night.

She is the Mary Lou Retton and the Nadia Comaneci and the Olga Korbut of the '96 Olympics. It wasn't just athletics, it was theater.

But Strug did much more than they did. Those great gymnasts merely performed. It required skill, not fortitude. Strug knew that by taking the final vault her precious goals of medaling in the individual events — including floor exercise, at which she is perhaps the world's best — would probably vanish.

What greater sacrifice is there than making your teammates a priority? What better show of maturity than to put someone else's good ahead of yours? "I knew I did more damage on my second vault," she said.

Not that it wasn't and won't be appreciated. When Strug returned to the Georgia Dome for the medal ceremony, she was given such an ovation by 32,000 fans that it raised small bumps on your skin.

All that remains is for President Clinton to phone.

In 1976 at the Montreal Olympics, the men's gold medal came down to the rings competition in which Japanese star Shun Fujimoto needed to score 9.7 or better to get the gold medal away from the Soviets.

But Fujimoto had broken his leg at the knee while finishing his floor exercise routine. He kept the injury to himself and went ahead with the side horse routine, earning a 9.5. He then scored a 9.7 on the rings, which won the gold medal. He was the only one who knew how badly the pain would be on his dismount.

He did it anyway. Japan won the gold medal. It was exactly the situation Strug faced last night.

Fujimoto's landing compounded his injury, dislocating his knee. We don't yet know what physical damage Kerri Strug did by insisting on completing her final vault last night, winning the first team gold medal in U.S. women's Olympic history.

We do know, however, that we'll never forget it.

Someone asked Kerri if her performance yesterday will be long remembered in Olympic history.

"Well," she said in her tiny voice, "I definitely hope so. We won the team gold and went down in history.

"I hope everyone realizes that."

EDITOR'S NOTE: Two torn ankle ligaments in her left ankle prevented Kerri Strug from competing for an individual medal at the Atlanta Games. Nevertheless, she became a national star because of her winning vault, earning a trip to meet President Clinton and appeared on the cover of Sports Illustrated and Wheaties cereal boxes. Strug retired from gymnastics soon thereafter and enrolled at UCLA. She later graduated from Stanford and worked as a schoolteacher in the Bay Area and Washington, D.C. Now, she works as an auditor in the Office of Juvenile Justice and Delinquency Prevention in the U.S. Justice Department. Strug was inducted into the United States Olympic Hall of Fame on Aug. 3, 2008.

# Victory worth its weight in gold

*Tuesday, September 26, 2000*

*SYDNEY, Australia*

In 1947, when he broke baseball's color barrier, Jackie Robinson said he avoided looking at the crowd "for fear I would see only Negroes applauding."

Fifteen years later, Australia granted Aborigines the right to vote.

We have a lot in common, Australia and America. We had 100 years of slavery. They had 200 years of racial persecution. We imprisoned Indians. They stole the children of their indigenous people while exiling their parents.

We both have used sports to assist in our ethnic reconciliation. For us, it was Jackie Robinson. For them it is Cathy Freeman.

At the great Stadium Australia last night, bias and bitterness ran dead last. I don't know how television played the reception and reaction to Cathy Freeman's gold-medal run at 400 meters, but if you were here you were left groping for words.

The closest thing I've seen in American sports was the night Cal Ripken Jr. surpassed Lou Gehrig's consecutive-games streak and was bathed in a victory lap that raised goose bumps from here to Halifax. But that special moment was just baseball, viewed by a small pocket of Americana.

Freeman's victory lap was history.

Today's Sydney newspaper headlines were completely lacking in cynicism. PRIDE OF THE LAND. ... A CATCH IN THE NATION'S THROAT ... AUSTRALIA'S LONGEST MINUTE ... A NATION STOOD STILL FOR CATHY ... CATHY'S GAMES ...

Aussie television ratings records were shattered. Until the Sydney Olympics, the most-watched show in Australian history was the 1997 funeral of Princess Diana, estimated at 4.6 million viewers.

The opening ceremonies almost doubled that at 7.4 million, the intrigue being none other than Cathy Freeman, who put the torch to the Olympic cauldron.

Last night's Freeman-wins-400 telecast? An estimated 7.9 million viewers. She's a Super Bowl and the final episode of "M*A*S*H" unto herself.

You ask yourself why this is such a big story. Why did this enormous crowd of 115,000 totally ignore Michael Johnson's gold-medal

214

victory 15 minutes after Cathy Freeman circled the track carrying both the flags of the Aborigines and Australia?

Because the Australian government stole Cathy Freeman's grandmother from her family 60 years ago and exiled her in a penal colony on Palm Island. She was generically labeled as "troublesome." There was no trial, no explanation. That was life for the Aboriginal people in the mid-1900s.

It wasn't much different from what we did to Indians in the late 1800s when we killed them, uprooted them, and ultimately put them in minimum-security-type settlements on remote patches of no-man's land.

Cathy Freeman represents progress.

"I'm sure what happened tonight will make a difference toward people's attitudes," she said. "I've made a lot of people happy, from all sorts of backgrounds, who call Australia home. I hope this will be a symbol for change."

In 1912, Jim Thorpe, an Indian, was the world's foremost athlete, the first to bring great acclaim to people of his ancestry. He won a gold medal in the decathlon in Stockholm, Sweden, and when presented his medal by the King of Sweden, he said, naively, "Thanks, King."

Now, almost a century later, Cathy Freeman doesn't have to say anything. It is our turn.

Thank you.

# In Olympics, even a rower can make big waves

*Saturday, September 30, 2000*

*SYDNEY, Australia*

I was standing next to a TV screen Thursday night, watching the day's Olympic highlights, when a man I'd never seen walked up and started a commentary about the coxed fours.

"I thought we had the Brits," he said, nodding toward the screen. "How can a man with diabetes row 2,000 meters of water at age 38 and still be so extraordinary?"

Right, I said.

The man continued to talk about Steven Redgrave, the greatest rower the world has ever known. He talked about Redgrave the way I would stand next to a TV set in Tucson and talk about Mark McGwire hitting 70 home runs.

"He's won the gold at five consecutive Olympics," the man said. "He switched from the coxless pair to the coxed four and still he wins the gold. My hat is off to Steven Redgrave."

I felt like applauding, and not for Steven Redgrave, but for the Media Village volunteer who knew so much and was so passionate about this British Olympic hero whose name was altogether foreign to me.

It's like this every four years. I walk into the Olympics thinking I know sports. I walk out humbled, floored by the realization that what I know about the total Olympics isn't much more than what I know about what really makes this laptop computer work.

I spent too much time at the swimming venue again this time. Too much time watching baseball games and Marion Jones and everything else that comes in a red, white and blue, mainstream media package.

I missed Steven Redgrave, and who knows what else?

NBC can't possibly begin to deliver the real spirit of the Olympics because it is too big. We get the American vision of the Olympics, and that's a shame because there is so much more. We don't get to see the domination of Chinese table tennis players and the reaction of their fans, and we don't get to see the Romanian delegation that spills out onto Darling Harbor, singing happy songs because Mihai Covaliu has won the men's individual sabre fencing gold medal.

I spent 30 minutes watching the semifinals of the field hockey game between Holland and Australia the other night and was absorbed by the great difficulty of the game, and by the chanting, raucous, sell-out crowd that filled the Olympic Park Hockey Center. I was amazed; there must've been several thousand people displaying Holland-red paraphernalia.

Did all these people come here from Holland just to watch field hockey? Don't these Dutch know that the Olympics are an American idea? Did they even know that Tommy Lasorda was here, wearing a gold medal? And who were these people, 15,000 strong, who filled the hockey arena every day of this Olympiad?

Yesterday morning, I took a 10-minute walk from the Main Press Center to the State Sports Arena, curious to see if anyone was watching the day's taekwondo semifinals. There are 5,000 seats. There were 5,000 spectators, and a healthy split of them were from Denmark.

They came all this way to watch taekwondo?

They were watching Muhammad Dahmani of Denmark compete against Warren Hansen, a homeboy from Australia. At the conclusion of the match, won 6-5 by Hansen, the man from Denmark refused to leave the court. He raised two fingers on his right hand, as if to make a V, for victory. He walked around the court displaying the V to the judges and the fans. He was visibly angry.

The place almost came apart. Whistles. Boos. Finally, security officials were summoned and forcibly removed Dahmani from the court.

I walked to the press interview zone in the hopes I could learn why the man from Denmark was so upset. A reporter from Australia told me that Dahmani had complained that the judges had exhibited favoritism to the hometown Aussie.

"Same as yesterday," the man said. "When Lauren won the gold at 49kg, the bronze medalist from Chinese Taipei also refused to leave the court because she thought the judging was unfair."

That's it. Common knowledge. Everybody knows this stuff. An Aussie journalist on a first-name basis with the country's taekwondo gold medalist. Who doesn't know Lauren Burns? Or Steven Redgrave?

I wish I could say I'm going to exit the Sydney Olympics with a better insight into the love Greece has for its weight-lifters, and I wish I could say I had a memorable experience watching the passion that the Turks have for their wrestlers.

I get the sinking feeling that the more Olympics I watch, the more I'm missing.

# CHAPTER SEVEN

# Unforgettable characters

## Snowden leaves UA with a smile

*Saturday, July 2, 1983*

*"Once there was a fleeting glimpse of glory."* — From "Camelot," and then replayed on Fred Snowden's TV special

On his last day in the employ of the University of Arizona, Fred Snowden had his new sales pitch practiced and probably, polished.

"If everything falls into place," he said, "It bodes for a great future. I'm hoping I can sell great ice cream like I sold great basketball."

But in a two-hour special broadcast Thursday night on Channel 11 — Snowden's last hurrah — he didn't try to sell anything.

He wasn't weakly sentimental, self-serving or critical of the school that showed him the door as the coach after the 1981-82 season.

"I don't want to get into reasons for what happened the last few years," he said and left it at that.

Never mind that a TV special 15 months after Snowden resigned as the UA's basketball coach was untimely and, I think, unnecessary.

I thought Snowden had long ago tired of those who dredged up the past. Surely the public remembers Snowden's last three seasons (34-47) as much as the first seven (133-61). Maybe it's not fair, but that's the way it is.

But Snowden always has loved the limelight and thus could rationalize a final appearance.

"We only had one subpar year," he said in his farewell special. "Much has been made of our three losing seasons, but they really weren't that bad when you reflect on it."

He also left his detractors a thing or two to chew.

Remember, for example, how Snowden's successor, Ben Lindsey, complained about the poor academic support system he inherited?

Albeit unsubstantiated, Snowden denied this Thursday.

"I take a lot of pride in the fact that 88 percent of my players graduated," Snowden said.

The academic community at UA probably gagged.

It was a sometimes entertaining, sometimes touching, yet maudlin and overbearing production.

The score from "Camelot" plays. The announcer says something about the "aura of Fred Snowden permeating Southern Arizona — Tucson was Camelot and Snowden was King Arthur."

You can guess most of the rest.

"When I came here, our goal was to win right away," Snowden said. "Second, our goal was to win a national title."

The UA was certainly in the big time for a while. Especially in the 1975-76 season, when it won the Western Athletic Conference title and met UCLA in the Far West Regional final.

"Had Eric Money and Coniel Norman developed for four years, stayed in school and continued to progress," said Snowden, "there's no question in my mind that we would've won the 1976 national championship. I have no question of that."

Indiana went 32-0 in 1976 and won the NCAA basketball title. Money and Norman quit school after their sophomore seasons, in 1974, to play in the NBA.

Yet the UA won 24 games in 1976 with Jim Rappis, Bob Elliott, Al Fleming, Larry Demic, Jerome Gladney, Herman Harris, Phil Taylor and others. Add Money and Norman and well, Snowden's got a point.

Interviews with some of Snowden's former players put his years at the UA in perspective. The message was: The kids had fun.

Len Gordy, who also coached under Snowden said, "I had roomed with half of these guys, and we had done bad things together. We missed bed checks and things like that. Suddenly, coach Snowden was telling them to call me 'Coach.' I had to laugh."

Joe Nehls: "I was so awed by UCLA. Even before we beat them (in 1979), I was in the bookstore buying sweatshirts with 'UCLA' written all over them."

Eric Money: "A guy from Sports Illustrated bought me a couple of drinks before he interviewed me. I was playing Muhammad Ali. The story came out before we played at UTEP and headlines in El Paso were smeared across the paper: 'Big Mouth Comes to Town.' It was the most emotional game I played, college or pro."

The decline of Snowden's program was touched upon.

Russell Brown, on what went wrong with the UA basketball program: "It was the press. We really couldn't concentrate with all the outside stuff going on. That was the key."

Greg Cook, once suspended for fighting at practice: "I didn't want to hurt Coach as much as I did."

When Demic left the court following his last home game, he was shown shaking hands with teammates. Then he embraced Snowden, crying.

Snowden displayed emotion, too. Addressing the team before his final game a year ago, his voice broke. "Remember one thing," he said, "be the best of the man that you are." The team huddled around him and Snowden cried. "And remember," he said, "Arizona means something."

After that final game, a 96-78 victory over Oregon, Snowden had not lost his humor despite a 9-18 season.

"We'll celebrate tomorrow after we find out what the NCAA tournament committee is going to do," he told the team.

Snowden now enters private business, in an executive capacity, with Baskin-Robbins ice cream stores.

"So many things have come down the last few years that would've killed most of us," Gordy said. "But Fred's still smiling, still kicking away.

"I say the guy has nine lives."

EDITOR'S NOTE: Fred Snowden ran his own private management consulting company, working for Baskin-Robbins until the company hired him as its vice president of urban affairs and development in 1985. Later, he served as the executive director of the Food 4 Less Foundation in Los Angeles. Snowden died in Washington D.C., on Jan. 17, 1994. He was 57. He was in the nation's capital at the time to attend a White House ceremony for urban development with President Clinton. Snowden was inducted into the UA Sports Hall of Fame in 1988.

Fred Snowden ushered in an exciting new brand of basketball at the UA. His high-scoring Wildcats went 133-61 in his first seven seasons.

JACK W. SHEAFFER

RON MEDVESCEK

Ricky Hunley is congratulated by Arizona coach Larry Smith after the Wildcats beat host ASU on Nov. 26, 1983, the final game of Hunley's collegiate career.

# Football a far cry from what mother wanted for Hunley

*Friday, September 23, 1983*

PETERSBURG, Va. — Even now, tears well up in the eyes of Scarlette Hunley. "I get misty every time I talk about it," she said. "But the good Lord must've wanted Ricky Hunley to play football awfully bad."

Ricky, now a senior All-America linebacker with the University of Arizona, didn't appear destined to play the game while in high school.

"I had so many terrible times with that boy and football," Scarlette said. "I have shed many, many tears. I just didn't want my boys to play football."

It was late summer 1979, and the Petersburg High School football team was together for practice. Ricky was not supposed to be among that number. He had missed his junior year, 1978, with a painful muscle injury to his lower back.

"We took Ricky to three doctors in town, three more at a special clinic and two up in Richmond," said his father, James. "Every one of them said he was gonna be all right. That he just needed the year to heal.

"But he couldn't convince his mother because he walked funny, kind of like a man with a cane."

Scarlette remained convinced that 1978 was a harbinger of more injuries.

"It seemed like I spent forever rubbing that awful liniment on Ricky's back," said his older sister, Renita. "Boy did it smell. We did everything to make Ricky feel better. But oh, how he missed football. He just wasn't himself that year."

Scarlette wasn't sure a cure was the best medicine.

"One day, Ricky limped all the way home from school," she said. "Every step he took, a tear dropped from my eye. I insisted that Ricky wouldn't play anymore. I put my foot down."

But when it came time for the '79 season, Ricky was ready to play. The pain in his back had disappeared.

Showdown time.

"He came to me one day before his senior year and said, 'Let me do it my way. Let me play.'

"My heart was in my mouth," Scarlette said. "I knew I had to say yes."

• • •

Reginald "Buster" Hunley and younger brother Wayne, eldest of 11 children of James and Scarlette Hunley, weren't active in athletics.

Buster, 28, eventually went into the service and is a certified mechanic. Wayne, 27, ... well, Wayne dances to his own drummer. "If you asked me where Wayne is tonight," Scarlette said, "I couldn't tell you. But we love him and he loves us. He knows he's got a home here."

To say the Hunleys are a close family would be as inadequate as saying Ricky Hunley is a good football player. "Families are forever," Scarlette said, and you know she meant it.

It is because of much love that Ricky could be classified as the All-American who wasn't supposed to be.

"I was overprotective of Buster and Wayne," said Scarlette, who insists on being called Scarlette, even by her children. "I was just so afraid my children would get hurt. I babied 'em because they were — they are — my babies."

When he was 10 years old, Ricky secretly tried out for a youth football team. He soon fractured the middle finger of his right hand, had it splinted and told Scarlette he hurt it at the playground. Or somewhere.

The next day, unbeknown to his mother, he played in a game.

"Rick was so overwhelmed at his team's victory that he couldn't hold it back," Scarlette said. "I didn't even know he was playing football. I could've choked him!"

But the horse was out of the barn, and the race was on.

"By the time Ricky was in sixth grade," James said, "he had had sprained ankles, broken toes, wrists, everything. We went to the hospital with him almost once a week. He was the most fragile child I have ever seen."

• • •

If Ricky Hunley thought the path was clear, he had underrated his mother.

"I'll never get used to watching my boys play football," she said. "I can never get used to watching my kids get beat up. It's awful."

Scarlette did not consent to watch Ricky play football until he was a senior at Petersburg. She listened to the 1979 state championship game on the radio. It was the Crimson Wave's first state title in 35 years.

"I only go to senior homecoming games," she said. "and only when I have to."

Almost predictably, Ricky and younger brother LaMonte, a junior starting linebacker at UA, sustained minor injuries the first time Scarlette saw them play. "I would stand up and yell, 'I don't want to see my boys get killed. Take them out!'"

Said Renita: "One time, when LaMonte got the wind knocked out of him, Scarlette stood up and yelled 'Oh my! My boy's dead!' All the people around us, the principal and all, told her to hush up. That's the way it is at every game."

Hush, hush, sweet Scarlette.

• • •

Hunley's high school football coach, Norm Jenkins, died of cancer last spring. He was 45. The only coach remaining from Petersburg's 1979 state championship team is Bernie Brand.

"Ricky was one of those kids you didn't have to teach," Brand said. "He was a natural."

"He really only played one full season for us. He didn't play much as a sophomore, and he missed his junior year because of a back injury. But it didn't seem to bother him at all. He had the best attitude I've ever seen. He just simply believed he could do anything. And he was the hardest worker on the field."

How good was Ricky, circa 1979?

"As for his ability, he's the best I've seen and I've been here 30 years," Brand said. "He just had a tremendous gift and he took advantage of it. I saw Ricky last summer and he's still the same person he was four years ago. Always optimistic. Always positive."

• • •

The Petersburg school system was integrated in 1962. Peabody and Petersburg high schools became one. "Peabody was all-black and Petersburg was all-white," Scarlette said. "But they kept the name of the white school."

This year's Petersburg varsity football team has one white player. Of the six coaches, two are white.

"We called a lot of (white players) over the summer and asked them to come out for the team," said Quintin Hunley, a senior tight end at PHS with aspirations to play college baseball. "But they just didn't. There were about four or five white players on Ricky's team."

James grew up in Iowa. Scarlette has been in Petersburg all her life. She said racial tensions don't affect her.

"We are all God's children," she said. "He loves us all. And that's what I taught my children — love everybody because that's what the Lord wants you to do."

• • •

Roland C. Day Field, dedicated in 1970, is rimmed by mature oak, maple and pine trees and sits in a hollow, almost in a valley. The serenity is unmistakable.

The field is rock-hard. Whatever grass is there has been beaten down by too many cleats, too many winters and too little maintenance.

A weathered, four-lane track circles the field. A handful of portable bleachers are on each sideline. A sign on a concrete wall on the southwest end of the stadium, painted in burgundy and gold, says: "Petersburg Crimson Wave. State champs '79."

Ricky Hunley played there.

Two Petersburg players are running stairs after practice, punishment for taking too long on a water break.

"I'm gonna be the next Ricky Hunley," says one of them, No. 58. "He used to run these stairs, too. I'm gonna be the next Ricky Hunley."

• • •

A visitor asks James Hunley if Ricky has any mementoes, or perhaps a scrapbook. It is a silly question.

James repairs to an upstairs bedroom and returns with a large — we're talking big — suitcase. James has to drag the suitcase. Inside are so many newspaper clippings it seems as if Ricky Hunley must've campaigned for president. Who else gets so much publicity?

"Wait until Ricky starts playing pro football," said Renita, laughing. "We'll probably have to add a new room to the house just so we can keep all of his newspaper articles."

It hasn't always been this way, though.

When LaMonte was a senior at PHS, Scarlette thought reporters wrote too many articles expecting LaMonte to fill Ricky's rather large shoes. "So I cut them off," she said. "I wouldn't let the reporters talk to LaMonte anymore."

• • •

The stucco, earth-tone row house at 1910 Matoax Ave. has two chimneys, two stories, two wall-unit air conditioners and two proud parents.

There is an ever-present buffet line in the kitchen. Chicken is the night's feature. The atmosphere is serve yourself, sit down and let's talk.

The Hunleys live in a middle-class area, but it hasn't always been that way.

"We lived in the projects, the bad area of town when Ricky was growing up," Scarlette said. "We didn't have any money, but I always made sure there was enough food on the table. I wouldn't ever have my children go hungry. I have always said, 'Hungry stomachs lead to sticky fingers.'"

The Hunleys moved from the projects about four years ago to a historic, three-story house at 606 Harding St. "When we moved in there," Scarlette said, "people thought we were wealthy. They didn't know how long it took, and what it took, to get us there."

Tales about their stay there are almost legend.

"The house was haunted, nothing less," sad Reginald, who goes by Buster. "A rich old dentist used to own the house and his son hanged himself in one of the upstairs rooms. There were many nights I was wishing for a gun or a big old pipe when I got scared. The place was haunted."

"Not only was it haunted," said James, laughing, "but we never got it heated. We had two big furnaces and $600 heating bills in the winter. But we never could get that damn place warm."

The old house had its charm for the Hunleys. It also had slave quarters.

"My momma (Anna Mae Good) lived in the slave quarters out back for three years," Scarlette said. "I told you it was a historical home, but we're glad to be out of it."

• • •

Visitors are welcome, almost encouraged to drop by the Hunley household.

So it is with that in mind that Scarlette tells of college football coaches who came in waves to recruit her son Ricky.

"It wasn't a traumatic experience …" she begins to say.

"Oh, Scarlette, it sure was. It was one trauma after another," said Renita, Ricky's older sister, 24. "Did you forget the Maryland coach?"

Scarlette hasn't forgotten the Maryland coach.

The Hunleys had arranged to accompany Ricky on recruiting visits to Purdue and Notre Dame, but bad weather postponed their driving plans. Ricky was to visit the University of Arizona, mostly because an aunt lived in Sierra Vista.

"Arizona was my second choice. I think we all wanted Ricky to go to North Carolina," Scarlette said. "But I never wanted him to go to Maryland."

"A coach for Maryland insisted — insisted — that Ricky could go nowhere but Maryland. He stayed in our house for four hours one night and gave us a long pitch about Maryland. He just pushed too hard."

It soon got to be too much for Ricky, too.

"We just had to cut it off," Scarlette said. "Ricky came in one morning, sat down on the arm of my chair and said, 'Scarlette, I'm tired of people bugging me. I'm tired of it all.' So I called the school and said nobody is allowed to see Ricky. Nobody!"

The Maryland coach persisted and got past Scarlette's security system. That's when the Hunleys hit the fan.

"The Maryland coach tried to work some psychology on me," Scarlette said. "He told me Ricky shouldn't go to a school in such a far-away place as Arizona. Then he told me Ricky wasn't good enough to play at Arizona."

Wrong approach, Coach.

"I stood up, opened the front door and told the coach to leave and never come back. No one tells me my children aren't good enough. I told him not to let the doorknob hit him where the Good Lord split him."

• • •

Former UA coach Tony Mason was the key to getting Hunley to Arizona.

"Tony Mason is a darling. We love him," Scarlette said. "He's a living doll."

The Hunleys had dinner at Mason's home in Tucson before the UA-ASU game last November. "We would never go to Tucson without going to see if Tony Mason is all right," Scarlette said. "We love that man."

• • •

Ricky and LaMonte Hunley went home for Christmas last year. It was a special time because Petersburg High was to retire Ricky's football jersey, No. 89, at halftime of a home basketball game.

"Ricky's the only one that has his jersey retired," said the youngest brother, Derek, a sophomore at PHS. "LaMonte wore his number after Ricky left, but then they retired it."

There is one other retired jersey in the PHS trophy case. It belonged to Moses Malone, Class of '74. *That* Moses Malone.

• • •

The Hunleys plan to fly to Tucson for the UA-Washington game in November. "We won't drive there anymore," James said, "because two

228

years ago we tried to drive there and our car broke down four times. We ended up spending two days in a small town in Tennessee. We never did get to Tucson."

That doesn't mean the community is lacking. The Hunleys reach out and touch. A lot.

"We've had phone bills as high as $299," Scarlette said, rolling her eyes.

"Come on Scarlette, admit it. We've had phone bills as high as $400," Renita said, laughing. "That's when the real trauma hits."

James, who is disabled and has had five back operations, no longer works as a barber and said the money is hard to come by. Scarlette said it isn't.

"When the phone bill comes," she said, "I just close my eyes and then ask for donations. We get a little bit from everybody."

Scarlette is a food supervisor at Petersburg Social Services department. She works 8 to 5.

"We don't have much money," she said. "We make up for it in love."

A particular treasure of hers is a newspaper clipping in which Utah coach Chuck Stobart said in effect: If one Hunley doesn't get you, the other one will.

It is in reference to Arizona's recent 38-0 victory over Utah in which LaMonte, not Ricky, was honored highly. In fact, LaMonte was named the Pac-10's Defensive Player of the Week.

"I hope Tucson appreciates my boys" Scarlette said. "I don't like being away from them, but I know they've got a good home there. But you only get to keep them for a short time. Then I get them back."

EDITOR'S NOTE: Ricky Hunley was a consensus first-team All-American as a senior in 1983, and was named the Pac-10's Co-Defensive Player of the Year. He is still widely regarded as the best and most accomplished player to ever play for the Wildcats. In 1998, the star linebacker became the first UA player to be inducted into the College Football Hall of Fame. Hunley still holds school records in career tackles (566), career solo tackles (323) and career assisted tackles (243). After college, he was the seventh overall pick in the NFL draft and spent seven years in the league, reaching the Super Bowl twice with the Denver Broncos as a starter in 1987 and 1988. His playing career ended in 1990, and he quickly joined the coaching ranks. Hunley served as an assistant at USC, Missouri and Florida before jumping to the NFL. Following one season with the Washington Redskins, he was the linebackers coach for the Cincinnati Bengals from 2003 to 2007. He lives in Cincinnati with his wife and two daughters. LaMonte Hunley was an All-American as a UA senior in 1984 and spent two years in the NFL with the Indianapolis Colts. He lives in Tucson and is vice president of Arizona Health, an exercise equipment dealer. Their mother, Scarlette Hunley, recently moved back to the family's hometown of Petersburg, Va., where she works with the youth in the community.

The bust of John "Button" Salmon outside McKale Center bears the former Arizona quarterback's immortal phrase, uttered on his death bed in 1926.

# Arizona finally bears down in marketing campaign

*Friday, September 14, 1984*

"Bear Down" is all over town. On billboards. On radio. On TV. At bus stops, on the sides of buses. On stickers that cling to your clothes and stickers that cling to your car.

It is a major marketing campaign underwritten by the University of Arizona that is probably more than a half-century overdue.

It is also proof that sometimes you don't immediately recognize the stuff from which legends are made unless it's hand-delivered by Knute Rockne.

But I do know this: Before there was "Win One For The Gipper" there was "Bear Down, Arizona." Same sport. Same concept. Different marketing approach.

Ronald Reagan has yet to say he made a career mistake by portraying George Gipp and not John "Button" Salmon in the movies.

Notre Dame won for the Gipper at Yankee Stadium in 1928. The world was watching. When "Bear Down" was created, at Las Cruces, N.M., in 1926, the Pony Express probably already had left town with that year's mail.

It has been 57 years since "BEAR DOWN" was painted in enormous block letters on the top of the new gymnasium at the UA. Twenty-five years later, in 1952, UA bandmaster Jack Lee put "Bear Down" to music.

There seemed to be no rush.

"Until now, virtually no attention has been paid to the 'Bear Down' legend," Martin Gentry, 81, said. He is a retired lawyer who started at guard for Arizona football teams from 1925 to 1929. "I'm surprised. I don't think it particularly needs a lot of publicity."

There are other views.

"I think it took all this time (58 years) for the legend to really take hold," Ralph Deal, 80, said. He is a retired purchasing agent who was a UA football letterman in 1927.

"I painted the letter 'B' on the roof of Bear Down Gym back in 1927, but there weren't that many airplanes in those days. Very few people ever saw it, and very few people talked about it or seemed to remember it — until now."

UA football coach Larry Smith leads his team in the 34-word song after each football game, win or lose. The UA is spending thousands hoping the slogan takes hold and becomes as identifiable in the Southwest as say "Hook 'em Horns" is in Texas.

But unfortunately, "Bear Down" is, at root, a tragedy.

On the last play of the last football game of his life, John "Button" Salmon, 22, threw a 30-yard touchdown pass to John McArdle. The pass was thrown on Saturday evening, Oct. 2, 1926. Salmon, a senior from Bisbee, had helped the UA varsity beat the UA freshmen 20-0.

Salmon and a teammate, Ted Diebold, drove to Phoenix the next day, to visit Diebold's family. On the drive home that night, Salmon failed to negotiate a curve while driving on the highway north of Florence. He was thrown from the car and severely damaged his spinal cord. He was paralyzed immediately. Diebold was treated for cuts and bruises and released overnight.

On Oct. 18, Salmon, the UA's student-body president, died. Football coach J.F. "Pop" McKale canceled practice for two days. UA president C.H. Marvin canceled classes that day. Salmon's body would lie in state for 24 hours.

"I used to date Button's sister," Frank "Limey" Gibbings, 80, said. He is a retired UA coach and was a reserve quarterback on the 1926 team.

"He was one of my closest friends," Gibbings said. "He was one of the best baseball players around, and he always used the term "bear down." It's a term you get from baseball. Button always used it.

McKale took a UA traveling squad of 24 players to Las Cruces for a game against New Mexico State on Oct. 23, five days after Salmon died. Arizona, 2-0, had outscored opponents 89-0 in its victories. New Mexico State was 0-2 yet was tied with Arizona in a scoreless game late in the third quarter.

"It was a very emotional time," Gentry said. "We almost lost, and we should've won very easily. We were all uptight. We were all thinking about Button."

Before the game, McKale addressed his team.

"We knew that (McKale) had visited Button at the hospital every day," Gentry said. "So just after the pre-game warm-ups, McKale told us to gather around. It was a very emotional moment.

"Mac said that he had asked Button if he had a message for the team. And Button had told him 'Tell them . . . Tell them to bear down."

The anecdote was not published in The Arizona Daily Star that year. And not until Deal coordinated an effort and raised enough money to buy the paint to spell "Bear Down" on the roof of the new gymnasium — a year later — was Salmon's message to his teammates heavily publicized.

Just as there were no witnesses when George Gipp and Knute Rockne had their famous chat in the hospital, people are asked to take Salmon's "Bear Down" line on faith.

"Mac was a good talker," Gibbings said. "He was very emotional and could always get the team stirred up. I never heard him use the term 'Bear Down,' but I don't think anyone ever doubted that he told us exactly what Button said."

Deal agrees.

"In all honesty, McKale wasn't beyond making something out of something, stretching it a bit," Deal said. "But I'm sure it was the truth. It was exactly what I would've imagined Button to say."

Gentry said McKale once told him exactly what Button said before he died.

"I know exactly what was said, but I'd rather not comment on it; that's between Mac and Button," Gentry said. "The school's got a good thing going, and I want to see it stay that way."

Leo Golembiewski has been the face of the highly successful Arizona Icecats for three decades and counting. They won the national championship in 1985.

KELLY PRESNELL

# The best of times are now for the Icecats

*Friday, November 30, 1984*

*"Things are always at their best in the beginning."* — Blaise Pascal, 1656
*"It ain't gonna get any better than this."* — Me, 1984

These are the good old days of Icecat hockey, age 5. This is the max. Sellout crowds. Live TV. Winners. The wave. How can it get any better?

It can't.

Leo Golembiewski, the coach of the Icecats, disagrees. This is natural. But he wants more out of the program than the guy who pays $4.50 (Talk about the price of success: Last year's most expensive ticket was $3) to get through the gate.

"What we've done is humbling. Our fans are remarkable," Golembiewski said. "From their perspective, I'm sure it's exciting. But that doesn't mean we're going to let up and start Mickey Mousing around."

This is where the Icecats coach starts sounding like someone out of Fantasyland.

Golembiewski said he wants his club-level program to become NCAA Division I.

He wants to give his players scholarships. He wants to schedule better opponents. He wants to establish better academic-quality controls. He wants to play more home games. He wants the White Sox to win the pennant. (That's what he said.)

But Golembiewski isn't going to get his way very soon, if at all, and the reason is elementary. Money.

A move to the NCAA would require scholarship commitments, recruiting budgets, coaching salaries and unusually costly travel expenses to play schools, for example, in the Western Collegiate Hockey Association — Denver, Minnesota, Wisconsin, Northern Michigan and so forth.

The Icecats can't yet make enough money to become self-sufficient, or close to it, on the NCAA level.

"What we needed is 10 to 12 weekends a year at the TCC,"

Golembiewski said. "Once we get that many home dates, it'll be possible to show (UA director of athletics) Cedric Dempsey that we can make a profit or break even."

Trouble is, the Tucson Community Center is so frequently booked that the Icecats barely managed six home weekends this year and seven in 1985-86. Golembiewski is already working on the 1986-87 home schedule.

Dempsey, for his part, isn't in position to throw a few scraps toward the Icecats.

A two-year NCAA sanction that doesn't permit the UA to play its football games on live television is expected to cost the school an estimated $1.25 million in revenues through next season. Dempsey won't be taking on boarders at this point.

"Our position hasn't changed in regard to the hockey team because of our budgetary reductions," Dempsey said. "It's probably even less likely to change until our TV sanctions are completed and the TV issue is settled."

Big deal.

It's my belief that if you polled the first 5,000 fans through the door at tonight's UA-Southern California game at the TCC, 60 percent of them couldn't tell you if the UA was a club team, an NCAA team or an NHL team.

They just want to see a puck on ice, a beer on draft and a team with "UA" scrawled on its shirts. That's entertainment.

I'm not saying the fans are unsophisticated. They're just grateful to have hockey.

Golembiewski doesn't disagree. He said a move to the NCAA isn't necessary to keep drawing a capacity crowds of 6,850.

"Hockey players and coaches are not used to this type of acceptance, especially at this level," he said.

"And maybe the fans are satisfied with what we've accomplished and where we are. But I'm not. I don't see fans looking at Division I status as something that would necessarily have to happen.

"I sense that they are pleased with the team, with our winning record and with the excitement at the TCC — as long as we keep it up."

Which is at question here.

How long can the UA continue to have a vibrant hockey program playing on a club level? Will the honeymoon end, the novelty wear thin? Are those crowds of 6,850 people the same 6,850 people at each game?

Is hockey at the TCC just a trend that's about to flame out?

I doubt it. A base for hockey has been established, and Tucson isn't getting any smaller.

"As long as we entertain the fans and work hard," Golembiewski said, "I believe we'll get stronger and stronger. I don't think this is as good as it's going to get."

Yet the Icecats are in a situation not unlike BYU's football team. The restrictions — club hockey and the WAC — are a little staggering. Sometimes it gets old beating up on the same broken teams every week.

The Icecats sooner or later are going to have to find a new challenge, the total solution of which isn't scheduling an exhibition game or two against an NCAA team each season. That is under study.

The most formidable challenge awaiting the Icecats is to prove they can profitably move to NCAA Division I, perhaps five years from now. Perhaps sooner. Perhaps not that soon.

And when that happens, it's likely the Icecats would be down for a few years. It would take time to build a recruiting base. It's likely the Icecats wouldn't win as often.

And therein lies the gamble. Winning has been the hallmark of Golembiewski's teams. The draw. Would Tucson support a loser while the program tested its NCAA teeth? If not, would the program die a financial death before it could get over the hump?

I'm not trying to detract from the excitement the Icecats have created, but rather I'm trying to say that it might be wise to appreciate it.

It's not going to get much better than it is today.

EDITOR'S NOTE: The Arizona Icecats won the American Collegiate Hockey Association national championship in the 1984-85 season, setting a club record with 28 wins. The Icecats finished as national runners-up three more times over the next six years and made the national tournament 21 straight years from 1983 to 2003. But despite their consistent standing as one of the premier Division I teams in the ACHA, the Icecats have never attained member status from the NCAA. Coach Leo Golembiewski reached the 600-win plateau during the 2008-09 season, his 30th at the helm of the Icecats.

ARIZONA DAILY STAR 1989

Sean Elliott, the best basketball player in Tucson's history, speaks to the McKale Center contingent after breaking the Pac-10's scoring record in 1989.

# Sean a gem of city: Brilliance has made Tucson shine

*Sunday, February 19, 1989*

In the movie "It's a Wonderful Life," Jimmy Stewart, who feels like a louse, is able to see life as it would've been without him.

He was, to his surprise, an impact player.

In "Back to the Future," Marty McFly is a time-traveler who discovers the future wouldn't have been nearly so much fun without him.

Same with Sean Elliott.

What if Elliott, for example, had chosen to be a baseball player? It was, after all, his first love in sports.

Who would've made all those jumpers in the clutch to beat UCLA?

What if, on his doctor's advice, Elliott had given up sports after tearing up a knee in a 1982 soccer game?

Who would've made up the 182 points Elliott has scored in the NCAA tournament?

What if Cedric Dempsey had not fired Ben Lindsey in 1983, and instead given Lindsey three seasons to coach the UA basketball team? Lute Olson would've gone from Iowa to Kentucky. Could Lindsey have recruited Elliott?

No, you say. He could not.

Can you imagine Sean Elliott wearing the orange and blue of UTEP? What if Elliott had signed with UCLA? Don't even think about it, you say. Would Brian Williams be here? Matt Othick? Sean Rooks? Would Don DeVoe be Arizona's coach?

What if?

What if, on the day Amphitheater's freshman basketball team beat Elliott's ninth-grade team at Cholla High School, 100-18 — that's right 100-18 — Elliott had decided he might get more fulfillment and less frustration out of an after-school shop class?

"Hello, Elliott's Cabinet Shop, this is Sean. We do all kinds of woodwork."

I bring this to your attention because in each life there is a meeting of great chance.

Or maybe it's better defined as a meeting of geography.

In 1984, Lute Olson found Sean Elliott in his backyard and the lives of 650,000 Tucsonans have never been the same.

What's it like to have the nation's best collegiate basketball player in your town? From your town? Doesn't it make the quality of life a little better? Doesn't it put a little more juice in those calls from back home?

"Hey, Dad, did you watch that Arizona game on CBS the other day? Right, Dad. I hear you. Elliott. ... Know what? That wasn't even his best game of the week. He grew up here, you know that, Dad? I used to see him shoot around at the playground. ... Sorry about the vacation plans this summer, Dad. But I guess we're going to take the time off and use the money to go to the NCAA regionals in Boise. It might be Elliott's last game, you know. ..."

Players like Elliott, teams like Arizona, always seem from someplace else. They're never your guys. They're always from California or Carolina.

But this time Michael Jordan grew up in Tucson. Larry Bird is the guy from down the street. Danny Manning is on our team, not beating it.

Tucson's reaction to Sean Elliott has been unconditional. He is not loved the way Steve Kerr is loved.

Kerr is a son. Family. The passion for Elliott is more sophisticated, less affectionate.

Every time Elliott misses a shot there seems to be a slight gasp. How can he miss?

Every time he does anything that does not click and tick and proceed exactly as planned — 4 for 15 against 'SC; 10 points at Oregon — something has to be wrong.

But nothing is wrong.

He gets 31 against Duke, goes for 32 against UNLV, 31 against Villanova. He positively wrecks UCLA and Stanford. When it counts, Elliott has always been there.

Our guy. Our town. His town.

He does what he does in this state better than anyone in our lifetime. He gets the basketball to places where it can't go. Where only Magic can take it. His picture should be posted on all tavern walls. In schools. His jersey, 32, should hang from the ceiling, never to be worn again.

In the course of a normal life, there will never be another No 32. Not in this town.

In "The Natural," Roy Hobbs says that all he ever wanted was for people to see him walk down the street and say, "There goes Roy

Hobbs, the best there ever was."
In Tucson and to Sean Elliott, it is no movie. It is real.

EDITOR'S NOTE: Sean Elliott won the John R. Wooden Award for the 1988-89 season as the best player in college basketball and broke the Pac-10's all-time scoring record on Feb. 18, 1989. He was selected third overall in the NBA draft that summer by the San Antonio Spurs, the team with which he spent 11 of his 12 seasons in the pros. Two months after he and the Spurs won the 1999 NBA championship, Elliott announced he suffered a kidney disease that required a transplant. In August 1999, he received a kidney from his older brother, Noel. The two-time All-Star returned to the Spurs the following season and retired in 2001. The UA retired his jersey No. 32 in 1996, and the Spurs did the same in 2005. He now works as a TV broadcaster for the Spurs in San Antonio.

Steve Kerr talks with Lute Olson after the UA won the NCAA championship in March 1997. Two months later, Kerr helped the Chicago Bulls win the NBA title.

DAVID SANDERS

# Glory day for Kerr: Ex-Cat always handled pressure well

*Sunday, June 15, 1997*

On Friday night in Game 6 of the NBA Finals, game tied, six seconds to play, Steve Kerr took a pass from Michael Jordan and had an open 18-footer.

It was the chance of a lifetime.

Thousands of basketball players come and go and never find themselves in precisely the right moment at precisely the right time.

All that was left was to stand up to the pressure.

Steve Kerr had played more than 12,000 minutes in the NBA — roughly 720,000 seconds. In an instant, without warning, the 720,001st second of his NBA career would be the ultimate confluence of opportunity and reward.

The Shot would be his to take.

After a lifetime spent introducing himself to pressure, Steve Kerr didn't hesitate.

Jerry Marvin was the basketball and baseball coach at Pacific Palisades High School in 1983, Kerr's senior year. Do you know what Marvin remembers most? That Kerr was a terrific baseball player.

"He was a control pitcher with a good breaking pitch and a bite to his fastball," Marvin remembers. "He was a third baseman with a clutch bat."

Palisades reached the city finals at Dodger Stadium, and Marvin still regrets not pitching Kerr that day.

"He was unbelievable as far as pressure was concerned. The bigger the moment, the better he'd be. Baseball, basketball, it didn't matter. He was the guy you wanted when the game was on the line.

"He was a real pressure player."

This is pressure: In August 1983, Kerr was at the airport in Beirut, Lebanon, preparing to fly to Tucson to register for his freshman year in college.

He was traveling alone, embarking on the grandest experience of his life, sight unseen. Kerr had never been to Tucson, never had time to take a campus visit after Lute Olson offered him a scholarship in late July of '83.

Hell, Olson didn't publicly announce Kerr's addition to the UA squad until Aug. 29 of that year, 12 days after school had been in session.

As Kerr was waiting to board his plane that day, a 122 mm Druse rocket exploded, rocking the Beirut airport. He was 18 years old, and he thought it could be his last few moments on Earth.

Less than 10 seconds later, another shell hit a runway as a plane was landing. Bedlam. Somehow Kerr was able to escape the shelling and return to the house of his father, Malcolm, near the American University of Beirut. Most of the buildings at the university were scarred by bullet holes.

That's pressure.

Several days later, pulling strings, Malcolm Kerr, president of the American University, arranged for his son to fly out of a U.S. Marine base nicknamed "Sandbag City" where 1,200 Marines were encamped.

He would fly on a diplomatic jet through Cairo, Egypt. But just as Kerr arrived at the air base, the flight was scuttled.

Finally, three days after trying to leave Lebanon, Kerr agreed to a harrowing plan. It was decided that he would be driven, before dawn, by a friend of the family past Druse outposts, through Syria to Amman, Jordan. There he would catch a flight to Cairo and then to the United States.

The drive took 10 hours, requiring several stops at military checkpoints.

Kerr reached Tucson two days later. His father would be dead, killed by assassins, 4½ months later.

Maybe that's why taking a jump shot under duress, even an 18-footer with the NBA title at stake, doesn't seem to rattle Steve Kerr.

A year later, after his freshman season at Arizona, Kerr and his mother, Ann, accepted an invitation from an old family friend and flew to Washington, D.C., to visit him.

Kerr and his mother met Vice President George Bush at the White House and, after catching up on old times, were taken to the Oval Office to be introduced to President Ronald Reagan.

"I understand you play basketball for Arizona State ... " Reagan said, standing up to shake Steve's hand.

Kerr blushed. "Don't say that," he said. "It's Arizona."

Word was getting out, if slowly.

Kerr was one year removed from the summer of his senior year, when he had written a check for $300 and sent it to Colorado basketball coach Tom Miller, deposit on a dorm room at CU. That was before

Olson had scouted him, in late July of '83, and before Cal State-Fullerton had offered him a late scholarship.

Kerr was going to be a walk-on at Colorado and try to make the Buffaloes' basketball team, one that was coming off an 8-19 season.

There was no thought given to the wild notion that someday he'd take the most important shot of an entire NBA season.

After his junior season at Arizona, in which he had become an All-Pac-10 point guard, Kerr wasn't sure what he would do with his life.

"Sometimes I think I want to coach basketball," he said. "I know I want to stay in Tucson for a couple of years after I graduate, work and stick around while I decided what I want to do. I love it here. I like it a lot better than L.A."

No mention of the NBA. No pretensions.

It was that summer that Kerr wrecked his knee while playing for the United States' gold-medal-winning World Championship team in Spain. Two doctors, Tim Taft, in Spain, and Kim Hewson, in Tucson, told him the injury was possibly career-ending.

That's pressure.

He left Madrid, Spain, early on a Friday morning, wheeled out of a hotel by former UA assistant coach Scott Thompson, who helped Kerr get from a wheelchair into a waiting airport van to begin the sobering journey home.

"There are worse things than this," Kerr said, his eyes red from a night without sleep. "I'll be OK."

I turned away, tears in my eyes, afraid the doctors were right and he was wrong.

Who could've known?

In the days after Kerr shot a crippling 2 for 13 in the 1988 Final Four against Oklahoma, his draft projections weren't good.

NBA scouts insisted that Kerr's Final Four shooting performance was tied to the quickness of Sooner guards Ricky Grace and Mookie Blaylock, both of them blessed with pro-type speed.

Kerr fretted that he wouldn't even get drafted.

One day in May of '88 Kerr dug his old baseball gear out of a box and went to the Hi Corbett Field annex and had his name added to the official roster of a city league baseball team.

He warmed up, took a few cuts, and midway through the game was inserted at third base. His city league team included a few UA coaches, among them Dick Tomey and Rick LaRose; the opposition was a bunch of hot shots from area high schools and community colleges.

When Kerr finally got in the game, at third base, he made a remarkable bare-hand play, charging a slowly hit roller and throwing a runner out at first base. He had played the game before.

In his first at-bat, however, he was hit by a pitch that certainly wasn't a change-up or a knuckleball. The ball drilled him in the ribs and he walked to first base, wondering if this wasn't the smartest thing he had ever done.

The next batter, as luck would have it, doubled to the gap and Kerr sprinted around the bases, fearing he would have a collision at the plate. Fortunately, the throw home was late and Kerr scored standing up.

The NBA was a month away and he was bearing down on a catcher at full speed?

That was pressure, but it wasn't good pressure.

He put his baseball gear away for good. If he had any future in basketball, he was going to keep himself healthy enough to give it his best effort.

In the 10 years since he returned to basketball, his right knee fully rebuilt, Kerr has bounced around some. He was traded by Phoenix to Cleveland, and by Cleveland to Orlando. He sat on the bench in long spells, stacked up behind some not-so-immortals such as Jimmie Oliver, Litterial Green and Chris Corchiani.

In his first seven years in the NBA his highest average was 3.2.

He was traded by Phoenix for Mark Buford.

Cleveland traded him for Amal McCaskill.

When he finally signed a free agent contract with the Bulls, in 1994, Jordan left the team to play baseball.

Kerr seemed, almost chronically, to be in the wrong place at the wrong time. Who could've known what was in store?

Who could've guessed that with six seconds left in the Game of His Life, world championship on the line, Michael Jordan would see him standing there.

Open.

Nothing but net.

EDITOR'S NOTE: Steve Kerr won another championship with the Chicago Bulls in 1998, then won two more with the San Antonio Spurs in 1999 and 2003. He is one of only 22 players in history to win five or more NBA titles. His 15-year career in the league ended in 2003, and he still holds the NBA's record for career three-point percentage (.45403). After serving as a television analyst for TNT from 2003 to 2007, Kerr was named general manager and president of basketball operations for the Phoenix Suns, a position he still holds entering the 2009-10 season. His jersey No. 25 was retired by the UA on Jan. 9, 1999.

# Baffert beat 'million to one' odds to become horse racing success

*Wednesday, May 6, 1998*

*SONOITA*

I am rushing to beat the clock, maybe 14th in a line of 20 or so eager to put a few shillings on the sixth race at the Santa Cruz County Fairgrounds.

There are 17 other lines like the one I'm in, deep and slow, and it's three minutes to post. We all wait to put our $6 on the quarter horses from Duncan and Douglas and Safford and Nogales.

On a good day, more than $150,000 is wagered at the dusty little track at the intersection of highways 82 and 83. On a good weekend, 8,000 people crowd into the wooden bleachers the same way they've been doing it each spring across the last 44 years.

The Elgin Club sells cotton candy and hot dogs and all manner of Mexican food. The kids all come to play. Some of those kids are 75. Some are 5. Some play the horses. Some play in the dirt.

If you want a snapshot of small-town Americana the way it is in Southern Arizona, this is the place.

In 1987, quarter horse trainer/cattle rancher Willie Baffert made the short drive from Nogales through Patagonia and entered Hollie's Effort in the Santa Cruz County Futurity. It was a sprint, 350 yards, and Hollie's Effort won by a head. That victory fetched almost $41,000 for Baffert and the horse's owner, Holly Lee Golightly.

Willie Baffert paid less attention to that day's Kentucky Derby, simulcast in the Fairgrounds' betting pavilion. Alysheba won the 1987 Kentucky Derby at Churchill Downs, which is as far removed from the Santa Cruz County Fairgrounds as Earth is from Mars.

Or at least it used to be.

Willie's son, Bob, was with him, part of the training team when Hollie's Effort won the '87 Santa Cruz Futurity. Today, 11 years later, Bob Baffert is one of four trainers in horse-racing history to win back-to-back Kentucky Derbies, and the first in 25 years.

What are the odds that a former jockey/trainer from Nogales who 11 years ago was working the Arizona county fair quarter horse circuit could become America's best (and most well-known) thoroughbred trainer?

"A million to one," his father said with a laugh. "A million to one."

The Baffert name is hardly new to Southern Arizona. At the turn of the century, Tucson's largest grocery wholesaler, Baffert and Leon, stood at the corner of Toole and Stone, and stood there for more than a quarter-century, operated by Bob Baffert's great-grandfather. The Baffert clan has spread so much that Willie and his wife, Elinor, will not go to the Preakness to watch Derby winner Real Quiet run next week because they will be attending the graduation of their grandson, Andrew Braccia, in ceremonies at the UA.

There is more than a little destiny involved in this local-boy-makes-good saga.

The son of French immigrants, Willie Baffert got his first horse when he was 6 years old, a pony his father, Pierre, bought from the ore-mining firm in Cananea, Sonora. "I haven't been without a horse since that day," Willie Baffert said. "It became a way of life with me."

Willie thought he might make a career with the railroad. His father was the Nogales terminal superintendent for Southern Pacific, and Willie spent his teen-age years loading cattle on and off railroad cars.

The war years detoured Willie to the Army, an infantryman in the Philippines, a first lieutenant whose ranching days seemed to be at an end when he followed his heart — read: Elinor — to Cal-Berkeley at the end of World War II.

"I majored in business administration," he said. "While Elinor was going to school at Cal, she lived with the family of the vice president of Crown Zellerbach Corp. His daughter was her best friend. So I always figured I'd be working for Crown Zellerbach, selling paper for a living."

How many Kentucky Derby trainers grow up in San Francisco?

Ultimately, the Bafferts returned to Nogales, got a start on a 2,500-acre spread, and when Bob was born in 1951 he was surrounded by horses and cows and chickens and not cable cars.

"When Bob was a little boy we'd get up on Saturday, load the horses in the trailers and head off to Duncan or Douglas for the county fair races," said Willie. "It was a family thing. We'd stay overnight at a motel, and run our horses. As he got older, he would ride, which took away the worry of having to find a jockey. I don't know how scientific it was: After the race we'd feed 'em, rub some lotion on their front legs and get 'em ready for the next race."

The Bafferts would spend the winter running their horses at Rillito Downs in Tucson, and the summer would be spent at the track in

Prescott. Had Rillito not gone bust in 1982, shutting down for six years, forcing him to move to California and work with thoroughbreds, Bob Baffert might never have quit the quarter horse circuit, might never have left home.

He might still be at Sonoita the first weekend in May, wearing a cowboy hat, his name engraved across the back of his belt, staying at the Motel 6 in Douglas, watching the Kentucky Derby on ESPN.

Luck?

"No," said Willie Baffert. "This is no fluke. He's won at every level. He was trainer of the year at Santa Anita and Del Mar, he was the Eclipse Award winner as national trainer of the year. He's won two Kentucky Derbies and the Preakness. It's not luck."

But it is a million to one.

EDITOR'S NOTE: Ten days after this column ran, Bob Baffert's horse, Real Quiet, won the Preakness to give the Nogales native another chance at horse racing's Triple Crown. Real Quiet then lost by a nose in the Belmont Stakes, leaving Baffert one win shy for the second straight year. Baffert won two-thirds of the Triple Crown again in 2001 (Point Given) and 2002 (War Emblem), and his horses also won the Breeder's Cup in '07 and '08. Baffert's career earnings of $134.8 million through 2008 ranked fifth all-time among trainers. In August 2009, he was inducted into the National Museum of Racing's Hall of Fame.

Pam Reed, this decade's leading female ultramarathoner, treks her way to-ward an unofficial world record along the I-10 frontage road in March 2005.

# Tucson woman finds exhilaration in exhaustion

*Friday, August 2, 2002*

Just before 10 a.m. on July 24, Pam Reed crossed the finish line of the Badwater Ultra-Marathon and began to cry.

She had been running for 27 hours 56 minutes, and when she was done, she led the field by more than five hours. It made Lance Armstrong's ride through the Alps come off as a Tour de Breeze.

Reed thought of the other 61 runners still on the course, who wouldn't finish until midafternoon, when temperatures in Death Valley, Calif., would exceed 120 degrees.

"I hate crying, but I couldn't stop," Reed said. "I was so over-whelmed by what I had done. And I kept thinking about those poor people; it was so hot, it was scary. Some of them had the bottoms of their shoes melt."

Pam Reed is 41, a Tucson mother of three and stepmom of two who is 5 feet 4 inches, maybe 105 pounds, and about as fragile as a sumo wrestler. In April, she prepared for the Boston Marathon by running the course in reverse in 3 hours 38 minutes, and then, without stopping, turned around and ran the official race in 3:30.

But it was 60 degrees in Boston that day. When she ran through Death Valley last week — passing through the most uninhabitable hell-hole in this country, through Stovepipe, Furnace Creek and Badwater basin, where, at 282 feet below sea level, the overnight low is often 100 — it frightened her.

"I knew I could run 135 miles," she said. "But Death Valley? In July? It was unlike anything I had ever done."

Reed did not stop. She did not get sleepy. She did not consider quitting. She did not run for fun. She intended to win — and she did.

"My goal was to beat 30 hours," she said. "I blew that away. I felt like I could run forever."

The Badwater Ultra-Marathon has been part of the American Ultra-Running Association's race calendar for about two decades. At first, it was a dangerous publicity stunt, no saner than snake-hunting or cliff-jumping. But the race endured, growing from a handful of male daredevils to this year's robust field of 71.

Reed was the only female.

She took a crew of Tucson friends with her to Death Valley, including distance runner Suzy Bacal, who followed closely in a car with medical equipment and supplies. For 27 hours, Reed consumed more than 30 cans of vitamin-rich sports liquids, constantly chewed ice and, with the exception of half a peanut butter sandwich, declined to eat.

"I ran aside Pam for three hours during the heat of the day and I was pretty wasted," said Bacal. "I almost heat-stroked out when I got back in the car. And that was after three hours. Pam ran for more than 27 hours."

You ask: Why does Pam Reed . . . why does anyone . . . do this? She did not win a cent for her victory. She has since been interviewed by reporters from Sports Illustrated, Runners World and the Los Angeles Times, but the payoff is neither publicity nor money.

"I just do this for me; I do this for my sanity," she said with a laugh.

Sanity? Running when it's 123 degrees outside?

"My husband, Jim (a Tucson CPA), and I have five kids at home, between the ages of 7 and 17. Running allows me to get away and focus on other things. I don't find it exhausting. I find it exhilarating."

Those who know Pam Reed — she has worked as an aerobics instructor in Tucson, and as a fitness director at the Jewish Community Center — do not find this run-through-hell much of a surprise.

In 1988, she ran the 111-mile El Tour de Tucson cycling course a day before the race, then hopped on a bike and rode it on race day. In 1996, she ran the Bisbee-to-Sierra Vista Mule Marathon, roughly 50 miles, on a Saturday. By Monday, she was at the Boston Marathon.

She plans to run the 100-mile Leadville (Colo.) Ultra-Marathon later this month, at an average elevation of 10,000 feet, and tune up for that by running the Wasatch 100, Utah's longest road race, next week.

Not bad for a former Michigan high school tennis player who stayed in shape by jogging three miles ("it seemed ridiculously long to me then," she said) and evolved into a distance runner when she moved to Tucson in the 1980s.

"She's like Forrest Gump," Bacal said admiringly. "She just keeps going, one step after another. She's a hero."

When Reed and her crew left Death Valley last week, she vowed never to return to Badwater. How many times does one need to climb Everest? But on Thursday, in the mountain air of her family's vacation home in Jackson, Wyo., she softened.

"When I crossed the finish line that day, I said, 'That's it. I'll never do that again.' But now I don't know. I might. It wasn't really that bad."

EDITOR'S NOTE: After becoming the first female to win the Badwater Ultra-Marathon in 2002, Pam Reed won it again the following year. In 2005, she ran 301 miles, nonstop, along the Interstate 10 frontage road between Marana and Picacho Peak to break the unofficial world record of 262 miles — male or female. In 2009, at age 48, Reed participated in the Self-Transcendence Six-Day Race in Flushing, N.Y., where she ran 490 miles.

# Heart of gold: UA softball coach perseveres despite beloved wife's death

*Sunday, December 26, 2004*

*CASA GRANDE*

The most challenging step of Mike Candrea's gold medal journey, 14,000 miles to Greece and back, a softball-across-America tour that stopped in 43 cities, did not confront him until he got home.

Turning off Interstate 10 at McCartney Road in early September, driving the isolated stretch of desert north of Casa Grande, this man of great detail knew he had left one thing undone.

As he stood outside his Pinal County home on rural Martin Road, Candrea faced the grief of entering an empty house.

"I paused in front of the door," he says. "I knew that Sue wouldn't be there. The whole Olympic thing was over and I was back home, alone. It was a big step for me."

Last week, five months after Sue Candrea had died of a brain aneurysm in a small-town Wisconsin hospital, her husband of 27 years stood in "her kitchen" as their son, Mikel, finished washing the breakfast dishes.

Sue Candrea paid the bills, bought the groceries, cooked the food, cleaned the house. Now it's a team effort.

One of the many plaques in the warm and comfortable home says: "WE INTERRUPT THIS MARRIAGE TO BRING YOU THE SOFTBALL SEASON."

At 49, Mike Candrea has blazed through life's stop signs and punched the accelerator. The softball season is on. His schedule is not full; it is overflowing. He does not have an open weekend until June. He has spent just one night alone since returning from his triumphant if lonely Olympic odyssey.

Although it has yet to be announced, he will coach the United States at the 2008 Beijing Olympics.

"I would not want to see someone given the burden of trying to live up to what we accomplished," he said.

He has no plans to leave college coaching. In fact, he was so eager to return to his spot as Arizona's coach that he moved the fall season up two weeks.

Last weekend, his annual winter softball camp in Tucson attracted

215 young girls, up from the usual 125 or 150. This time there were campers from everywhere: Virginia, Canada, Illinois, Kansas, Montana, Washington. Ordinarily, it's a regional camp.

"We didn't even advertise," Candrea said. "I used to take a few photos with the girls, but this year I must've taken hundreds."

Candrea was not awarded a gold medal in Athens; no coaches are included in the medal ceremony. Nor was he pictured on the cover of Sports Illustrated that proclaimed his incomparable softball squad "The Real Dream Team."

But, unmistakably, it was his team. He significantly changed the roster from the 2000 Sydney Olympics. He spent four years in meticulous preparation, involving biomechanics, physiologists, nutritionists, psychologists and even the Navy Seals to get Team USA ready for two weeks in Greece.

Final score: America 51, World 1.

It was similar to the excellence Candrea produced while winning six NCAA championships at Arizona.

The sad irony was that at the precise moment of Candrea's career victory — "On Top of the World," Sports Illustrated proclaimed — his personal life had come tumbling down.

Not that Candrea has been left to grieve alone. His mother lives in a house on his property. Mikel has moved home and usually accompanies his father on the daily commute to and from Tucson. His daughter, Michelle, lives nearby, in Phoenix. A sister lives down the street. In-laws surround him.

The world's best softball player, USA pitcher Lisa Fernandez, calls frequently. He gets more e-mail from the softball community than he ever imagined. Lute Olson, whose wife, Bobbi, died in 2001, took him to lunch. Ex-Wildcat basketball standout Richard Jefferson sought out Candrea in the Olympic village and gave him a hug.

One phone call last week was from former UA football coach Dick Tomey.

" Dick said he was thinking about me and wanted to talk," Candrea said. "He was sitting in his car in a parking lot somewhere. Amazing.

"The web of friends created by softball has just floored me. There's so much more to life than winning a ballgame. I think people are scared to leave me alone. "

After Team USA rolled to the gold medal, dispatching Australia 5-1 (in the closest U.S. softball game of the Olympiad), inscrutable Japan coach Taeko Utsugi approached Candrea before the medal ceremony.

Utsugi, an intense, drill-sergeant type of coach, handed Candrea $100 in American bills. An interpreter indicated the money was meant to purchase flowers for Sue. The Japanese coach hugged Candrea, stepped back and then, with both hands, popped him in the chest. And then she did it again.

"It was her way of saying 'stay tough,'" said Candrea, his eyes filling with tears. "Staying tough; it's a universal language."

Candrea isn't sure how long he'll coach at Arizona. His UA salary, about $95,000, is far less than what he makes from speaking engagements, video instruction, summer and winter camps, endorsements for equipment manufacturers and as a USA Softball coach.

But he burns to win another NCAA title, the seventh, and he has no plans to relocate to Tucson. His passion for coaching has not ebbed.

"My tranquility, my peace of mind, comes from the drive home each night," he said. "I guess someday I should move to Tucson. I mean, if I go play golf somewhere I drive to Tucson, but I've still got so much here. My family. My friends. Sometimes I feel as if Sue is still around. Besides, if I moved to Tucson I'd spend all my time in the office. This is better."

When he was 41, Candrea said publicly that he could not picture himself coaching at 50. Now, committed to another Olympic push, revitalized by his daily relationships with the Wildcat team and his UA staff, his life unalterably changed, he puts no age, no date on his plans.

He's healthy, down 25 pounds to about 175, a reflection of his latter-day running program. He has a summer home in Pinetop that he'd like to visit more frequently. He'd like give some attention to his once-sharp golf game.

His calendar is full.

This weekend, Candrea planned to visit Sue at the Casa Grande cemetery, another difficult journey, a place he has not been since that awful July day.

"I've grieved, and I continue to grieve," he said.

"But I'm making strides in the right way. In the last year, I've gone through the highest of highs and the lowest of lows. In some ways, I'm just getting started."

# Remembering Polkey: California hometown holds service in high school gym

*Monday, October 3, 2005*

*HANFORD, Calif.*

Bullpup Gymnasium seats about 1,800 for basketball games and it was often full to overflowing when the Hanford High School girls won the 2001 state championship.

But when the baskets are raised and folding chairs are set up on the court for special occasions, capacity climbs to about 2,300.

On Sunday, sadly, the chairs were on the court, the baskets were up and about 2,000 people from this agricultural area in Central California came to say their goodbyes to Shawntinice Polk.

"It's ironic," Hanford High School principal Steve France said, "but we never lost a game in this gym when Polkey was playing."

On Sunday, it was much more than a loss.

It was a funeral.

Polk — Polkey to most who knew her and a three-time All-Pac-10 basketball center — died last Monday in Tucson of a blood clot that traveled from her leg to her lungs.

"Polkey was dynamic, energetic, stubborn and delightful," said France. "I would like to say that we came out here today to say hello to her, to welcome her back home, but that's not the way it is."

UA athletic director Jim Livengood, standing alone near a bus that would take the UA women's basketball team to a nearby airport, said that Sunday's memorial was not the end of Polkey and her association with the school.

"This is just the beginning," he said, quietly. "We now have to learn, day to day, how to deal with this loss. It's going to be very difficult."

Sunday's service was especially difficult for UA women's basketball coach Joan Bonvicini, who recruited Polkey out of the same gymnasium five years ago.

When the public viewing began at noon, Bonvicini walked alone from one baseline to the other until arriving at the place where Polkey lay in an open casket.

257

The coach stood motionless for a few minutes, a handkerchief to her mouth. She bent over and said something into Polkey's ear.

An hour later, Bonvicini returned and did the same thing.

Then she walked around the gym, looking at mementos of Polkey's career, displayed on two walls, including her high school jersey No. 00.

"It was on this floor that Polkey showed up as a freshman, trying out for the team," said Hanford girls basketball coach Dwayne Tubbs.

"Before she was a freshman, we had a rule that freshmen couldn't play on the varsity. She knew it. She told me that she was unclear about her chances to make the team."

Tubbs laughed, his puffy eyes hidden by dark glasses.

"I didn't tell her this, but she's the reason we changed that rule," he said. "That was Polkey. She could never understand what all the fuss was about."

As shocked as the Tucson basketball community was by Polk's death, the small town of Hanford first reacted with a sense of disbelief.

"Just impossible," said France. "Not Polkey. It still doesn't sink in.

"I remember a day, her senior year, that we had a signing party in this gym. She was to sign her letter to attend Arizona and she had a real glow about her."

On the lawn outside the gymnasium, as the funeral procession began its move to a nearby cemetery, dozens of people could be heard sobbing.

"This is a deep wound," said the Rev. James Tubbs. "We have an ache on the inside that can't be breached."

Don Fielder, a history teacher at Hanford, remembered a talk he had with Polkey during her senior year. It was about homework. The teacher wanted her to do better. Polkey, stubborn, questioned the value of doing homework.

"I told her, 'Polkey, you have an opportunity for someone to pay for your college education. If you don't do your homework, you'll be throwing away a lot of money. If you do your work, someday you'll come back here and tell me that you're rich,' " Fielder recalled.

A year or two later, the door to Fielder's history class swung open and Polkey, a star in the Pac-10, walked in unannounced.

" 'Mr. Fielder,' she said, 'I'm rich.' "

And so are we, for the brief privilege of having known Shawntinice Polk.

EDITOR'S NOTE: The University of Arizona posthumously retired Shawntinice Polk's jersey No. 00 on Feb. 18, 2006. She is the only player in program history to receive such an honor.

Until her tragic death in 2005, Shawntinice Polk was a transcendent sports figure in Tucson as the star of the Arizona women's basketball team.

White Sox manager Ozzie Guillen jokes with players during spring training in 2004. Of his famously zany antics, Guillen said, "I'm not an actor. I'm the truth."

A.E. ARAIZA

# Mouth of the South (Side): Ozzie Guillen has an opinion on everything, but nobody on the championship side of town seems to mind

*Sunday, February 26, 2006*

Ozzie Guillen admits twice to being at the Chicago-based "The Jerry Springer Show" last season. Uninvited. Unknown. Undetected. Just another witness to some daytime bedlam.

"I wanted to see the real thing," he says. "It's all an act."

He is asked if he, too, is an act. The unfiltered opinions. The uncensored language. The daring against-the-book strategy. The willingness to take on anyone.

"I'm not an actor," he says. "I'm the truth."

Imagine Ozzie Guillen on the "The Jerry Springer Show," on stage, not in the audience. Now wouldn't that send the ratings into orbit? Imagine a breathless baseball commissioner Bud Selig.

In a world without Ozzie Guillen, baseball would not have created any buzz in a decidedly cold Hot Stove League.

In his quiet time over the winter, Guillen told HBO that billionaire Bill Gates could not have survived Guillen's Venezuelan upbringing, and that former Chicago Bulls coach Phil Jackson was "not good," but rather blessed by good players. He confessed that the day he interviewed to become White Sox manager, in 2003, he was hung over.

He told Sports Illustrated that Alex Rodriguez is a butt-kissing hypocrite and that he, Guillen, is more popular in his home country, Venezuela, than Hugo Chavez, its leftist president.

In between, he set off a minor furor in Chicago and Washington by skipping the White Sox celebratory visit to the White House. And, oh yes, in January he became a United States citizen, telling reporters after the ceremony that his answer to the question, "Who is the mayor of Chicago?" was "Ozzie Guillen."

In the staid old game of baseball, Ozzie Guillen is doing the half-pipe on a daily basis.

There has not been anyone like Ozzie Guillen in baseball. Not now, not ever. Casey Stengel managed with house money. Tommy Lasorda was scripted. Leo Durocher was image-conscious, and at times, mean-spirited.

Guillen, fearless, is doing this by-the-seat-of-his-pants routine literally by the seat of his pants.

"Ozzie is so out front that no one is offended by what he does," White Sox catcher A.J. Pierzynski says. "He is consistent."

On Chicago's first full day of workouts in Tucson, Guillen sat in a golf cart and told stories about himself, rather than watch his pitchers and catchers execute cutoff plays.

"To me," he said, "I'm the face of this (expletive) ball club."

In a 30-minute interview, the (expletive) button was pushed every eight or nine words.

He said he spent the previous night, his first in Tucson, watching a CNBC program on the U.S. penal system. It was his way of explaining how far he has come and how much he appreciates the opportunity baseball has given him. (He earned about $23 million in his career, a glove-first shortstop who three times made the American League All-Star team.)

"If Venezuela jails were like those here, people would be saying, 'I did it! I did it!' It would be like the Motel 6 to them. They would get food. A bed. Showers. In Venezuela, I have been to the prison. There are 33 people in one cell."

The education system? "I was driving by Cholla High School this morning," he said. "It would be the best college in Caracas. It's a (expletive) palace."

The White Sox won 99 games in Guillen's second year as manager. They went 11-1 in the postseason, sweeping the Astros in the World Series. It caught the establishment by surprise. Guillen was discovered overnight. The underdog story never fails.

"I thought Ozzie was in over his head," ESPN's Peter Gammons said last week. "We were all wrong on that."

Now 42, Guillen was raised in Venezuela by his mother, a school administrator, yet he did not graduate from high school. He was signed by the Padres before he was 17, sent to the minor leagues, unable to speak English. His survival skills did him well.

He spent 13 seasons as Chicago's shortstop and put in a relatively brief time on the coaching staffs in Montreal and Florida. His uncommon energy attracted the long-moribund White Sox.

General manager Ken Williams has suggested that Ozzie deploy the no-comment card periodically. Instead, Guillen has not met a question, no matter how politically incorrect or insensitive, he doesn't like.

"I don't give a (expletive)," he said.

Guillen now has a beach house and a boat four hours from his Venezuelan home. He said a perfect day would be sitting on his boat, drinking coconut milk and scotch while looking at the "blue water." While in Tucson this spring, he said he expects to play golf five days a week.

Baseball? Who's got time for baseball? He laughs and adds a few expletives. You don't know if he is kidding. You never know when he is kidding.

Next subject: religion.

"How did they come up with that heaven and hell (expletive)?" he asked. "How does anybody know? They put you in the ground and throw a lot of dirt on your little butt." He laughed. He was rolling.

"Hell is getting up every morning in Chicago and turning (sports talk) radio on. But I love it. They rip me. I don't mind at all. Maybe sometimes I'll hear something that will actually help me."

At this time and place, Ozzie Guillen does not need much help. The White Sox have pitching, speed and defense. Their bullpen is tight. They changed personnel just enough to transition from satisfied to hungry. They are what the Yankees wish they could be.

And yet the man on HBO, the man featured in Sports Illustrated, the man most prominent in the Chicago dailies, is Ozzie Guillen. True to his own words, the spitfire manager has become the face of baseball's best club.

EDITOR'S NOTE: The Chicago White Sox left their spring training home in Tucson in 2009 for a new facility in Glendale, a complex they share with the Los Angeles Dodgers.

A running list of Jay Dobyns' adventures: local schoolboy, college football star, federal law enforcement agent, biker-gang infiltrator, nonfiction author.

KELLY PRESNELL

# Life as Hells Angel a perilous existence for ex-UA receiver

*Tuesday, May 2, 2006*

The last time I talked to Jay Dobyns, maybe 1998, a chance meeting at McKale Center, he told me he was "neck-deep in violent crime" and someday I should write a book about it.

His arms were covered with menacing tattoos, one of them a skull. His head was shaved. He wore two earrings.

It was not the Jay Dobyns pictured on the cover of Arizona's 1984 football media guide.

I saw him four or five years later, idling on a very large, very loud motorcycle near Speedway and Craycroft. He had a pistol tucked into the back of his black leather pants. I could clearly see the gun as he sat at the stoplight. I looked away, hopeful he would not recognize me.

He looked more like a Hells Angel than a Hells Angel himself. I drove away thinking that someday soon I would be reading Jay Dobyns' obituary.

This was not the same man who once was pictured in 12-foot-high billboards all over Tucson, a marketing vehicle for the 1984 UA football season.

Upon graduation from Sahuaro High School in 1980, Dobyns caught 103 passes for the Wildcats. He was a personable and approachable athlete, an epitome of the toughness that defined Larry Smith's UA football teams. The latter-day Dobyns did not suggest toughness. He suggested violence.

Dobyns had been shot in the back at point-blank range in 1987, a hostage while on a Tucson undercover assignment for the U.S. Bureau of Alcohol, Tobacco and Firearms. It was his first week as an ATF agent. He should have died. It was in all the local papers.

But I naively assumed he would be given a nice settlement, a monthly disability check and go into something that did not involve bleeding.

Now we know that getting shot did nothing to change Dobyns' career plans. He is one of the lead subjects of a recently released book, "Angels of Death — Inside the Biker Gangs' Crime Empire." I read it over the weekend. It all but made me ill. Whatever the ATF pays Dobyns, it cannot possibly be enough.

The book's authors, Julian Sher and William Marsden, quote Dobyns as saying, "I'm not a worrier; it's not my thing."

This from a man, who, after recovering from his gunshot wound in 1987, was transferred to Chicago. In his first assignment, he was hit by a car; the man driving the car was shooting at Dobyns with a machine gun. After that, Dobyns successfully infiltrated the Calabrese organized-crime family.

Sher and Marsden write that both the Hells Angels and the Aryan Brotherhood have enlisted hit men to find and kill Dobyns. They write that Dobyns and his family have moved repeatedly, from safe house to safe house, from state to state, to dodge revenge-bent biker gangs that Dobyns infiltrated and the government indicted in 2004-05.

"The ATF would've had to look long and hard to find a better candidate than Jay Dobyns to penetrate the Hells Angels," Sher and Marsden write. "Everything about him was pure outlaw biker. His tall, lean, muscular body and his fiery, challenging eyes seem to warn you to keep back, this guy could explode. He had rings on every finger and chains around his neck."

Tom Mangan, public information officer of the Phoenix office of ATF, on Monday declined to comment on Dobyns and the book.

For several years, Dobyns was a Hells Angel. He lived their life. He attended their weddings and their birthday celebrations. Sometimes he would be gone from his wife and two children for a month at a time, all to gather evidence that would someday put a biker in jail.

"I could see my family slipping away," he says in the book. "My kids don't care that I'm trying to be a Hells Angel. My kids don't care that I was trying to impact crime in the community. All they want is for Dad to come home, to be there and love them. This kind of work eats families alive."

While a UA football player, Dobyns was a possession receiver. That is another way of saying he was willing to go across the middle and get hit. At the time, I thought the toughness thing was related strictly to Dobyns' zeal to be a football player. Now, upon reading "Angels of Death," I understand that the toughness thing is part of his being.

His obsession with catching footballs is probably unprecedented at the UA. He once estimated he had caught more than 10,000 passes as a young ballplayer, all so that he would be prepared for the Big Moment, such as his last-minute, game-winning catch to beat UCLA 27-24 in 1983.

His life as an ATF agent has a similar theme. He is obsessed not with catching footballs but with catching felons. The big difference for Dobyns is that this pursuit might never end.

# Smith happiest at UA, shed tears that proved it

*Tuesday, January 29, 2008*

In his seven seasons as Arizona's football coach, Larry Smith always seemed to lead the league in tears spilled.

His team stunned No. 1 USC in 1981. The coach choked up.

In 1982, the Wildcats went to Notre Dame and shocked the undefeated Fighting Irish. It turned into a tear-jerker.

And after each of the UA's celebrated victories over Arizona State — five in succession, 1982-86 — Smith would emerge from a joyous Wildcat locker room sniffling, dabbing at his eyes.

"Those doggone guys just wouldn't quit," he would say. "I love every one of those dang guys."

Inevitably, his indomitable wife, Cheryl, would tug at his arm and say, "C'mon, Larry, they've heard it all before. Let's go; we've got kids to get to bed."

He didn't take himself too seriously.

On a Sunday afternoon at the conclusion of his final Arizona season, a few days before New Year's Eve, 1986, Smith drove to the home of UA athletic director Cedric Dempsey. Smith was going to resign. He would accept a lucrative contract to become the coach at USC. He barely made it into Dempsey's living room before choking up.

"He was so emotional; he came in and started hugging me, crying, saying he really didn't want to go," Dempsey said Monday. "He said 'I've got to go, Ced, it's USC. I've got no choice. I feel like I've got to chase the rainbow.' Larry went to USC, but he was probably as happy in Tucson as he ever was anywhere."

Larry Smith died Monday. He was only 68, built like John Wayne, seemingly indestructible, but danged (one of his favorite words) that he couldn't beat the double team of lymphoma and leukemia the way he used to beat ASU and UCLA. He was an old-school guy, a blue-collar Ohio laborer's son who would play at Bowling Green and coach with Bo Schembechler at Michigan. When he left coaching in 2002, Smith returned to Tucson so he could be with his five grandchildren.

During a scrimmage at Arizona Stadium last spring, Smith chased a grandson rather than watch the blocking and tackling.

"I'm going to take him to the carwash," Smith said, exiting early. "He loves going through the carwash. I get such a kick out of watching him."

Priorities: aligned.

Sitting in the press box at an Arizona football game last fall, Smith spoke fondly of his days as a high school ballplayer when a "big night out" in Lima, Ohio, was watching TV while munching popcorn and eating apples. You can't talk about the life of Larry Smith without putting a white picket fence around it.

"My vision of Larry is of a very muscular, big, good-looking guy," said former UA head coach Jim Young, who brought Smith to Tucson as his defensive coordinator in 1973. "And that's how I'm going to think of him."

Smith's UA career had the predictable turbulence of any college football coach. He battled with the fans when he thought they booed his quarterback unfairly. He failed by a whisker to get to the Rose Bowl in 1985 and 1986, unable to prevail in must-win games against UCLA. And when he left for USC, he did so almost overnight, without a proper goodbye.

He told me several times he regretted the timing of his departure and wished Arizona fans could forgive him.

Smith's best player, UA Hall of Fame linebacker Ricky Hunley, learned of his coach's death Monday. He booked a flight at the Cincinnati airport and immediately left for Tucson.

"The influence he had on my life goes beyond words," said Hunley. "I had absentee fathers in my life, in and out, but Larry was always there. My mother loves him dearly. She is so upset, crying."

As part of his team's underdog persona, Smith recruited Sunnyside High School's 5-foot-6-inch David Adams, a tailback who in 1986 made the All-Pac-10 team and gained in excess of 1,000 yards. Smith was the only major-college coach to visit Adams' home.

Smith was uncanny that way. He invited 1987 consensus All-America safety Chuck Cecil to be part of the team when no other major-college team gave him an offer. He persuaded Phoenix South Mountain basketball player Byron Evans to play football for the Wildcats. In 1986, Evans became the Pac-10's premier linebacker and went on to prominence in the NFL.

But it was Smith's relationship with Adams that probably best reflects the spirit of Smith and those UA football teams, 1980-86.

"Coach Smith came to my house and met my mom," Adams said Monday. "She liked those old-school guys like him. He would say 'yes ma'am' and 'no ma'am.' He told her that he would take care of me and give me an opportunity.

"My mom said 'David, I don't know a thing about football, but I know a lot about people. You go play for Larry Smith. There's a man you can trust.'"

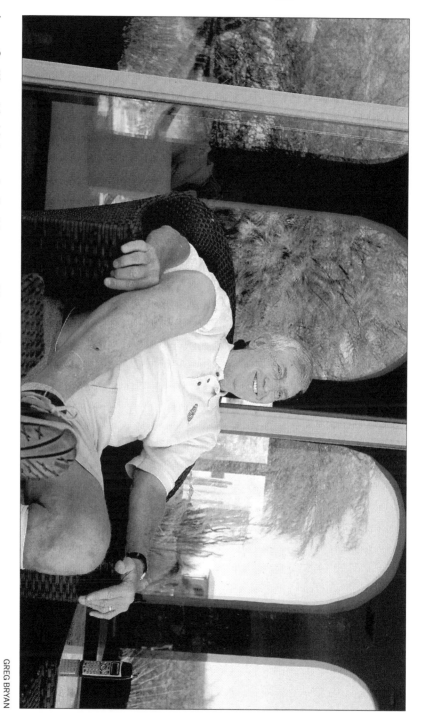

Larry Smith guided Arizona football to some of its most historic wins. His legacy, though, is less about football than it is about being "a man you can trust."

GREG BRYAN

# CHAPTER EIGHT

# Hansen's lists

## Some records appear safe at UA

*Thursday, June 7, 2001*

Before it could be said that Jennie Finch's 32-0 pitching record is unassailable, along comes the UA's top incoming softball recruit, Marissa Marzan of Fresno, Calif.

She had an ERA of 0.00 in 26 games this year. Marzan pitched 13 no-hitters. She walked a mere six batters in 184 innings. These are not typos.

In UA softball terms, unassailable has taken on a new meaning. Finch's 32-0 record trumped Susie Parra's 33-1 school record. Parra had erased Debby Day's once-untouchable 32-5 record.

This trend suggests that one of Mike Candrea's pitchers is ultimately going to finish 34-0, or maybe even 40-0. Is nothing sacred?

I will, however, give you 10 modern UA records that, like Joe DiMaggio's 56-game hitting streak and Wilt Chamberlain's 50-point scoring average, have little to fear.

**1. Ontiwaun Carter carries 815 times.** Say this for Dick Tomey: He wasn't shy about giving Carter the ball and letting him take a pounding. By the time he completed his UA career, he not only became the first UA tailback to carry the ball 800 times, he became the first to reach 700 carries. No one else has more than 649. Wildcat freshman Clarence Farmer rushed 138 times last fall; he needs to average 222 carries per year to reach Carter. Farmer weighs 210 pounds and is the visual definition of durable. Yet it was Carter, maybe 170 pounds on a day he ate a steak, who went four years without serious injury.

**2. Vance Johnson long jumps 26 feet 11¼ inches.** Long-jump 26-11 these days and you're on the Olympic team. (Johnson missed a 1984 Olympic spot by 3 inches). This nation is not producing 26-foot long jumpers in bunches, and rarely at all. That UA record is so secure that the second-best leap, 26-9, set by current UA associate AD Gayle Hopkins in

1964, came during an era the event was known as the broad jump.

**3. Alison McCutcheon bats .466 for her career.** In three years as a UA outfielder, McCutcheon batted .534, .490 and .450. She hit 'em where they ain't: slap bunts between third and short, bloopers to center field. It was 50-50 she'd beat out any infield grounder. Her .466 career average is better than any hitter in college softball in 2001 (high: .458). McCutcheon's speed set her apart from the rest, and gives her another record unlikely to be toppled anytime soon. She stole 67 bases in 1998. No Wildcat had more than 38 this year; no one in college softball reached 50.

**4. Ryk Neethling scores 216 points in the NCAA swimming finals.** Win a national swimming title and you receive 20 points. Over four years, you would need 10 NCAA championships and 16 points elsewhere merely to equal Neethling's prodigious haul. You would need to be Mark Spitz. There's more. Neethling helped the UA score another 132 points on relay teams. And "helped" isn't an appropriate word. Without Neethling on the anchor leg, the UA's 132 relay points might have been closer to 32.

**5. Steve Kerr shoots .573 from three-point distance.** Kerr didn't just get hot in 1988; he was incandescent. No other Wildcat has even shot 50 percent from three-point range in a season (Chris Mills is second at .483). And it's not like Kerr qualified with a minimum of attempts. He made 114 treys that season, the only player in Pac-10 history ever to hit 100. No wonder he has earned more than $15 million in the NBA.

**6. Dan Schneider strikes out 186 batters.** In the mid-'80s, Joe Magrane was a dominating UA left-hander, a first-round pick of the St. Louis Cardinals who would start two World Series games. He pitched an overload of 149 innings in his best season at Arizona, 1985, and yet he, like every other Wildcat pitcher in the last three decades, failed to come within 45 strikeouts of Schneider's total. The Milwaukee Braves were so impressed with Schneider that they paid him a $100,000 bonus to leave the UA after the '62 season, believed to be a major-league record bonus at the time.

**7. The UA men's golf team is ranked No. 1 in five of six years.** Competition at the top level of college golf is so intense, that it's unlikely a Wildcat team — men's or women's — will ever match or exceed what Rick LaRose's club did from 1987-88 to 1992-93. Those teams produced a U.S. Amateur finalist, five first-team All-Americans and four PGA Tour pros.

**8. Tommy Hinzo steals 88 bases in two seasons.** The swift second baseman, a leadoff batter on Arizona's 1986 NCAA title club, stole 43 bases in '85 and 45 a year later. No Wildcat has stolen even 30 bases in a season since. This year's UA leader had 12. College baseball has become a game of three-run homers.

**9. Tedy Bruschi gets 19 quarterback sacks.** By the time Bruschi completed his UA career, he had 52.5 sacks, tied for the NCAA lead. But it was his sophomore year, 1993, in which he was credited with 19 sacks that is out of reach. Consider this: No other UA player has had more than 14.5 sacks in a year — and that was Bruschi, in 1995.

**10. Arizona wins 71 consecutive games at McKale.** From Dec. 4, 1987, to Jan. 11, 1992, the Wildcats went 71-0 at McKale Center. Two of those victories came against Duke. Don't count on Lute Olson putting together another run at the school-record 81-game streak (1947-52). The Pac-10 has a forest of Top 25-types now, which it lacked a decade ago. The change in the way the game is played, with marquee players splitting after two or three seasons, also suggests that the Wildcats — that anybody — will not be able to load up with upperclassmen and win 71 straight again, anywhere.

EMMETT JORDAN

Lute Olson piloted the UA men's basketball team to a 71-game winning streak at McKale Center from 1987 to 1992 — one of the school's remarkable records.

Sean Elliott holds a news conference in the Arizona Wildcats' locker room after setting the all-time Pac-10 Conference scoring record on Feb. 18, 1989.

# The 7 best days in Tucson sports history are ...

*Sunday, February 25, 2007*

Greg Hansen has picked his greatest days in Tucson-area sports history. These events all took place in and around Tucson. So, for example, the Arizona men's basketball team's NCAA championship in 1997 is not among them.

• **Jan. 19, 1945:** The inaugural Tucson Open is held at El Rio Country Club. The field includes Sam Snead, Byron Nelson and the first woman ever to play in a tour event, Babe Zaharias. The '45 event established Tucson as a regular on the PGA Tour.

• **March 10, 1951:** The New York Yankees made their spring training debut at Randolph Park. All the epic names were there: Joe DiMaggio, Mickey Mantle, Yogi Berra and manager Casey Stengel. A capacity crowd of 5,380 attended. The Yankees' visit to Tucson gave legitimacy to Tucson's presence on the big-league spring training circuit and helped to change the modern image of Tucson.

• **Dec. 17, 1976:** The Arizona Board of Regents agrees to admit the University of Arizona into the Pacific-8 Conference (now known as the Pac-10), a move aggressively pursued by then-UA President John Schaefer. In effect, it separated Tucson from mid-tier Western cities like Albuquerque, El Paso and Salt Lake City. The Wildcats begin league competition in September 1978 in an Arizona Stadium football game against Oregon State, winning 21-7.

• **Feb. 18, 1989:** Sean Elliott becomes the Pac-10's career scoring leader, pouring in 35 points in a McKale Center victory over UCLA. Elliott, from Cholla High School, finished with 2,555 points. UCLA's Lew Alcindor, later Kareem Abdul-Jabbar, had 2,325 in his career. Arizona, en route to a 17-1 Pac-10 record, was ranked No. 1 at game time.

• **Sept. 13, 1991:** Twenty-three years after being awarded a Pacific Coast League franchise, the Tucson Toros win their first championship. A two-out, bottom-of-the-ninth single by Joe Mikulik scored pinch runner Trenidad Hubbard with the deciding run in a 4-3 victory over Calgary. An overflow crowd of 8,919 attended at Hi Corbett Field.

• **Nov. 8, 1992:** Desert Swarm comes of age as the UA shocks No. 1-ranked and defending national co-champion Washington 16-3 at Arizona Stadium. The Tedy Bruschi-led defense triggered a three-year period in which the Wildcats won 24 games and were generally considered the NCAA's top defensive team.

• **Feb. 26, 2006:** The PGA Tour announces that Tucson will from 2007 to 2010 be the site of the WGC-Accenture Match Play Championship, one of the eight most prominent golf events in the world. The purse of $8 million more than doubles the $3 million purse of the encumbered Chrysler Classic of Tucson.

DAVID SANDERS

Tucson Toros players spark a wild celebration on the turf at Hi Corbett Field after they won the Pacific Coast League championship in 1991.

# A century of Tucson sports: 11 who made a difference

*Summer 1999*

At the end of the century, after becoming familiar with the history of sports in Tucson, I thought many people who had made a mark had been forgotten or overlooked.

The timing was right to find the following 11 people, reflect on their careers and, selfishly, get to know them. I felt like I had missed something by not being around when they were significant contributors to the Tucson sports landscape.

**Greg Hansen**

PHOTO ILLUSTRATIONS BY AARON J. LATHAM

# A century of Tucson sports: Fred Enke

*Sunday, June 6, 1999*

Mo Udall typed and Fred Enke looked over his shoulder. The words were foreign to college football in 1948: no-cut contract; signing bonus; a salary of $12,000.

Until then, Mo Udall's business expertise was giving his basketball teammates haircuts: 25 cents per head. But this was '48, the war was over, and sports were changing.

Fred W. Enke, UA's most distinguished athlete of the half-century, had two years of college eligibility remaining — his father, Fred A. Enke, was part of the Wildcat coaching staff — and here he was hammering out contract terms with the Detroit Lions. He had some leverage — the New York Yankees of the old All-America Football Conference had drafted him, setting off a mild auction — and he was coming off a season in which he led the NCAA in total offense, 1,941 yards, the first Wildcat ever to make The Associated Press All-America (third) team.

"Mo was my agent," Enke says now, chuckling at the memory. "He was probably the first agent in college football. He was pretty sharp. After he typed up all the clauses, he insisted that he be paid $100 for putting the contract together. And he insisted on a $100 bill. I can't tell you how nervous I was handing that money over to him."

Until that time, Enke didn't have a car, or even a sport coat. What he had was an athletic career in Tucson that was second to none. He was the baseball captain and an All-Border Conference outfielder, a starting guard on the first UA basketball team that reached postseason play, the 1946 NIT. He had barely completed half of his college eligibility when he took the money and began a seven-year NFL career.

"No one tried to stop me, not even Pappy," he says, his endearing term for his father who coached at UA from 1925 to 1961.

Fred W. Enke is 75 now. Both of his knees and a hip are now wired with titanium, the result of all of those days playing one ballgame after another. He is a millionaire, a retired farmer whose farm in Casa Grande — at one time he owned 3,200 acres on which he grew cotton, barley, wheat, lettuce, you name it — is a not-so-subtle reminder that one of the state's ranking sports legends lives there. He has a lighted tennis court, which is his current passion, a putting green, a volleyball

279

court, basketball standards and a driving range.

"I was in good shape until I was 65," he says. But that's just him. He still carries himself with dignity, and barely a limp. He has a presence.

"When he walks into one of our reunions," says Bob Carter, a boyhood friend of Enke's who has returned to Tucson after a corporate business career in Michigan, "people turn their heads and watch him."

**Not just good, the best**

Heads turn in admiration just like they would for any person who might be considered Tucson's greatest athlete ever. And the closure of this century marks a perfect time to incite the debate. Who was Tucson's best athlete? Enke? Joe Batiste? Michael Bates? It is not necessary to disqualify any of those who come to mind, but rather to accept that it is impossible to make an exact determination.

Few, if any, were more successful in America's three major sports than Fred W. Enke. Few, if any, were staged for a career in athletics the way Enke was.

"Freddy was good in everything," says George Genung, who played on the '46 UA basketball team with Enke. "And not just good, the best."

The Enke family is German in origin, Minnesotans via immigration. (It's pronounced "UN-ka" in Germany, but "Ink" in Arizona.) His father was, similarly, a three-sport star, at the University of Minnesota, who earned a degree in engineering and had several adventures before settling in Tucson in 1925. In South Dakota, the elder Enke built roads and coached at South Dakota State University, followed by a stint at Louisville. It was either serendipity or just plain luck that in the summer of '25, Fred A. Enke attended a coaching clinic in Indiana at which the great Knute Rockne lectured. One of the things Enke learned from Rockne was that the dusty school in the desert, the relatively new University of Arizona, was searching for a man who could coach basketball, start a golf program and assist with football coaching.

Enke was on a train to Arizona as soon as he could make arrangements. He was hired by Pop McKale for $3,000, and several weeks later drove his wife, Ollie Charline, and 8-month-old son, Fred William — who would be the couple's only child — cross-country in a Model T. It was July. They decided to stay anyway. Across the next 36 years, Fred A. Enke won 511 basketball games as UA's head coach.

His son listened and learned.

"It seemed like I always had a lot of friends, and looking back it's probably because all of the sports equipment was at my house," Fred W.

Enke recollects. "Pap would always have a bat or some basketballs. We just played. We didn't have any formal training — there weren't any camps like kids go to these days — we just played. Sometimes we'd play all day. High school was my best time."

It's unlikely any Tucson schoolboy had a more prolific athletic career than Enke.

### High school to flight school

At Tucson High, he was a first-team All-State athlete in football (1941-42), basketball (1943) and baseball (1943). The Badgers won state titles in all three sports during his days on the varsity. He might've gone elsewhere to college to dodge his father's long-reaching shadow, but in May 1943, graduation day, he chose the U.S. Navy over Arizona and Minnesota and everywhere else.

It took 22 months to get through Flight School and get his wings. He was a dive bomber, a Navy pilot, a hot shot. "We were really going to get them," he says. "But the reality is that the (atomic) bomb saved my life. Six kids on my last baseball team at Tucson High were killed in the war. I would've been No. 7 if we had ever invaded Japan.

"A lot of life is luck."

He had a choice to stay in the Navy for another four years or to get out in December 1945 and return to school. He was 21. Single. He went to Philadelphia with some friends to watch the Army-Navy football game. The temptation to be a pilot was a strong one, but ultimately he and his boyhood friend Lincoln Richmond decided to "go home and play for Pappy."

College basketball in the winter of 1945-46 was vastly different from the game played today. Enke traveled from Philadelphia to Tucson via train and when he reached the family home on Mountain Avenue, just north of Speedway, his mother told him to continue on to San Diego. His father's basketball team was preparing to start the season in a holiday tournament.

So they drove to San Diego. Life began again.

"We weren't even registered in school then," Enke says. "But the war had changed a lot of things. They asked us if we 'intended' to go to school. If so, you could play right away. When we got to San Diego we ran into guys we hadn't seen in three or four years, all of them returning from various war experiences. We shook hands and went out and played."

They won 25 games.

It was the first of several banner seasons under coach Enke that would ultimately lead to berths in six postseason tournaments and several Top 20 polls through 1952. Enke wasn't the star; the best player was his buddy, Richmond. The rest of the team included Genung, Mo and Stew Udall, Tim Ballantyne and Marvin Borodkin. "That's when Tucson really started taking to basketball," Enke says. "Bear Down Gym was filled."

### Gridiron natural

He made his mark in football, a single-wing quarterback in coach Miles Casteel's system that emphasized his instincts, be it running or passing. In a 1947 game against Kansas, Enke accounted for 364 yards of total offense, which was the school record for another 22 years and remains No. 6 in UA history. He had a powerful arm, was a fearless runner, and his instincts were unparalleled.

"He was born to be a ballplayer," says Carter. "He was a natural."

From 1948 to 1951, Enke played quarterback for Detroit, was traded to Philadelphia for a year and completed his career in 1953-54 for the Baltimore Colts. With the merger of the NFL and the All-America Conference, the NFL had all the financial leverage. Enke's starting salary, $12,000, was cut to $7,500. He was good, not great, but had prepared himself for life after football, returning to Tucson in the off-season and getting two degrees, including a master's in education administration.

"I was all set to be a teacher and coach" — he applied to replace Warren Woodson as UA head coach in 1957 but was inexplicably turned down by UA President Richard Harvill — "but it paid about $3,500 a year, and I had bought a nice piece of ground in Maricopa that required a lot of attention."

That nice piece of ground multiplied many times, making him a wealthy man and requiring his attention for the next three decades. He sold much of his property to the UA in 1984 for an estimated $5.2 million.

In a treasured place at his farm in Casa Grande, Enke has what he calls his "stuff room." There is memorabilia from every conceivable part of his, and his father's, athletic careers. State championship trophies. Newspaper headlines. Valued old jerseys. It goes beyond that. At the NFL Hall of Fame in Canton, Ohio, in a section displaying those who played without face-masks, there is a large picture of Enke, Detroit Lions quarterback, being grabbed by a Bears lineman at Wrigley Field in Chicago.

Nor is he forgotten. As recently as a month ago he received unsolicited in the mail a Lions jersey with his name across the shoulders. A fan wanted him to autograph the jersey and return it. "I checked it out," he says. "The jersey cost $179."

It's hard to miss the Enke name on the UA campus. Fred W. Enke's name is one of few in the school's Ring of Honor at Arizona Stadium. And outside the UA football office, just across from Enke Drive, is Enke Plaza, a grassy sanctuary honoring his father, who died in 1983.

"Once in a while, during the football season, we'll get out a blanket and have a tailgate gathering right there, at Enke Plaza," he says. "It really hits you: Pappy came here almost 75 years ago, and now they've got a street and a nice little plaza named in his honor. He really made a mark. We were inducted together, in the original class of the UA's Sports Hall of Fame, in 1976. A lot of good things have happened to the Enke family at the UA."

AUTHOR'S NOTE: Fred W. Enke is retired and continues to live on his sprawling farm on the outskirts of Casa Grande. The wear and tear of pro football required him to have hip- and shoulder-replacement surgeries, but he still insists on an occasional game of tennis.

**THE FRED ENKE FILE**
**Born:** Louisville, Ky., 1925
**Family:** Wife, Marjorie, three children
**Education:** Tucson High School; UA
**Occupation:** Retired cotton farmer, Casa Grande; NFL quarterback from 1948 to 1954.
**Athlete he most admired:** Lincoln Richmond, former UA all-conference basketball player.
**Memorable moment in sports:** At the 1946 NIT at Madison Square Garden in New York City, Enke and his UA teammates played with glass backboards for the first time. "It was quite a difference shooting. We fell behind 16-1 and got licked pretty good."
**Best team played on:** 1943 Tucson High baseball team went undefeated to win the state title. Enke was the state's MVP as the Badgers started a 52-game winning streak that would extend over the next two years.
**Quote to remember:** "That lad will become one of the league's best." — NFL Commissioner Bert Bell upon watching Enke in a 1948 game at Philadelphia.

# A century of Tucson sports: George Bland

*Sunday, June 13, 1999*

In the spring of '44, George Bland wrote a letter to his mother, Iris, describing the military cemetery in Epinal, France, in which his brother Ted was buried.

"It's so beautiful here," he wrote. "The cemetery overlooks the Moselle River. I stayed most of the day to be with Ted."

France was free and Germany had surrendered, but the price for George, as millions of others, was inestimable. Ted Bland, 29, was dead.

For the first 19 years of his life, George Bland had been identified most as a second baseman with some pop, and a left halfback who could scoot. And he wasn't even the best athlete in the family. That would be Ted, the most accomplished UA football player of the school's first 35 years, its first All-American.

If you heard the name "Bland" in Tucson it carried athletic clout.

But on that day in France, George Bland, carrying the scars of German shrapnel in his legs, understood that life was much more than ball games. His perspective had forever changed.

"I had gotten out of the war with my health and I was happy for it," he says now. "My mind wasn't shot, and I was appreciative for that. When I got back in Tucson I was walking downtown and I saw a kid on the street that I knew from high school. We called him Stumpy; he was a husky kid, as strong as an ox. I never did know his real name. I saw him in front of the old Penney's store and I called out to him. 'Hey, Stum ...' and just as I said that I saw that he had lost a leg. He had been in the war and he wasn't as fortunate as I had been. I saw quite a few that came back in terrible shape, and Tucson wasn't a very big town in those days. Four or five of my good friends — friends from my baseball and football teams — had been killed."

Who knows what the youngest sons of Allen and Iris Bland would've been had not World War II intruded.

George planned, like Ted, to be a football star at Arizona. But when he returned from Europe 2½ years later, his place in the backfield had been taken by a young hot shot from Texas, Art Pollard.

So George hit the books, which was a nice option considering the 30-month horror he had been through. The books couldn't hit back.

Ted's athletic career was over by the time he was sent to North Africa

285

to fight Gen. Erwin Rommel's troops in 1942. There was no pro football tryout for a 155-pound quarterback whom the local dailies labeled "Tucson's Mighty Mite." And his promise as a baseball player was scuttled when the New York Giants dispatched him to dreary Palestine of the East Texas League, a minor-league post so remote that it encouraged prospects to find work elsewhere.

Ted Bland could take a hint. He found work with the railroad, the Border Patrol and, ultimately, the Army.

## Living with the railroad

Seventeen years before George Bland was born, his father and pregnant mother climbed aboard a train in Houston and headed west. Allen Bland had $5 in his pocket, no job, no real education and no real plan.

It was 1908. The train stopped in Tucson. Allen and Iris got off. Just like that.

It was part adventure, part deliverance and that's what drove Allen Bland. He would no longer walk behind his father's mule, plowing 80 acres of land. Whatever lay ahead, it would be a better life.

It took Allen one day to get a job, at the Southern Pacific Railroad, and it would last a lifetime. The union of Allen and Iris Bland produced the UA's first All-America football player, Ted; and a state championship baseball player, George.

The Southern Pacific Railroad dispatched Allen and Iris to an even more desolate setting, Lordsburg, N.M., beginning a 15-year tour of the Southwest's railway junctions: Bowie, San Simon, Wellton, Sentinel, Yuma. Wherever the Southern Pacific line went, Allen Bland was a useful hand, changing the batteries that kept the signal lights operating; recharging the ones that had gone dead.

The Blands frequently lived in boxcars. "My mother told me it was hell in summertime," George Bland remembers. "Just pure hell."

But it was a living, and Allen Bland worked his way through the system, ultimately getting a much-anticipated assignment in the brake yard in Yuma, and, finally, to Tucson in 1923. This is where they would make a stand and raise their family, three boys, all athletic, all ultimately engulfed by the great world war.

George was the last of the kids, 17 years behind Allan and 11 behind Ted. And who wouldn't want a big brother like Ted Bland? He became a near-legendary figure in pre-war Tucson. A star quarterback, star shortstop, Big Man on Campus. There was nothing Ted Bland couldn't do. Four decades later, when the University of Arizona inaugurated a sports Hall of Fame in 1976, Ted Bland, Class of '35, was in the third group of inductees.

Mighty Mite wouldn't be forgotten.

**A hard 112 pounds**

In the spring of 1942, George Bland was a second baseman who was mildly annoyed that he hit sixth in Tucson High's batting order.

When the Badgers won the state championship on a beautiful Saturday morning in May, Bland went 3 for 4 and scored the winning run in the bottom of the ninth as the Badgers rallied to beat Phoenix North High 3-2.

"(Coach) Hank (Slagle) left me there all year and I didn't like it," Bland says now. "But we won it all, so I guess he knew what he was doing."

Whatever athletic genes were passed on by Allen and Iris, Ted got his share and more. George, by contrast, weighed 112 pounds when he entered Tucson High in the fall of 1939. But it was a hard 112 pounds. Growing up in economically depressed Tucson in the '30s wasn't ideal, especially in summer. There was no air conditioning.

"There was vacant land all around the neighborhood where we lived," he says. "We didn't know it was hot. Hell, that's the way it was. We didn't know anything else. We'd do what all kids did; play cops and robbers, chase coyotes, catch Gila monsters. It was fun. In junior high, we'd play tackle football on a dirt playground. Tackle. No equipment. Our old coach, Frank Sancet, was a tough old guy. A real disciplinarian from the old school. You got tough in a hurry with him around."

On Dec. 6, 1941, George and his high school sweetheart, Avonne (now his wife of 56 years) went to the senior prom at Tucson High. The next morning he heard his mother talking about bombs and Pearl Harbor and war.

"If you could see lightning and hear thunder," he says, "you knew that the war would touch us all."

**Perils of a paratrooper**

From his first training camp, Fort Riley, Kan., where he and Avonne were married, George was assigned to Fort Benning, Ga. He had volunteered for the paratroopers, and not because it was a romantic notion. His Tucson childhood buddy Dan Olney had told him that paratroopers got an $50 extra per month.

So George Bland, ex-second baseman, became a paratrooper.

Letters from home confirmed the worst: George's high school acquaintances were, he recalls, "starting to drop like flies." Five or six of his teammates on the '41 Tucson High football team had already been killed in action.

"It was sad, so sad," he says. "My oldest brother, Allan, was in

Burma, and Ted was in North Africa and I was getting ready to parachute into France. My mother was just a wreck."

Jump school had a simple premise: Four practice jumps in daylight, one night jump, and then on to a staging area in Andover, England, for the Big Jump into occupied France. But it was not as uneventful as it seemed. While sitting on the ground near a drop zone one evening at Fort Benning, Bland and his fellow paratroopers watched as a lumbering C-47 flew overhead to unload the night's first 24 trainees, a dozen per group.

One of the plane's engines exploded and to the horror of those on the ground, the plane did a nose-dive. "Bing, straight down," George says. "Only the two men nearest the door, the jump master and one other guy, got out. Everyone else was killed."

Finally, in August 1944, Bland went overseas with the 17th Airborne Division and he hadn't been there for long when a letter from his mother carried the worst news: After surviving a year of brutal combat in Italy as part of the 36th Infantry Division, Ted had been killed in France.

Compounded by the anxiety of a planned airborne drop into France and an extended separation from Avonne, George's great adventure ebbed. He had heard all about the invasion of France and understood fully that Germany was stubborn about retreating.

What was he doing in the middle of this mess?

He almost froze to death one day en route to the Battle of the Bulge but survived, ironically, when he was hit by shrapnel from a German shell that tore into his thigh, a wound that removed him from combat.

### Giving dentistry a shot

George did not resume his football career at UA, as so many of his pre-war buddies did. He used the GI Bill to get back in school.

"My oldest brother, Allan, put the seed in my mind about being a dentist," he says. "He didn't want me winding up at the railroad. I was still growing up and the war hadn't interrupted my life that badly. I knew I had to get on with it."

Accepted by the Harvard School of Dental Medicine, George moved with Avonne to Massachusetts and began the long haul that would require six years. They would get by, at times, in student housing that cost $16 a month. The GI Bill paid for much of his Harvard tuition. He pieced together the rest.

"They were the happiest times of our life," he says. "We were starving, but it was a great time."

While in dental school, all three of the Blands' children were born: Steve in 1947; Andy in 1950; and Sally in 1952. Upon finishing his internship in Kansas City, George moved back to Tucson, borrowed $6,000 from the Southern Arizona Bank and hung out his shingle; he was one of four oral surgeons in the burgeoning city of Tucson.

His athletic interests changed. He replaced baseball and football with golf, and was among the first 50 Conquistadores, a distinguished service group that for more than three decades has operated the PGA Tour's Tucson Open. He served on the Conquistadores Board of Directors for a decade.

"I've moved outhouses, worked in security, parking, you name it," he says. "I got a kick out of helping with pro golf. Any time you can help your community it gives you a sense of accomplishment."

In 1987, after 35 years of private practice, George retired.

"I met most of my close friends through football, in high school and at the UA, and these are wonderful friendships that have held up over the years," he says. "What else can I say? My kids still talk to me, and my wife seems to love me. You can't get it much better than that."

AUTHOR'S NOTE: George Bland, 84, is retired and lives near the UA. He and his wife, Avonne, spend the summers on the beach near San Diego.

**THE GEORGE BLAND FILE**
**Born:** February 1925, Tucson
**Family:** Married, Avonne, three children
**Education:** Tucson High School; UA; Harvard School of Dental Medicine
**Occupation:** Retired oral surgeon
**Most admired athlete:** Joe Batiste, a former Tucson High football player and world-class sprinter. "There's really no one to compare him to. I think the guy could high jump 6-8 without any training. They wouldn't let him play basketball because (he was black), but I can imagine he'd have been the best at basketball, too."
**Outstanding game:** In the 1941 football season, the Badgers upset undefeated Inglewood, Calif., 27-6 before a crowd of 5,500 at THS. Bland scored the game's first touchdown and recovered a fumble leading to the second score.
**Memorable moment:** "When we won the state baseball championship in 1942, I got three hits. I'll never forget the pitcher from (Phoenix North). I had gotten a lot of hits off fastballs, so they would only throw me curves. And that day I hit those, too."
**Quote to remember:** "When I was in the Army in France, I was in a demolition platoon. We spent time trying to find booby traps. That's not my favorite line of work. Luckily, we didn't find any."

# A century of Tucson sports: Bill Hassey

*Sunday, June 20, 1999*

Pop McKale's way of recruiting Bill Hassey was to stop by Joe's Arizona Liquor Store on Meyer Avenue. Not to buy or imbibe, but to talk baseball with Bill's dad, Joe. He'd pitch the virtues of education and remind Joe that if the scouts from the Yankees and Cardinals were becoming a nuisance, the surest way to get rid of them was to ask for a $1,000 bonus.

That was 1946. Bill Hassey took no one's money and no one's scholarship. He joined the Army. It would be a few years before he cut short his UA career after his freshman season and took $400 to play center field and join the Yankee farm system.

"I was going to be the replacement for Joe DiMaggio," he says now, chuckling. "I'd never heard of Mickey Mantle."

A quarter-century later, Jerry Kindall went to Bill Hassey's house to recruit his son, Ron, and offer him a chance to play for the Wildcats.

Kindall's way of recruiting was less talk and more visual than Pop McKale's. Kindall juggled his schedule so that he could watch 12 Tucson High games in 1972. He wasn't alone. The ranking college baseball coaches of the day, USC's Rod Dedeaux and ASU's Bobby Winkles, were sprinkled through the bleachers as the Badgers went 25-3 and won the state title. Tucson's star shortstop, Ron Hassey, hit .503.

When the moment of truth came — after Ron had taken visits to USC, Texas and Arizona State — Kindall offered something less than a full scholarship.

Ron balked.

Kindall knew that the Hasseys were close to Winkles, the Sun Devil coach who had won national championships in 1965, 1967 and 1969. Bill Hassey and Bobby Winkles were teammates on the Casa Grande Cotton Kings, a national semipro power of the '50s. Winkles played short; Hassey was the center fielder. But were they close enough for a Sun Devil to win over a Wildcat house?

Winkles talked about Ron Hassey's fit into the lineage of great Sun Devils. There would be Reggie Jackson and Sal Bando, Rick Monday and Ron Hassey. Winkles offered a full ride.

Ultimately, Kindall realized that a baseball-playing Hassey didn't come at reduced prices. He coughed up a full scholarship. Four years later, with Ron driving in 86 runs, Arizona won its first NCAA championship.

A generation later, 1998, UA coach Jerry Stitt sat in Ron Hassey's living room and invited Ron's son Brad to play for the Wildcats. Brad accepted.

Don't ask if Grandpa Hassey was excited. "I don't think I missed even a practice this year," Bill says. "It's like I'm starting all over again."

**Tucson's baseball families**

There's not much debate about Tucson's leading baseball family of the century. It's a three-way tie, hopelessly deadlocked among the Hasseys, Kellners and Pagnozzis.

Of the 25 former high school players from Tucson who have reached the big leagues, Tom Pagnozzi, a Rincon catcher for St. Louis, and Alex Kellner, an Amphi left-hander for the Philadelphia A's, are the only two to play in an All-Star Game.

Three Pagnozzis were drafted and played professionally. Three Kellners reached Class AAA or above, and another played for the UA's 1980 national championship team.

The Hasseys remain a work in progress. Bill, 72, spent two years in the Yankees minor-league system; Ron, part of the Oakland A's 1989 World Series champions, spent 13 seasons as a big-league catcher; Brad, a sophomore second baseman at the UA, playing in a collegiate league in New York this summer, is embarking on what he hopes is a professional career.

A case can be made that Bill Hassey was the best high school baseball player in Tucson history.

From 1944 to 1946, he was on the official all-state team. Three years. As a sophomore in 1944, when Tucson High won the fifth in a string of seven consecutive state championships, Hassey was selected the state's MVP.

A sophomore. He batted .556 in the state tournament.

What does it mean to make the All-State team as a sophomore, junior and senior? Just four Arizonans have done it since 1940 — Hassey, Mesa pitcher Phil Ortega, Westwood infielder Dick Harris, and Flagstaff catcher Jamie Dugan.

Modest to a fault, Bill Hassey attempts to shrug off his high school career.

"I can't remember all that much about it," he says. In an attempt to change the subject, he talks about the 1945 Tucson High basketball team.

"We won the state title," he says. "Oh, boy, did we have a lot of good ballplayers on that team: Hosea Thomas, Jim McKissick."

What he doesn't say is that he also made the all-state basketball first-team.

### A Lebanese lineage

There was little reason to expect the descendants of Joseph and Sophie Hassey to be professional athletes.

The family lineage is 100 percent Lebanese. Joe, who grew up in Michigan, drove a cab in Detroit. He didn't play baseball or any sport. Sophie, who is from Newfoundland, was a stay-at-home mom. They moved to Tucson in 1927 so that Joe, ailing, could breathe the clean desert air.

He got a job driving a produce truck, often making the Tucson-to-Los Angeles haul twice a week. In the mid-'30s he bought a liquor store on Meyer Avenue.

Bill, their oldest child, started high school in the wake of what might have been the best core of athletes ever at one high school in Tucson. Linc Richmond, Joe Cherry and John McIntyre were all-state basketball players. Fred Enke, Marshall Littlefield, Joe Valenzuela and Fred Batiste had led the Badgers to state football titles. The baseball program was so good that you couldn't keep track of the first-team all-staters: Bud Grainger, Billy Crowell, Frank Kemph, Gil Carrillo, Emil Rey.

"I'll tell you how much talent we had: In 1946 we played the UA junior varsity and beat them pretty badly," Hassey recalls. "Pop McKale didn't like that at all."

On the day that the Badgers won the 1945 state baseball title, a banner headline in the Star read: "Russians say Hitler and Goebbels committed suicide as Millions of Nazis Surrender."

Hassey got three hits.

By the end of the 1946 high school season, Hassey had a choice to take a full scholarship to play for McKale at Arizona or to join the Army. He took the Army, went to boot camp at Fort Bragg, N.C., and was shipped to the Aleutian Islands where he spent 18 months deciding he should have gone to school.

"McKale wrote me frequently," he says. "The Army wanted me to re-up for three years and join the intelligence agency, but I got out as soon as I could and was back in Tucson for the spring semester in 1948."

Hassey was the Wildcats' starting centerfielder that year, batting .312, catching everything in sight. Against his parents' wishes, a Yankees scout lured him to Ventura, Calif., and offered him $400 to sign and $125 a month. And thus he gave up his college eligibility and drove to Class D Sweetwater, Texas.

It wasn't exactly a garden spot. When Bill and his wife, Delores, checked into their tiny Sweetwater apartment they turned on the lights and almost left town on the spot. "The cockroaches in our apartment outnumbered the people in the town of Sweetwater," he recalls.

Welcome to the minor leagues.

### Injury ends career

Hassey's professional career was scuttled when he suffered a knee injury during spring training the next year. The Yankees sent him to Pampa, Texas, a Class C team in an oil-well town. He batted .299. The reality was that the Yankees were looking for power-hitting outfielders and he was a leadoff man.

A year later, he began a 40-year career in the liquor wholesaling business, and was out of organized baseball. Sort of. Back in Tucson, married and with children (Bill and Delores celebrated their 50th anniversary in October 1999), he played as much baseball and softball as ever. The Casa Grande Cotton Kings were one of America's finest semipro baseball teams, sometimes playing 75 games a year. And on the nights Hassey wasn't playing baseball he was a regional star in some wicked fast-pitch softball leagues.

He was one of the first group of inductees into the Southern Arizona Softball and Baseball Hall of Fame. He played until he was 40. By then he had other interests: Ron had shown a proclivity for baseball, and Bill was a willing teacher.

"Ron was originally a right-handed batter, but he held the bat all wrong so I switched him around and made him a lefty, which is a big advantage for a ballplayer," Bill says. "We'd play Wiffle ball in the backyard all the time. I coached or helped to coach just about every team he ever played on. By the time he was 13 or 14, you could tell he had a chance to be an outstanding ballplayer."

Funny how life offers the same challenges to fathers and sons. After Ron Hassey's junior year at Arizona, 1975, he was drafted by the Kansas City Royals and was tempted to leave school.

The Royals offered a $1,200 bonus, a relative pittance in 1975. The urge to get started in pro ball was nonetheless tempting.

Bill Jackson, the K.C. scout, sat with Bill and Ron Hassey in a Tucson restaurant and told them that although Ron had the ability to be a major-league hitter, he had no real position. He was an All-America third baseman at the UA, but his range was limited.

Jackson told the Hasseys that Ron would be best advised to return to school and become a catcher. The problem was that the Wildcats had two good catchers, Don Houston and Bob Woodside.

With the help of UA pitching coach Jim Wing, Ron Hassey converted to catching. "Best decision we ever made," Bill says. Ron was in the big leagues in two years and ultimately caught more than 1,000 major-league games (including perfect games from Len Barker and Dennis Martinez) and made several million dollars.

"I've always loved baseball," Bill Hassey says. "I've been to World Series games that Ron played in and I've watched him play for the Cubs at Wrigley Field. But I go to all the high school games and I'm down at Tucson Electric Park watching the Sidewinders whenever I can. I enjoy the game at every level.

"I'm rejuvenated now because Brad is playing at the UA. I even go to their practices. That'll give me two or three more years to be at the ballpark. Maybe it'll keep me out of trouble."

AUTHOR'S NOTE: Bill Hassey died in Tucson in 2003. He was 76.

## THE BILL HASSEY FILE
**Born:** Detroit, 1926
**Family:** Wife, Delores; four children: Joe, Ron, Janet, Mary Ann
**Education:** Tucson High School; attended UA, 1948
**Occupation:** Retired, wholesale liquor distributor
**Most admired ballplayer:** "I thought Alex Kellner was the best player I ever saw in Tucson. He was a big old lefty and it was an event just to go out and watch him pitch. After his major-league career, we coached a Little League team together. I played with (former Tucson High standout) Lee Carey in Casa Grande. He was just a great ballplayer."
**Unforgettable moment:** "We were at the 1989 World Series at Candlestick Park when the big earthquake struck. I remember looking at the girders above me and they were just shaking, back and forth. Ron came out of the A's dugout and motioned for us to come down on the field where it would be safer."
**Did you know?** Bill's son Joe, a former general manager of the Tucson Toros, is a national-level racquetball player who has won several state and national age-group racquetball championships.
**Baseball was a different game then:** "When I was playing in Sweetwater, Texas, in 1948, the fans would stick dollar bills through the screen behind home plate after you'd hit a home run. You'd jog by the fence and take them one at a time. The first time I hit a homer down there I got 36 $1 bills. That was pretty good money in those days."

*Tom Black     John Black*

# A century of Tucson sports: Tom Black and John Black

*Sunday, June 27, 1999*

There were times after football practice that John Black walked the seven miles from Tucson High School to the family's combination gas station/dairy farm north of Oracle Jaynes. He'd get home at 10, milk the cows and go to bed.

There were times he got up the next morning and had to walk back, seven miles, hitchhiking if he could, hoofing it when he couldn't.

"Dad didn't believe in football," says John's brother, Tom. "He thought it was a silly game. He'd say, 'If you want to play, get there the best way you can. I've got important things to do.' He was all about work."

One morning in 1934, John Black left home at 6, walking again, so that he could catch a bus that would take the Tucson High junior varsity team to a day game in Douglas.

He got to within a half-block of the school when the bus pulled out. He ran and ran and ran, shouting for the bus to stop. He saw the JV coach look out the window at his 120-pound hamburger-squad end. The coach turned away. The bus rolled on.

"That just tore me up," John Black says now. "If that's how insignificant I was — given what I was going through to play football — the easiest thing would have been for me to quit."

Quit?

The sons of Bonnie Christian "Bon" Black learned a lot of things growing up with a Depression-era father who worked as a miner, a farmer and a dozen other things to keep them a step ahead of the poorhouse. One of the few things they didn't learn was how to quit.

They could tell you about the time Bon, forced out of the slumping copper-mining business, moved from Douglas to Clifton to Tucson trying to pay the rent. They could tell you about the time their father put all his money on a table and gave it to a man eager to sell his little root beer stand on the corner of Drachman Street and Miracle Mile.

"My word is my bond," Bon Black told the man. "I expect yours is, too."

And two weeks later, a bill collector showed up at the root beer stand and told Bon that none of the equipment — the compressor, the refrigerators, the furniture, the stock — had been paid for; he had been bilked.

The Blacks lost their root beer stand. Desperate, John and Tom would sit on the fender of Bon's 1931 Ford station wagon, driving slowly through the neighborhood, selling their mother's tamales.

When that failed to provide a living for the family of five, they moved back to Clifton, back to the mines in a rented square box of a house. It burned to the ground one night and, as if by miracle, the only thing left untouched was Bon's wallet with the only money the Black family had.

Grow up like that and you learn to find a way out of any situation.

"By the time I was 10," Tom Black says, "we had moved back to Tucson and lived on the far north edge of town, out in the country, living on a seven-acre farm of a friend of my dad's. We'd run the service station from 6 a.m. until midnight, pumping gas, and we'd milk the cows. My dad still had his old '31 station wagon, and he would haul kids from out in our area of town into Tucson to school and back. Each kid would pay 75 cents a week. That's how we made a living. We learned how to work."

How ironic that Bon Black's sons found a game, football, as the way out of their hardscrabble beginnings.

**Football ties are strong**

By the time John Black completed his college eligibility at the UA, 1940, the New York Giants offered him $165 a game to be a pro. Twelve games a year.

His wife, Mary, shook her head. No. What kind of a life was that?

The two-time All-Border Conference halfback had grown to a sturdy 175 pounds. He usually played both ways, offense and defense.

"It was an insult to be taken out of the game," he says.

One place he stayed was in school. UA coach Miles Casteel hired John to coach the Wildcat freshman team, and it sounded like a worthy career. Coach, teach, raise a family.

Similarly, Tom had emerged as a football player of note. He followed in John's path at Tucson High, both playing on the powerhouse Badger teams of coach Rollin Gridley, who won five state titles from 1937 to 1945.

As timing would have it, it was Tom, not John, who got to play in the biggest of all games: at Notre Dame in 1941, the UA's most anticipated game of the school's first 40 years of athletic competition.

It took four days via train to get to South Bend, Ind., and there were complications. Tom's chemistry professor told him that he would be docked 10 percent for each missed class. If you go on the trip, in other words, you flunk chemistry.

Tom and three other football players in the class protested, taking it to Pop McKale, the athletic director, and ultimately to the president's office. The F's stood, Notre Dame won 41-7, and it would be another 39 years before the schools would meet again.

Big-time football hadn't yet reached Tucson.

But World War II did. Tom joined the Air Corps and John the Navy. Both were involved in the horror. On a carrier in the Pacific, near the Philippines, a Japanese kamikaze pilot aimed his death plane at the deck of the CVE Salamaua. John was arming planes with torpedoes at the time of impact. More than 60 men were killed. "A lot of the guys were on fire," he recalls. "Pure hell."

Tom also was in the Pacific, but it wasn't until midsummer of '45 that he was sent overseas, to Leyte in the Philippines. "The week we got there," he says, "the war with Japan ended."

It didn't mean that he wasn't in harm's way. As a guard for 2,000 Japanese prisoners of war in Manila, Tom drove a military jeep into the path of a sniper's machine gun burst. He rolled from the jeep and lay in a gutter next to five dead soldiers, blood still pumping out of their bodies.

"The war was over," Tom says, "but the hatred remained. It wasn't a safe place at all."

He had a sense of urgency to get home, back in school, ready for the 1946 college football season, his final season of eligibility. As good fortune would have it, Tom was discharged almost the day football practice began.

That's where his luck ended. At the UA, he suffered a disabling knee injury in midseason, against Texas-El Paso, and his playing days were over (much like John, who, as a senior in 1940, missed a berth in the East-West Shrine game with a shoulder injury). But Tom was no longer an aimless 19-year-old waiting for the war to inevitably send him around the world. He was 26, savvy, and he held on to football for all it was worth.

### Coaching becomes a career

The Black brothers have much in common besides blood. They were all-state football players at Tucson High. They served in the same World War II theater. They both coached the UA freshman team. They both decided on careers as high school coaches.

Phoenix Union, the state's largest school, chose 29-year-old John Black as its head coach in 1947. There were 150 applicants. When asked by the school board whom he thought the state's best coach was, John said, without much hesitation, "my brother, Tom."

But Tom, who had left the UA to become the head coach at Casa Grande High in 1947 — the Cougars won the state championship in Tom's only season there — was then the head coach at rival Phoenix North. What happened next was one of the most compelling rivalries in a century of

Arizona sports.

Phoenix North and Phoenix Union, the city's two largest high schools, met each year on Thanksgiving Day. The crowds were bulging to capacity, about 16,000. ("We outdrew ASU in those days," John Black says.) Their parents would sit on one side during the first half, the other during the second half.

It was the athletic event of the year in Phoenix. The two young guns, coaches from Tucson, had taken over Maricopa County.

In the first, much-anticipated meeting, in 1948, they tied.

A year later, again on Thanksgiving Day, again with 16,000 fans watching, the Black brothers met again. Their teams tied again. John's team won the 1948 state championship, beating, of all teams, Tucson High, for the title.

In three years since leaving Tucson, Tom Black had become, with his brother, John, the hottest commodity in high school coaching in the state of Arizona. That's a long way from selling tamales on the fender of their dad's '31 Ford.

Little did they realize that their coaching careers would end before either of them were 32 years old. John would go into business with his father-in-law and become a cattle rancher in Missouri; Tom, who feared being recalled to the Korean War, and who declined an opportunity to be a junior college coach in Los Angeles, moved to Kansas, where he became an FBI agent.

### Returning to Arizona

Tom Black opens a folder and picks out the letters from another lifetime. How long ago? Most of them were mailed with 2-cent stamps. All of them are signed by J. Edgar Hoover.

"... my sincere appreciation for the apprehension of a dangerous fugitive. ... your work for the Bureau is outstanding. ... your investigation into the murder led to the capture. ..."

He was an accomplished FBI agent, but his heart was in Arizona. Same with John. The cattle business had all but gone bust in the Midwest drought of 1954-55, and although he had a passion for working the 460 acres, fixing fences and being a cowboy, John took the gamble of his life by returning to Phoenix and starting an insurance business.

"I hated to leave the ranch," he says, "but it's the best thing I ever did."

The Blacks flourished in their insurance foray. Tom ultimately moved to Tucson in the late '50s to open a branch office. John, who laughs now at the thought of it, admits, "I went to ASU to get my master's, but don't tell anyone."

Both got their hands back into UA football without delay. John became president of the Phoenix Towncats, then the school's athletic booster group. Tom was the head of the Tucson Towncats. They were up to their necks as Wildcat activists, helping to get Jim LaRue — an old friend from the Big Eight — the football coaching job in 1959, helping players find summer employment, twisting a few arms to help with fund-raising.

Together, they've endured every conceivable era of Arizona football. They both watched the Blue Brigade of Tex Oliver, the school's best teams of the first half-century. They knew and worked for McKale. John played in the same backfield as Hoss Nielson and Tom Greenfield, perhaps two of the top 20 players in school history. Tom played both ways against Frank Leahy's Fighting Irish in South Bend. John's son, John Jr., was a two-year Wildcat football letterman in 1969-70. They held steady through the Bob Weber and Tony Mason days. They've been there, game after game, hearts on their shoulders, to support Larry Smith and Dick Tomey.

"We haven't missed much in 70 years," John says. "But it would sure be nice if we could get to a Rose Bowl while we're still alive."

AUTHOR'S NOTE: Tom Black died in the spring of 2004. He was 81. Big brother John died in August of the same year, at 85.

## THE JOHN BLACK FILE
**Born:** Douglas, 1919
**Family:** Wife, Shirley (deceased); wife, Mary. Three children
**Education:** Tucson High School; UA; master's from ASU
**Occupations:** High school coach; cattle rancher; insurance executive.
**Tie to the '90s:** "In the early '60s, I was active in helping UA football players find employment. One year we got a job for a tough kid from Pennsylvania, Howard Breinig. We got him a job with a moving company. After a week or so, the owner of the company phoned and said, 'If you've got any more like him, send them over.' Breinig went on to be a UA captain; he coached Sahuaro High to the 1994 state 4A football title. He is in the Arizona Coaches Association Hall of Fame.
**Most admired athlete:** "Joe Batiste. He was so good in track and field that he could beat anybody on our team at Tucson High in their event, whatever it was: javelin, pole vault, mile run."
**Two great coaches:** "I played on the last football team Pop McKale ever coached, the 1937 UA freshman team. And not only did I play for Rollin

301

Gridley at Tucson High, who I consider one of the finest coaches ever, anywhere, but I coached against him in 1947, his last year at Tucson."

## THE TOM BLACK FILE

**Born:** Douglas, 1922

**Family:** Wife, Ann; two children

**Education:** Tucson High School; UA

**Occupations:** High school coach, FBI agent, insurance executive

**Lesson well learned:** "My high school coach, Rollin Gridley, had such an impact on us that I've heard my teammates say that when they're around Grid, they won't smoke or drink or cuss, even 40 or 50 years after they've left school."

**Brother vs. brother:** "My Phoenix North team tied John's Phoenix Union team both times we played, and each game was played on Thanksgiving. My mom, Alice, would sit on John's side in one half, and my side in the other. She'd pray for a tie, and she got what she wanted. She knew we all had to go home together for Thanksgiving dinner after the game."

**How football helped:** "When I was in high school, a counselor asked me what I wanted to do. I said, 'play football.' And it was football that got me a college education and helped me to grow up. I'm not so sure I wouldn't have wound up in jail, or somewhere, if not for football."

# A Century of Tucson Sports: Eddie Leon

*Sunday, July 4, 1999*

Eddie Leon was 15 the first time he went to Yankee Stadium. He arrived at the grand ballpark in a caravan of four station wagons that parents of his Tucson all-star team had driven cross-country.

Two of the station wagons got lost in Harlem and never did get to the game.

"I was one of the lucky ones that got to see Mickey Mantle play that day," Leon remembers. "It was bigger than life. I dreamed, like most kids who played baseball, that someday I'd be playing there, too."

Leon returned to Yankee Stadium seven years later, 1969, as a rookie shortstop for the Cleveland Indians. Now he would be playing against his idol, his team.

He walked from the Indians clubhouse to the visitors dugout and stood on the top step. The view was breathtaking. He looked first at the faraway facade on the upper deck in right field, where one of Mantle's legendary home runs had ricocheted a few years before. He remembers getting "all tingly."

It was a million miles from the El Rio Little League.

The last time Eddie Leon was in Yankee Stadium, he was 29 and he was wearing a Yankee uniform. Lou Piniella and Graig Nettles were his teammates. George Steinbrenner signed his checks.

"The manager, Bill Virdon, called me into his office and told me they were going to release me," Leon says now. "It was June 15 and I had been sitting on the bench for two months without getting an at-bat. I had been a ballplayer since I was 4 years old, so it was a pretty tough time. Baseball had been everything for me, and suddenly they were telling me I couldn't play anymore."

How does someone retire when he's 29?

**Accelerated growth**

Forty-nine former UA baseball players have reached the major leagues. It's enough that the roster spans from A, George Arias, to Z, Bart Zeller.

Ron Hassey spent 13 years in the big leagues. Hank Leiber lasted 11 seasons. Dwight Taylor was in and out in two weeks.

More rare than longevity is a first-round draft pick. Since the draft began in 1965, UA has produced just five: Leon; pitcher Lance Dickson, 1990, Cubs; pitcher Joe Magrane, 1986, Cardinals; outfielder Terry Francona, 1980, Expos; and catcher Alan Zinter, 1989, Mets.

Dickson reached the majors in two months. He lasted 17 days, injuring his arm, never to regain his form. Zinter has been a career minor-leaguer. Magrane, who started two World Series games, was just hanging on by the time he was 27. Francona, cursed by injuries, parlayed his baseball instincts into a managerial career.

The message seems to be: Be prepared for life after baseball.

And that's where Leon has been most successful. At 53, not far from playing shape, he has spent two decades working in real estate and development in Tucson. His UA degree — he graduated in engineering in nine semesters — gave him the necessary background to make more money in the last 10 years than he ever did in major-league baseball.

His father, Enrique, whose lineage stretches to northern Sonora, had neither money nor athletic skill, but what he did have was the ability to teach his son the value of education.

"My dad worked at Hughes, doing leather work for the interior of airplanes, but it was an uneven business," Leon says. "He'd get laid off periodically, and when I was 7 he was transferred to Los Angeles. It was rough, so he decided to go back to Tucson. He was hired as a custodian for TUSD, and ultimately became the head janitor at Rincon High School."

Eddie was a wonderfully talented, if small, ballplayer. There was a reason for that: While attending second grade in L.A., he was put into an accelerated-learning program. When the Leon family returned to Tucson, he should've been in third grade. He was so advanced they put him in the fifth grade.

That's nice for someone whose career lies in academia, but it can be destructive to a ballplayer.

"I was always playing with kids two years older than me," he says. "In some regards, it helped me. It forced me to keep up, playing against older kids. When (former UA pitching coach) Jim Wing coached our summer league teams, I was 13 years old playing against 15-, 16-year-olds. I was always the youngest and the smallest.

"When we'd go to a game, I'd have to ride in the coach's car with Beth Wing while all the other players would go in their own cars. Beth still kids me about that."

Leon's accelerated education was beneficial. By the time he was a high school senior, he was an all-state shortstop and an A student. Arizona coach Frank Sancet, who was economical, didn't offer a scholarship. Eddie was instead awarded an academic scholarship, which was substantially short of the books, fees, tuition and (in those days allowable) $15 a month for an athletic scholarship.

"They were cheating the kid," says Ray Adkins, Leon's baseball coach at Tucson High. "I kept telling Sancet that he didn't have a dime in his pocket, and (Leon) was keeping the coaches employed."

The rub of being stiffed by the baseball coach — "Sancet told me he was out of scholarships," Leon says — ate at him.

Word spread. After a standout freshman season, Leon had phone calls from the coaches at USC and UCLA. Both offered full rides. Leon told Sancet he was going to play for Rod Dedeaux at USC. NCAA baseball rules allow immediate eligibility to those who transfer out of their conference. Sancet knew Leon was serious.

The next day, Leon had his baseball scholarship.

**Contract hard ball**

The Minnesota Twins offered $28,000. Eddie Leon wanted $80,000. But more than that, he wanted a little respect.

This was 1965. In the first amateur draft in major-league history, the Twins used their first pick, No. 9 overall, on the sophomore shortstop from UA. They wrongly assumed negotiations would be easy.

Leon was 19. His family had no money. The Twins were a glamour team, headed for the '65 World Series, with the American League MVP, shortstop Zoilo Versalles, and marquee stars Harmon Killebrew and Mudcat Grant. The Twins tried to confuse Leon with the way the bonus was structured. They said it was $28,000, but Leon, an honor student, called their bluff.

Two years worth of salaries, a bonus, and an incentive clause had been rolled into the $28,000. "What you're offering me," Leon said, "is $7,500, not $28,000."

He held out.

This was unusual because, in 1965, nobody held out, and especially not a 19-year-old from Tucson High, to whom $28,000 had to appear like all the money a man could print.

Two Twins scouts flew into Springfield, Ill., where Leon was playing in a summer collegiate league. They all went to dinner and played hardball.

"They sat there and broke down my game and said I couldn't do anything well," Leon recalls. "They said I didn't run, that I had no power, couldn't hit for average, didn't field well and couldn't throw. Geez, why did they bother drafting me?"

Leon knew then he wouldn't be playing for the Twins.

"I told them to take me to Minnesota for the All-Star Game and let me throw with Zoilo. If I couldn't throw better than him, I would take their offer."

So Leon returned to Arizona for his junior season. He was a first-team All-American. The Wildcats (40-15) finished fifth at the College World Series, and he inched closer to a degree in engineering. He assumed his value had doubled.

"Your junior year is the last time you have any leverage," he says. "The Cubs made me their first pick and offered me $50,000. I asked for $50,000 and a car. The Cubs wouldn't go for it. We were a car apart."

Over the summer, Leon's stock rose. He was the MVP of an All-Star tour through Japan, Korea and Hawaii. He had gotten bigger. But the Cubs thought they had a shortstop for the next decade, Don Kessinger, and not only didn't offer Leon a car, but told him he'd have to switch to third base or left field. No deal.

So there he was. Back in school, a senior who was again the first-team All-America shortstop (the first UA player to be so named twice), drafted by Cleveland. No leverage. Indians scout Bob Niemann offered $20,000. "It's the best we can do, Eddie," he said.

After two minutes of conversation, Eddie Leon signed a contract and was headed to Pawtucket, R.I., to play minor-league baseball. He was married. Real life began. "I used that bonus," he says, "to buy my first house."

### 'Top of the heap'

A No. 1 draft pick attracted a lot of attention in Tucson in the '60s.

"I first saw Eddie play at Spring Junior High School," says Adkins, the Tucson High baseball coach from 1960 to 1972. "I pegged him right away. He was a natural. My God, he could go into the hole, plant his foot and make the throw to first as well as anyone I ever saw. He was just unbelievable. He was so smart, you only had to show him something once and then it was like he'd been doing it for years."

Adkins had three state championship teams at Tucson High. The last one, 1972, went 25-0, and is the only post-World War II baseball team in Arizona to be undefeated. He had dozens of players go on to college and pro careers, including Ron Hassey.

"Old Eddie was at the top of the heap," Adkins says. "He wasn't a big guy, and he was a year or two younger than the rest of his classmates, but he had a presence about him. He was so confident. He was such a good athlete that he could've been the best tennis player at the school."

Pat Darcy, a Rincon High pitcher who went on to play in the 1975 World Series for the Cincinnati Reds, remembers Leon's reputation.

"I was a little younger, but everybody knew who Eddie was. There were many, many outstanding ballplayers in Tucson in the '60s, but Eddie was the one we all talked about. He drew us all to the games at the UA, especially when they played ASU."

Leon was a central figure in what was probably the greatest college baseball game ever played in this state.

In 1967, Arizona and ASU tied for the WAC championship, necessitating a one-game playoff in Phoenix. The winner would advance to the NCAA tournament. The loser's season was over. It would be the last game Leon ever played for Arizona.

Attendance was 8,324. Fans were allowed to sit in the outfield, with a rope separating them from the playing field. ASU's Gary Gentry pitched all 15 innings of a 2-1 Sun Devil victory, striking out 18.

"We lost on an opposite-field nubber," Leon says, shaking his head at a memory 32 years old. "The year before, with 10,000 people at Hi Corbett Field, we beat ASU in a playoff to get to the College World Series when I hit a three-run triple in the seventh inning.

"That was great baseball, baseball that will never be duplicated in this city. Both cities were galvanized by that rivalry then. It was a special time. I'm happy to have been a part of it."

AUTHOR'S NOTE: Eddie Leon, 64, lives in Tucson, where he has become a near-scratch golfer when he's not dabbling in the property business. One of the bats he used as an Arizona All-American is on display at Kindall/Sancet Stadium.

## THE EDDIE LEON FILE
**Born:** Tucson, 1946
**Family:** Wife, Joy; three children
**Education:** Tucson High; UA
**Occupations:** Former major-league ballplayer (Cleveland, New York Yankees, Chicago White Sox); engineer; real estate developer
**What you probably don't know:** After leaving the Yankees in 1975, Leon played two years in the Mexican Baseball League, for Hermosillo and Tampico, and was part of the 1975 Caribbean World Series championship team. "When I got back to Tucson, people

asked me to play in the semipro leagues. I told them I wasn't sliding anymore, and I wasn't practicing, either. And that was that for my career."

**Most admired ballplayer:** "(White Sox first baseman) Dick Allen was the best I ever played with. Jim Palmer was probably the best pitcher I faced. He didn't make you uncomfortable, like Nolan Ryan, but he had everything it took to beat you. I hit a home run off Ryan, but the first time I ever faced him, he struck me out on three pitches."

**The shortest home run:** At old Yankee Stadium, when it was 296 feet down the right field line, I hit an opposite-field homer that curled around the foul pole. It went 297 feet. I figured if it counted for Ruth and Maris, it counted for me."

Eddie Leon

Mary Roby

# A Century of Tucson sports: Mary Roby

*Sunday, July 11, 1999*

Mary Roby was born in 1926 in the tiny Arizona mining town of Miami. Her parents didn't speak English, neither had attended a day of school, and when Mary was 5, her father died from decades of inhaling toxins in the gold and silver mines.

Her mother, Kate Pavlich, scratched out a living by becoming efficient in everything from wiring a house and fixing the roof to feeding boarders. She would live to be 96, and if she stood for anything, it was that no barrier was too great.

When it came time for Mary's older sister, Katherine, to go to school, the little school in Miami sent her back home. And why not? She only spoke Croatian, as did the rest of her family.

That didn't stop Kate Pavlich. Nothing stopped Kate Pavlich, a Croatian immigrant who was the eldest of 13 children of a family raised in Lead, S.D. She not only sent Katherine back to school, she went with her.

"You teach-ee," Kate said in the only English she knew. "She learn-ee."

And by the time Katherine Pavlich graduated from Miami High School, she was the class valedictorian.

Talk about your role models. Mary Roby didn't have Mia Hamm or Sheryl Swoopes: She learned from a higher dimension. She had Kate and Katherine Pavlich.

"With examples like that," she says now, "how could I fail?"

No barrier would be too great for Mary Roby, either.

**Little by little**

In 1970-71, one in every 27 girls in high school participated in sports. At the University of Arizona, the landscape was similar. There were no scholarships. The budget for women's sports was $20,000. Swimmers who qualified for the national championships stayed home because they couldn't afford travel expenses.

UA was in something called the Intermountain Conference, and among its 12 sports were badminton, archery, fencing and field hockey. McKale Center would be completed in two years, but the women's athletic department wasn't invited to move in until 1982.

It's not even accurate to say that, in 1971, UA had a women's intercollegiate athletic department. There was no trainer. No sports information

311

office. All women's teams — clubs, extramurals, intramurals — were under the auspices of the department of Physical Education for Women.

Mary Roby was hired in 1959 as the director of the Women's Recreation Association — budget: $8,000 — and the only real competition was a biannual gathering with ASU, NAU and some of the state's junior colleges in which everyone got to work up a good sweat.

Roby was, at times, the head coach of the gymnastics team (from 1962 to 1969 the UA had five gymnastics coaches).

"Every year I bought one set of uniforms," she remembers. "Not one set for every team, one set for the entire department. The volleyball players would turn in their uniforms after the season and the softball team would use them. Coaches would be responsible for getting them cleaned, and turn in their receipts from laundromats."

The message here is that no one, not even Roby, UA Class of '48, could foresee the emergence of UA women's athletics into a $750,000-a-year enterprise by 1980, and into one whose annual budget exceeds $8 million today. But it doesn't mean that Roby, whose high school years at Miami did not include a single athletic competition against another school, lacked vision.

"We struggled, pushed, begged and crawled, and little by little we grew," she says. "I saw everything. I came through it all."

By the time Roby retired, in 1989, Arizona was recognized as one of the NCAA's nine or 10 most prominent women's athletic departments.

"I wouldn't change one minute of my professional career," she says. "Not a minute."

### Getting the best

In 1975, the UA men's and women's sports departments merged. Dave Strack ran the men's side; Roby the women's.

It is of significance that her all-female coaching staff of pre-1975 soon became integrated. Her first male hire was Chris Murray, then the women's track coach at Iowa State. She would follow in 1980 with: Jim Gault (gymnastics); in 1985 with Dick Jochums (swimming); in 1985 with Mike Candrea (softball); and in 1989 with Frank Busch (swimming).

Ideally, she wanted to hire as many female coaches as possible, if for no other reason than to provide opportunities for a growing profession. Pioneers have a way of looking out for other pioneers.

"When it came down to it, I hired the best person available," she says. "I was torn somewhat, especially early in the process, but never when it came down to getting the best."

Murray didn't want to leave Iowa State when he flew to Tucson for an interview in 1979. He had family in Iowa. He was successful. Arizona was a gamble. Its attempt at women's track began in 1976 and foundered.

"My first impression of Mary was so strong that I changed my mind on the spot," Murray says. "A week before I left Ames, we adopted a baby daughter. Mary and (husband) Fred soon became her godparents. Of all the places I've worked and all of the people I've worked for, Mary is the best. I continue to look at her not only as a mentor, but as a role model.

"She was a mover and shaker in the industry, but what separated her from the others is that she wasn't in it strictly for the cause of women's athletics. A lot of early (women's) administrators lost sight of the student-athletes and battled only for the so-called cause. Mary didn't go that way. That's why she was able to hire male coaches. To her, the girls came first and she gave them the best that she possibly could."

Said Cedric Dempsey, Arizona's former athletic director and later executive director of the NCAA: "Mary could hold her own and more in any setting, in any company, male or female."

Roby's reach was at times greater than her financial resources. She phoned Tennessee's legendary Pat Summit and asked if she would be interested in coaching the Arizona women's basketball team in the '80s. (She wasn't.) She hired the United States' No. 1 female volleyball player, Rosie Wegrich, to coach the Wildcats (a 12-year period in which Arizona finished in the top 20 on 11 occasions).

Her most notable hire was Candrea, five times a national champion at Arizona, an unknown whom Roby plucked off the Central Arizona College campus in 1985.

Her most accomplished protégé is Barbara Hedges, who worked in Roby's WRA department from 1969 to 1973 and coached the UA's gymnastics team for four seasons. Hedges, at Washington, is now one of two female athletic directors in the NCAA Division I. The other, Debbie Yow at Maryland, is also part of Roby's past. "I tried to hire her to be our basketball coach one year," Roby recalls. "It wasn't difficult to see that she had what it takes."

Says Murray: "Mary never sought the credit. In fact, she would always make you try to feel important. I never heard her talk about herself, yet she was a giant in women's athletics."

**A shorter line for P.E.**

Of all those who have coached and administered in UA's athletic program this century, the most unlikely might be Mary Roby.

Unlikely in that she grew up speaking Croatian. Unlikely in that her small mining-town high school, Miami, didn't sponsor a single girls sports competition. Unlikely in that she initially planned to be a business student at UA in 1944. ("The line for registration was much shorter for physical education," she says with a chuckle. "So I switched lines.")

In her undergraduate days she didn't get cheated. She tried them all. Her favorite: field hockey. She got a letter sweater, a reward based on a points system that existed at Arizona until 1972. She was a student of Ina Gittings, the UA's most legendary female physical educator of the first half-century. When Roby graduated in 1948, the budget for women's sports at Arizona was $4,800. Ten years later, it was $7,200. There was little growth, little money, little hope to change either.

"Doctors warned girls against the physical evils of playing full-court basketball," she remembers. "The climate was not at all good."

Instead of accepting a teaching position, she got a master's at exclusive Smith College of Northampton, Mass., followed by a doctorate at USC. When she went to work as a professor of physical education, she assembled a good base of experience at Colorado, ASU, Cal and Texas. Then, in 1959, she came back to Tucson and began the battle to take women's sports into the big time.

She credits two major developments for the growth of women's sports. One, the visibility of the Olympic Games, in which television ratings for gymnastics and ice skating surged ahead of men's sports and generated participation in all girls sports. Two, the implementation of Title IX in 1972.

"Title IX was our godsend," she says. "It was a law. We were concerned, always, where the money was coming from, but we could no longer be ignored."

The federal law mandated that female athletes receive equal rights on the playing field. When it happened, Roby was ready. By 1974, the budget for women's sports at Arizona was a robust $60,000, triple the amount of 1972. By 1977, it had almost tripled again, to $169,000.

"We still had to fight for everything, even after it became a law," she says. "But it wasn't the money as much as it was the attention that led me to believe we had arrived. In the early days, the reporters would always call me when they wanted some news on a team. But within a few years, they were calling my coaches. That's when I knew we had arrived. Interest spread quickly."

In 1989, when women's sports at UA were flourishing, when the golf and softball teams were on the brink of national championships, and after she hired Frank Busch to turn the swimming team into an elite program, Roby retired.

The Pac-10 had absorbed women's sports in 1986, and Arizona matched the nation's glamour schools, Stanford and UCLA, stride for stride.

"It was a good time for me to leave," she says. "I felt we were accepted and respected."

AUTHOR'S NOTE: Mary Roby, 82, lives in Tucson with her husband, Fred. She remains active in various community projects.

## THE MARY ROBY FILE
**Born:** Miami, Ariz., 1927
**Family:** Husband, Fred
**Education:** UA; Smith (Mass.) College; USC
**Occupations:** Retired as UA's associate director of intercollegiate athletics; physical education professor and women's athletic administrator at Texas, ASU, Colorado, California
**The Dempsey connection:** Roby's husband, Fred, hired Cedric Dempsey as a physical education teacher at the UA in 1964. When Dempsey left to be the athletic director at Pacific in 1969, he asked Mary to be his senior women's administrator. She declined. When the UA's athletic directorship opened in 1982, Roby sent Dempsey, then at Houston, three postcards. "The first said, simply, 'on your mark,' the second said, 'get set,' and the third said 'go,' with the directions to Tucson."
**Four big letters:** "I believe that a lot of the success of women's sports came when we left the AIAW in 1986 and became part of the NCAA. Our championships took on new meaning. People were much more aware of women's sports when we joined the NCAA than they were in the AIAW."
**Pay attention:** When the UA left the Intermountain Conference in 1979, it joined the old Western Collegiate Athletic Association. "To give you an idea of how much attention people paid to us, I joined the league first and told the athletic director later," Roby says. "No one seemed to know."
**Keeping busy:** Today Roby is an active photographer, has a passion for designing web pages and, last fall, was the oldest woman cyclist to complete the 62-mile Tour of the Tucson Mountains.
**Working with men:** Roby fired four coaches in her tenure at the UA, including a successful swimming coach, Dick Jochums, in 1988. "It hurt me every time I had to fire someone, and it was the worst part of the job," she says. "Some people I gave second chances, some I didn't. We wouldn't tolerate cheating."

*Clay Hitchcock*

# A century of Tucson sports: Clay Hitchcock

*Sunday, July 18, 1999*

If you use 70 years wisely, you have time to be a biology teacher and learn to play the clarinet. Time to fight forest fires. Time to raise eight children. Time to be a historian. Time to be a tank commander. And time to be a track coach.

You have time to map out and rebuild a 400-mile trail from Fort Apache to Prescott. You have time to win a state track championship, time to finish second in the state basketball tournament, time to get a master's degree, and time to sit back, take it all in and say: "I once went 12 years in a row without missing a day of work; I got a kick out of every day."

Every morning at 6, earlier if it's too warm at sunrise, Clay Hitchcock gets his 70-year-old bones out of bed and runs a mile. There's so much to be done, so much that has been done. If you ask Hitchcock for details, he snaps open a briefcase and produces details.

A picture of his great-grandmother, Sally Manus Peacheater, who lived to be 103? It comes with a story. A photo that brought back memories of his old Tucson High teammate, Roger Johnson, the first basketball All-American in UA history? "He'd stop by my house after school and relieve me of all my comic books," Hitchcock says. "He just loved comic books."

Unsolicited, Hitchcock has jotted down the record holders, one through five, in every track and field event at Pueblo High School from 1955 to 1988. Nothing is rounded off; tenths of a second separate good from great. He has a yellowed newspaper clipping stating that he was the Arizona Biology Teacher of the Year in 1960-61. He reaches into his pocket and produces a lifetime pass to all UA athletic events — yes, that includes two seats at McKale Center whenever Lute Olson's team performs — a long-ago reward for three letter-winning seasons on the Wildcat track team.

If you're not careful, if you probe into his religious beliefs, he can give you chapter, verse and history of the Mormon Church, dating to 1830.

"I've always loved learning, and when I was in the fifth grade, I decided I would like to be a teacher," he says. "I coached the track team at Pueblo for 32 years and I'd always be asked by other teachers when I was going to quit. I'd just say, 'Whenever I get worn out.' I guess I never did."

317

### Self-taught hurdler

There isn't much in Clay Hitchcock's family background to suggest that he would spend more than half his life in the pursuit of athletics.

His father, Clayburn, was a Cherokee Indian who worked the oil fields in Oklahoma. His great-grandmother, Sally, was one of the few survivors of the brutal "Trail of Tears," an 800-mile forced march of Cherokees from Florida to Oklahoma in the 1830s in which more than 4,000 people died.

"We moved to Tucson when I was a few months old on the advice of a doctor who said I would die unless we got to a drier climate," Clay says. "It took us three weeks to make the trip in a broken-down Model T Ford. When we got here, my father couldn't find work because he was an Indian, which was one strike against him in those days, and to make it worse, it was the Depression."

The Hitchcocks moved into a tiny shack near the Santa Cruz River and 29th Street. Rent was $5 a month. Clay's father trapped coyotes and sold their pelts for $2. After living in abject poverty for three or four years, until Clayburn got a job with the railroad, he then built an adobe house near St. Mary's Hospital.

"I remember my father stamping in the mud, getting the mixture of adobe just right," Clay remembers. "He built it from scratch, the same way Indians made their homes centuries before."

Clay's mother, Helen, a Caucasian, got a job as a telephone operator and later was hired to be a body-double for Barbara Stanwyck on Western movie sets at Old Tucson.

By the time Clay got to Tucson High in 1945, he went out for the track team, picturing himself as a long jumper. But when Badgers coach Doc Van Horne got a look at Hitchcock, he pointed him to the cinder track and instructed him to run the hurdles.

Clay's response?

"Is that what those white things are? Hurdles?"

It was the beginning of a wonderful relationship.

Self-taught — "Doc didn't know much about the hurdles," he says — Hitchcock finished second in the first hurdles competition he entered as a THS sophomore. As a senior, he was fourth in the state championships.

At Arizona, first as a walk-on, later as a scholarship athlete, Hitchcock picked up lessons in the hurdles whenever and wherever he could. His coach, Limey Gibbings, was, like Van Horne, not much of a technician.

"Limey would come out to practice with a big old cigar in his mouth and say, 'Get busy,' and then go about his business," Hitchcock says. So he would sound out his teammate, Fred Batiste, brother of former Tucson High hurdler Joe Batiste, a former American junior record holder.

Later, when a past-his-prime Joe Batiste returned from the service and enrolled at Arizona State, Hitchcock got to run against him. They would talk techniques even as they were in the starting blocks. Little by little, Hitchcock became an authority. Not just in the hurdles, but in all track and field events.

After completing a stint in the Korean War, patrolling the Czech border with an assignment to keep an eye on Russian troop movements as part of his duties as a tank commander, Hitchcock got a master's degree, in biology, and acquired a simple goal. He wanted to teach and coach.

He had learned Spanish in school and put it to use immediately as a teacher and coach at Pueblo High School, which was his first choice. Why Pueblo?

"Those kids are my kind of kids," he says. "It's a poor section of town, and I was crazy enough to think I could help some of them."

### Clay molds Frederick

No story about Clay Hitchcock can be told without a detour to Dale Frederick. As much as, for example, the Pop McKale story can't be told without mention of Button Salmon, as much as the career of Dick Tomey can't be defined without a chapter on Tedy Bruschi, Hitchcock and Frederick are similarly connected.

By the time Frederick turned out for the Pueblo track team in 1962, unannounced and unknown, Hitchcock had coached the Warriors to the 1959 state championship. But he had been unable to develop a star in his beloved hurdles event. No one was more unlikely to be that person than Dale Frederick, who, in a 1964 newspaper article, described himself as a "street urchin."

Perfect. Just another down-and-out Pueblo kid who Hitchcock could help.

"The first time I saw Dale, he was among the many kids out for the team that I made run a lap around the track just to get a glance at them," Hitchcock says. "He was a tall, skinny kid, but, my goodness, he stood out right away. I could just see him running over those hurdles. He had no background in hurdles, in track, really, but he had that look."

Frederick placed fifth in the state meet as a sophomore, and then, Hitchcock says, "we got serious." He told his hurdler all the stories about Joe Batiste, they inaugurated a serious weight-training program, and when Frederick was a senior, in 1964, he broke Batiste's state record in the 120 low hurdles, at 13.8 seconds. (Batiste's record, 14.0, had stood for 26 years.)

The West's top track schools sought the Pueblo star. But UCLA and Oregon couldn't get him away from UA coach Carl Cooper, and Frederick went on to win the 1966 WAC championship for the Wildcats. He was second in the NCAAs and held the UA hurdles record from 1966 to 1984. Frederick's attempt to make the 1968 Olympic team ended when he pulled a muscle (he earlier defeated one of the three U.S. hurdlers on the '68 Games roster).

The Frederick-Hitchcock bond had a much greater success than on the track. Frederick went on to become, as Hitchcock, a biology teacher. He was a helicopter pilot in Vietnam, the principal at Rincon High, then, superintendent of the Pittsburgh Public Schools. Next, he was hired as the superintendent of the Mesa Public Schools system.

Just a street urchin, huh?

"Clay was a model for all students at Pueblo," Frederick says. "He was articulate and spent a lot of time highlighting other aspects of life."

**'I should be in his class'**

A coach's influence may best be measured by a reflection of 30 years.

From 1966 to 1969, Burney Starks ran for Pueblo's track teams, he admits, only because the football coach, Ed Brown, strongly recommended it.

Talk about an odd couple. Hitchcock, the part-Cherokee, 40-something coach and teacher, and Starks, an African-American, one of 10 children of a Tucson soil chemist. How would they ever hit it off?

"The thing about Clay was that you would walk by his classroom and you could hear kids laughing, you could sense some excitement," says Starks, who now works for the Tucson Unified School District as a marketing and recruiting specialist. "You would tell yourself, 'I should be in his class.' "

After playing football at the UA, spending 20 years in the Army, and working for the Tucson Urban League, Starks continues his relationship with his old Pueblo High coach.

"He was a great teacher and a super person," says Starks. "Any time I would go back to Pueblo there would be a handful of teachers I would automatically stop to see, and Clay was one of them. A lot of his former students are that way with him."

In 1988, Hitchcock retired after 33 years as Pueblo's head track coach. In that span, Pueblo had more than 15 head coaches in football, basketball and baseball, but only one in track. He never wore out.

He is asked if one season, or one meet, or one athlete, stands above

320

all others. He shakes his head, no, and retrieves a list of times and distances that Pueblo athletes recorded over 33 years.

There are more than 70 names on the list.

"All of them," he says. "They all stand out. I enjoyed them all."

For Clay Hitchcock, it was 33 years well spent.

AUTHOR'S NOTE: Clay Hitchcock died on Easter Sunday in 2005. He was 75.

## THE CLAY HITCHCOCK FILE

**Born:** Hominy, Okla., 1929

**Family:** Wife, Beverly; eight children

**Education:** Tucson High School; UA (bachelor's 1952; master's 1955)

**Occupations:** Army lieutenant; biology teacher and track and field coach at Pueblo High School; forest naturalist, U.S. Forest Service; firefighter, U.S. Forest Service

**So much for a racing career:** As a soap box derby racer in his teen years, Hitchcock was matched against future Indianapolis 500 driver Bill Cheesbourg in a race down "A" Mountain. Hitchcock lost control of his racer and crashed through a barrier onto some rocks. "End of career," he says.

**Do you remember?:** Former Pueblo High football center Ron Thomas turned out for the track team to stay in shape. Hitchcock asked him to run a lap so he could get an idea what event he should pursue. Thomas ran the 400 meters in 50.4 seconds. Amazing. "He came back to me, asked his time and said, 'Is that a good time?' By the time he graduated, Ron had a scholarship to Oregon and ran the 100 meters in 10.6 seconds to win the state championship."

**Earth, wind and fire:** During Hitchcock's 27-year career of spending summers working with the U.S. Forest Service, he helped to fight fires in places ranging from Yosemite National Park to Northern Arizona. He also was an investigator, determining origins of forest fires. "I was trapped once when wind took a fire up by Prescott and put it out of control," he says. "The fire jumped the road and I had one option: drive my pickup through the flames and hope for the best. I floored it for about 50 yards and got through it unharmed."

**Most admired athletes:** "Joe Batiste was at the top. He could win a track meet all by himself. I have always thought Lee Carey, one of my classmates at Tucson High, was as good as any baseball player Tucson has produced. He almost made it to the Cleveland Indians."

# A century of Tucson sports: Norm Patton

*Sunday, July 25, 1999*

For a long time, Norm Patton couldn't figure out the interest some of his basketball players at Marana High School had for the game. They would come to his house in the summer, on Saturdays, and ask for the keys to the gym. This was decades before high school basketball was practiced on a 12-month calendar. And many of the kids lining up for those Saturday games weren't gym rats at all.

Basketball was a growing industry in Marana during Patton's nine-year coaching stay. The Tigers were undefeated state champs in 1969, and again in 1972 — 24-0 and 25-0, respectively — and in between, in 1970, they had an "off" year, losing twice but winning another state championship.

But summer games were new.

Patton began to notice that some of his players would leave the court after 10 minutes. Others would feign interest in hoops, and then be gone, off to the showers 30 minutes after shooting their first jumper. Then Patton figured it out. Because so many of those who played basketball — played sports — at Marana came from impoverished situations, they got into the gym so they could have access to the showers.

"Many of my top kids came from the Rillito area, and some of them didn't have running water at home," Patton remembers. "Do you know how difficult it is for a young man to say, 'Coach, I need to get in the gym so I can take a shower this week.' If I learned one thing at Marana, it was the importance of gaining the trust of my kids, and in turn, trusting them. The reward to me was having those young men know they could come to me with their problems, any problem."

And, boy, did they come to him. Over the years, more than 10 players coached by Patton (and some he got to know through teaching, not coaching) moved in with the Pattons for various reasons and various stretches.

"I don't know if I've ever come across anyone so caring as Norm and his wife, Sandra," says Darryl Jones, a Scottsdale home builder who played on Patton's Pima College teams in 1976-78. "They took me in, a kid from a small New Mexico town, put me up at their house. Norm got me a job at the college cafeteria. He didn't know me from Adam, but he made me feel special. He was probably the only coach I had in my career that made me feel wanted as a person, and not just as a basketball player. He wasn't just a coach. He was, and remains, a friend."

Patton's first state champ at Marana was a lesson in diversity. Four players were black. One was an American Indian. Three were Hispanic. Three were Caucasian. He looks at a team photo, 30 years old, and can't keep from beaming. "What a nice mix, huh? The kids got along well. Experiencing the different cultures benefited me and the kids."

He says, modestly, that he "must've been lucky."

But there was no luck involved. For 27 years, whether it was at Marana or at Pima College or, later, in 13 seasons at Central Arizona College in Coolidge, the kids Norm Patton coached got along well because he accepted them as he would a son.

In the middle of his run of state championships at Marana, Patton befriended a student — not an athlete — whose family situation was unstable. Patton's house was already crowded with four young daughters — Lori, Kelly, Vickie and Patricia — but Norm invited Bobby Rice to bunk at Camp Patton for as long as he needed.

"We have five bedrooms," Sandra explains. "We just doubled up the girls, and Bobby (or whomever it happened to be at the time) moved in."

Rice, who didn't play on any of Patton's basketball teams, flourished. He was accepted to Duke University. He became a Rhodes Scholar and got his law degree at Harvard. One of many Patton success stories.

### Making a small town proud

Barney Patton was a rancher, a Texas rancher who moved his young family to Glenwood, N.M., when Norm was a head shorter than the cattle he tended. It was 30 miles, on dirt roads, to the nearest high school, in Cliff. The "big city," Silver City, was 65 miles away. One of Norm's jobs was to pump water for all of the family's needs from a well. If the wind didn't blow, if the windmill didn't turn, the only available water was from a nearby stream.

So you can't say that Norm Patton grew up dribbling a basketball, watching Hank Iba coaching videos, learning basketball from the masters. He played the game in the dirt.

When he was 16, Norm went to work for the Forest Service, watching for forest fires in the New Mexico wilderness. From May through August, he would often be alone, with horseback the only means of travel. He loved it. He could've had a lifetime with the Game and Fish Department, or the Forest Service. The jobs were his for the asking, and he thoroughly enjoyed the work. But he became obsessed with basketball, shooting for hours on a lone hoop in the tiny town of Glenwood, which, in retrospect, wasn't so tiny at all. It wasn't so small that you couldn't make a name for yourself.

In the 12-person senior class at Cliff High School in 1957, Patton and his basketball-playing buddy, Charlie Bearup, are pictured sitting next to one another in the annual team photo. A quarter-century later, Patton was reading a story on the year's Converse All-Americans, a list of the nation's premier girls and boys high school basketball players.

Vickie Patton of Marana High School was on the girls All-America team. Brett Bearup, Charlie's son, was on the boys All-America team. What are the odds? Vickie went to Cal-Irvine, then to UA and NYU and has dual degrees in hydrology and law. Brett went to Kentucky to play for the Wildcats.

Norm and Charlie, who went to Eastern Arizona College together in 1958, and who a year later took separate paths — Norm to coach and Charlie to work in pharmaceuticals — didn't just get out of a small town. They made that small town proud.

So maybe it was fitting when Patton was hired to teach history and driver's ed at Marana High in 1965 — he'd have to wait a year to get the basketball coaching slot — that he was working familiar terrain. A small farming town bulging with potential.

"Before Marana, I spent a year at Bayfield High in Colorado, just north of Durango," Patton says. "It was 1962 and I made $3,700 a year. We almost starved. I coached three sports, lined the field before the football games, set up the refreshment stand and drove the bus. Ha, ha, ha. I took over a football team that hadn't won a game in four years. We went 4-4-1 and it was like we had won the Super Bowl."

Norm and Sandra just loved it, but they couldn't support their growing family on $3,700.

Through a contact with another old friend from Cliff, Brad DeSpain, then a teacher at Marana High, Patton was offered a job at MHS. His first contract was for $5,500. "Woo-wee," he says. "We were rich."

### Only one losing season

Jerry Robinson was a mostly gangly, often-nervous junior when Norm Patton arrived at Marana High. He had averaged four points a game, trying to uphold the family tradition: His brother Paul went on to become the NFL Rookie of the Year for the Cincinnati Bengals;

another brother, Cleo, went on to be a Pac-10 football referee.

By year's end, Jerry Robinson averaged 16 points a game and was on the all-state team. A year later he was all-state in football and basketball. He is now a banking executive in San Diego, still in touch with the Pattons.

"I'm sorry," Robinson says, clearing his throat, "I sometimes get a little tearful when I talk about Coach Patton. Sometimes, when I give seminars through my business, I'm asked what type of person impacted my life, and I tell them about Coach Patton. I tell them that here was a white man who took a little old farm kid like me and gave me direction and leadership when I needed it most.

"I was floundering when Coach Patton came to Marana, with no idea what to do with my ability. He helped me get started. He is a person I could talk about for a long time. He sacrificed for me. I'm grateful to this day."

But even the intimacy between Patton and the family he created in Marana couldn't go on forever. In 1973, after compiling a 158-34 record for the Tiger basketball program, he was tempted by the creation of a coaching position at Tucson's new junior college.

"About the same time, I was offered the job as principal at Marana, but I was still young (34) and wanted to stay in coaching," he remembers. "The Pima College job was attractive because they wanted to keep it local, and I had been on a roll for a while and thought we could keep all the local kids in Tucson and really get it going."

But coaching basketball, or any sport, at Pima College, was considerably more difficult in the '70s than it is today, which is significant. The Aztecs offered no scholarships, had no history to draw from, no urgency to excel. Patton saw that in a hurry; in the first basketball game in PCC history, the team's uniforms weren't ready. The first season, 1973-74, was to be the only losing season in Patton's 29 years of coaching.

All of Pima's rivals in the competitive Arizona Community College Athletic Conference — Eastern, Western, Yavapai, Mesa, etc. — offered more. Tucson athletes could attend those schools, eat at a training table for free, stay in dorms, play to win. All Pima offered was a chance to play to win.

And, ultimately, Patton found a way. He kept the top basketball players at home, like Kenny Ball and Chuck Goslin and Greg Cook. In 1980, he coached the Aztecs to their only ACCAC championship, improved his PCC record to 111-83, and then decided 17 years was enough coaching. The combination of getting away to watch his girls play basketball and quit banging his head against PCC's slow-moving wall led him to retire. He was barely 40 years old.

"In the end, I just felt like Pima wasn't committed to doing the best it could do," he says. "They just let things evolve. We finally got it going there, but it liked to have killed me."

A year later, with Patton in temporary coaching retirement, the Aztecs went 4-21.

### Complete circles

A lot of things can go wrong in a small town like Cliff, N.M. For instance, Norm's father, Barney, had a heart attack after finishing with some ranch work. He got off his horse, complained of chest pain, and got into the pickup. By the time young Norm Patton, driving like mad, reached the nearest hospital, 30 miles away in Silver City, Barney Patton, 59, was dead.

There have been some trade-offs. Playing basketball at Cliff got Norm a scholarship to Eastern Arizona College, which led to a scholarship at New Mexico State, which led to his coaching job in Colorado, which led to his coaching job at Marana.

He met his wife, Sandra, while playing for Cliff against rival Silver High School. Sandra was a cheerleader for Silver High. One day a few years later, while in Silver City, Norm phoned Sandra's father, Monte, a mechanic his family knew, and mentioned that "your daughter is very pretty."

Monte arranged a date.

While at Silver City, Sandra went to school with George Young, who went on to become the greatest long distance runner in UA history, and one of the best in American Olympic history. (Young ran in the 1960, 1964, 1968 and 1972 Olympics). The New Mexico connection worked again in 1981.

Young, then the athletic director at Central Arizona College, asked Patton if he would come out of retirement to coach the Vaqueros basketball team. Patton balked. It's a 75-mile drive, one way, to Coolidge, and he wasn't about to move his family from Marana.

Young persisted. Patton resisted.

Ultimately, tempted by the possibility of coaching at a school committed to excellence, Patton agreed to coach for one season, replacing Gary Heintz, who had joined Fred Snowden's staff at UA in August 1981.

It turned into a 13-year gig, perhaps the hallmark of a long coaching career: four ACCAC Coach of the Year awards; a 269-118 record; 13 consecutive years in the region playoffs; more than 25 players sent to Division I schools.

"We had a chance to win two national titles," Patton says. "We finished sixth in the nation in 1992, and might've had the best team. It was a wonderful experience. We sent players to Marquette, UTEP, George Washington, Nebraska, Hawaii, Seton Hall ..."

The circle was completed in 1994 when Patton's old assistant at Pima, and his predecessor at CAC, Heintz, replaced him. Patton was still a young 55, and busied himself watching his youngest daughter, Patty, coach Catalina Foothills to the 1997 state 4A championship. They are the only father-daughter combination in Arizona history to coach state champions in basketball.

Patty is 32 now, and that special night at America West Arena, when the state interscholastic association honored the Pattons, father and daughter, capped a wonderful ride.

"I was so happy for Patty," he says. "I know what she was feeling because there is no feeling like winning that first state championship. Now she's doing what I did. She's doing all she can to get No. 2."

But that isn't quite the end of the story. Friday afternoon, while Patty was coaching her team in a tournament in San Diego, Norm and Sandra Patton drove to the gym near Marana to watch their 8-year-old granddaughter, Kenzie, play her first organized basketball game.

AUTHOR'S NOTE: Norm Patton, 70, lives in Marana with his wife, Sandra. In recent years, he has watched daughter Kelly Fowler coach the 2005 Canyon del Oro High School softball team to the state championship, and granddaughter Kenzie Fowler, a pitcher, win three state titles at CDO and twice be selected the national softball player of the year.

**THE NORM PATTON FILE**
**Born:** Hatch, N.M., 1939
**Family:** Wife, Sandra; four daughters
**Education:** Cliff (N.M.) High School; Eastern Arizona College; New Mexico State; UA (master's)
**Occupations:** Retired educator, coach and cattle rancher
**Some heartaches along the way:** "One of the first players I ever recruited at Central was a kid from Buffalo, N.Y., named Leonard Jackson. His family situation was a mess. I picked him up at the airport and he didn't have a nickel. He didn't have a suitcase; his clothes were in a cardboard box, held together by tape. He became a first-team All-American and signed to play for Oregon. But once

Leonard got out into the real world, he kind of got sidetracked. He never did get to Oregon."

**Most admired athlete:** "At Pima, we had Greg Cook, who had played at Sunnyside, and then later at the UA. When he was right, he was big-time. He had NBA talent."

**Mistaken identity:** While coaching at Pima College, Patton was invited to give a coaching clinic in Hermosillo, Mexico. The morning after his clinic, attended by about 200 coaches, a local newspaper ran a banner headline identifying Patton as the head coach of the Phoenix Suns. "I got to the airport," he says, "and there must've been 1,000 people wanting me to sign a certificate from my clinic. The officials there delayed the plane for two hours until I signed every last certificate."

**Welcome to the big time:** In Patton's first coaching job, 1963 in Bayfield, Colo., he discovered that there wasn't enough equipment to outfit his football team for the opening game, and the school didn't have a budget to purchase any. He phoned nearby Fort Lewis College and asked if he could have their leftovers: helmets, shoulder pads, hip pads, anything. "We drove down to Fort Lewis in an old school pickup and loaded everything into the back. My wife, Sandra, ended up painting 40 helmets blue and gold. When we went to line the field for the opener, we had nothing to do it with. I ended up going down to a flour mill and lining the field with flour."

Larry Hart

# A century of Tucson sports: Larry Hart

*Sunday, August 1, 1999*

Shortly before the 1964 high school football season, Flowing Wells coach Larry Hart discussed the merits of the Caballeros with Star sportswriter Ed Jordan. At issue was whether the Cabs had any merit.

Jordan said they didn't. Hart insisted they did.

"You might not win a game again," Jordan started.

"We'll win at least five," Hart rejoined.

This made Jordan laugh. The Caballeros were coming off 0-7-1 and 0-10 seasons, and had failed to post a winning football record in the school's first nine years. "If you win five," he said, fearlessly, "I'll eat my hat."

Boom. The Cabs steamroll the month of September. Hart commissions a baker to whip up a cake in the shape of a hat. And almost before the newspaper ink is dry — CABS BEAT BISBEE FOR 5TH STRAIGHT — Hart and several carloads of Flowing Wells football players are standing in front of Jordan's desk.

The memory brings a smile to Hart's face.

"Ed ate his hat."

There was a lot of hat-eating in those days. Larry Hart's football teams at Flowing Wells went on to play in the state championship game an inconceivable six times across 10 seasons, including '64. At one stretch, from 1970 to 1972, the Caballeros went 34-1-1 in regular-season games.

Yet the anecdote about the sportswriter's hat is out of character. Hart wasn't about frosting or flash. In four decades as a high school football coach, Larry Hart was as flamboyant as a hammock. He spent almost 20 years as a high school principal, and it fit.

"Larry was like an icon. He was THE coach," said Ben Jimenez, a Tucson homicide detective who was the Cabs' starting quarterback in 1975. "We were so well-disciplined. You looked up to him, you listened to him, and, in a way, you feared him. But it was a healthy type of fear."

A visitor asks Hart how many state championship games he reached, and Hart demurs. "Oh, I have it in a book somewhere," he says, twisting the conversation to an unexpected route.

"I never believed in playing championship games at the high

331

school level," he said. "I always felt the kids should play 10 regular-season games and then be free to follow other pursuits. Championships have forced specialization. They've forced year-round football, weight-lifting, summer passing leagues, film sessions and many things I'm not in favor of. High school football has become a miniature version of college football, and coaches have been given too much latitude. I was a part of all that."

It is inescapable that Larry Hart's coaching days at Flowing Wells will forever be defined by six appearances in the state championship game. What else attracts so much attention in football? The irony is that he looks back and sees something much different.

He sees that his former quarterbacks have become husbands and fathers and engineers. He sees a much bigger picture than a 14-13 state championship victory over Snowflake in 1975, a cleansing victory that ended a streak of five humbling losses in the state championship game. He sees his most celebrated player, linebacker Mark Jacobs, working with kids up and down the hallways at Flowing Wells, giving back to his old school.

For 11 years at Flowing Wells, Hart served burdensome dual capacities as football coach and principal, one of the rarest of all combinations in the education system, unprecedented in Tucson's larger schools. What would motivate someone to work those buckling, 14-hour-a-day jobs that never seem to end?

Ego? Power? A few dollars more?

"My whole philosophy was to help kids reach their potential," said Hart. "In teaching, you could reach a few students. But there is no medium where you can have an impact on the kids as through coaching. The reward isn't winning a state championship. It's working with the kids."

### His forte was work ethic

As an entry, the Hart brothers, Larry and Bobby, are as accomplished as any set of brothers in a century of Tucson sports. Both were standout, three-sport high school athletes at Amphitheater; both played college football, and played it well (Larry at Idaho, Bobby at Arizona); both spent 30 years coaching (Bobby at Amphi, Larry at Flowing Wells and Ajo).

The Harts belong in the same distinguished company as Tucson's top brother combinations, the Batistes, the Bateses, the Kellners, the Dawsons, the Duncans.

"I was fortunate enough to coach them both, and to coach with and against them," said George Genung, basketball coach at Amphi for more than 30 years. "They're as different as night and day — Bobby is very outgoing and Larry is very reserved — but they had a great impact on this town for a long time."

They were virtually inseparable. In the early '50s, Bobby Hart was a one-man track team at Eastern Arizona College in Thatcher (then called Gila Junior College). At the JC national championships one year, Bobby became an All-American by finishing second in the low hurdles and, again, second in the high hurdles. A Tucson newspaper ran a picture of Bobby Hart at the finish line.

The caption identified Bobby as Larry.

"Bobby was a very fine athlete, much better than I was," said Larry. "My forte was work ethic."

They grew up in the rural Marana area, the son of Paul and Hazel Hart. Paul was a Kansan who moved to Tucson in 1921 to attend UA and became an auditor and insurance executive. Hazel came from a family of dairy farmers in north Phoenix. They had six sons and a daughter, struggled financially in Depression-era Tucson, and the boys created their own entertainment. Mostly they played baseball with makeshift equipment on dirt-and-rock lots.

"For as long as I can remember," said Larry, who grew up watching and being influenced by UA football and basketball stars of the '30s and '40s, "I wanted to be a coach."

During his playing days at Amphi, Larry was fortunate to have two of those former Wildcats, Genung and Merle McCain, on the coaching staff. He was impressed by McCain's toughness and by Genung's sincerity, and told himself that when he became a coach, he would model himself after them. "They were what I thought coaches should be all about," he said.

After establishing himself as a top halfback at Amphi, Larry longed to play for the hometown Wildcats, much like Genung and McCain, and one night was invited to meet with UA football coach Bob Winslow.

Winslow offered several Amphi football players scholarships, with one proviso. They would have to commit to him by that night or forget it. They forgot it, and all of them went to Thatcher to play for the Gila Monsters. Larry worked in the laundry to make ends meet while starring for the EAC football team.

Two years later, he accepted a scholarship to Idaho, worked his way into the Vandals' starting lineup as an offensive and defensive halfback and completed his degree in four years.

"In the summers, I would come back to Tucson, on the train, and coach the Amphi American Legion baseball team," he said. "During my senior year at Idaho, I opened the mail one day and in it was a contract to teach and coach at Amphi. It offered me $3,033 a year."

Hart gave up plans to work for a commission in the Air Force and came home.

"My first year I coached baseball, football and basketball. I was a scout for the varsity football team and one season I drove to Yuma three times to scout Yuma and the teams they were playing. I'd get home at 3 in the morning and be up early for our 10 a.m. junior varsity games. In track, I had to learn coaching techniques out of a book. Coaching didn't pay much, $200 per sport per year, but I wouldn't have wanted to do anything else."

### A special time

Ajo was a thriving mining town of about 8,000 in the mid-'50s. The mines worked on a 26-and-2 schedule: 26 days on, two days off.

There wasn't much to do in a small town whose mines were open 24 hours a day. When the high school football team was having a good year, it wasn't uncommon for townsfolk to load up six buses on Friday afternoons and follow Larry Hart's team out of town.

Hart took the Ajo job in 1956, recommended by Arizona athletic director Pop McKale. It wasn't a tough act to follow. Ajo was working on its fourth coach in four years, and Hart took over a team that had gone winless. He did that, too. In his third season, Hart's club was 0-8-1.

"It might've been one of my best coaching jobs," he said. "We had no talent whatsoever, but the kids were just excellent in giving what they could."

Ajo in the mid-century was a good place to raise a family. That's why Hart stayed for eight years. Ultimately, the isolation got to him. "I couldn't go see the UA play very often because it was about a 2½-hour drive," he said.

During Hart's days at Ajo, Flowing Wells had gone through four football coaches from 1956 to 1962. When Bob Maxwell left after going 0-10 in 1962, Hart was hired in midsummer, with barely enough time to meet anyone before school started.

Dick Griesser, a former UA All-America baseball player, was on the coaching staff at Flowing Wells and vividly remembers his first impression of Hart.

"We met at Larry's house and, boy, was he organized. He

explained how he wanted to do things. He implemented a 'system,' meaning that the junior high team and the freshman team and the JV team would all be running the same plays. This was new. We followed everything to the letter. I sensed that things would be changing for the better."

Although not quickly. The Cabs went 0-7-1 in Hart's debut, completing the season with 19 players. Eleven were dismissed from the team for disciplinary reasons. But a year later, the Cabs had a sportswriter eating his hat on the way to a 7-3 regular season and a berth opposite Winslow in an agonizing state championship setback. The final score was 7-0.

Everything had changed for the Cabs. Hart implemented a study hall at 6:30 a.m., before such things became fashionable. Grades were checked weekly, for eligibility.

"It didn't take long for Larry to get it going, and get it going in the right way," Griesser said. "I could see that if a kid had any talent at all, Larry would bring it out of them. Kids wanted to play for him. He treated them with respect. It was an enjoyable situation."

But just as Hart got it going, he left. He accepted the job as principal at Agua Fria High School in Avondale in 1966. The Cabs, under Ted Sorich, who had been on Hart's staff, did well, going 6-2-2 and 6-2-1. But Hart missed coaching, and in 1968, he returned to Flowing Wells.

"That's when we really got it going," he said. "It was a special time."

The next eight years would be among the finest any Tucson high school ever experienced. The Caballeros went 66-14-1 and played for the state title in 1968, 1971, 1972, 1973 and 1975. They weren't winning with extraordinary manpower; only two Caballeros from those years went on to play Division I football (at Arizona): Mark Jacobs, a dominating linebacker, and lineman Paul Schmidt.

If anything was wrong, it was the timing.

The Cabs were somewhat overlooked because their rise as a small-schools power coincided with three Tucson High state championship teams, loaded with all-staters and college recruits. And when THS ebbed, Palo Verde roared to a 13-0 record in 1973, capturing headlines locally.

Finally, when the Cabs broke through to win the '75 state title, Amphi had a higher profile, winning the big-schools state championship.

"Thank God we won it in '75," Griesser said. "We had lost five state championship games, and two or three of them were just excruciating, lost on fumbles in the last few minutes. You would hear rumors that 'Larry couldn't win the Big One,' and it was hard to get away from that. There was a big cloud over all the success he had. When we beat Snowflake that year to win it all, the frustration of all those previous years just washed away. Larry didn't have to carry that with him any longer."

Today, tempered by a quarter-century, Hart is remembered not for losing five state title games, but for being an overwhelming success.

"The reward wasn't in me winning the state championship, it was in watching the kids in that crowning moment," Hart said. "If there was any frustration, it was that we would go 9-0 in the regular season and people would say, 'What went wrong?' Our failure to win those games clouded too much of what the kids accomplished."

After the Cabs won their long-awaited state title in 1975, Hart got teary-eyed, and when the team reached the locker room, his voice broke on more than one occasion.

"Seeing him emotional like that was a first, a surprise," said Jimenez, the quarterback. "We were always so in sync, so well-prepared, that we just went out and did our job. He was a tough old guy, but every once in a while you could see that we got to him."

AUTHOR'S NOTE: Larry Hart, 79, lives in Tucson. He is an active volunteer for the Pima County Sports Hall of Fame and for the Southern Arizona chapter of the National Football Foundation, College Hall of Fame.

## THE LARRY HART FILE

**Born:** Tucson, 1931

**Family:** Three children

**Education:** Amphitheater High School; Eastern Arizona College; University of Idaho; Arizona State University

**Occupations:** High school coach, teacher and principal; retired 1987

**Honors:** Pima County Sports Hall of Fame

**What might have been:** While attending the University of Idaho, Hart was employed part time as a special deputy in Moscow, Idaho. He lived in the jail on weekends, attending to prisoners. "We captured two bank robbers from Illinois, wanted for murder," he said. "I would serve them food in their cell, with the sheriff standing beside me with a shotgun. I saw too many horrible things to consider that as a profession. Five high school kids were killed in a car crash — too much snow and drinking — and I was at the scene."

**Long days:** When Flowing Wells made its 34-1-1 regular-season run in the early '70s, Hart also served as assistant principal, the president of the Arizona Coaches Association and on the board of the Arizona Interscholastic Association. "I'd go to work at 6 a.m. and get home at 10 p.m.," he said. "They were very long days."

**Ties to Larry Smith:** When Larry Smith became the defensive coordinator at Arizona, under Jim Young, he visited Hart to inquire about linebacker Mark Jacobs. Hart gave Smith four game tapes on a Tuesday. Smith came back the next day, offering a scholarship. In 1980, when Smith became Arizona's head coach, Hart joined the staff as a volunteer for a year. He worked mostly with scout team defensive preparations.

**Among the best:** Hart ticks off a list of those whose athletic abilities he admired through the years, among them Tucson High infielder Lee Carey, Douglas High running back Gib Dawson, and his own linebacker, Jacobs. "He was probably the most intense player I ever coached," he said. Jacobs became an All-WAC linebacker at Arizona.

**Memory serves:** As a senior at Amphi in 1949, Hart played in the state championship basketball game against Tucson High. "To this day, I can't forget those scores. We tried to hold the ball. It was 5-3 after one quarter and 11-7 at half. We lost 49-26."

# A century of Tucson sports:
# Bud Grainger

*Sunday, August 8, 1999*

They were boys before the war. Bud, Chappo, Corky and Frank.
"If you saw one of us, you saw all four of us," John Henry "Bud"
Grainger says now. "People said we lived on the wrong side of the
tracks, but it was fine by us."

Some of the boys didn't grow up to be men.

Cornelius "Corky" Moore was killed at Iwo Jima, shot by a
Japanese sniper the day before the Marines planted the flag on Mount
Suribachi. Frank Kempf, an all-state catcher at Tucson High, was killed
by German artillery on the way to Berlin.

By the time Bud Grainger was honorably discharged from the
Marines late in 1945, his old gang was gone and Tucson was a lonelier
place on both sides of the tracks. Arnold "Chappo" Riesgo, one of the
Four Musketeers, survived the war but soon moved to Florida to play
baseball. Life got on without an intermediate stop.

Maybe that's why Bud had such a great appreciation for life.
Maybe that's why he didn't seem to stop, plowing ahead for the next 55
years as if he were making up for the time his boyhood chums didn't
have.

Bud played baseball in the Brooklyn Dodgers' chain. He got a job at
the bank, as a lowly messenger, and worked his way into a vice presi-
dency. He raised a family, umpired more than 1,000 baseball games,
and when he got through with that, he not only volunteered his time to
coach in the American Legion system, he wound up running the entire
Tucson operation. Still does, and he's 76, with the scars of a triple
bypass as evidence that it'll take more than that to keep him down.

So how'd he do? How's he doing?

"I've known Bud since I was a kid. We grew up in the same neighborhood on the same side of the tracks, and I've umpired hundreds of
ball games with him," says Don Moore, Corky's brother. "It's always
been a privilege to know him. He's fair, he's professional and he's the
type of guy that you can count on as a friend for life."

Don Moore stops in mid-sentence. His voice breaks and he points
to an old photograph that shows his late brother, Corky, in a pose with
an early '40s championship baseball team from Tucson High. There's

339

Corky and Frank ...

"Those kids," he says, "had so much promise."

**The influence of baseball**

It was almost ordained that the Graingers would be a baseball family. Bud's grandmother, Nora Carter, who lived in the Los Angeles neighborhood that housed old Wrigley Field, was not only a regular at the ballpark, she died there, of a heart attack, watching the Hollywood Stars in the Pacific Coast League.

Bud doesn't necessarily want to die at the ballpark, but when he attended the funeral of Hank Leiber, one of the most accomplished baseball players ever at UA, and a former All-Star for the New York Giants, he did pick up some pointers.

At the conclusion of Leiber's services, an organist played, "Take Me Out to the Ballgame."

"I thought, 'OK! That's great. Hank would've loved it,'" Bud says. "I hope when my time comes they play it for me, too."

Baseball was an easy choice for the neighborhood kids in Tucson in the '30s. What else was there to do? There wasn't any money. Bud and Chappo and Frank and Corky built their own baseball field, kicking away the rocks and recruiting Bud's father, Jack, to help build a back-stop and correctly measure the base paths.

If you could get six kids, you had a game. It was called work-up. One or two guys batted, and when one made an out, the others rotated until it was their time to bat. It was the American sandlot game of the '30s and '40s and '50s — as much as video games are today's staple entertainment.

That's what Bud and Chappo and Frank and Corky would play. Day after day. Hour after hour.

"We'd go watch the (professional) Tucson Cowboys play and when someone would hit a foul ball over the fence, we'd run and get it before one of the team officials could retrieve it," Bud says with a laugh. "We'd hide the ball down a gopher hole and go back and get it later. That was the only way we could get a baseball. We sure couldn't afford them."

By the time Bud and Chappo and Corky and Frank got to Tucson High, the school's vast baseball tradition beckoned. The Badgers won the state championship for eight consecutive years, from 1939 to 1946. Bud was the all-state second baseman in 1941.

"We just didn't lose," he says. "We were very good. Baseball was the way of life for us. It was a good way to grow up, a good influence. It kept us out of trouble."

Bud was going to be a baseball player. In 1942, the Dodgers offered him $75 a month and UA coach Pop McKale offered him a scholarship. He took the $75, lured by the promise of a $500 bonus if he stuck with the Class D club in Olean, N.Y., through the summer.

He didn't get the $500 (he was beaten out by future Philadelphia Phillies manager Danny Ozark). But he did meet Betty George there. She would become his wife for 53 years and counting. As baseball trades go, it was a good one.

### A treasure

By Bud's count, he worked 192 Arizona-ASU baseball games. He umpired through the eras of Bobby Winkles and Frank Sancet, and Jim Brock and Jerry Kindall. In 1975, he had his greatest honor (and again in 1978) when he was selected to the umpiring crew for the College World Series.

He umpired from 1946 to 1984, working at every conceivable level. High school, youth leagues, the minor leagues, colleges.

"Bud was a treasure, just an absolute treasure," says Lou Pavlovich Jr., editor of the Tucson-based Collegiate Baseball magazine. "He was a hustler. He had the game's best interest at heart. He wasn't a showboat. He was just good."

You don't have enough time to read about all his umpiring stories. That would take a book.

There was the time at the NCAA Regionals in Austin, Texas, when the beloved Longhorns lost a close game and some fans chased Bud and fellow Tucson umpire Bill Rosenberry to the locker room. They pounded on the door with chairs. They threw jars of Vaseline at them.

"We had been staying at the same hotel as the ballplayers," Bud remembers. "We moved the next day."

There was the time he was umpiring an Arizona-Iowa game when Hawkeye coach Otto Vogel became unhappy. He called Bud a "homer," which was, during his career, the one word he would not tolerate.

"Pretty soon, the whole dugout was calling me a homer," Bud says. "I just detest that word. If I prided myself on anything over the years, it was to bend over backward to be fair. So I went to the Iowa dugout and tossed Vogel out of the game. And then I tossed his whole bench out of the game. He told me I couldn't do that. I said I could. It got pretty quiet after that."

There was the time at USC's Dedeaux Field in 1978 when Bud blew an interference call at second base in a tight pennant race between the Trojans and Wildcats. The UA's Kindall sprinted to second base, confronting Grainger.

"It took Jerry about three steps to go 100 yards and get right in my face," Bud says. "Before he could say a word, I said, 'you're right; I blew the call and I can't change it now.' But I was always a good listener. I let Jerry have his say. When he got back to the dugout, he kept riding me and I went over and told him that was all. He knew not to cross the line. He was always a gentleman."

Grainger estimates he worked maybe 500 UA games over the years, half for Kindall, half for Sancet. He ejected Sancet once; he ejected ASU's Brock and Winkles once each. It says a lot for maturity and professionalism, not just for the Wildcat and Sun Devil coaches, but for Bud. The feelings between UA and ASU, especially in baseball and especially in the '60s and '70s, were so raw that it took an extraordinary umpire to keep order.

One of the treasures of Bud's career is a letter from Brock, written in 1984. After more than a decade on opposite sides, as umpires and baseball coaches are, Brock wrote that he respected Bud and hated to see him retire.

"He told me I was a good official," Bud recollects. "That's the most an umpire can ask."

Says Moore, a fellow WAC, Pac-10 and high school umpire in Bud's years: "Bud was an aggressive umpire. He was very meticulous and strived for perfection. Hey, you wanted to go on the field with him because you knew he would take charge."

## Bud and the Kellners

In a century of Tucson baseball, Bud Grainger bridges all the generations. He played for Tucson High's legendary Andy Tolson, and he played for the young Hank Slagle, who, by percentage was the most successful high school baseball coach in Arizona history.

He played for Chuck Hollinger, who was no less than the Caretaker of Baseball in this town for 75 years, a youth-league coach and umpire of distinction. (He taught Bud how to throw a knuckleball.) And he umpired for McKale, Sancet and Kindall. There's virtually no baseball life in Tucson in the 20th century that didn't touch Bud Grainger or wasn't touched by him.

"Frank was like a second father to me," Bud says. "I considered him a mentor. But that didn't mean our paths didn't cross. The time I had to throw him out, he called me gutless. I told him to cool it and he said, 'You're still gutless.' The next day, it was behind us."

But the one connection Bud Grainger has that ties him to Tucson baseball for posterity is his link to the Kellner family: Alex and Walt, of Amphitheater High, became major-league pitchers; Walt's son, Joey, pitched for Arizona's 1980 NCAA championship team; and Walt's youngest son, Frank, reached Class AAA with the Tucson Toros.

He played against Walt and Alex, and was Walt's teammate on a semipro team that finished third in the nation at the 1949 National Baseball Congress World Series. He and Walt coached Joey and Frank in youth leagues and in American Legion.

"Bud's not only the best umpire to ever come out of Tucson," Walt Kellner says, "but he's one of the first men you would want to be involved coaching your sons. We were fortunate that way." (Says Bud: "As good as Alex was, I could hit him. But big old Walt, no way. That guy was the toughest pitcher I ever faced.")

One of the most compelling Tucson baseball stories of the century connects, naturally, to the Kellners and to Bud Grainger. As follows: Shortly after Leiber had retired from baseball, coaching and playing for the Tucson Cowboys, young Alex Kellner was a pitching phenom for the Philadelphia Athletics. One day in February, they happened to attend the same workout.

Ultimately, Kellner was pitching and Leiber was batting. Grainger, playing third base, backed up, almost to the grass.

"Hank was the best to have ever come out of the UA," he remembers. "Alex was the best pitcher Tucson ever produced. Kellner vs. Leiber. Everyone stopped to watch. I was in awe. Leiber lined a shot back through the middle. Boy, those were the days."

Indeed.

AUTHOR'S NOTE: Bud Grainger, 86, is retired and living in Tucson. You can often see him behind home plate at Kindall/Sancet Stadium, supporting the umpires.

## THE BUD GRAINGER FILE
**Born:** Tucson, 1923
**Family:** Married (Betty), three children
**Education:** Tucson High School
**Occupations:** Banker, umpire, coach, Marine Corps
**Best of the lot:** "With all due respect to Eddie Leon and Lee Carey, Emil Rey was one of the best to ever come out of the area." Rey was a first-team all-state shortstop at Tucson High from 1938 to 1940.
**Life in the trenches:** While umpiring a Class C Tucson Cowboys game in the '50s, Grainger called a Cowboys runner out at third on a

343

close play. "He got up and bumped me, and I put out the palm of my hand to stop him," Grainger says. "We wore ties in those days, and he grabbed my tie and tore it off, ripping my shirt in the process. He paid for my shirt and was suspended. He later apologized and we became best of friends. I don't carry grudges."

**Tucson's class of umpires:** "There have been so many outstanding umpires from Tucson. Bill Lawson is outstanding. Terry Mann. The DiMuro family. I'm not sure Bill Rosenberry wasn't the best we've ever had. He was tough. He was outstanding. He's been at the College World Series several times."

**The bank caper:** In 1981, when he was vice president of Southern Arizona Bank, Grainger was taken hostage in an early-morning robbery that netted a then-United States record $3.3 million. The intruders held a gun to Grainger's head and threatened that his wife was also in their custody. No one was injured. The robbers were caught a few days later.

**A long list of talent:** In Grainger's many years as an American Legion and youth league coach, he was fortunate to coach a future major-league pitcher, Andy Hassler of Palo Verde High School. "I couldn't say who the best is," he says. "I coached a lot of the future college players, Jim Filippelli, Rick Valley, Willie Morales Sr., Dave Breucker. There were a lot of them."

# The best of the best

I began an annual list of Tucson's top 100 sports figures in 1996 for one reason: Tucson had become big enough to easily accommodate such a list. I was eager to put it in perspective and acknowledge the remarkable performances of everyone from distance runner Pam Reed to Champions Tour golfer Don Pooley.

Initially, it was tempting to include former UA athletes no longer living in Tucson, such as Annika Sorenstam, the first No. 1 selection. But by the second year, I thought the list would be better if it did not reflect ex-UA athletes, unless they had grown up in Southern Arizona.

Otherwise, Annika Sorenstam or Kenny Lofton would be near the top of the list each year. I wanted diversity; I wanted the Top 100 to reflect Tucson sports at its foundation: top performances by people living or raised in Tucson. High school coaches. Gymnasts. Everybody.

Nor did I want it to be a list dominated by UA athletes. If the local newspaper doesn't recognize the achievements of rodeo stars such as Colter Todd and Cesar de la Cruz, and wrestling dynamos like Nate and Nick Gallick, nobody will.

**1996**
1. Marisa Baena, UA women's golf
2. Kerri Strug, Team USA gymnastics
3. Damon Stoudamire, Toronto Raptors
4. Jenny Dalton, UA softball
5. Amy Skieresz, UA cross country/track and field
6. Scott Gaskins, Salpointe Catholic High School swimming
7. Jim Reffkin, Pima College women's and Salpointe tennis coach
8. Mike Candrea, UA softball coach
9. Steve Kerr, Chicago Bulls
10. Bob Baffert, horse trainer

**1997**
1. Chad Carvin, Team USA swimming
2. Nancy Evans, UA softball
3. Chad Cislak, Sabino High School baseball
4. Miles Simon, UA men's basketball
5. Chris Johnson, LPGA Tour golf
6. Shelley Duncan, Canyon del Oro High School baseball
7. Julie Brase, Catalina Foothills High School basketball
8. Mike Bibby, UA men's basketball
9. Erin Aldrich, UA volleyball/track and field
10. Nathan Wize, Sabino High School football

## 1998

1. Dick Tomey, UA football coach
2. Amy Skieresz, UA cross country/track and field
3. Ryk Neethling, UA swimming
4. Mike Bibby, UA men's basketball
5. Frank Busch, UA swimming coach
6. Adia Barnes, UA women's basketball
7. Nancy Evans, UA softball
8. Chris McAlister, UA football
9. Jim Scott, Sahuaro High School girls basketball coach
10. Trung Canidate, UA football

## 1999

1. Jason Terry, UA men's basketball
2. Ryk Neethling, UA swimming
3. Dennis Northcutt, UA football
4. Will Smith, Palo Verde High School baseball
5. Erubiel Durazo, Arizona Diamondbacks
6. Nick Frost, Salpointe Catholic High School wrestling
7. Jenna Daniels, UA women's golf
8. Judy McDermott, Tucson Conquistadores operations manager
9. Yewki Tomita, Team USA gymnastics
10. Melinda Almazan, Regis College volleyball

## 2000

1. Sean Elliott, San Antonio Spurs
2. Gil Heredia, Oakland Athletics
3. Jenna Daniels, UA women's golf
4. Frank Busch, UA swimming coach
5. Gord Fraser, Team Canada cycling
6. Dana Burkholder, UA volleyball
7. Paul Seiler, USA Baseball operations manager
8. David Coronado, Sunnyside High School football/wrestling
9. Dave Rubio, UA volleyball coach
10. Abdi Abdirahman, Team USA track and field

## 2001

1. Lute Olson, UA men's basketball coach
2. Jennie Finch, UA softball
3. Brianna Glenn, UA track and field
4. Dave Rubio, UA volleyball coach
5. Lorena Ochoa, UA women's golf
6. Yuliana Perez, Pima College track and field
7. Jesus Cota, Pima College/minor-league baseball
8. Richard Sanchez, Sunnyside High School football coach
9. Dana Burkholder, UA volleyball
10. Dick McConnell, Sahuaro High School boys basketball coach

## 2002

1. Don Pooley, Champions Tour golf
2. Mike Candrea, UA softball coach
3. Pam Reed, endurance runner
4. Ricky Barnes, Amateur/UA men's golf
5. Lorena Ochoa, UA women's/professional golf
6. Jennie Finch, UA softball
7. Lute Olson, UA men's basketball coach
8. Sue Brooks, local marketer (LPGA golf)
9. Jim Reffkin, City of Tucson director of tennis
10. Luke Walton, UA men's basketball

## 2003

1. Amanda Beard, Team USA swimming
2. Jim Livengood, UA athletic director
3. Eric Larkin, Arizona State wrestling
4. Tairia Mims, UCLA/Team USA softball
5. Richard Sanchez, Sunnyside High School football coach
6. Ricky Barnes, UA men's golf
7. Mike Candrea, UA softball coach
8. Lute Olson, UA men's basketball coach
9. Jason Stanford, Cleveland Indians
10. Andy Lopez, UA baseball coach

## 2004

1. Mike Candrea, Team USA softball coach
2. Amanda Beard, Team USA swimming
3. Stacy Iveson, Pima College softball coach
4. Chris Nallen, UA men's golf
5. Dan Tobias, UA soccer coach
6. Robert Cheseret, UA cross country/track and field
7. Frank Busch, UA swimming coach
8. Nate Gallick, Iowa State wrestling
9. Andy Lopez, UA baseball coach
10. Luis Cota, South Mountain College/minor-league baseball

## 2005

1. Nate and Nick Gallick, Iowa State wrestling
2. Robert Cheseret, UA cross country/track and field
3. Frank Busch, UA swimming coach
4. J.J. Hardy, Milwaukee Brewers
5. Todd Mayfield, Palo Verde High School football coach
6. Mallory Miller, UA soccer
7. Trevor Crowe, UA baseball
8. Channing Frye, UA men's basketball
9. Pam Reed, endurance runner
10. Gord Fraser, professional cyclist

## 2006

1. Chip Hale, Tucson Sidewinders manager
2. Frank Busch, UA swimming coach
3. Alicia Hollowell, UA softball
4. Stacy Iveson, Pima College softball coach
5. Chris Duncan, St. Louis Cardinals
6. Jerry Coons Jr., professional car driver
7. Whitney Myers, UA swimming
8. Ian Kinsler, Texas Rangers
9. Bobby and Kyle DeBerry, Sunnyside wrestling
10. Kenzie Fowler, Canyon del Oro High School softball

## 2007

1. Bernard Lagat, Team USA track and field
2. Taryne Mowatt, UA softball
3. Michael Thompson, Amateur/Alabama golf
4. Lacey Nymeyer, UA swimming
5. Preston Guilmet, UA baseball
6. Jake Arnold, UA track and field
7. Michael Garten, WGC-Accenture Match Play Championship golf director
8. Jeff Scurran, Santa Rita High School football coach
9. Antoine Cason, UA football
10. Caitlin Leverenz, Team USA swimming

## 2008

1. Frank Busch, UA swimming coach
2. Ian Kinsler, Texas Rangers
3. Lacey Nymeyer, UA/Team USA swimming
4. Jackie Vasquez, Arizona State softball
5. Ryan Perry, UA/minor-league baseball
6. Lara Jackson, UA swimming
7. Kenzie Fowler, Canyon del Oro High School softball
8. Adam Hall, Palo Verde High School football
9. Colter Todd and Cesar de la Cruz, rodeo team roping
10. Michael Thompson, Alabama golf

## MOST APPEARANCES IN THE TOP 10

6- Frank Busch
4- Mike Candrea
3- Lute Olson
3- Amy Skieresz
2- Ricky Barnes
2- Mike Bibby
2- Robert Cheseret
2- Jenna Daniels
2- Nancy Evans
2- Jennie Finch
2- Kenzie Fowler
2- Stacy Iveson
2- Ian Kinsler
2- Ryk Neethling
2- Lacey Nymeyer
2- Pam Reed
2- Damon Stoudamire
2- Michael Thompson

# CHAPTER NINE

# UA vs. ASU

## UA: 'All that matters is we beat ASU'

*Sunday, November 27, 1983*

*TEMPE*

Less than 30 seconds had elapsed since Arizona's Max Zendejas kicked a 45-yard field goal to beat Arizona State 17-15 yesterday at Sun Devil Stadium.

The press box elevator was loaded and ready for descent.

Four Arizona coaches arrived at the elevator, hugging, hollering and being — well, what's an antonym for solemn?

"Ultimately euphoric," offensive coordinator Steve Axman said later.

Or something similar.

Almost simultaneously, four ASU coaches — heads down and lips bitten — reached the elevator. No vacancy. The car was crammed.

"Winners ride," someone yelled from the back of the elevator, "and losers wait for the next bus."

This day, the UA rode.

"There's nothing else I could ask for," Zendejas said. "I couldn't have dreamed for a better ending."

So maybe you get the idea; the circumstances aren't the least bit complicated. It was a one-game season for both teams.

"Nothing else matters," UA quarterback Tom Tunnicliffe said. "Stats, points, who cares? All that matters is we beat ASU."

There was a seemingly perpetual happiness in Arizona's dressing room. It was as if a victory over the Sun Devils magically removed the losses from the UA's 7-3-1 record.

And I don't disagree.

Whatever scars were inflicted in the UA's first 10 games have been soothed. The UA had fallen from grace. It got it back.

349

"We didn't go 11-0 or 10-1, but we had a great year," linebacker Ricky Hunley said. "I would have to term it as close to the ultimate success as you can get."

Through the anguish of losses to Stanford and Oregon and the disappointment of a tie with Cal, Arizona seemed to sense the season could be repaired on Nov. 26.

And it was.

"We went out winners and that's all you can say," tackle Marsharne Graves said. "We improved our (6-4-1) record from a year ago and we beat ASU. There's not much more."

Even if you want to get picky, the UA has a ready argument.

"Sure, it's going to be hard to look back and second-guess those three losses," receiver Jay Dobyns said. "But I'll take a 7-3-1 any time. A lot of people wish they were 7-3-1. I'm grateful to be 7-3-1."

UA fullback Chris Brewer, who gained 73 yards, 19 in critical situations on the deciding possession, had a long, brown cigar stuck between his teeth.

"I bought this cigar this morning," he said. "I was hoping like hell I'd get a chance to use it. But I'm going to save it, not smoke it. It's a souvenir."

Most significant of Brewer's runs was a seven-yard gain on third-and-three at ASU's 44 with less than two minutes to play.

"We would have gone for it on fourth down had Chris failed," UA coach Larry Smith said. "But he didn't. He really bailed us out."

To that time, ASU's defense had been especially impregnable. Arizona hadn't come close, even to Zendejas' range, since midway through the second quarter.

"We hadn't moved the ball well," Tunnicliffe said. "but we had been able to run some, and I knew all we had to do was get in Max's range.

"I liked our strategy."

What Smith did was push all the UA's chips into the pot when the UA got the ball with 4:44 remaining, down 15-14.

"We'll play these," he seemed to suggest.

"It was a gamble," Smith said. "I thought all week the game would come down to who had the last kick, and I'm glad it was us.

"I told Axman that we had to get to the 35 and to get us that far. But mostly I was just happy to get the opportunity to put Max on the field."

Axman, who calls plays from the press box, wasn't waiting for the two-minute offense.

"But when it got to the clutch," Brewer said, "our offensive line was there."

Arizona's deciding drive resembled the final series in last year's 16-13 victory at Notre Dame. Arizona worked the final 4:16 off the clock in South Bend, Ind., and Zendejas kicked a 48-yard field goal as time expired.

"It was old hat to us," Axman said.

"The Notre Dame game came to mind," Zendejas said.

"We've been through so many similar situations that we drew strength from it," Tunnicliffe said.

Axman and Smith didn't waver.

"We felt ASU would lay back and expect the pass, so we decided to run it chunk by chunk," Axman said. "We wanted to move the chains, get a few first downs and run basic plays left and right.

"I'll tell you, this game doesn't go into the memory bank with a lot of others. This one is more than beating UCLA or USC. It's special."

Many of the UA players had been crying, most of them moved by a rendition of "Bear Down Arizona" played by the UA band after the game.

"It doesn't get any better than this," Brewer said. "When we all went back on the field and the band played our song, it was a moment I'll never forget.

But mostly, yesterday's game was one the UA-ASU historians will not soon forget. Could a rematch be arranged? Is today too soon?

Maybe Brewer put it in perspective best.

"It's hard to leave here after the thrills we've had," he said. "I wish I had another year.

"I want to come back for more."

# Something magical about The Streak

*Saturday, November 23, 1991*

Turn on the radio this week in Tucson and you hear the voice that broke a gazillion UA hearts.

"That can't be Frank Kush singing 'Bear Down, Arizona,' can it?" you ask.

Don't be ridiculous. Frank Kush can't sing.

"But I'd recognize that voice anywhere — underwater, driving a Harley," you say. "If you live in Tucson, that voice has made your hair stand on end since the Eisenhower administration."

But Frank Kush trying to sing the lyrics "fight, fight, Wildcats fight" on a Tucson radio station? The week of the UA-ASU game? Is that possible?

"Change stations," you say. "Maybe we can catch Bo Schembechler singing 'Buckeyes Forever.'"

The Streak hasn't just warped the psyche of Sun Devil fans, it has reduced the greatest of all Sun Devils, Frank Kush, to a radio appearance in which he admits he long ago memorized the words to Arizona's maddening fight song.

"But in those days," Kush said with a laugh, "you'd never catch me singing it."

Yes. Those days.

Fifteen times in 17 seasons, from 1965 to '81, "those days" were Sun Devil days. For almost two decades, Wildcat fans went to bed in anguish and woke up in anguish over their school's frustrating inability to beat ASU with any more regularity than once every 8.5 years.

And then, out of nowhere came The Streak and life has never been the same in this little old town. No one has been able to explain The Streak. No one wants to. Leave it alone and let it grow.

"There's no magical type of thing that happens," said ASU coach Larry Marmie.

Larry, have we been watching the same games?

No matter how good ASU has been — only twice have the Wildcats had the best record entering the game — it has not been a factor.

The Sun Devils have gained more total yards in The Streak, 3,184 to 2,863. It did not help.

More? Arizona has never completed more passes than ASU in any of the nine games. ASU has led in the second half of five games. By the

352

time the Wildcats had more first downs in a game than ASU, The Streak was already at 5-0.

The momentum factor does not compute. The Wildcats have won five games in which they were coming off a loss. The Sun Devils have lost five times in which they were on a roll, coming off a victory.

The Sun Devils have taken a seven-game winning streak into the game. And lost. And the Sun Devils have taken a six-game winning streak in and lost. By contrast, the Wildcats have never gone into a Streak game with more than two consecutive victories.

Larry Marmie and Darryl Rogers and John Cooper may not believe in magic. Maybe they should look at the tape of the 1984 finish at Arizona Stadium. ASU quarterback Jeff Van Raaphorst is hit as he prepares to pass and the ball comes to rest on guard Randall McDaniel's shoulder pad. Teetering. ASU is 25 yards from the winning score, two minutes on the clock.

And the ball just teeters on the shoulder pad. If it rolls off and hits the ground it's an incomplete pass. ASU probably wins the game and The Streak is extinguished at two.

How often have you seen a football rest motionless on a player's shoulder until an enemy linebacker snatches it away?

Magic? You tell me.

How often does nose guard Joe Drake (UA, '82) get two safeties in a game? In a career? He did it twice against ASU. In 1988, UA quarterback Ronald Veal threw three touchdown passes to beat the Sun Devils. In the other 10 games that year, he threw one TD pass. How do you explain 29 Sun Devil turnovers in The Streak, and only 12 by the Wildcats?

How do you explain ASU scoring just one touchdown in the fourth quarter since 1983?

"It's not like we go out and blow them away," said UA coach Dick Tomey.

In 1982, two days before Arizona innocently entered Game 1 of The Streak, a 5-4-1 puffball against the 9-1 Sun Devils, Wildcat tackle Jeff Kiewel tried to put the rivalry in perspective. "If you beat ASU, it's a game you'll always remember," he said. "If you lose, it's a game you will never forget."

The Wildcats have been remembering for nine years. The Sun Devils have been trying to forget.

About midnight on the night Arizona knocked ASU from the Rose Bowl in 1985, my colleague Jack Magruder and I drove to the Fiesta Inn in Tempe. Stopping for a red light at the intersection of Priest and Broadway, we noticed a man in an ASU sweatshirt sitting at a roadside stand. He was slumped over, shivering in the chill.

A single 60-watt bulb barely illuminated the man's handwritten sign, which read "Roses $1."

"Too bad we don't have a camera," Magruder said. "If you could take a picture of that, you'd never need to write another word about this streak."

And now we have Frank Kush singing "Bear Down, Arizona."

You get the feeling that The Streak is just starting to gain momentum.

Jeffrey Foster's block of a punt by Arizona's Matt Peyton was converted into an ASU touchdown in the November 1994 game, but the UA won in a classic finish.

BENJIE SANDERS

# Arizona triumphs — by inches; Cats get life from failed do-or-die try

*Saturday, November 26, 1994*

At game's end, a man was leaning over a railing maybe 10 feet above the path leading to Arizona's dressing room, a sign dangling from his hands:

I'm Dying

Beat ASU

Last Wish

It was that kind of game. And it is again that kind of series.

My guess is that the man isn't dying at all — he was just dying to beat the Sun Devils. And isn't that the way it always is with Wildcat football? When all else fails, there's always Arizona State.

Beating ASU is the biggest eraser of all, a little piece of late-season magic that has soothed Arizona's ailments for 11 of the last 13 seasons.

When the Wildcats all but danced into their locker room last night, bone-tired, it was as if they had been through three games. They appeared dominant early, taking a 9-0 lead. They appeared doomed through the middle of the game, falling apart as they fell behind 27-15. And in the final 12 minutes the Wildcats played their best football of the year to win 28-27.

"We looked like a different team at the end," said UA nose tackle Chuck Osborne.

One tidy little plot to the game was, that for the first time in more than a decade, the Wildcats seemed to enter a game against ASU with a nothing-to-lose attitude.

I mean, the games of consequence had already been played, and lost, in Eugene, Ore., and at the L.A. Coliseum. The Rose Bowl slipped away, followed shortly by any real chance to play in a bowl coalition game on Jan. 2. Win or lose last night, Arizona was almost certainly bound for the Freedom Bowl, and what's really the difference between being 8-3 or 7-4? Between being ranked No. 16 or No. 24?

Well, what the Wildcats quickly discovered was that the nothing-to-lose concept was entirely wrong. If you lose to the Sun Devils, you have to take it home and live with it forever.

"That (47-yard missed field goal by ASU's Jon Baker) kick would've changed everything," said All-Pac-10 linebacker Sean Harris.

357

"It would have been four losses and we wouldn't have even had a decent season any longer. We would've been looked at as failures and everything.

"Sometimes you don't realize how much it means to beat ASU until you get out there on the field. They talk so much stuff. When their lead got bigger their mouths got bigger. But when their lead was shrinking you could hear a pin drop."

You got the feeling that Harris (or any Wildcat) would rather date Tonya Harding than lose to the Sun Devils.

If there was an irony that might've been lost in the plays and mis-plays, it was that Duane Akina's offense was backed into just the corner that the Sun Devils had hoped for — forcing the Wildcats to win with their passing game.

Put it all on Dan White and his receivers in the final 12 minutes, trailing by 12 points. There wasn't enough time to run the ball and pull it out. And besides, Ontiwaun Carter was in a neck brace at University Medical Center, meaning the UA's safety net was gone. Plus, its only able-bodied fullback, Charles Myles, had been knocked out of the game with a knee injury.

There was just enough time to see if the Wildcats could pass what Akina has long described as "the final test" of Arizona's offense. Two long drives in the fourth quarter. Touchdowns, not field goals. Against a defense that knew what to expect.

To add to the drama, White had taken a painkilling shot at half-time to numb the agony in his right shoulder, injured early in the game. How long would he be able to stand in there? The next hit might be his last.

In the press box, Akina felt a little buzz.

"I wasn't saying, 'Oh, boy! Oh, boy!' but I enjoyed the challenge," he said. "We didn't want to have to depend purely on the pass, we mixed in some nice runs with Gary Taylor, but we did have to throw and score with the throw to win it. But you know, I think Dan enjoyed the situation."

If so, he was about the only person in an audience of almost 59,000 people who didn't feel the anxiety.

It's unlikely that anyone will get carried away and say that Arizona's offense has now evolved into a passing circus, or even one that will strike fear into Utah's defensive backs in their preparation for the Freedom Bowl. But can you imagine the UA offense of '93 or '92 or '88 or anytime in the last 10 years winning with the pass the way White and his array of receivers did last night?

Everybody but Joe Smigiel caught a pass.

The winning touchdown came on a play Akina calls "35 Nancy" — in which White did a little tango to escape (really) the rush and fire a sidearm pass to Lamar Harris. More irony: That particular play had been on Akina's mind two weeks ago in Los Angeles, when the Wildcats instead opted for a run and had their notable failure on fourth-and-2 at the USC goal line.

Better late than never, I suppose.

At the end it came down to a single kick, Baker's 47-yarder, the kind of kick that Arizona has made a living on through the years. Brett Weber beat ASU with a similar kick in '79; Max Zendejas won games in the exact situation at Notre Dame and against ASU in '82 and '83, respectively. Later, the Wildcats used Doug Pfaff and Gary Coston to beat Oklahoma and Washington with similar boots in the Tomey years.

All or nothing, and in the last 15 years it has usually been "all" for the Wildcats.

In a twisted sort of way, you could say that the beginning of this Desert Swarm era came when Steve McLaughlin missed an all-or-nothing kick in an 8-7 loss to top-ranked Miami two years ago. Hatched from that defeat was a three-season run in which Arizona has experienced some of the best moments in its history.

In a UA perspective, it seemed fitting that this game, one that for all intents closes out the Desert Swarm era, was decided by another missed kick.

"I was standing there watching (Baker's kick), watching it curve and saying 'please! please!'" said the UA's Harris. "I don't know what I would've done if it had gone through. I would've just died, I guess."

As usual in this wonderful series, that was a feeling that was going around.

SARAH PRALL

Arizona QB Keith Smith hurdles Sun Devils linebacker Pat Tillman in the first half in 1996. It was one of the few things the Wildcats did right in a 56-14 loss.

# UA fans, brace yourselves: Things may only get worse

*Sunday, November 24, 1996*

A scene you never thought you'd see at Arizona Stadium: Sun Devil fans dancing on the goal posts, defying police, rocking, rolling, doing everything but stealing the silverware.

As it turned out, the goal posts at the old stadium were indestructible, much like the Sun Devils themselves. When the lights were turned out, 45 minutes later, the goal posts were still standing.

It was Arizona that had fallen, 56-14.

Oh, yes, it can get worse: Arizona opens the '97 season on the road at Wazzu, Ohio State and UCLA.

Much worse: Dick Tomey will be under a job watch all year, preseason ticket sales will go into the dumper, and would-be Wildcat recruits will have to ask, seriously: Why go to Tucson and miss all the fun stuff in Tempe?

For the first time in 15 years, the UA no longer holds as a shield its superiority over the Sun Devils. Minus its annual feel-good victory over ASU, a cosmetic process that covered so many deficiencies — transforming so many .500 years into misleading, stay-the-course celebrations — the UA has been exposed.

This was its worst football season since 1980.

Worse than the injury-beset team of 1991 that went 4-7 but was stocked with the young players who would make 1992-94 so exceptional. And it was worse than Tomey's first team in 1987, a 4-4-3 mix of leftovers from the Larry Smith years and the core of Tomey's first two bowl teams.

None of the excuses will fly.

There was never an assumption that this would be a transitional season and, therefore, underneath the brave talk that the Wildcats would surely find a way to scuttle ASU's national championship express, there can be but one conclusion: It isn't working.

Imagine what might've happened had the Sun Devils not had so many turnovers. How many would they have scored, 70? More?

Instead, Arizona State won by a Kushian 44 points and slammed shut the history books with a bit of thunder. The Sun Devils exorcised all of those nagging nightmares: Cecil's interception, Max's kicks,

361

Tunnicliffe's bombs and Osborne's sack.

The old bag of magic dust has been emptied.

"They're complete," said UA quarterback Keith Smith. "I don't know what they were doing, but it was working."

The Sun Devils played at a dimension totally unfamiliar to Arizona, with a speed and sharpness that didn't betray their bid to become a national champion. Two Pac-10 teams previously finished the conference season 8-0 — the '91 Washington Huskies and the '88 USC Trojans. This ASU team might not have the pedigree, or the character, but it has a similar ability.

What was particularly laudable was that the Sun Devils labored under as much pressure as any ASU team ever had in Tucson. On alien ground, with few friends about, with 15 years of misfortune closing in, the Sun Devils rose above all of it.

But only on the scoreboard.

What started out as a thundering zoo of Wildcat fans, a record crowd of 59,920, was turned into a mute gathering that left the stadium shocked, blinded by the Sun Devils' low blows and other assorted cheap shots.

It was the worst exhibition of class, or the lack of it, since the renegades from Miami played here five years ago.

"It was hard to keep my composure," UA safety Mikal Smith said. "I wanted to rush the field; we all did. The type of football they played starts at the top, with the coach. It puts a big black mark on everything they've accomplished this year."

In a game played for life, limb and the right to put a "We may not be No. 1, but at least we beat the Sun Devils every year" sticker on the old pickup, the Wildcats were fortunate to get out of it with life and limbs intact.

The Sun Devils played with a ruthlessness that stretched the boundaries of sportsmanship.

"We just didn't beat them," said Sun Devil lineman Shawn Swayda. "We punished them."

Not that it was anything to be proud of.

A brutal cheap shot by ASU guard Glen Gable, an immobilizing blindside, illegal block on UA defensive lineman Daniel Greer, threatened to turn Arizona Stadium into a war zone in the fourth period.

Gable was ejected, setting an NCAA record of some sort. Gable had replaced ASU guard Pat Thompson, ejected for scuffling in the first half. Two right guards, two ejections. A third player, a linebacker, was ejected for taunting. Thirteen ASU penalties for 125 yards were more indicative of the Sun Devils' outing than 651 yards total offense.

If it wasn't so ugly and so potentially explosive, it might've been laughable.

And if it hadn't come at the expense of an undefeated team, it might be dismissed, looked upon as isolated incidents by a few imbeciles.

"I couldn't believe what they were doing," Keith Smith said. "The game's supposed to be fun. You've got to have respect for the game. I really didn't see any from them."

One lingering question: Is there any hope for Arizona in the short term?

The obvious, optimistic approach is that ASU was 3-8 as recently as 1994, and limped home at 6-5 last year. No one nominated Bruce Snyder as a coach who had that something special. The Sun Devil team that the Wildcats beat 31-28 last November was almost, to a man, the same Sun Devil team that we saw last night.

But to dream that Arizona can have a similar turnaround, and so quickly, is unrealistic.

The closest comparison is that the Wildcats can now appreciate how the Sun Devils have felt since 1981. And that is, next year's game can't get here soon enough.

DAVID SANDERS

Early this decade, Loren Woods' talent and physical presence helped Arizona relegate ASU to its familiar also-ran status in the intrastate hoops rivalry.

364

# ASU still isn't ready
# to play with big boys

*Thursday, January 27, 2000*

*TEMPE*

Year after year, whenever the UA visits, Arizona State creates the feel of a Vitale-worthy, big-game basketball precinct.

There's a local legend, Eddie House. There are gold towels waving from every seat. Hip music. High rollers in the floor-level seats. Ad panels raking in the dough, and a deafening thunder when the Sun Devils run onto the court.

In the Pac-10's most aesthetically pleasing basketball venue, Arizona State can style with the big boys.

Oh how the Sun Devils ache to be able to play ball with Lute Olson.

And oh how it hurts when Olson's Wildcats plant another loss on ASU's kisser, turning their wannabe neighbors into a mood you find only at the morgue.

Is there any rivalry in America that has had such awkward timing to match one team, Arizona, that is on a 17-year roll, against another, ASU, that has been in a down cycle for precisely 17 years?

Just when you think the Sun Devils have cut into the competitive abyss, and just when you think that the thin Wildcats can be had, Arizona blows out to a 35-point lead, humbles ASU 82-55, and whatever gap seemed to have been closed is torn open.

The current ASU coach, Rob Evans, has only been part of the grief for three games, but he knows fully what predecessors Steve Patterson and Bill Frieder felt.

After the Sun Devils lost at UCLA last weekend, Evans came into the interview room and, in an oblique way, cited Arizona for the setback.

"After being embarrassed by Arizona (two days earlier), UCLA had resolved to come out hard against the next team," Evans said. "We happened to be the next team."

The Sun Devils were the next team again last night.

Embarrassed by an 80-72 loss at USC, the Wildcats vowed that whoever came next — ASU, Oregon, the New York Knicks — they would get their best shot.

ASU got next.

Olson and his lieutenants weren't shy about reminding their play-ers about a perceived air of confidence coming from the Sun Devils. Whether real or imagined, the Wildcats fed off it. "There had been comments made that this was the year they were going to get us here," Olson said.

But it wasn't bulletin-board material that beat ASU last night. It was Arizona's suffocating defense and the presence of center Loren Woods that limited the Sun Devils to .328 shooting, their worst night of the season.

Remarkably, the Wildcats paired ASU's low with their season-best shooting night, .559.

Game over.

"We got on a run in the first half," said Luke Walton, "and the run never quit."

No one is going to say that they expected Walton and Rick Anderson to outshoot Eddie House, not even Walton and Anderson themselves. But they did, coming back from a 2-for-12 performance at USC to make 9 of 14 baskets last night. Olson's term for that: Breakout games.

"When I made the first one, I didn't even think about (the slump) anymore," Walton said. "It just came back naturally."

The genesis of Arizona's box-and-chaser defense that took House out of the game didn't come in any of Olson's closed-to-the-public practices this week. They came from way back, in 1991-92, when the Wildcats designed a box defense to deal with USC's Harold Miner, who was to Pac-10 basketball a few years ago what House is now.

In those days, Arizona put Matt Muehlebach on Miner and the results were terrific. Miner had three bad nights, one good one. UA associate head coach Jim Rosborough started designing a defense for House last Friday morning, a few hours after the Wildcats won at UCLA.

He became so consumed with stopping House that he made up a list of "Eight Ways to Defend House" before leaving the team hotel yes-terday. When Rosborough got on the bus as it departed for Wells Fargo Arena, he handed out a sheet to each of his players.

Michael Wright took one look at the sheet, read the list item by item, and said, wryly, "Who is this guy, Jordan?"

The fault isn't with House, nor is the credit strictly to Gilbert Arenas and Jason Gardner, the Arizona guards who Rosborough sicced on House. Much of the issue was decided by those ASU players not named Eddie House.

The young Sun Devils aren't ready to contend for the Pac-10 title yet, and it showed decisively last night. Freshman power forward Shawn Redhage, who was third in shooting percentage in the league, didn't make a basket and looked intimidated. ASU's point guards, Alton Mason and Kyle Dodd, missed all but one shot. Center Chad Prewitt, a sophomore, was slow to the ball, slow to get downcourt.

There's not much doubt in the Pac-10 that ultimately Rob Evans is going to have the Sun Devils challenging Stanford, Arizona and UCLA in the upper tier, but it isn't going to happen any quicker for him than it did for Henry Bibby at USC or Bob Bender at Washington.

You take your lumps along the way, and last night ASU took a few of them, but probably not the last of them.

# The Day Lute Roared
# an afternoon to behold

*Sunday, January 4, 2004*

*TEMPE*

Lute Olson was on foreign turf, surrounded by unfamiliar faces from the Phoenix dailies and a tabletop of unfamiliar microphones from Fox 10 News, XTRA 910, ABC 15 and a dozen more.

It was a group willing to listen, and Arizona's basketball coach had a message he wanted to deliver to this new audience.

"It's been a great run in Tucson," he began, touching on his milestone victories, his plans for the future and the event of the day, a dominating 93-74 victory over the Sun Devils.

To the victor goes not only the spoils but the coveted newspaper space and TV time.

On this unfriendly piece of ground, in which he has won 17 of 21 games, Olson dispensed one of his most effective coaching performances of the last 30 years. It was a clinic, actually, and those mouthy lunkheads in the Sun Devil student section should have been charged a second admission to witness its on-court execution.

No wonder the Wildcat coach, steamed at the profanity directed at him in the final minutes of a walkover, pointed to the scoreboard and later said "you should learn to keep your mouth closed when you are down 30-something points."

"Frankly, it's disgusting," he said, among other things.

Thus, it will be widely said and frequently written that Saturday's game was The Day Lute Roared.

"It's awesome that Coach O showed that kind of emotion for us," said UA center Channing Frye. "He got out of his bubble a little bit."

But all of that misses the point. On a day that Arizona had too much of everything for the Sun Devils — too much quickness, too much speed, too much toughness and mostly too much talent — the real story was that Olson and his staff were too much for their Sun Devil colleagues.

It's too simple to write that Coach A out-smarted Coach B when Team A has superior personnel, but that's what happened at beautiful Wells Fargo Arena on Saturday.

The Wildcats came well-prepared and exposed ASU's weaknesses

368

so thoroughly that the game was decided before halftime.

Arizona's 1-3-1 zone defense, with Salim Stoudamire running the baseline to double-team Ike Diogu, exposed the Sun Devils as a one-dimensional, plodding, shooting-challenged team with too many players unable to respond to a big-game challenge.

The Wildcats forced an inside-oriented ASU club to become a perimeter shooting team. In the end, Diogu spent far too much time standing 15 feet from the basket, from where he doesn't need to be guarded.

Arizona's coaches couldn't have asked for a better reaction to their defensive strategy. Not only was Diogu neutralized, he was outplayed by Frye, who sees the word "IKE" and becomes so motivated that he plays like a future lottery pick.

Olson is neither a screamer nor a win-one-for-the-Gipper coach, but he is a master at subtle psychology. To motivate his players, every time someone writes that Diogu is All-This or All-That, Olson makes sure that Frye reads the content.

"We were just hyped up," said Frye, who informed a group of reporters that his mission was to show the people in his hometown that he has gotten better and that he's not a pushover.

"I respect (Ike)," he said. "But they have to respect me."

In three outings against Diogu, Frye has averaged 18 points, 8 rebounds and is shooting an absurdly good 68 percent from the field. Diogu's numbers against Arizona: 16 points, 8 rebounds and 38 percent shooting.

Many of Diogu's problems when facing Arizona is that he doesn't have Luke Walton or Hassan Adams nearby to deflect the attention.

When Diogu and his teammates got the ball, Arizona's quickness became manifest. There were hands everywhere, slapping at the ball, creating doubt, closing space, forcing the Sun Devils to rush.

"People talk about our quickness as it relates to foot speed," said UA associate head coach Jim Rosborough. "But what really works just as well is the quickness of our hands. Mustafa Shakur and those guys on the perimeter are really good at knocking the ball free."

As long as it remains Diogu vs. Arizona, the Sun Devils are going to be in trouble. ASU is going to need another recruiting class — and for Diogu to resist an opportunity to enter the NBA draft — to be competitive against the Wildcats.

Where is Chad Prewitt when you need him?

"We can smother Diogu as much as possible," said UA sophomore

Andre Iguodala. "But we also considered this a big game today. It's time we began to show what we can do and play a complete game. This was probably our most complete game."

After Saturday's game, ASU coach Rob Evans spoke candidly when he said that "the team we play next (Stanford) is better than this team. It's not going to get any easier in this league."

Amen, Rob. Amen.

# Rivalry's intensity will live forever

*Wednesday, November 23, 2005*

On Sunday, the Arizona State athletic department purchased a half-page ad in the Mesa-based East Valley Tribune, advertising tickets to the UA-ASU football game. About 10,000 remained unsold.

"Plenty of tickets available" is a cry not customary in this grand rivalry.

Could this be the same UA-ASU football series that Frank Kush and Chuck Cecil so anticipated for 365 days each year? The biggest, most meaningful sporting event in this state, no exceptions, from 1950 to 1999?

Oh, how the Wildcat-Sun Devil football rivalry used to absorb our attention. Read on:

Early 1970s. An Arizona State assistant football coach rings the doorbell at Gene Arneson's residence in Southeast Tucson. The Sun Devil coach is in town to recruit Tom Arneson, the youngest of Gene's three football-playing sons.

All-WAC linebacker Mark Arneson and his younger brother Jim Arneson, an All-WAC guard, answer the door. It is an awkward moment for the two Arizona Wildcats and brother Tom, all graduates of Palo Verde High School.

"We talked outside for a few minutes," Mark Arneson, the UA's 1971 football MVP, remembers. "We didn't invite him inside. I guess he could tell by our body language that this was going to be a tough sell."

The Arnesons talked briefly with the Sun Devil coach. Mark Arneson went 0-3 against the Sun Devils in his UA career, 1969-71. Jim also went 0-3 from 1970-72.

"It didn't take long to get to the truth," Mark Arneson says now. "The ASU coach finally said, 'This is a lost cause, isn't it?' And we said, 'We don't want any part of Arizona State.'"

• In his decade as an NFL scout, Pete Russell, the UA's 1988 and 1989 Bronko Nagurski Award winner, has been on virtually every college campus in America. He has met and become friends with ex-Huskies, ex-Trojans, ex-Ducks, you name it.

In his travels, Russell met St. Louis Rams scout Dave Boller, who in the 1980s was an equipment manager and ASU's director of football operations.

"We're both pretty easygoing guys, and we have a good relationship," Russell said. "But he tells me all the time that I'm the only Wildcat he's ever liked."

• Doug Penner played at Sabino High School and became an Arizona starting offensive lineman in the 1980s. He later became a graduate assistant coach at the UA. Before that, in middle school, he sold Cokes at Arizona Stadium.

Penner now works in New York City, sales manager for the vast Viacom Outdoor Corp. located on Broadway, in the heart of Manhattan.

He lists, in order, detail by detail, indelible moments from Arizona's 8-0-1 streak against ASU from 1982 to 1990.

• Steve Boadway and Craig Vesling sacking Jeff Van Raaphorst to force a fumble and win the '84 game.

• Byron Evans stripping the ball from Anthony Parker in the end zone, 1985.

• Chuck Cecil's interception return in '86.

• the Hail Mary pass to Derek Hill, who handed off to Melvin Smith in '88.

The 1989 game in Tempe remains a Penner favorite.

"I was a graduate assistant in '89, for the game in Tempe," he says now. "Their quarterback, Paul Justin, had guaranteed a victory, a story that was printed in one of the Phoenix papers. I got a clipping, made a hundred copies and put it in the locker of every single player.

"We were so psyched up and ready to play that our great defensive end, Anthony Smith, a No. 1 draft pick that year, insisted that he could play even though he had a torn-up knee and was out of the game. He got dressed and took one of our freshmen, Mike Bundy, into a hallway and started to block him, firing off an imaginary snap from center. He wanted the coaches to see that the could play. He was just beating the heck out of Bundy, whacking the walls. But the coaches wouldn't let him play. We were ready, put it that way."

Arizona won 28-10.

• Justin Lanne was an Arizona safety from 1967 to 1970. His football career ended in the ASU-UA game of his junior season.

"I got clipped on a reverse play and it just shredded my knee," he said this week. "I've still got four or five staples in there, holding everything together."

Lanne is an executive in a Tucson commercial real estate company.

"I don't know if I could say I hate them; that's probably too strong," he said. "But I sure learned to respect them. The Kush teams of those years were just outstanding. They had so much quickness, so many good players. Art Malone, J.D. Hill. We had played good teams — Syracuse and Michigan — but ASU's athleticism was something else. It just blew us away."

No hard feelings?

"I do remember they ran a lot of illegal stuff, picks in the secondary. I would keep screaming at the refs, 'That's illegal. Call it!' They never did. We never beat them."

• Heath Bray was recruited to Arizona in 1987 out of North Carolina. He now lives in Phoenix — he has a Saturday morning radio show there that pertains to his specialty, financial investments — but during UA-ASU week he morphs into his Wildcat linebacker/special teams days.

"I'm going to the game with (ex-Wildcats) Max Zendejas, Donnie Salum, Ty Parten and Paul Glonek," he says. "I am granted one day per year of pure irrationality by my friends and family, and that day is Friday. (Former UA defensive coordinator) Rich Ellerson always referred to them as the 'Evil Empire.'

"I was asked once for a Fox Sports Arizona special what the rivalry means to me. I said it's a battle of good vs. evil. You see the Devil running on the field dressed in mustard and rust colors. And then you have a superior academic institution from Tucson, wearing the colors of our country."

The UA-ASU game? Still on.

JAMES S. WOOD

Alexis Greene and the UA gymnastics team were responsible for ending the Wildcats' 0-11 streak against ASU in all sports in the 2007-08 school year.

# Cats blow Devils' streak out of water

*Sunday, February 17, 2008*

*TEMPE*

A few minutes before the annual UA-ASU dual swimming meet Saturday, a Sun Devil official tacked up a sign that said "GO DEVILS! FORK 'EM" behind the starter's platform.

Indeed, the "Fork 'Em" theme has been getting a lot of mileage in Sun Devil territory.

From Labor Day through Valentine's Day, the Sun Devils had successfully used the "Fork 'Em" approach in 11 consecutive athletic competitions — an 11-0 sweep over the Arizona Wildcats — which is believed to be a record of domination/futility never before seen in the UA-ASU rivalry.

The Sun Devils swept Arizona's women's volleyball and basketball teams, rolled over Arizona's soccer team, twice upset the men's basketball team, finished ahead of the UA women's golf team last week, and beat the UA men's and women's cross country teams so badly that, in the ASU Invitational, the Sun Devils prevailed by giving their "A teams" the day off and routing Arizona with, ahem, "B teams."

And in the second cross country match of the year, in Tucson, ASU swept the Wildcats again.

It wasn't Bear Down as much as it was a series of beatdowns.

Not until Friday night at Wells Fargo Arena did the beatdowns cease. UA gymnastics coach Bill Ryden stopped the awkward streak, directing the Wildcats to a 195.925 to 195.725 victory.

"I'm pretty speechless about the whole thing," Ryden told a student reporter afterward. "It truly was a historic moment in our program."

It was the first time since 1987 that a UA gymnastics team had won in Tempe. And it was the first time in the 2007-08 calendar sports season that the Wildcats didn't go home losers.

Never had the UA been forked so often.

Arizona swimming coach Frank Busch was made fully aware of this Sun Devil Sweep business long before he sent his No. 1-ranked men's team and his No. 4-ranked women's team into action Saturday at ASU's Mona Plummer Aquatic Center.

He, and not some high-profile coach from the UA football or basketball office, was asked to speak to a group of big-money boosters before Thursday's UA-Cal basketball game. When in doubt against the Sun Devils, the surest thing Arizona has going is Frank Busch, whose women's team has not lost to ASU since 2000, and whose men's team has rocked the Sun Devils' world each season since 2001.

"I attended two UA functions during the week," Busch said, "and it amazed me how many people from Tucson knew exactly how this thing with ASU had been going. The message I got was that this thing was getting pretty desperate."

On Saturday afternoon, Busch and his swimmers built on what Ryden and his gymnasts began Friday. Incredibly, the UA men's and women's swimmers won 27 of 28 events in ASU's water — and tied the 28th event, a dead heat in the women's 200 freestyle relay.

"We're deep, we're strong, but I've never seen anything like that in a Pac-10 dual meet," said UA assistant coach Rick DeMont. "We're good and they're not."

Arizona won the men's meet 199-85. The Wildcat women's team won 177-111. Almost unfathomably, Arizona finished first and second in the day's first 22 events. Or, it captured 44 of 44 possible first-and-second-place finishes to that point.

It was Senior Day for the Sun Devils, who took about 10 minutes before Saturday's meet to introduce their men's and women's seniors. None of them had ever — have ever — defeated an Arizona team.

So lopsided were the day's events that the leading ASU women's swimmer, senior Caitlin Andrew — whose name is prominently listed on a poolside board that details event-by-event Sun Devil career record-holders — finished fourth behind Arizona's Anna Turner, Lara Jackson and Lindsey Kelly in her strongest event, the 50 freestyle.

One uncomfortable moment came during a 15-minute break midway through the meet. The public address announcer read the team scores backward. Like this:

"ASU 37, Arizona 112, in women's competition."

"ASU 27, Arizona 119 in the men's meet."

Nobody seemed to be fooled.

Busch said he tried not to "rub it in" on the Sun Devils because his women's team, which finished No. 2 nationally last year and is probably stronger this season, did not use all the regulars. Busch, instead, used several top scorers in non-counting "exhibition" races.

Not that any of this should be breaking news. Busch has quietly built Arizona into one of the nation's two or three strongest swimming programs the last decade. He replaces Olympians with Olympians. On

Saturday, those Olympians, such as senior Albert Subirats, who is probably the NCAA's top male swimmer, were unusually motivated.

"We found out about the ASU streak about three days ago," said Subirats. "Sure, we wanted to beat (the Sun Devils), but we are also undefeated in dual meets and ranked No. 1 in the nation. We had great motivation all week."

Busch is a gentleman, if nothing else. He talked to his team about its future — the Pac-10 and NCAA meets — instead of the differential against Arizona State.

"Right now, our program and ASU's program are just in different places," he said. "But you don't beat them and then apologize, either."

Fittingly, as Busch and his teams left the aquatic center, the "FORK 'EM" sign had been removed.

DEAN KNUTH

K'Lee Arredondo and the Wildcats couldn't stop a changing of the guard in the UA-ASU softball rivalry in 2008, the year the Sun Devils won the NCAA title.

# With 42 wins, Devils have earned their due

*Thursday, April 10, 2008*

The ceremonial introduction of players before Wednesday's UA-ASU softball game suggested that the long-submissive Sun Devils would be defiant, not compliant.

Whether it was calculated or just a gut reaction, each of the 21 Sun Devils occupying the first base line turned her back on a pre-game scoreboard video celebrating the Arizona Wildcats' eight NCAA championships.

As if to say: Who cares?

As if to suggest: That was yesterday.

Or perhaps they were scanning Hillenbrand Stadium's standing-room-only crowd to make sure the great Sun Devil killers, Mike Candrea and Caitlin Lowe, were really not there.

Whatever, it was an altogether rare and hellish night for the Wildcats. The top-ranked Sun Devils won a regular-season game in Tucson for the first time in 17 years, and they did not just win 8-1. They arrived.

"First time we've ever won on this field, 29 straight," said ASU coach Clint Myers. "We knew."

It was so convincing that the Sun Devils hit four home runs off Taryne Mowatt, who 10 months ago was winning an ESPY for her pitching excellence.

So for the first time in two decades, the rivalry is back. Really. Back on.

"We all knew it was 29 straight, so me and the other four seniors were determined not to go out without winning here," said Sun Devils star outfielder Jackie Vasquez, a Catalina Foothills High School grad. "We were ready; we expected it."

Not that this should come as breaking news. In his first two seasons at ASU, Myers coached the Sun Devils to 54-17 and 53-15 records, reached the College World Series twice and pretty much let it be known that the UA-ASU series would become the equivalent of the Duke-North Carolina basketball rivalry.

Beating Arizona in Tucson is his latest step in establishing ASU as a national-title threat.

"It's a state of mind," said Myers, who won six NJCAA titles coaching softball at Central Arizona College. "You have to bust your (butt), but you also have to expect something like this out of yourself."

ASU is 42-2, and all who claimed Myers had built that record against a pre-conference series of lightweights have learned a new, if painful, math: The Sun Devils are already three games up on Arizona in the Pac-10 loss column.

Catch 'em if you can.

And, no, it is not that Candrea is off for the year, coaching the USA Olympic team. It is not that interim head coach Larry Ray is in over his head, or that Mowatt is lost without former pitching coach Nancy Evans.

It's that ASU is exceptionally talented.

The Sun Devils deploy possibly the college softball player of the year, center fielder and leadoff batter Kaitlin Cochran. That's not all: Senior Katie Burkhart, who is 23-2, is probably the season's most dominant pitcher, and that is saying something, considering Texas A&M's Megan Gibson is 22-0, and Virginia Tech's Angela Tincher is 20-4 and pitched a no-hitter against Candrea's touring Olympic team.

In most years, it is Arizona that has a Cochran and a Burkhart. The Wildcats are good, a top-10 club likely bound for the College World Series, but the Sun Devils have a special look to them.

By comparison, Ray was not handed a vintage Arizona powerhouse; he is trying to replace the top three hitters from the '07 national champs; Lowe, Chelsie Mesa and Kristie Fox combined to hit 25 homers, drive in 134 runs and hit a cumulative .371 last year.

Three of the first four batters in Arizona's lineup — Brittany Lastrapes, Lauren Schutzler and Stacie Chambers — are first-year players, future stars, yes, but not yet Lowe-Fox-Mesa.

More troubling for Arizona is that Mowatt, a senior, is 16-8 and struggling. In mid-April last year, Mowatt had 23 victories and then emerged as the nation's most resourceful Big Game pitcher.

On Wednesday, the Sun Devils greeted Mowatt as if she, too, were a freshman. The first three Sun Devils reached base and scored. So much for fearing the reigning NCAA championship pitcher.

So much for all those years of losses at Hillenbrand.

Myers has recruited expertly; he knows Candrea and UCLA cannot get every good player out of Southern California, as has often been the case for 20 years. Myers, for example, signed freshman Krista Donnenwirth, probably the nation's top power-hitting high school player, out of Orange County last spring.

Donnenwirth is the kind of player Arizona almost always had in its lineup. But on Wednesday, she hit a three-run homer in the first inning to give her the Pac-10 lead in RBIs with 51. You will be seeing a lot more of her.

And do not forget, the Cats must see her twice next week in a two-game set in Tempe.

Gulp.

# CHAPTER TEN

# Lute Olson

## Olson weathers hectic transition, heated recruiting

*Saturday, May 28, 1983*

You probably can best identify a newcomer to Tucson by the way he attempts to rationalize 100-degree weather in, of all months, May.

"Listen," said the man with white hair and, as yet, no tan, "it feels much hotter when it's 85 degrees in Iowa. For 100 degrees, this isn't bad at all."

Yeah, and the crickets aren't bad, either.

Already, though, Lute Olson has made moves to counteract the change in climate that goes with the territory as the new basketball coach at the University of Arizona.

And I'm no longer talking about the weather.

The basketball program Olson inherited from Ben Lindsey, by way of Fred Snowden, is considerably different from the one Olson left at Iowa. Olson is going from a 21-10 team to one that was 4-24.

The good news is that Olson has shown a capacity for taking bad situations and making them not as bad.

Yet I've got to believe that when Olson got his first full look at the basketball program he now has charge of, he must've had a few second thoughts. He doesn't deny it.

"To say it has been a traumatic two months would be an understatement," he said yesterday. "The first week was the toughest. That's when you face all the problems of moving and coming into a new situation and leaving all the strong relationships we had at Iowa.

"And then," he said, "we found out how much help they needed here. ..."

Olson didn't have time to bemoan the near-chaotic (who are we kidding: the UA basketball program was fully chaotic last season), and maybe

383

that's why he didn't reconsider his decision and return to Iowa.

Moreover, people have backed off before. Kansas State's Jack Hartman, for example, once accepted the basketball-coaching job at Oklahoma State — and quit two days later.

And upon Snowden's resignation at Arizona, Hartman twice accepted the UA job and retracted.

But Olson didn't have time. He undertook a barnstorming recruiting gig of six weeks that left him gasping.

"About the only time I was in Tucson was when I flew back on weekends to show the recruits around town," he said, not to mention that he was getting his first glimpses of the town as well. "It sure tested my endurance."

Olson began one day in Tucson at 4:30 a.m. and visited recruits in Birmingham, Ala., Memphis, Tenn., Phoenix and, he said, almost everywhere in between.

"I finally ended up going to bed at 1:30 (a.m.) in Los Angeles. Some days I crossed three time zones and worked about 24 hours before getting back to bed."

The result?

"It was a miracle," Olson said yesterday. "A miracle is what it was."

And miracles are what the UA basketball program needs so desperately. So are we to believe that the four recruits signed by Olson in his first six weeks as Arizona's basketball coach are a harbinger of sellouts at McKale Center?

"I've never been one to worry about expectations," he said. "My worry is to get the fans interested and get them in the arena.

"I feel, from the people I've talked to, they know what kind of job is ahead of us and that it can't be done with a snap of the finger."

Olson signed 6-foot-9-inch Van Beard from Seattle, 6-7 Eddie Smith of Dodge City, Kan.; 6-7 Pete Williams of Walnut, Calif.; and 6-1 Michael Tait of Bellflower, Calif.

Of those, Smith and Tait are said by scouting services to be capable of starting at major colleges next year, and Williams isn't far behind.

Under the circumstances — nine of the 18 recruiting visits allowed by the NCAA had been used by Lindsey — Olson had no room for error.

"Usually if you can sign four kids with 18 visits, you've done well." Olson said. "But we wanted to sign five kids with nine visits, and we badly needed those five kids."

What's more, insofar as Olson was hired two weeks before NCAA letters of intent could be signed, he was at a tremendous disadvantage.

"Most of the kids we hoped to recruit had already scheduled the maximum five campus visits, so we had to convince them, first, to cancel a visit and come to Tucson.

"Next," Olson said. "with the limited number of visitations we had left, we had to ask the kids, all things considered, could we count on them signing with us if they liked Tucson and the University of Arizona.

"Considering none of them had been here, that's a tough question, but we couldn't bring in a kid on a risk that he was giving us a 1-in-5 chance and nothing else."

Olson used seven visitations to sign four players.

"The old staff had been in contact with Smith (Kansas junior college Player of the Year), but he told them he wasn't interested," Olson said. "But we got him to cancel a visit to Minnesota, and once he visited here, he canceled a visit to UCLA and signed with us."

Smith also was sought by Tulsa, Texas A&M, Marquette and Kansas State.

Tait, who seems likely to start at point guard as a freshman, told Lindsey's staff last fall that he wasn't interested in Arizona. Williams, from Mount San Antonio Junior College, told Arizona to stay away last fall.

Beard had not been contacted by the previous staff.

"We came out of the woodwork on most of these guys," Olson said. "We still have a scholarship available, but we won't give it just to take somebody, especially somebody similar to what we have in our program."

Olson said he does not expect any returning players to leave.

But now, if you don't mind, he is going to kick back; he may even find time to put something in two large, blue bookcases in his office that have gathered dust and nothing else.

"We bought a house (near Sabino Canyon), but our furniture is still in Iowa," Olson said. "We're trying to sell our house there, and we're trying to settle in here."

But, the evidence is, his work has just begun.

Lute Olson and wife Bobbi chat moments before his first press conference as the new head coach of the Arizona men's basketball team on March 29, 1983.

JOE PATRONITE

EMMETT JORDAN

Thirty-one days before his first game as the Arizona coach, Lute Olson goes over a practice drill with guard Brock Brunkhorst on Oct. 27, 1983.

# Laying a foundation for UA basketball no rush job

*Friday, October 28, 1983*

For longer than you or I care to remember, college basketball has been a diseased product in Southern Arizona. If there's anything beyond intensive care, that's where it was. And has belonged.

The once-proud, once-victorious University of Arizona has been a franchise with a weakening pulse. The last time Arizona won 20 games was in 1977. Andy Woodtli, now a freshman center for the Wildcats, was in sixth grade then.

Then, from above — or at least from Iowa — came Lute Olson to re-create the magic, reignite the torch and refill McKale Center with life, laughter and the American greenback.

It is 28 days until the UA is unmasked and opens the season in McKale Center against Northern Arizona.

Olson met the state's audio, video and print media yesterday. He talked at length about shooting, recruiting, his players and his plans.

And I came away with the same feeling I have every time I have encountered him: Does anybody really doubt that he will soon have UA's flags flying and the stands full?

Just don't expect a rush job.

A losing season is freely predicted, indeed expected, this year. This is not fast food.

Olson won't win as quickly as Fred Snowden did. Snowden took a 6-20 team to 16-10, an immediate gain of 10 wins. Olson was given the remains of a 4-24 team. Something along the lines of an expansion team. If he has a 10-win turnaround — to 14-14 or thereabouts — I imagine he'll surprise even himself.

My hunch is that when Olson begins to win, it will be sustained. It will go beyond what Snowden wrought. But it may take Arizona a few years to pay on the interest before it makes a move to the first division.

There is no Kiddie Korps among Olson's first batch: no Coniel Norman or Eric Money to help make the transition.

But Olson made it clear yesterday that he will not compare his program to those of past UA coaches. If Arizona loses its first 10 games, I don't foresee Olson calling a news conference to complain that he's operating with six players from Ben Lindsey's program.

Which isn't to say he won't be able to laugh while the UA grows.

"We'll run one offense that is similar to what Indiana runs," he said, laughing. "But whether it looks the same, I don't know."

It doesn't take Johnny Wooden to detect precisely why the UA has had four losing seasons in succession.

A lack of work. Work is probably what Olson does best. It's what he does all the time.

"We feel it's our job to reach out, not to sit back and wait for people to come to us," he said. "We can't sell our program by sitting at home by the phone. People have got to see you.

"We began our in-home recruiting visits Sept. 1, and I'm afraid I couldn't count all the ones we've been in."

Instead of taking a vacation last summer, Olson and his assistants recruited and scouted. And then they recruited and scouted some more, almost until practice began two weeks ago.

On the UA's first day of practice, Olson planned a session of two hours and 15 minutes. "We ended up going 3½ hours," he said. "It took us that long to get everything done."

After work comes image. And the UA's image has not suffered by hiring Olson. He is a one-man marketing campaign.

"We try to make it impossible for a young man to go through a day without getting something in the mail with an Arizona logo on it," he said.

"And we try to make it impossible to go to a camp or a clinic without seeing an Arizona T-shirt. Since May we've sent out brochures, posters, anything to advertise Arizona basketball."

How would you like to be this man's secretary? Or pay his postal bills?

But I suspect the thing we're going to like best about Olson is his ability to communicate. He said he will operate on an out-front basis.

Before the UA season opens, Olson will have the players evaluate themselves and their teammates. Coaches will do the same. After that, Olson will meet with each player for at least a half-hour.

Roles will be defined, discussed and perhaps, debated. It's a healthy situation.

"We'll have a very definite pecking order," Olson said. "I'll know who the No. 7 player is and he'll know it, too. I just want to make sure we're not keeping secrets from each other."

Don't expect the UA's basketball program to be a secret much longer, either.

Arizona celebrated this win over ASU to end the 1984-85 regular season, but no one was sure if the Cats' 21-9 record would be enough to make the Big Dance.

BENJIE SANDERS

# NCAA waiting game

*Sunday, March 10, 1985*

*The NCAA selection committee*
*cordially invites the University*
*of Arizona to attend*
*the grand opening of*
*The Road to Lexington,*
*A 64-team basketball tournament,*
*the inaugural rounds of which commence*
*Thursday, March 14, 1985,*
*at a regional near you*
*R.S.V.P. by March 10*
*No substitutions please*

Everyone will be there. The Beasts of the East. The Tar Heels from Tobacco Road. Billy and Wayman and the boys. Louie and his Magic Sweater. Tark and the Techs, Louisiana and Georgia.

Our regrets to Bob K., Joe B. and the Crums from Louisville.

And, hey, UA, thanks for the memories.

Am I dreaming? Or is Arizona's 1984-85 basketball season about to reach the dream-come-true stage?

Not even The Shadow knows, let alone Arizona coach Lute Olson, whose team dispatched Arizona State 68-48 yesterday at McKale Center to conclude its regular season with a 21-9 record.

"I don't know," Olson said yesterday. "It's up to somebody else ... I'm sure I'll be nervous all night.

Truth is, the Wildcats have all but packed their bags and made arrangements for someone to water the plants during this week's opening rounds of the NCAA tournament, of which they plan to get 1/64th of the action.

I can't blame them.

But you know how the NCAA operates. It usually overbooks. Somebody's going to have to get off and board a plane to the NIT. There will be compensation, of course, but not much. There will be recognition, of course, but not as much.

I advise you not to hold your breath until further notice. By 3 p.m. Tucson time the selection committee is to make public its 64-team field.

In an otherwise confusing selection process, Arizona's situation is

391

easily understood. It's likely the NCAA will choose between the UA and Oregon State. Or, if the Pac-10 gets lucky, the NCAA will take both.

The Wildcats and OSU each finished 12-6 in the Pac-10, tied for third place with UCLA. The Beavers are a game better overall, 22-8. UCLA? Forget it. The Bruins have a 16-12 overall record after hanging on to top Oregon 72-69 last night in Eugene. Unless John Wooden has final approval of the 64-team field, UCLA is out.

The leading question is, will the NCAA select as many as four teams from the Pac-10? Will it even select three? The UA seems to be No. 4, if you agree that co-champions Washington and USC are the best chances, and Oregon State is No. 3 because it has a better overall record. It's a tough call.

Views differ on how the UA would react if not invited to the NCAA.

Arizona State coach Bob Weinhauer said yesterday, "The key thing is, Arizona has the opportunity to go somewhere. It doesn't matter where. It's been such a long time since the school has been in a post-season tournament that there should be no disappointment no matter which one it goes to."

The UA said this was your basic case of bunk.

"I'd be really disappointed if we don't go to the NCAA," guard Brock Brunkhorst said. "I don't see how we could be in the Top 20 two weeks ago and not in the top 64 now."

Sophomore guard Steve Kerr said, "I have to admit my hopes are pretty high for the NCAA. I'd be real disappointed, but I guess having an NIT game at McKale would be something to fall back on."

Olson made a long and strong case for the UA but finished with the most realistic remark: "There's nothing I can do about it."

Here's a part of his filibuster:

• "All (nine) of our losses were close," he said. "We could've won them all." The UA lost by margins of nine, one, three, four, one, four three, two and four. An average of 3.4 points per loss. Impressive.

• "Brunkhorst (starting point guard) was out for a month. We lost to Missouri and, in essence, three league games while he was out." Sad but true.

• "How could this team have been ranked in the Top 20 a week ago and suddenly not be one of the top 64?" Well?

• "It was my feeling we had to win today, and win convincingly." Mission accomplished.

Olson, however, will not be invited to plead his case to the NCAA selection committee in Kansas City.

"We're not out of the woods yet," he said. "But I hope all of these factors are looked at."

Weinhauer said that the Pac-10 would be lucky to get three teams into the NCAA. "There's a possibility of four," he said, "but not five."

Sorry, UCLA.

If it helps the UA breathe easier, there is a precedent on its side. In 1980, when the NCAA tournament was a 40-team field, four Pac-10 teams received NCAA berths — OSU 26-4; ASU 22-7; Washington State 22-6; and UCLA 22-10. The NCAA said UCLA was the 40th team selected. UCLA subsequently met Louisville for the national title.

"We'll live with whatever decision the committee makes," Olson said.

Bet on the NCAA.

EDITOR'S NOTE: On March 10, 1985, the Arizona Wildcats earned a berth in the NCAA tournament. It marked the start of the program's current streak of 25 consecutive years of playing in the Big Dance.

ARIZONA DAILY STAR 1992

In a '92 game versus UCLA, Lute Olson got a technical foul — a penalty the Bruins said provided "a boost" as they ended the Cats' 71-game home winning streak.

# Olson's 'T' untimely, filled with mystery

*Monday, January 13, 1992*

The instant Tom Harrington placed his left hand on top of his right hand to form a "T," Lute Olson recoiled in horror.

The damage would be great and he knew it.

"Lute looked much like Lee Harvey Oswald looked at the moment Jack Ruby shot him," wrote Mark Whicker of the Orange County Register.

The airline industry has a term for what happened to the Wildcats with 5:55 remaining in Saturday's UCLA-Arizona game.

Pilot error.

"It's the first time I've ever seen coach Olson lose his cool and do something to hurt his team," said Bruin guard Gerald Madkins.

I don't know who was more surprised — Olson or the Bruins.

"I didn't think I'd ever see that happen here," said UCLA forward Don MacLean. "I think it gave us a boost."

But there was much more to UCLA's 89-87, streak-breaking victory than the regrettable technical foul.

The most pressing question is: What could Lute Olson have possibly said that drew a technical foul from 30 yards away?

But how could Harrington have heard Olson above the din of 13,965 fans? A view of the tape shows that Olson was not out of the coaching box, nor was his body language excessive or demeaning to the officials.

We will never know. The Pac-10, much as the NCAA, does not allow its officials any public comment on specific plays or games. Not even via a prepared public statement or a pool reporter.

Bad rule, guys.

And why would Olson risk a technical on what appeared to be an otherwise harmless and routine call in which MacLean drove to the lane and was fouled by Wayne Womack?

One statistician sitting near the Arizona bench said he heard Olson shout "bull..."

But that's unlikely because one member of the basketball administration said there is only one documented instance of an Olson profanity in all his years at Arizona. "The harshest term he uses is 'jackass,"' said the official. "And that's only on rare occasions."

You would hope in a game of such magnitude that Tom Harrington would be looking to not call a technical unless someone really got out of line.

UCLA led 76-74. Time remaining: 5:55. Let the Bruins and Wildcats decide the outcome. Not Tom Harrington.

Olson's response? "There was nothing said." And even if Olson did yell "bull...," Harrington was on the opposite side of the court and could not possibly have heard it.

Maybe he reads lips.

The Bruins got three extra points out of the technical. They needed two of them to win.

It was the only regrettable incident in a wonderful game, one that was exactly what UCLA coach Jim Harrick said four days earlier it deserved to be called.

A classic.

What would have happened had Harrington not called a technical on Olson? Would the McKale streak be at 72? It is impossible to say, but it is, to this hour, a question all the Arizona people ponder and may continue to ponder all season.

"I'm not going to say anything about the refs," said UA guard Matt Othick. "We'll see those guys down the road again somewhere. They read the papers like anyone else."

The game's other major issue was not as volatile or mysterious.

It came with 10.9 seconds remaining in a game tied at 87. Olson replaced Othick, a senior, with freshman Damon Stoudamire and assigned Stoudamire to guard Bruin senior Darrick Martin.

That's a lot of confidence in a freshman playing his second Pac-10 game.

Moreover, Stoudamire had been conspicuous by his absence for most of the second half. He played seven minutes.

He yields three years of savvy and about an inch of size to Martin. Othick, by comparison, has played in a world of pressure situations and has a 2-inch height advantage over Martin.

It's a tough call, either way.

"Coach took me out because I had four fouls," said Othick. "He wanted to make sure I was available for overtime."

Even the best laid plans. . . .

The first rule of coaching in a tie game, final 15 seconds, is don't foul. That's precisely how Sean Rooks beat UCLA at McKale Center a year ago. Olson knew the Bruins wouldn't risk a foul, so Rooks got a basically uncontested shot to win the game.

Olson went with Stoudamire, who is quicker than Othick, and had replaced him in the lineup for defensive purposes with 50 seconds remaining — and then removed again with 49 seconds after a UCLA turnover on an inbounds play.

"I feel I forced (Martin) to take a shot we wanted them to take," said Stoudamire. "I'm pretty sure that was not the shot they wanted to take."

Maybe Martin would've gotten open against Othick anyway.

But to those who flailed away at Olson's defensive plan in the final 10 seconds, remember this: At the end of the first half, with the Bruins working the final 12 seconds to get a shot, Stoudamire slapped the ball out of Martin's hands and stole it with one second remaining.

Olson has a good memory.

What's more, UCLA had turned the ball over on three of its previous six possessions before the Martin game-winner, so whatever defensive plan Olson had ordered served to get the Wildcats back in the game.

No, the Bruins didn't benefit from bad coaching as so many of those fans in Tucson seemed to suggest on Saturday's radio shows.

They benefited from UCLA's totally rebuilt defensive system. Jim Harrick hired defensive coach Steve Lavin from Purdue this year and has the Bruins playing better defense than they've played in 10 or 15 years. Every shot Sean Rooks attempted was a battle. This was a new-look UCLA defense.

And UCLA benefited from MacLean, who had a career performance much the way Arizona's Matt Muehlebach and Brian Williams had career performances against UCLA a year ago, when the final bounce went the Wildcats' way.

The question remaining about Saturday's game is something that only Tom Harrington and Lute Olson will ever know for sure — did he or didn't he?

# Olson holds grudge like no one else

*Monday, March 28, 1994*

Lute Olson has made Tucson feel good about itself in a way no other individual ever has. It has even been suggested that Olson himself changed the image of Tucson from desert outpost to a city of winners.

I won't argue with that.

A politician can't do what Olson has done here. Nor can an astronaut or a movie star. Some cities are indelibly altered by statesmen and scientists. Our city was won by a basketball coach.

Olson took a franchise in disrepair and brought it up to code. No one ever told him no. The budget was open-ended. He wanted it, it was done. No fuss. Whatever money was granted to the Arizona basketball program and its coach, it was money well-spent.

He has seven Pac-10 championship rings, two Final Fours and five Coach of the Year awards with the Wildcats.

Olson has been the basketball coach at the UA for 11 years, and in this short-attention-span world, that runs about five years over the average. Twenty-three coaches have come and gone in the Pac-10 since Olson took Ben Lindsey's place one April morning, 1983.

Either way, 11 years is an awfully long time in one place, and the likelihood of boredom/irritation grows with each new season. If a coach stays long enough at one school, he will become an institution. Stay long enough anywhere, and you will develop friends and enemies alike. That may not be good, but you can't avoid it in any profession. Basketball coaches are just more visible.

There is a larger problem: Coaches are the last great dictators in American society, and they believe they can get away with anything — because they usually do. Witness Jerry Tarkanian's long and scandalous run at UNLV, and Bob Knight's reign of terror at Indiana.

Olson has total control at Arizona, just as Knight does at IU. The difference is, Olson has not abused the power.

But undeniably, the games off the court are always played by his rules. When Olson is winning, his occasional insufferableness and irritability with the media are applauded. When the NCAA Tournament didn't go so well, his insufferableness and irritability were taken as signs of weakness — a loss of poise and composure.

Lute Olson has not changed. But the view of him, the angle on him, most certainly has. A Final Four berth closes out a lot of overdue

398

accounts. Olson is now baying at his critics, and that is not altogether unexpected or unfair. In this very space a year ago, it was suggested that Arizona wasn't getting enough return on the hundreds of thousands of dollars it was paying him.

But whatever it was I had to say last year was lost in a firestorm of criticism. Talk shows. Man on the street. Why, even Olson's perennial sounding board and unwavering ally from the afternoon paper scolded him fiercely.

Two first-round NCAA exits threatened to put Olson's image into a shadowy place in college basketball history. What shocked me more than anything was Olson's reaction. He genuinely believed that the criticism, any of it, was unwarranted. So what if the Wildcats had suddenly gone bust? After paying on the principal for all these years, Olson thought he could ride out any storm on the interest.

What was once this wonderful and innocent pageant, Wildcat basketball, had somehow turned into something else. It turned into something hyped beyond all recognition, doomed to disappoint.

People in the game who have known Olson over the years saw a change in his personality — tighter, grimmer, less happy. I've seen grudges before, held a few myself, but I've never seen a man cling to one the way Olson does.

It became so big, so uncontrollable, that it became a mission. After many notable Wildcat victories this year he would walk into the press room and fire away. Each victory was treated like a sweet step of vindication, leading to the biggest possible victory, a slot in the Final Four.

Harder men than Lute Olson have known when to give it up and move on.

But no. Saturday at the Los Angeles Sports Arena, in his moment of glory, Olson was in no mood for celebration. There was anger in his eyes.

He raged on, borrowing time that would normally be spent detailing his team's late-season excellence and from his own coaching performance, which, based on what I've seen in March, should qualify him as the NCAA Coach of the Year. Instead, he roared away, both guns blazing.

Predictably, many of the nation's Sunday sports columnists ripped into Olson and overlooked the UA's elegant season.

This was the lasting image of Arizona basketball that many in the throng of media took home to tell and to re-tell their audiences. The problem wasn't in believing him.

The problem was in not feeling sorry for him.

# Coaches give up; Pac-10 is Lute's

*Friday, November 11, 1994*

*LOS ANGELES*

This is Lute's league.

The other coaches no longer fight it, and they no longer beat their fists on the desk in frustration. They have given in and accepted Arizona as the model of excellence for Western college basketball and signed over the deed.

They all want to be like Lute.

They all want what Lute has.

The best they can hope for is to be full partners with the Wildcats.

Where there used to be animosity and resentment from some old coaches — Cal's Lou Campanelli, UNLV's Jerry Tarkanian, Oregon's Don Monson and UCLA's Walt Hazzard come to mind — there is now respect.

By going to the Final Four again last spring, and by having enough talented personnel in stock to be a Top 10 program for at least another four seasons, the power struggle on the West Coast has ended. Arizona may not win the Pac-10 every year, but there is no longer the persistent hope that the Wildcats will fall back and Lute Olson will let up. That much was obvious at the Pac-10's annual media day gathering at the Airport Hilton yesterday. "Sometimes," said Pac-10 commissioner Tom Hansen, "we overlook how good we really are."

And he wasn't talking about UCLA. The Bruins went 7-7 down the stretch last year and were booted from the NCAA tournament by Tulsa. And he wasn't talking about Cal. The Bears suffered a first-round NCAA flameout against Wisconsin-Green Bay and lost their two franchise players, Jason Kidd and Lamond Murray. And the commissioner certainly wasn't talking about any of the other missing-in-action Pac-10 basketball programs.

He was talking about Arizona, winner of seven of the last nine Pac-10 titles.

"Thank God for Arizona," ASU's Bill Frieder said. "Getting to the Final Four last year gave the league the credibility it needs."

That's typical of how the league seems to feel now about the Wildcats.

There is no longer an edgy feeling when UCLA's Jim Harrick and Lute Olson are in the same room, sitting 5 feet apart during lunch, as

400

they were yesterday. They have developed a mutual respect, borne both by Harrick's never-ending battle for acceptance in L.A., and by Olson's persistent success against the Bruins, 11 victories in the last 15 games.

The bitterness has subsided, in part because UCLA spends half of its time fighting off its local critics and the other half wondering how to combat a wicked 1994-95 schedule that includes Kentucky, Duke, LSU, Louisville, Notre Dame, UMass and the Pac-10 regulars. "Unbelievable," said Harrick, who then braced himself for the inevitable questions about Tulsa and said that injuries were mostly to blame. Predictably, that answer didn't go over well at all.

"Everyone thinks I'm sniveling," Harrick said.

But there is no time for sniveling this year. Arizona and the Bruins have too much at stake.

They have also become, in effect, allies. They are partners in help-ing the Pac-10 improve nationally, which therefore helps them help one another. The Bruins and Wildcats both have been picked No. 1 nation-ally in various preseason magazines this month, and maybe for the first time the rest of the league has finally caught on.

The rest of the league must improve. "There won't be much for-giveness at the top," said Stanford's Mike Montgomery. "Those people aren't willing to take a step back."

Media day always gets tricky in the Pac-10 because every November, without fail, the league's coaches fall in line and say this is the best the league has ever been.

And it never turns out that way.

That was Topic One again yesterday, but this time the coaches may be on to something. Oregon State, 6-21 last year, is fortified by a group of new players, some of them with impressive credentials. Embattled Beaver coach Jim Anderson said he had two all-conference players, Brent Barry and Mustapha Hoff. Washington, 5-23 a year ago, is unquestionably making a move upward. Oregon, 10-17 last season, is talking about the NCAA tournament.

Who's going to finish last? Unlike most Pac-10 basketball seasons, there does not seem to be a perfectly awful team destined for that spot.

"The thing that I liked last year was that Arizona won the confer-ence with four losses," said second-year Washington coach Bob Bender. "That shows me, from top to bottom, that there is strength in the con-ference. You often see that the ACC champ has five league losses; that's because the ACC is so strong. That's what we need to get to."

Olson doesn't disagree. That has long been his wish. His 17-1 and

16-2 conference champions were good, but he might've preferred a more rigorous road to prepare for the NCAA tournament. "When you go on the road this year," Olson said yesterday, "I don't know if you can say, 'This will be a win,' at any stop. It'll be treacherous. If you can win four or five on the road and do the job at home, that should be enough to win it."

A year ago Stanford finished fourth in the Pac-10 and the Cardinal has four returning starters plus 7-foot-1 freshman Tim Young, of whom Montgomery says, "He's going to be an extremely good player in this league." In a normal year, the Cardinal would be thinking of the top three.

This may not be a normal Pac-10 year. "It's going to be tough to stay at No. 4," Montgomery said. "Even though we've improved, the bottom teams are much better. That's healthy for the league."

You may be surprised by some of those who are thinking big.

Washington has sold 3,500 season tickets, and former Bob Knight/Mike Krzyzewski aide Bob Bender is turning heads. The UW has scheduled home games in its ancient barn against Michigan and Missouri, and the Huskies are recruiting the way Todd Bozeman did at Cal (well, maybe no Jason Kidd, but they've got some real players this year, and more on the way). Benderball they call it. And the Ducks are about to be heard.

"We've re-done all the seating at Mac Court," UO coach Jerry Green said. "We're making the students more involved, seating them around the court on all sides. We've sold more than 3,000 season tickets, and I think we've got some people excited."

And wouldn't that be nice if it came true? More excitement. Less sniveling.

Lute's league might be on to something at last.

DAVID SANDERS

The defining achievement of Lute Olson's brilliant career, winning the 1997 NCAA championship, put him in a class with the game's all-time great coaches.

# Altered Olson not ready to retire

*Sunday, April 6, 1997*

John Wooden went until he was 66, cut down the nets one last time and walked away.

At 70, Joe Paterno is still full of thunder, still riding hard. Dean Smith, 66, continues to set the pace. Adolph Rupp stayed until he was 71, much too long, hanging on until he was depicted as faded glory, living in the past tense, getting by with what used to be.

Bear Bryant coached until he was 69, unyielding to the end. He was dead six weeks after he quit.

Ray Meyer stayed on until he was 68, desperate to get The Ring, so close, yet so sad. By the time Don Shula stepped down, at 66, the cruel parlance of the trade was that he had lost it.

How do you know when to let go?

On Friday afternoon, Lute Olson climbed the long stairs at McKale Center and settled in for his final press conference of a very long season. He wore a navy turtleneck sweater with a Nike swoosh on the collar. He looked positively ebullient. Tall, handsome, fit.

He was on top of the pile.

At 62, Olson has no more worlds to conquer in college basketball. He was four days removed from putting the cherry on one of the greatest coaching sundaes ever, and he treated inquiries about retirement as if they were fleas.

"I get the questions, 'If you win the title will you retire?'" he said. "What's that got to do with retiring?

"You retire because you get fired, and I don't think that's on the agenda. You retire because you're sick of the job or don't have energy to do the job. I don't think any of those factors are present. Winning (the title) has nothing to do in how much longer I'll be here."

No one questions whether Olson still has the bear's growl.

He can be a formidable presence, whether you are an idiotic Cal fan getting in his face after a paralyzing loss, or whether you are Rick Pitino, plotting enemy strategy.

If this is what 62 looks like, 50 must be for kids.

"People get locked up into age," he says. "But the most important things are your energy level and whether you can you still communicate with kids."

Olson's contract runs through 2001 and, barring health problems, there's no reason to think he won't fulfill that contract. Why? It's a combination of three things:

• He has bridged the generation gap.

After the period from 1990 to 1993, when Arizona had a plodding, unimaginative inside game and a preponderance of attitude cases in the clubhouse, Olson told associates his enjoyment for the game was ebbing. He gained almost 20 pounds. The stress of NCAA losses to East Tennessee State and Santa Clara was eating him up inside.

But Olson had the patience to become part of the next generation, the group of players led by the delightful Damon Stoudamire, which subsequently evolved into Reggie Geary's group and, now, Miles Simon's and Mike Bibby's.

You can't help but like these guys, Jason Terry and A.J. Bramlett. They are the latter-day Kerrs and Elliotts.

Those who have been around UA basketball for Olson's duration noticed a change in his public speaking this year. He returned to his '80s mantra — "fun group" and "good people on and off the court" — which was noticeably missing from his vocabulary in the early '90s.

The Disease of Me has been eradicated from the Wildcat locker room.

• Olson's earning power has never been greater.

Drawing $523,223 per annum from the UA, Olson will get a $50,000 bonus for winning the national title and, possibly, a salary adjustment. His attractiveness on the endorsement market is growing. A national title could bump his take from Nike to something close to $200,000 annually.

• After all these years, he seems to be at peace with himself.

During Arizona's 6-0 run through the NCAA tournament, Olson was accommodating to a fault. Not quite charming, but on the fringe of it. Even in the adversary's lair — a series of 10 lengthy press conferences in three weeks — Olson showed the side of him customarily reserved for moms and dads when he's hoping to close the deal with a high school All-American.

For most of the '90s, Olson had raged at the media and fair-weather fans. He didn't seek respect but seemed genuinely hurt when it didn't arrive. Whether because of pride or ego or spite, he stubbornly resisted the urge to let himself be liked (except by those always-obedient worshippers at McKale).

At times he was sensitive to criticism beyond all reason.

But this year, especially in March, he took the high ground.

You can see the change. You can see the glow.

Olson can't possibly know where the next four years will take him. If he loses too many games, he'll lose some of his luster. The gloss is important, but less so after you have The Ring.

But there is no reason to expect Olson's teams to back off at all. His consistency is so amazing that not even Duke can match it. In the Olson years at Arizona, only North Carolina has stayed in step, year by year.

Three times to the Final Four.

TV games all the time. A fantastic schedule. A tested tournament team. Arizona has played, and defeated, all the marquee teams of the era. Michigan, Duke, North Carolina, Kentucky.

Across 14 years at Arizona, Olson's teams have played 33 NCAA tournament games. Is there a greater measuring device than that? Do you know how many NCAA games ASU has played during that span? Five.

This is no time to stop, because Olson realizes, as we do, that while getting to the top was fun, when it's over it's not as much fun. The chase is the fun.

And now everyone is chasing him.

# Bobbi Olson leaves special legacy at UA

*Tuesday, January 2, 2001*

Section 16, rows 3 and 4, has for years been the happiest place at McKale Center.

Bobbi Olson sat there, surrounded by her friends, her children, her grandchildren, and by strangers she made feel welcome. The pep band would announce her arrival — "Hi, Bobbi!" — and she would smile and wave. Whatever the level of tension and scope of the game, the people in Section 16 seemed above it.

Bobbi's routine was to walk onto the court at floor level about 20 minutes before tip-off. Some games, it would take her the full 20 minutes to get from the south baseline to her seat in Section 16. Who didn't know her, stop her and count her as a friend?

There was a clear sense that you knew her, even if she didn't know you. This was the way she made Tucson her home. We'd all be friends.

At what other arena does the coach's wife have such a presence? Such a relationship?

For most of last season and all of this one, Section 16 has been without Bobbi Olson. Her fight against cancer made her visits infrequent. Before each game, fans would turn and scan Section 16, hopeful that Bobbi would be there and that she and her husband would begin that night's post-game press conference with an announcement that the real loser was cancer, and not Oregon or Cal.

"We beat it," they would say. "It's gone."

As idyllic as Lute Olson's basketball career has been, grief has intruded on much too regular a basis. His first Wildcat assistant coach, Ricky Byrdsong, was murdered two years ago. The father of Steve Kerr, the UA's most beloved player, was assassinated. The man who brought the Olsons to Tucson, Cedric Dempsey, fought and won a heroic battle against cancer.

Why does this program, so wildly successful, have to deal with so much pain?

Sean Elliott suffered kidney failure. Luke Recker was almost killed in an automobile crash. One of Olson's former UA assistants, Scott Thompson, had to retire from his coaching position at Cornell this year, decked by cancer. Another of his former UA assistants, Tony McAndrews, survived, miraculously, a plane crash while on a recruiting trip.

Through it all, Lute could lean on Bobbi and Bobbi could lean on Lute and they found a way to get through the hurt.

Lute Olson and Bobbi Russell were married on Nov. 27, 1953, a few months after they graduated from a small North Dakota high school. They would become a traditional American family.

He worked his way through school, a small college in Minnesota. She worked as a secretary. Later, she was a stay-at-home mom. He drove an oil truck for Texaco. He worked as a roofer and a painter, and taught driver's education. She had five kids.

He quit his career as a high school basketball coach in Minnesota and they moved to Colorado, bent on a career in education administration, believing it was a better way to support a growing family. A year later, they packed and moved to Southern California, hungry for the opportunity to get back into coaching.

They camped in Yosemite. They'd go to the movies when they found time, especially when Lee Marvin was on screen. When they took the family to a restaurant, they'd often caution the kids that they'd have to order water with their hamburger, because they couldn't afford a Coke or a root beer.

Theirs was a beautiful relationship long before they came to Tucson on a beautiful April day in 1983. Dempsey introduced Lute to an audience of reporters. Lute then introduced Bobbi.

He made it clear from that day that it was Lute and Bobbi and not just Lute Olson, basketball coach.

For those who know her only from afar, the enduring snapshot of Bobbi Olson came on March 27, 1988, at the Seattle Kingdome. The Wildcats defeated North Carolina to earn the school's first berth in the Final Four, and before Lute joined his celebrating team, he spotted his wife, who had skirted security guards and moved swiftly onto the court.

Television cameras captured the happy embrace as Lute lifted her off her feet and kissed her.

"They are always together, a perfect balancing act," the Star's Jon Wilner wrote in 1993. "He is the shy husband tossed into the spotlight. She is the vibrant, outgoing wife with the calming presence.

"She even admits: 'He takes great comfort if I'm along with him. It's easier for him to walk in a room with me there. I go on the road with him because it makes him feel like he's at home. It gives him something normal in his life. One time I missed a road game and I got four phone calls, asking me to be there for the next game.'"

Right now, the next game doesn't seem to matter much. When Bobbi Olson died yesterday, she left a lot more than an empty seat in Section 16.

She left a legacy of family and friendship that means far more than any of those banners hanging from the ceiling at McKale Center.

# Olson's '86 team won with less talent

*Wednesday, August 23, 2006*

*"Fine, put us in jail. The Russians can play an intrasquad game for the gold medal."* — Lute Olson, talking to Spanish police about not being able to practice at a Madrid gym 24 hours before the 1986 World Championship game.

In an attempt to rescue America's international basketball dignity, Mike Krzyzewski and Jerry Colangelo are in the process of winning the World Championship.

The finals will not be played until Sept. 2 in Saitama, Japan, but, come on, now that Coach K is involved, and the selection process eliminated the I've-gotta-get-my-points hot dogs, we have little to fear.

Humiliated at the 2002 World Championships, and again at the 2004 Athens Olympics, and aching for redemption, we have put our best basketball people on the job.

It must make Lute Olson laugh.

Twenty years ago this summer, Olson left Tucson with 12 amateur ballplayers and an assignment that today would be given to Tom Cruise for the "Mission Impossible" series.

Pressure? Olson was given the keys to an American program that had not won the World Basketball championship since 1954.

In preparation, Olson was allowed 10 practice sessions (and two walkover exhibition games) at McKale Center before embarking on an imposing overseas mission to play the pros from Russia, Yugoslavia, Italy and Brazil.

It was a daunting assignment made more so because four of America's five leading college players — Kansas' Danny Manning, Georgetown's Reggie Williams, Indiana's Steve Alford and Final Four MVP Pervis Ellison of Louisville — chose not to participate.

A month later, sitting in a hotel lobby in downtown Madrid, Spain — 24 hours before playing the Soviet Union for the championship — Olson said, frankly, "When we left Tucson, I really didn't envision us being here."

No kidding.

Before Olson's undersized squad shocked Yugoslavia a few days earlier, Yugoslav coach Kresimir Cosic bizarrely told an Oviedo, Spain, newspaper, "I could get together an all-star team of my old BYU team-

411

mates and match the team America brought to Spain."

The American team was such an underdog that it lost 98-83 to France in its first game, an exhibition in Paris, then survived a last-second layup missed by Puerto Rico to win 73-72, and then played poorly and lost to Argentina 74-70.

It was a fascinating and unpredictable month in which Team USA lost its top shooter, Steve Kerr, who tore apart his knee in a semifinal victory over Brazil, a period in which Olson spent six days outfitted in "Indiana Hoosiers" gear because KLM airlines lost his luggage.

There was tension everywhere, and not just because Olson was attempting to restore 32 years of lost American pride. In a week at Malaga, Spain, Team USA's hotel was guarded by 25 armed policemen (machine guns) and escorted to and from games and practice by a helicopter gunship.

But nothing was more tense than the showdown with Madrid police at a local gymnasium 24 hours before the gold medal game.

The Italians and Americans each showed up for a 1 p.m. workout. A policeman told Olson that he would have to leave. Thus provoked, Olson said he would forfeit rather than yield his team's final chance to practice.

Later that night, at the team's downtown hotel, Olson told me that he was dead serious.

"It wasn't a bluff," he said. "I wasn't going to let them intimidate us."

Olson's young players, led by Navy senior-to-be David Robinson, witnessed the showdown and responded 24 hours later with a once-in-a-lifetime performance, beating the Soviets 87-85 — after building an 80-63 lead.

It might have been the coaching gem of Olson's career. His starting lineup included second-tier collegians such as UNLV forward Armon Gilliam, North Carolina shooting guard Kenny Smith, Duke guard Tommy Amaker and Pitt power forward Charles Smith.

The leading subs were Kerr and Alabama's Derrick McKey. UA sophomore-to-be Sean Elliott was the third man off the bench.

Before he was injured, Kerr said that Olson's perpetual game face was the trigger behind Team USA's series of upset victories.

"When I get home to California," he told me, "I'm not going to touch a basketball for a month. This is work. But if it's the way to win a world championship, I won't complain."

Olson was thus set in the USA Basketball rotation, lined up to be

America's head coach at the 1992 Barcelona Olympics. But while he was waiting his turn, Olson was scuttled by an inept 1988 Seoul Olympics coaching performance by John Thompson, who could not beat the same Europeans whom Olson stunned two years earlier.

Once burned, USA Basketball and the NBA joined forces and formed the Dream Team for the 1992 Olympics. Olson was the odd man out.

Now, USA Basketball has added to its staff, with a high-profile GM like Colangelo and 12 NBA All-Stars. Some of it is overkill. Some of it is because, globally, basketball has improved considerably in the 20 years since Olson won in Spain.

The United States should win; we can all yawn in unison. But it was much more fun in 1986.

The final two years of Lute Olson's career were plagued by instability and raised many questions. The program often seemed to be without a voice.

MAMTA POPAT

# It's time for Wildcats, Olson to decide if they're in or out

*Sunday, March 9, 2008*

*EUGENE, Ore.*

As recently as four years ago in an NCAA interview room in Raleigh, N.C., Lute Olson recoiled at the bitterness of a 20-10 season and a first-round tournament loss to Seton Hall.

"A 20-10 record is not acceptable," he said. "And just one round in the playoffs is not acceptable."

So what will the proper term be after Arizona lost 78-69 to the Oregon Ducks on Saturday? At 18-13, the Wildcats are thus forced to play in the much-dreaded pigtail round of the Pac-10 tournament on Wednesday.

They can only hope they get the opportunity to lose a first-round NCAA tournament game.

What was once unacceptable to the Wildcats has now become a desperate goal, a switch of philosophies in almost record time.

Arizona came to Oregon positioned on the NCAA tournament's Bubble Watch. It returns home not with its bubble burst, but in a position for it to be popped at the Pac-10 Tournament.

The Wildcats now must play Oregon State late Wednesday night in Los Angeles. A victory in that game would send them into a Thursday contest against second-seeded Stanford. It's true that in the days of the 64/65-team field that 71 teams have gotten into the NCAA tournament with 12 or more regular-season losses, but that's nothing that can be taken to the bank.

Arizona completed the Pac-10 season 8-10, its first time under .500 since 1983-84, which isn't necessarily a record that will expel it from the selection committee's big board. Thirteen teams have finished two games under .500 in conference play, or worse, and gotten into the NCAA tournament since the field grew to 64/65.

That's territory customarily reserved for Ole Miss and Virginia Tech and Dayton. It is now Arizona territory.

On Saturday, arriving at Mac Court in need of a season-saving victory, the Wildcats once again failed to contain Oregon's distance shooting. Amazingly, the Ducks made 13 of their first 15 shots in the second half, most of them from what seemed to be the California border.

415

How come Oregon is always so deadly against Arizona and so seemingly ineffective against the rest of the league?

Coming here in a must-win situation was not a good idea from the beginning, especially in a season in which the Ducks have a senior-laden roster and it was, gulp, Senior Day.

In the second half, by the time the Ducks began raining three-pointers over the UA defense, fears started to arise that those close losses to UCLA, Stanford, Arizona State and Kansas might not be balanced by close victories over Illinois, UNLV and Wazzu.

Now, unfortunately, much of the focus will return to the absence of Olson.

A week after losing to Seton Hall in that 2004 game, the then-69-year-old coach seemed in full control and the Wildcats merely seemed to be encountering a rare bump, as they did after shocking first-round exits in 1992 and 1993.

On that week, eager for a resolution as sophomore Andre Iguodala played coy about bolting for the NBA, Olson said "either you're with us or you're not."

The Wildcats were always so resourceful and so deep that Iguodala's early departure was of little consequence.

Olson had total ownership of UA basketball, a solo voice, and even though he was a few months from turning 70, no one stepped forward to say his treasured basketball program had irretrievably begun to slip.

"We've got three tough guys coming in," Olson said that day in Raleigh. "It's not going to be a case of worrying if Mohamed Tangara is tough. He's tough. Daniel Dillon is tough. Jawann McClellan's high school team went 39-0. He's tough."

No one saw this coming. No one could've known that four years later it would be Olson in the "not" category of the "with us or not" equation.

No one could've guessed that Tangara would have absolutely no impact in four years, and that Dillon would not develop into the type of useful sixth, or seventh, man that forever seemed to make the difference between Arizona and most of the rest of the Pac-10.

No one could have suspected that some misfortune, McClellan's string of injuries, would prevent him from becoming an all-conference player that you would expect from a McDonald's All-American.

The story now isn't Wednesday's game against Oregon State, but what Olson plans to do, or attempts to encourage UA athletic director Jim Livengood to let him do.

It is still Olson's responsibility to get the program back on its feet, either with his total involvement or, lacking that, with his support from a peripheral position. It is incumbent upon Olson to share the responsibility for his team's slippage, a team that enters the Pac-10 tournament in the unfamiliar No. 7 position.

He owes his team, if no one else, an explanation for his absence. He owes his school a quick commitment; can he continue to be a productive college basketball coach or can't he?

The program's long-term future is more important than a game or two in the Pac-10 Tournament. More than anything else, the UA needs some honesty from Olson.

Can he coach again? Does he want to coach again?

His continued silence is unacceptable.

# Bill comes due for Arizona program engulfed in chaos

*Friday, October 24, 2008*

In the end, there was no teary farewell, no band playing, no banners waving, no fairy tale at all.

It was Jim Livengood flanked by two thinkers from the school's public relations brigade, Paul Allvin and Stephen J. MacCarthy, saying something in code that really meant "the lawyers will clean up all the details."

As Don Henley sings, "This is the end, this is the end of the innocence."

By the time the UA puts all the dollars together, Lute Olson's retirement won't be about happy memories; it will be about the chaos that has engulfed Camelot, the once-thriving UA basketball program.

The first guy to knock on the door will be the attorney for Kevin O'Neill, the vagabond coach who a few months ago was publicly announced as Olson's successor.

"When does Kevin start?" his attorney will ask? Let the bidding begin.

Then will come the unhappy calls from parents of UA ballplayers who pledged to become Wildcats because Olson assured them he would be their coach.

There will be no good answer.

"Sorry," they will be told. "Lute didn't tell us, either."

Olson had to re-recruit Chase Budinger and Nic Wise and Jamelle Horne, pledging that if they remained Wildcats, he would erase the sting of last year's dysfunctional drama.

Tough luck, huh?

It's not true that Livengood failed to put an exit strategy into place and was unprepared for this preseason crisis; in fact, he has been working on Olson's departure for months.

Livengood chatted formally with former Stanford coach Mike Montgomery about replacing Olson for this season. But the timing didn't work, and in the end Olson wanted to give it another shot and, well, nobody had enough power to tell him no.

It wasn't good business sense, but when a man coaches you to four Final Fours and 11 Pac-10 titles in what seemed like 11 years, he has

418

the hammer. It was his choice, and perhaps his unwise judgment, to put the program he so artfully built into so much jeopardy. But no one, not even the university president, was willing to back him down.

And so now the bill comes due.

The UA recruiting class of 2009 is all but bankrupt. The team the next coach puts on the floor, in 2009-10, could be as bad as the one Olson inherited in 1983-84.

Because of that, there is a simultaneous feeling of appreciation and one of melancholy. There is also the reality that Olson wasn't going to be able to re-establish Arizona as an elite-level franchise.

"My personal opinion is that this is the right time for Lute to go," said Matt Othick, Arizona's skillful lefty shooting guard from 1989 to '92, who is now a Las Vegas businessman. "I didn't want to see him struggle. He's a special coach, and only a few have ever matched what he accomplished, but things had taken a turn for the worse.

"I'm glad to see that he stepped away before his image could be tarnished."

As Livengood begins to woo a replacement — is John Calipari too much to expect? — it is with a sense of urgency.

The UA athletic program is beholden to Lute's annual yield of about $16 million. It is one of the five or six top-grossing college basketball departments. Season-ticket sales have dropped by almost 2,000 since 2006, and it is imperative — urgent for the health of the UA swimming, tennis, softball and baseball teams — that Arizona continues to produce similar basketball revenues.

Every bit as important as Olson's 24 consecutive NCAA tournament seasons are these figures:

• In 2006-07, the Wildcats produced $17,056,700 in basketball revenues.

• In 2007-08, the figure was $16,609,000.

No wonder they put his name at center court. In a self-supporting athletic department, Olson was an ATM. Can you fathom how many UA golf events in Hawaii and how many volleyball recruiting trips were funded by Olson's basketball program?

"Lute didn't have anything left to prove," 1988 Final Four center Tom Tolbert said on his San Francisco radio program Thursday. "Tucson wasn't on the map when he took that job. Tucson was nowhere. But he put it on the map, and he has meant a hell of a lot to that city and to those who played for him."

Or as 1988-91 point guard Matt Muehlebach, a Tucson attorney, said: "We all had visions of Lute going out in the Final Four, or by winning a championship. But this is probably for the best. I'm left with a tremendous, positive feeling about him and Arizona basketball."

In the end, that is what will be remembered. Lute's sloppy departure will be forgotten; his fabulous success will prevail.

What happens next is on Livengood. It's the ultimate challenge of his long career. His charge is to find a replacement who will win at Olson's level, generate income at Olson's level and carry the torch with similar command.

No one is going to be happy with anything less.

# CHAPTER ELEVEN

# Arizona basketball

## Black player found sanctuary at Bear Down Gym

*Wednesday, February 6, 1985*

Twenty-five years ago tonight, "Easy" Ernie McCray, a 6-foot-5 senior center, scored 46 points for the University of Arizona in a 104-84 basketball victory over Los Angeles State at Bear Down Gym.

In 1,630 games at the UA — 80½ seasons — no one has scored more.

Yet there was no celebration after the game. McCray, who played at Tucson High, would have liked to have gone to a nice restaurant near his home at Stone Avenue and Second Street.

"But most restaurants in Tucson in those days," he said, "only served blacks food to go."

He also would have liked to have stayed up late, perhaps reminiscing about the game over a few cold beers.

"But I couldn't do that," he said. "My living conditions were such that I hated them.

"I usually worked before and after practice as a janitor, a busboy — I had thousands of menial, odd jobs just to make ends meet.

"I was a young father with three children that year and sometimes my workload seemed pretty cruel."

McCray persevered and left the UA as its career leader in scoring (1,349), rebounding (10.8 per game) and free-throw shooting. Each of those records has been broken. But he holds six UA records and is listed 22 times in school record books.

Only Bob Elliott, Al Fleming and Bill Warner have scored more at the UA.

Oddly, McCray is not in the UA Sports Hall of Fame — 21 other

421

basketball players are. Yesterday he said he considers his UA career "bittersweet at best."

"I went through some pretty rough times emotionally. I think I would have gone under, mentally, without the cheers of the crowds at Bear Down Gym."

McCray graduated from the UA in June 1962 with a degree in education. He has been an educator in San Diego since and has been principal of an elementary school for five years.

"I guess you could say I have a love-hate relationship with Tucson and the UA," he said. "But the main thing was, I got my degree and that enabled me to quit all those degrading jobs and be what I always wanted to be — a teacher."

McCray seems genuinely surprised that his 46-point game remains a record. Joe Skaisgir, in 1962, and Coniel Norman, in 1974, had 44-point games at the UA. Fleming had a 41-point game in 1976.

There was little reason to suspect McCray, averaging 22 points a game with a career-high of 35, would break Eli Lazovich's school record of 38 that night.

But McCray had 24 points at halftime, and the announced crowd of 2,055 seemed to sense something special was in the works.

"That was such a horse-bleep period of basketball that the gym rats like me and the loyal fans lived to see Ernie's march to 500 (points), his march to the career scoring record, and his game-to-game scoring statistics," said Mike Clark, an Associated Press sportswriter in New York. He grew up in Tucson.

"Through the years, there must be 10,000 or 15,000 people who claim to have been in Bear Down that night."

Bruce Larson, a UA assistant in 1960 and later the school's head coach for 11 years, said McCray's 46-point game didn't progress unusually.

"That's typical," Larson said. "Ernie wouldn't stand out. He wasn't flashy. But after the game, you'd look at the box score and he'd have his points."

When McCray scored his 39th and 40th points of the game, with roughly seven minutes remaining, the ovation at Bear Down gymnasium was such that the game was stopped for more than a minute.

"My honest feeling," McCray said yesterday, "was that I didn't know why the game was stopped and why the crowd was cheering so loud. The whole gym was at a feverish pitch.

"When I found out I had 46 points, it was more of a stroke to my ego than anything else.

"With all the typical racial-type things I had to endure in Tucson, I got almost all of my satisfaction through the crowd."

McCray was 16 of 26 from the field, 14 of 16 at the foul line and had 14 rebounds.

"The thing I remember vividly about the game was that I couldn't miss," he said.

"A couple of times late in the game I just kind of took lackadaisical shots — we had a big lead — and I made 'em all. It was incredible. It just blew me away."

McCray is probably not well remembered at the UA. His years as a starter came during some of the Wildcats' worst seasons — 10-15, 4-22 and 10-14 — during coach Fred Enke's final three UA clubs.

It was the downside of an otherwise successful era.

"Unfortunately," McCray said, "a lot of times it came down to how many points I scored rather than how the team did."

Furthermore, McCray was just the second black basketball player to play a significant role at the UA. More pressure.

(Hadie Redd was the other, an All-Border Conference Player in 1955.)

"The first thing Fred Enke told me was that the future of black basketball players at the UA rested on my shoulders," McCray said.

"He said it was all up to how I played and how I comported myself around town. All I could say was 'wow' — but I had no doubts I would succeed.

"And I think now, looking back, I can say I handled it well."

EDITOR'S NOTE: Ernie McCray was finally inducted into the UA Sports Hall of Fame on Oct. 22, 1988, nearly three decades after he left the school. His 46-point effort against Los Angeles State still stands as Arizona's single-game scoring record, and he still ranks in the program's career top 10 in points per game (seventh, 17.8), rebounds per game (second, 10.8), rebounds (seventh, 824), and free throws (seventh, 537). McCray is a retired school principal and lives in his hometown of San Diego.

BRUCE MCCLELLAND

Steve Kerr exits the floor in Long Beach, Calif., after a 1986 NCAA tourney loss.
A knee injury that summer made this his last UA game until the '87-'88 season.

# Kerr told his career may be over

*Friday, July 18, 1986*

*MADRID, Spain*
When the dreaded news came, Steve Kerr met it like a man. There was no angry "Why me?" crying.

He is out of the World Championship gold-medal game.

He is out of the 1986-87 college basketball season.

He may be out for good, his competitive basketball career terminated with 4:07 remaining in Team USA's 96-80 victory over Brazil last night in the semifinals of the 1986 World Championships at Madrid Sports Palace. Kerr was driving to the basket, attempting to make a pass when a Brazilian defensive player cut off Kerr's passing lane.

"I was forced to change my mind in midair," said Kerr, a senior guard at the University of Arizona. "As I did so, I came down awkwardly, unsure.

"As soon as I hit the ground, I felt the outside of my right knee explode. Then the pain shot to the other side of the knee."

Kerr rolled over and over on the court, screaming in pain and clutching at the knee.

"As soon as he went down," said Sean Elliott, Kerr's teammate at the UA, "I knew his knee was gone."

And so did Kerr.

"I never felt pain like that in my life," he said two hours after the game as he prepared to leave the team hotel en route to a Madrid hospital, where his damaged knee was to be put in a cast.

"I haven't heard the doc say anything but bad things. He's been totally frank about it," Kerr said.

"The doc said that more often than not an injury like this is career-ending . . . can you believe it? . . . career-ending.

"Those are the words that are ringing in my mind."

Team USA physician Tim Taft of the University of North Carolina diagnosed Kerr's injury as the worst possible knee injury that an athlete can sustain.

Two ligaments have been torn — the anterior cruciate and the medial collateral.

"In the world of knee injuries," said Taft, "this is as bad as it gets."

Kerr is to leave Madrid early today, fly via Amsterdam, then Chicago, and is expected to arrive at his home in Los Angeles late tonight. Taft said surgery likely will be performed on Kerr's knee as soon as possible.

"There's no question Steve will be out next season," Taft said. "As for the following season (Kerr obviously will redshirt in 1986-87), there will be some limitations. He will never have 100 percent strength in that knee again.

"To most athletes performing at such high competition levels, an injury like this is career-ending. But of course I can't predict the future."

In three seasons at the UA, Kerr probably has become the most popular athlete at the school. He seems to be one of the most well-liked athletes the UA has ever had.

He was an All-Pacific-10 guard last season and was voted the league's most valuable player by the news media. A 6-foot-3-inch guard from Southern California, Kerr also had established himself as one of the nation's premier guards, by averaging 10 points per game at the World Championships.

Last night, he scored 14 points, which included three three-point field goals, his specialty. The NCAA has established a three-point field goal rule effective next season. Kerr, who had long anticipated such a rule, will watch its implementation from the bench.

Team USA coach Lute Olson, who is Kerr's coach at Arizona, was visibly stunned by Kerr's injury, as were others on the club.

"I'm sick to my stomach," said Scott Thompson, an assistant coach here and at the UA. "It's as if it happened to me."

Olson did not let his emotions slow his speech. He talked tactically about the immediate loss of Kerr.

"It makes a tremendous difference in the gold-medal game Sunday against the Soviets," said Olson, "Steve was our best three-point shooter, and our best inside passer.

"He was at the heart of any team he's on."

Kerr was carried off the court and propped up in a chair, in obvious pain, and lifted into the team bus about 10 minutes before his teammates boarded. Tears welled in his eyes after Taft gave him the diagnosis, and Kerr seemed to be affected even more by his teammates.

"Adversity makes us all stronger," North Carolina guard Kenny Smith told Kerr. "Steve Kerr will make it through this."

Tyrone Bogues, this team's playmaking guard, visited Kerr in his hotel room and seemed to be in disbelief when told Kerr may not play competitive basketball again.

"Your whole career?" Bogues asked, incredulously. "Noooo. No way. It can't be."

Elliott, who suffered a similar but less-damaging knee injury about six years ago — and still wears a brace to protect his injured right knee — tried to console his teammate.

"There are no pros and cons to an injury like that," said Elliott. "It's all cons.

"Mine wasn't as bad as Steve's is, and I even have some instability in my knee now.

"This hurts. This hurts a lot. Why Steve?"

By midnight, Kerr had spoken to his family in Los Angeles and made plans to return there. He also was attempting to make the best of a bad situation.

"The doc said I'll lose some quickness," Kerr said, forcing a smile. "I just said, 'I already used all the quickness I've got, and it's not much.'"

And then Kerr was helped to the shower, and prepared to leave for a Madrid hospital.

"Don't worry about me," he said. "I'll make the best of it."

EDITOR'S NOTE: See Chapter 7 for a column and update on Steve Kerr's basketball career.

DAVID SANDERS

Sean Elliott cuts down the net in 1988 while being hoisted by teammates after the Cats clinched a spot in the Final Four for the first time in school history.

# Wildcats silence the naysayers

*Monday, March 28, 1988*

*SEATTLE*

By the time Tom Tolbert had breakfast yesterday, he understood better than anyone the pressure and pitfalls, the hype and headaches of trying to make the last step to the Final Four.

"Arizona had better be good — or Olson's a liar" was the headline in one morning newspaper.

The Wildcats read that they were "arrogant" and "almost disrespectful." Their coach was said to be full of "bluster and bombast."

The UA had at last attracted the attention of the college basketball world — but it was the wrong kind.

"I felt everyone was waiting for us to screw up," said Tolbert. "Everyone was ready to say, 'I told you so.'"

Instead, in the end, it was Arizona that delivered a brief yet telling I-told-you-so.

"Two more," said Steve Kerr, the Wildcats' senior guard.

"Two mo', " Olson said, laughing.

Arizona bumped off the august basketball players from North Carolina 70-52 in the Western Regional championship game in the Kingdome yesterday. Afterward, even before the nets had been cut down, someone pinned a button to Lute Olson's lapel that read:

"Glad you're here. Going to Kansas City."

He is and they are. The mood was so giddy that someone mussed Olson's hair and he laughed: He thought it was funny.

But the Tar Heels couldn't mess up the remarkable basketball team that has won 35 games, a standard reached by only three teams in the game's history: Duke, Kentucky and Nevada-Las Vegas.

"People are saying we have an arrogant attitude," Olson said. "But that's wrong. We have a confident attitude. The kids have never said 'I think we can.' They always said, 'We can,' and, 'We will.'

"And they did."

Arizona made its moon landing yesterday with no subtlety. The Wildcats advanced to the Final Four via margins of 40, 29, 20 and 18 points. That's 27 points per victory. North Carolina got the same treatment the UA gave to the Oregons and the Washingtons.

So the UA can no longer be construed, or misconstrued, as a freak or a fraud.

429

"We were a pretty flawless team down the final 15 minutes of the game," said Olson. "Everything was at stake, everything was on the line, and the kids rose to the occasion."

"I can't imagine a more deserving team anywhere."

When it needed to play the game of its life, Arizona played the game of its life. Trailing 28-26 at half, the Wildcats knew that a fairytale season was about to be sent to the shredder.

It was only the second time this season that Arizona had trailed at halftime — it had lost the other time, at New Mexico — but this wasn't a lukewarm team of Lobos on the opposite side of the court.

It was North by-God Carolina.

"We knew we were in a tight spot," said Wildcat guard Craig McMillan, who has re-emerged in this tournament as an impact player. "But we have come too far to let it all slip away now. We just dug in. We weren't going to let them beat us."

It was shortly thereafter that Tolbert, who had disappeared in the first half with one basket and one rebound, committed his third foul.

"We were stagnant, it looked bad," said Wildcat assistant coach Kevin O'Neill. "We're not used to being in that situation."

Olson summoned Tolbert to the sideline for a man-to-man chat.

"Do you want to go to Kansas City?" Olson asked, not-so-politely.

"I told him yes," Tolbert said later. "Yes sir."

What followed was a performance that will earn Tolbert a special place in the hearts and minds of Wildcat fans for posterity.

In the ensuing 14 minutes, Tolbert outscored the entire Carolina team. By that time the Wildcats led 59-48, and the Gumbys were rehearsing their next hit rap song, "Kansas City," which they auditioned endlessly in the dressing room.

Tolbert's performance included two acrobatic, Ferris-wheel, from-where-the-sun-don't-shine layups that drove a stake through the Tar Heels' hearts.

"What Tom did," Olson said in admiration, "was outplay the guy (J.R. Reid) who had been the national high school player of the year for two consecutive years."

It was almost a requisite for an Arizona victory. Tolbert picked up for Anthony Cook, who got in foul trouble and faded badly, scoring but two points and spending 11 minutes on the bench.

"That's where chemistry comes in," said Cook. "Tom picked us up. It's that kind of balance that got us to the Final Four."

But otherwise, it was just another day at the office.

Arizona played a smothering, relentless defense, creating so many problems that the Tar Heels missed 69 percent of their shots in the second half. And the Wildcats persevered, looking for the open man and probing Carolina's defensive weaknesses so carefully that the Tar Heels were never in the right places to stop Sean Elliott or Tolbert or Kerr.

"I thought maybe we shook them up a little in the beginning," said UNC coach Dean Smith. "But they didn't stay shook in the second half."

Given the circumstances, at no time this season did the Wildcats play better than they played for the final 15 minutes. At no time in any season has a Wildcat team played better.

North Carolina led 42-40, Cook and Tolbert were in foul trouble, the season was slipping away. . . . And then — boom — Arizona outscored the Tar Heels 30-10.

The cream rose.

"We did better than anyone else has against them," Smith said, forcing a smile. "They only beat us by 18."

Arizona guards Khalid Reeves, with ball, and Reggie Geary stumble over a Santa Clara player in the midst of the most stunning loss in program history.

DAVID SANDERS

# Another dollop of March sadness

*Friday, March 19, 1993*

*SALT LAKE CITY*

The door to the Arizona locker room opened and Kenny Lofton was in tears; Matt Othick had a towel over his head. Jud Buechler sobbed uncontrollably.

Year after year.

The anguish is always the same.

This time it was Damon Stoudamire, the blood drained from his face. "Choke," he said silently, but loud enough to be heard in the tomb that served as Arizona's dressing room. "Choke. Choke. Choke."

Stoudamire repeated himself three times, symbolic perhaps of Arizona's now-notorious string of flameouts in the NCAA tournament.

"Yes," said freshman guard Reggie Geary, "choked."

That's never a nice word and it's a little harsh for anyone who isn't getting paid to play. But the last thing I want to hear is that Santa Clara played a magical game and that anybody unfortunate enough to be in the Broncos' path last night would've suffered the same fate.

Nonsense.

Santa Clara missed 62 percent of its shots. It allowed the opposition to outscore it 25-0 in one stretch. Maybe the Broncos were better than a No. 15 seed, but not much better. Maybe No. 13.

You don't have to part the Red Sea to win an NCAA tournament game, but that's now the way it seems to the Wildcats. This team that had been so vibrant, so full of personality and dash showed up last night and everything was different. Everything was slow and labored.

And so Santa Clara won 64-61 and Arizona's national reputation will never be the same. It will be stained through the '90s and into the 21st century. Arizona not only can't win the big ones, it can't even win the little ones.

"I heard a guy say we were overrated the other day," said UA center Ed Stokes. "I don't know. . . . Maybe he was right."

That's what they'll be saying from now until the 12th of Never. Bad league. Can't win the big one. Chokers.

"We shouldn't have been in the position we were in," UA assistant coach Jim Rosborough said. "It's hard for me to fathom.

"You don't want something like this for the program and for the rap we'll get around this country. But how do you explain the thing

433

with East Tennessee State (last year's first-round UA conqueror)? I don't know. I don't even know if you'll be able to get a good explanation from the (game) tape."

Lute Olson has coached collegiately for 20 years and this is the loss that will follow him to retirement. Publicly, he always holds up well in these awkward appearances. He answered questions patiently and thoughtfully, the same way he always does. The way he did after East Tennessee State. The way he did after Alabama. The way he did after UNLV. He said there is no jinx.

He could yodel that brave statement from the Utah mountaintops and no one would believe a word of it. This has happened far too many times to Arizona to be, simply, a trend or a freak.

Last year was the wake-up call. This year the Wildcats slept in and missed the whole thing.

"This is the second time it's happened in two years, and people can take it however they want to," said Stokes. "I don't want to go through this again. I know all about how it goes from last year."

What must pain Olson most is that this wasn't a team in assembly. He had long ago fitted all the screws and attached all the pipes. The Arizona team has been online, up and running, basically since New Year's Day.

How and why these things happen is one of the unsolved riddles of sports.

Chris Mills hadn't been in foul trouble all year. He averaged 2.2 fouls per game, yet he spent what turned out to be the most important 10 minutes of his senior year on the bench with four fouls. It was no different than Sean Elliott not getting the ball in the final 30 seconds of the 1989 Sweet 16, as the No. 1-ranked Wildcats invented a way to lose.

Arizona's second-best player, Stoudamire, had the worst game of his career. He was 0 for 7 from the field. He had six turnovers. It was Steve Kerr going 2 for 13 in the Final Four.

No jinx, huh?

The ramifications of this defeat will do more than just linger at McKale Center. It could forever rock Olson's program and inhibit its continuity.

There is a painful precedent: DePaul entered the NCAA tournament ranked No. 1 in 1980 and 1981. The Blue Demons lost to eighth-seeded UCLA in the first round in '80, and a year later, again as the No. 1 seed, lost their opener to St. Joseph's.

DePaul has never been the same.

The same thing happened to Oregon State. The Beavers, a No. 2 seed in 1980, lost their opener to Lamar. A year later, ranked No. 1 in the nation, OSU lost its opener to Kansas State.

The Beavers' program steadily eroded thereafter, and an asterisk has followed OSU as well as DePaul through the last decade.

I'm not suggesting that Santa Clara 64, Arizona 61 is the most shocking upset in modern NCAA history, but it's in an elite class with Richmond over Syracuse, and those Cleveland State, Austin Peay classics.

There is a price that will be paid, and the Wildcats will pay it via a loss of image and reputation.

"It seems everything we did, everything we accomplished is for nothing," Stoudamire said. "People aren't going to remember anything except we lost."

Someone asked Stoudamire to explain the game's last possession — a failed Stoudamire three-point attempt at the buzzer — and he went back through the final five seconds of the UA's year in painful detail.

And then he paused and said, "If I had to do it again. . . ."

If only those one-game seasons in March worked that way for Arizona.

# Game of Ages had improbable finish for Cats

*Friday, March 3, 1995*

*PULLMAN, Wash.*
Chapter One. Nah. . . . You wouldn't believe it. Pure fiction.

Won it. Lost it. Tied it. Won it. Lost it. Tied it.

It wasn't just the Game of the Year in the Pac-10, it was the Game of the Ages.

Isaac Fontaine's free throw to win it in regulation, balanced deathly still on the rim, 1.6 seconds remaining. No.

Damon Stoudamire, Mr. Steel, at the free-throw line to win it — twice — in the final 11 seconds of regulation. Miss. Miss.

The crowd gets a technical foul in the final moments of regulation. Yes, it's true. No matter what the Wildcats needed, they got it. And last night they needed divine intervention to beat Washington State 114-111.

It wasn't pretty. It wasn't a symphony. It was more like Woodstock. They'll celebrate the 25th anniversary of this one in 2020, and they'll be talking about it at least until then.

In the final three minutes of regulation, I was sitting in the pressroom at Friel Court, deafened by the happy buzz of the home crowd, ready to rush the court and celebrate their first victory over Arizona since, when, the War of 1812? I was damning my luck, cursing ESPN for starting this game at 10 p.m., so late, in fact, that the final score from the WAC game in Hawaii beat it.

And then I heard a wail, which I didn't think related to Wazzu's breakthrough victory and an almost certain berth in the NCAA tournament.

"Daaaaaaaammmmmmmmmmnnnn!"

It is about 100 yards from the pressroom to the court at WSU's spacious basketball arena. I covered it with Carl Lewis speed, maybe 10 flat.

Stoudamire was at the foul line, the game tied at 90.

"What!?" I yelled to a security guard. "How did that happen? Wasn't WSU ahead by 10 with a few seconds to play?"

Stoudamire missed.

It was midnight and the game had just begun.

437

Remember that day 11 years ago when Olson's first Arizona team went to ASU and trailed by 7 with 35 seconds to go. The Wildcats won it and afterward Olson said, seriously, that as long as he is on the bench he will never give up. No matter how far back, no matter how wide the deficit, there's always hope.

I filed that away as brave talk, thinking there would never be anything to match that in the Olson years. Or any years.

And then I saw Donminic Ellison standing at the free-throw line with 1.6 seconds left, game tied in the first overtime. No way, I thought. The UA has already tapped into its supply of miracles for the next century.

Miss.

Miss.

I'm going to try to be optimistic here and say that the next game the Wildcats lose will be the Big One, the one that really matters and ends their little excursion into the NCAA tournament.

What will be difficult is to determine just what the comeback victory means. Is it that this UA team has the brass to win under any circumstances this month? Or was it just a wild escape?

More than ever, the UA's season is redeemable. That is because the Pac-10 has never been this good before, and that's because not only does UCLA look like a legitimate champion, Wazzu and a bunch of others look pretty authentic, too.

What becomes important for Arizona now is not to let last night's exhausting exercise linger. And it probably won't, either, because Lute Olson has a way of not letting the Wildcats wander, and it won't because what is left in their locker room has enough experience, enough seasoning, to know that they can still sneak into the Sweet 16.

With two minutes remaining last night, Cougar fans chanted, "Overrated! Overrated! Overrated!"

Talk about bad timing.

By then Stoudamire only had 24 of his 40 points.

Talk about a slip of the tongue.

So, as always, the Wildcats made their annual therapeutic stopover in the Palouse. This makes it 11 straight here, 20 straight over the Cougars. It was another feel-good session against Washington State before the craziness of March really begins to gnaw at the UA's nerves.

Which, by now, must be shot.

## LETTER TO THE EDITOR

Get Hansen gone
To The Sports Editor:
Tell me it ain't so.

Tell me that Greg Hansen sees all of an Arizona basketball game prior to writing his column.

Tell me that Greg Hansen's March 3 column ("Game of ages had improbable finish for Wildcats") is incorrect.

Tell me that Greg Hansen was at courtside, instead of the Friel Court pressroom during the last three minutes of the Washington State game.

Tell me that he did not think the game was won by Washington State and had gone to the pressroom to file his story.

Tell me that your paper employs Greg Hansen to cover all of the game and not just a portion.

Tell me, please tell me, that Greg Hansen is returning to his beloved Utah State University.

Walt Roberson

EDITOR'S NOTE: Arizona's game at Washington State started after 10 p.m. Tucson time and went into double-overtime. Washington State was 10 points up with 1:18 left in regulation. The game ended shortly before 1 a.m., and because of deadlines, Hansen had 15 minutes to write his column. Televised coverage of the game was available in the pressroom. Several callers expressed astonishment that Hansen was even able to file a column in that amount of time. The column made approximately 90 percent of the March 3 home editions.

JAMES S. WOOD

There was a tremendous amount of anticipation for the arrival of heralded UA hoops recruit Jason Terry, whose career exploits surpassed all expectations.

440

# Highly touted recruit is likely to play a key role for Wildcats

*Sunday, March 5, 1995*

*SEATTLE*

You know what they say about Jason Terry: He does everything on the basketball court except sell popcorn.

But this time they were wrong. Standing 10 feet outside the Wildcat dressing room last night at Edmundson Pavilion, Terry manned a popcorn concession booth for the University of Washington.

"I've heard all the jokes," he said with a laugh. Or he thought he had. The 6-foot-1-inch point guard from Seattle Franklin High School was the target of one-liners from the Wildcat players, his future team-mates, before and after a late game against the Huskies.

Mostly, it was about the funny little beanie that the Huskies require their employees to wear.

But that's about the last time Terry will be the butt of any jokes in his hometown. After his No. 2-ranked Quakers play in the Washington state tournament this week in the Tacoma Dome — Franklin won the state title last year — Terry will instead become a visitor. An enemy.

"The people in the stands have been yelling at me all year, calling me 'traitor' and things like that," he said. Indeed, in yesterday afternoon's 63-59 loss to O'Dea High School in a district seeding game, Terry bricked a three-point attempt, and an O'Dea student grabbed a megaphone and yelled, "Terry, you ain't going nowhere!"

Ah, but he is. He's going to Tucson, part of the cast of Wildcats who will attempt to fill the point-guard vacancy created by Damon Stoudamire's departure.

Can he play? Let's put it this way: He has a chance to be the fastest guard in the Pac-10, immediately. He can get into the lane almost at will, by virtue of his quick first step. He resembles UCLA's Tyus Edney as a pure point guard but has the size of ASU's Marcel Capers, and he is the same type of selfless player as Capers and Edney. All he needs is seasoning, and you never know how long that will take.

Terry is a lot like Kenny Lofton, beep-beep, but a better pure basketball player.

And did I mention those long arms?

Lute Olson and UA assistant coach Jessie Evans arrived at halftime

441

of Terry's afternoon game. At the time, Terry had six points, preferring to distribute the ball and get his teammates involved. But that wasn't working, and in the final 16 minutes, Terry scored 14 points and carried Franklin against clearly superior O'Dea personnel.

Terry plans to spend the summer at a Bellevue basketball/fitness center and said he wants to add 10 to 15 pounds in a strength training program, which would put him at about 6-1, 180.

"He's a good kid, an intelligent kid, and there's no reason to believe he won't be as good at the next level as he is at this one," Franklin coach Ron Drayton said after the game. "Once he gets fine-tuned at Arizona, once he gets that day-to-day coaching and plays daily against better competition, he's going to be an excellent player for Arizona. He has all the tools."

Sure, Terry needs work. He is not the perimeter-shooting prospect that previous UA point guards Matt Othick, Steve Kerr and Stoudamire have been. But he's better in the open court than almost any guard the UA has had, with the exception of Khalid Reeves and Stoudamire. But the worst thing to do would be to label Terry as Stoudamire's replacement.

No one can be expected to "replace" Stoudamire, who is probably the second best player in Wildcat history. Terry understands that more than anyone.

"I can't fill in for Damon, no one can fill those shoes," he said. "But I love the challenge of going down there and competing with the other guys."

On Thursday, sitting in a coffee shop in a hotel in Moscow, Idaho, Stoudamire talked about the Wildcats in '95-'96, and what they must do to replace him. "I think they'll do it the way they did in the '88 season," with Kerr, Sean Elliott and Craig McMillan, Stoudamire said. "They'll probably use two or three guys to get the ball upcourt. Miles (Simon), Mike (Dickerson) and Reggie (Geary) will spread it around. There's more than one way to do it, Lute has proven that. As the season progresses, Terry will get more and more time. They'll be OK."

In the final minute of yesterday's game, Terry sprinted upcourt with the ball the way he had on every possession, trying to beat the defense into position. Franklin trailed 61-56 and needed a big play.

Terry whipped the ball behind his back at midcourt, leaving two O'Dea defenders stumbling. In fact, one of them tripped against Terry's foot and the basketball squirted out of bounds. Turnover. It was an aggressive play, ruined more by Terry's explosiveness than anything else.

And when Franklin got the ball back with 21 seconds, Terry was again charged with a turnover, his team's last chance vanishing as a pass was dropped by a Franklin teammate. But it was because the pass was too good, too crisp for a lesser-skilled player to handle.

In a college game, with better players, each of Terry's final turnovers in the last 56 seconds might've been converted into transition baskets. He's that far ahead of the high school competition. His best days are ahead. Last year, Terry played against UA freshman Michael Dickerson's Federal Way High School team in a game that attracted a lot of interest in the Seattle area. Dickerson scored 40, Terry 34.

It's not known whether he had time to sell some popcorn.

EDITOR'S NOTE: Jason Terry became one of the most celebrated players in Arizona basketball history, serving as an integral member of the program's NCAA championship team in 1997 as a sophomore. As a senior in 1998-99, he became the second player in UA history to be named NCAA Player of the Year by various national media outlets. (Sean Elliott is the other.) Terry was later declared ineligible for that season by University officials after it was discovered he accepted illegal benefits from agents while playing for the Wildcats. The school asked him for $45,363 in forfeited NCAA tournament revenues and banned him from the UA Sports Hall of Fame. Arizona said it did not know about the violations and only had to forfeit the 1999 NCAA tournament game, a 61-60 loss to Oklahoma. Terry was drafted 10th overall in the 1999 NBA draft by the Atlanta Hawks, with whom he played the first five seasons of his pro career. He was traded to the Dallas Mavericks in 2004 and helped the franchise reach the NBA Finals for the first time in its history in 2006. Fresh off winning the league's Sixth Man of the Year Award, Terry entered his 11th year as a pro in 2009-10.

JIM DAVIS

Miles Simon, left, and Bennett Davison join the Wildcats' on-court party in the wake of their improbable upset of No. 1-ranked Kansas in the 1997 Sweet 16.

# Wildcats to face first real tourney test in Jayhawks: Perfect game needed for UA to KO a killer KU

*Friday, March 21, 1997*

BIRMINGHAM, Ala.
Before anyone goes nuts over Arizona's success, please remember this is where the Wildcats should be. They have not been dependent upon karma to get to the Sweet 16.

This is not to diminish Arizona's tournament victories over South Alabama and College of Charleston-Cinderella. But the real test of a team as good as Arizona should not be against a squad from the Trans America Conference.

It should be, and will be, against Kansas. The Jayhawks have the best players, and everybody knows it.

The degree of difficulty is so imposing that if the Wildcats win tonight it could be regarded as the greatest victory in school history, surpassing (or at least equaling) the Final Four-clinching tearjerker over North Carolina in 1988.

The '97 Jayhawks may be the best team Arizona has ever played in the NCAA tournament, anytime, any year, anyplace, and that includes the '76 UCLA team that eliminated Arizona in the West Region finals (and then lost to Indiana at the Final Four).

Better than the 34-4 Oklahoma juggernaut of '88? Yes. Better than the 28-4 Missouri team of '94. Absolutely.

Better than the Arkansas national champions of '94? It's a tough call, but you get the idea. If Kansas goes on to win the title, the perspective will be upgraded.

The Jayhawks are nine deep and nasty, nothing at all like the syrupy, made-for-TV persona of their accomplished coach, Roy Williams.

"We have faced good teams (this season)," Lute Olson said yesterday, "but we haven't faced one as good as Kansas."

What is most humbling is that Olson has willingly invoked the perfect-game theory for the week. It will take a perfect game to beat Kansas. The Jayhawks, by comparison, have the greatest margin for error of the teams left standing in this March spectacle.

445

My one-man survey of the past 10 NCAA tournaments identifies just two teams superior to this Kansas club: last year's Kentucky Wildcats, and the 1991 UNLV team that had a 30-0 regular season and deployed, at core, three NBA lottery picks, Greg Anthony, Larry Johnson and Stacey Augmon.

None of the Laettner-Hurley-Hill Duke teams entered the Sweet 16 with the same aura of invincibility of this Kansas group. Close, yes. But better, no.

And yet, somehow, inconceivably, Kansas is being told that the Wildcats aren't paying proper homage to the mighty Jayhawk armada.

In the heartland this week, Kansans took great offense to what they construed as a no-respect theme coming out of Tucson. Olson exacerbated the issue by asking for clarification. "Who's David, and who's Goliath?" he asked.

Michael Dickerson and Miles Simon spoke bravely about their team's chances, and Jason Terry was widely quoted about his team's mission. "Payback," he said. Harmless stuff.

But by the time the Wildcats arrived in Alabama yesterday after-noon, all of the Kansas dailies were dispatching "trash talk/bulletin board warfare" stories back home.

In fact, the first question asked at Kansas' morning press confer-ence was on the topic of Arizona's brashness. "I don't worry about their approach," KU guard Jacque Vaughn said. "We're not as outspo-ken as a lot of other teams."

Vaughn has been informed, several times, that Dickerson said Stanford's Brevin Knight is a more formidable opponent. But you'd say that, too, if you had spent two nights chasing the Stanford point guard through a maze.

If Arizona is guilty of being outspoken, so is Martha Stewart.

Tonight's game won't spin on any pressroom rhetoric, but on the defensive pressure Kansas applies to Dickerson, Simon and Mike Bibby. "As a pair," Williams said yesterday, "Vaughn and (Jerod) Haase are the best defensive guards I've ever coached."

The Wildcats cannot win if Kansas neutralizes both Simon and Dickerson. Nor can they expect to win if Dickerson goes 4 for 20 as he did at Michigan; or 3 for 13, as he did at USC; or 5 for 16, as he did at UCLA; or 5 for 18 as he did at New Mexico; or 4 for 19, as he did at Cal.

Dickerson is the indicator. If he struggles, Arizona goes home. Such has been true all season.

Kansas has a few flaws, none of them as notable as, say, Arizona's strength in the paint. Kansas is as big, strong and deep up front as Cal — but with better players.

True, the Jayhawks are not a good perimeter-shooting team. But their three-point numbers match Arizona's — KU has made 182 treys, Arizona 194; KU shoots .378, Arizona .369.

The man to whom Arizona has no answer is Raef LaFrentz, KU's 6-foot-11-inch, 235-pound power forward. Consensus All-American. Lottery-pick-to-be. The most improved player in America.

LaFrentz scored one point in Kansas' 83-80 victory over Arizona in last year's Sweet 16 in Denver. Corey Williams took him apart. But the LaFrentz whom Arizona will see tomorrow is similar in jersey number only.

LaFrentz improved his field-goal percentage from 54 to 59 this year. His free-throw shooting climbed from 66 to 76 percent. His rebound average went from 8.2 to 9.3, and his scoring average from 13.4 to 18.6.

He is the difference. Put LaFrentz on Arizona's team, and the Wildcats soar to the Final Four. Put him opposite Arizona, and the Wildcats are reduced to the dim hope of playing a perfect game.

Still, I like two things about the Wildcats, and one of them is a fearless demeanor that stems from Simon's uncompromising personality. The second? I think Kansas is expecting a Jayhawk cakewalk in the Southeast Regional, with clear sailing ahead.

The Wildcats haven't gone quietly all season, and especially not against any of the five Sweet 16 teams they have played. Why start now?

DAVID SANDERS

Miles Simon, the Most Outstanding Player of the 1997 Final Four, shoots over the Kentucky defense en route to Arizona's win in the NCAA championship game.

# This was one for the ages

*Tuesday, April 1, 1997*

*INDIANAPOLIS*

The game never really ends now. It is in your heart forever, unceasing, a moment in time never to be forgotten.

You will summon to mind the glow of a three-week crusade in which Arizona's unprecedented run against the royal family of college basketball — Kansas, North Carolina and Kentucky — became one of the most remarkable testaments to heart and poise in the history of the game.

If you live in Tucson you will never again have to say, "Damn, that should have been us." Now you know what it is to be No. 1, and now you know that the winning exceeds the wanting.

"It was such a war," said Miles Simon, who, in the mad month of March, became the best amateur basketball player in the world. "It is the hardest thing I have ever done."

If you ever wanted to know what it is like somewhere over the rainbow, it is something like this: Lute Olson stood on the champions' platform on the middle of the court at the RCA Dome last night, his wife's red lipstick smeared around his mouth, a national title cap pulled taut over his mussed-up hair.

"Three No. 1 seeds went down," he said into the P.A. microphone, his eyes misting over. He said no more. The reaction from the 4,000 Arizona fans drowned out whatever else it was he wanted to say.

The holy trinity of Arizona basketball (or at least a passable version of it) crowded into the UA dressing room and let it be known that they, too, belonged to this championship party. Sean Elliott, Steve Kerr and Jud Buechler, denied the national title nine years ago in a suffocating blob of hurt in the 1988 Final Four, wanted to get a closer look at this fourth-seeded team that hardly did anything the easy way, which is precisely its charm.

"Losing (in '88) still hurts, it'll always hurt," said Kerr, "but this takes away a lot of the sting."

So in the end, Arizona's last game was its best game. It beat Kentucky 84-79 in overtime, never tapping the brakes, always advancing, refusing to submit to Kentucky's battalion of all-stars.

The chroniclers of the game will now have to revise history. No longer is Villanova's 1985 title unchallenged as the most inspiring, most

449

unexpected championship ever. 'Nova, a No. 8 seed, beat two No. 1 seeds and the defending national champion, Georgetown, for the title.

Arizona's route to the championship is, at worst, a photo finish for the top spot.

"This was one of the all-time marches," said UA assistant coach Phil Johnson. "Beating Kansas was like a national championship game to me. And then beating North Carolina was like a national championship game, too. It's almost like we had three national championship games. Every game was a mountain to climb, and I think that's why we won it all. We prepared for every game like it was THE game."

There will be no clamor for a refund.

Each of Arizona's six victories was excruciatingly tense. Two overtimes. Two more required comebacks from double-figure deficits in the final seven minutes. And two chess matches in which Olson moved his pieces to the right places before Dean Smith and Rick Pitino could figure it out.

"I may be a little bit biased," Olson said, "but I wish I could've been there as a spectator. It seemed to have everything you could want."

If Jermel President of College of Charleston makes a 12-foot jumper with four seconds remaining two weeks ago, Arizona goes home with a 20-10 record, a fifth-place Pac-10 team with reasonably good feelings about the season.

But Jermel President missed. Of such tales are championships made.

Last night Simon and Mike Bibby, the best backcourt in college basketball — and who would've thought that four weeks ago? — were superb. Most national champions find The Man to lead them through the six-game gantlet. Arizona found The Men.

Bibby's 6-0 run through the tournament was unsurpassed for performances-under-duress. It was as if, with five minutes to go, game slipping away, Olson would flip a switch and Bibby would bury a trey, beat a press, make a half-dozen free throws.

He became the first freshman point guard in history to start for a national champion. He wasn't even sure he believed it. "We thought we had a chance next year," he said, "but not this year."

Arizona's Road to Indianapolis actually began 14 years ago, on a warm April morning at McKale Center. That's when Cedric Dempsey, the school's athletic director, broke the bank to hire Olson away from Iowa.

Last night, Dempsey, now the executive director of the NCAA, stood at midcourt watching the UA cut down the nets, taking in the show.

"When I hired Lute," he said, "we talked about the opportunity to win the national championship someday. Did I really think it could be done? Sure, that's why I hired him. I really did.

"If you look at it, Lute has been the country's most successful coach over the last 10 years (he is No.1 in winning percentage) and I felt that under the right circumstances, he would someday get it done."

The right circumstances, believe it or not, involved the strangest confluence of all: a team with no seniors, a game shy of the Pac-10's second division, chopping down the game's redwoods, one after another, one as sure as another.

In the most important game in UA history, Donnell Harris and Bennett Davison made the plays in overtime that brought it to fruition.

On the bus from the team hotel 90 minutes before the game, Sean Elliott climbed aboard and delivered a final message. "Make sure you have fun," he told them. "Don't make this bigger than life."

But by beating Kentucky, at least for a few weeks or a few months, Arizona's basketball program takes on a larger-than-life aura. They will visit President Clinton at the White House. They will return home this afternoon to a parade and pep rally that may overflow the 58,000 seats at Arizona Stadium.

"I heard school is going to be closed on Wednesday," Davison said. "I'll bet they've never done that before for a basketball team."

DAVID SANDERS

Lute Olson can't contain his excitement and neither can his players during the second half of the UA's 84-79 overtime win over Kentucky.

# Wildcats' legacy made in March

*Friday, November 10, 2000*

In the wake of Arizona's shattering NCAA tournament loss to Utah in 1998, Lute Olson was quick to remind UA fans that the Wildcats won 30 games.

"I can't find a whole lot wrong with a 30-5 season," Olson said before departing The Pond in Anaheim, Calif., a 76-51 loser.

No one was buying it.

The '98 Wildcats returned the top seven players from their 1997 national championship. They expected history, not humiliation.

Same thing applies now. Thirty wins won't satisfy anyone. Arizona is hunting history.

How good are these guys?

No one is suggesting they will be the first team in 25 years to go undefeated, or that they will soon remind us of John Wooden's many national champions at UCLA.

No one has compared them to the indomitable 32-0 Indiana Hoosiers of 1976.

But on paper, this UA roster is better than the 1991 UNLV team, often labeled as college basketball's best team of the '90s. Larry Johnson, Stacey Augmon and Greg Anthony became No. 1 draft picks after the '91 season, but the Rebels' other starters, Anderson Hunt and Moses Scurry, were average. Their bench was inadequate.

On paper, Michael Wright can't match Larry Johnson, but it isn't that much of a gap. Richard Jefferson is no Augmon. Not yet. They are different players. Augmon was a slashing, transition player who played defense at an All-America level. Anthony, much like UA point guard Jason Gardner, was a tough son of a gun, unselfish and full of confidence.

But Gardner is better offensively.

In all other positions, from player Nos. 4-10, Arizona is better than the '91 Rebels. Jerry Tarkanian's team had nothing close to a resource like Loren Woods. Nothing resembling a two guard like Gilbert Arenas, or a bench with Luke Walton, Gene Edgerson and Justin Wessel.

But, alas, the '91 Rebs, much like the '98 Wildcats, failed to win the national title. A Duke team with six losses upset UNLV at the Final Four and the Rebels' place in history was diminished.

452

A year later, Duke won another NCAA championship, a 34-2 team blessed with Grant Hill, Christian Laettner and Bobby Hurley. It is Duke, not UNLV, that carries the label as Team of the '90s.

Arizona's current roster compares favorably to the '92 Blue Devils, a squad that buried Michigan 71-51 in the national championship game. Here's the shakedown:

Blue Devil coach Mike Krzyzewski is unorthodox in that he often doesn't define a lineup by the five accepted definitions. In other words, his '92 team lacked a center and essentially deployed a group of four wing players: Laettner, Thomas Hill, Grant Hill and Antonio Lang, with a point guard, Hurley. Laettner, versatile and smart, could play center or power forward and did. Grant Hill, a sophomore, could play anywhere. Duke's bench was thin: Cherokee Parks was adequate as a center. Brian Davis was a useful wing player.

Yet Duke went 28-2 in the '92 regular season and then ran the table with six NCAA tournament victories. Why? Because it made few mistakes, had an unmatched mental toughness and played defense better than anyone else.

There was no luck involved. The '92 Blue Devils beat SEC champ Kentucky to reach the Final Four and, once there, eliminated Big Ten runner-up Indiana.

Mix the '92 Blue Devils and '01 Wildcats, and you'd probably have a starting lineup with more Wildcats. And the bench would be dominated by Wildcats.

But what is yet to be determined over the course of four months are the intangibles: Will the Wildcats have the toughness, especially on defense, to win in March? Will they have the chemistry, the savvy, that is a characteristic of Krzyzewski's teams?

This UA team won't be judged on the regular season. A 30-5 record, or something similar, won't be viewed kindly if it doesn't include, at minimum, a Final Four appearance. At Arizona's level, regular seasons have become qualifying runs and not much more. Since Wooden retired a quarter-century ago, NCAA history hasn't been kind to regular-season powerhouses.

Check this statistic: From 1976 to 2000, there have been 12 major Division I teams go through the regular season with one defeat. All had date-with-destiny dreams. None – not a single one of the 12 – won a national championship.

That's how difficult it is.

Kansas went 32-1 in the '97 regular season. The Jayhawks were ranked No. 1 by everyone. And then along came Mike Bibby and Miles Simon, and the Jayhawks were reduced to a puddle of tears in the Sweet 16.

Similarly, the UA's 2000-01 season doesn't come with a tear-free guarantee. Don't judge this team by what it does in Maui or at UConn or Stanford. Wait until late March. That's when history awaits.

# Cats follow Lute's lead, show their toughness

*Monday, March 26, 2001*

*SAN ANTONIO*

Lute Olson put his arm around Sean Elliott's shoulders and walked with him to a quiet place adjacent to Arizona's crowded dressing room. When they thought they were away from prying TV cameras, the two men embraced.

Everyone wanted to hug the old coach, to keep him occupied, to keep his mind on what it is he has done and where it is he is going. His five children rarely left his side. His grandkids crawled on Papa Lute, happy faces all around. The wives of his assistant coaches, dabbing at teary eyes, hugged and held on. Steve Kerr. Matt Muehlebach. Jim Livengood.

It was a happy day, but it also one made sober to see a man so alone in a crowd.

The Rock upon which Arizona's basketball program rests, the 66-year-old coach who is making a solo journey for the first time in his distinguished career, showed no more emotion than he ever does when the Wildcats punch a Final Four ticket. Olson has eliminated some grand programs to reach earlier Final Fours — North Carolina, Georgetown, Missouri and Providence — but that was just basketball. This was life.

The toughest man at the Alamodome yesterday wasn't Loren Woods or Gene Edgerson or anyone wearing an Illinois uniform. It was Olson. His team followed his lead.

In a corridor outside Arizona's locker room, Olson's voice seemed to break for a brief moment when he was asked about the character of his team that three months ago was 8-5.

"Today's game," he said, "got down to where I thought the toughest team was going to be the winner."

There was no doubt that the Wildcats, 87-81 winners over the Illini in a game in which the meek could not have survived, were, as their coach, tough guys.

"There was nothing said like 'let's win one for Coach O,' but I think we won because of him," said Gilbert Arenas. "When I looked at

455

him today, I had a feeling of strength. Everything he told us about Illinois was the way it was."

Arizona was the aggressor, not big-shoulder, Big Ten Illinois. The Wildcats soared to a 21-10 lead and never took their foot off the gas.

Arizona won the inside game, the muscle game, in the second half when every possession was a pitched battle. The Wildcats outrebounded the Illini 22-17 in that period when, if you believed their national profile, they were expected to back down.

All of the statistical categories that are related to toughness — defense, rebounding, points in the paint — were won by the Wildcats. Richard Jefferson took out the Big Ten's best player, Illinois point guard Frank Williams, forcing him to miss 12 of 15 shots. Arizona scored 26 points in the paint, same as Illinois. But the Wildcats did so with 23 fewer field-goal attempts on the day.

Softies? Woods blocked seven shots, six in the second half.

A San Antonio columnist yesterday described Woods as "this stiff," and rattled on about what an ill fit he is in such a big event. Woods scored 16 points in the second half. If he didn't grab every rebound in the last five minutes, it seemed like he did.

When Woods needed to be tough or go home, he stood tall in a man's sense and not in a size sense.

"I didn't read that story," he said, beaming a smile that reached all the way back to his hometown of St. Louis. "But it doesn't matter. I'm going to the Final Four. They can write that about me up there."

Tough guys? The shortest man on the court, 5-9 UA point guard Jason Gardner, who historically plays like a giant when pressure goes off the chart, played 37 minutes against relentless defensive duress. He committed a single turnover. He took what were probably the two most significant shots of the game and made them both: a long three-pointer to break Illinois' momentum after the Illini took their first lead, 49-48; and an even longer trey to give the Wildcats a 62-56 lead with 5:34 remaining.

"That," said Illinois coach Bill Self, "was the shot of the game."

Gardner, who wears a game face to match that of his coach, did not enjoy the afternoon. He certainly enjoyed the flight home, but during the game he was too concerned about keeping the pressure on Illinois to soak in the magnitude of what it is to get to the Final Four.

"In timeouts," said UA assistant coach Jim Rosborough, "Jason took control. He was telling the guys what to do, making the calls. If he doesn't rise to the occasion, we don't win. The tougher the situation, the better he plays."

This was the most difficult of the four regional championship games Arizona has won. The Wildcats were clearly superior to the Tar Heels in '88, they routed Mizzou in '94, and although the '97 game against Providence went into overtime, the Friars didn't have the personnel Illinois has.

This took a coaching clinic by Olson and his assistants. Assigning Jefferson, and then Luke Walton, to guard Williams, rather than following convention and sending Arenas after him, was decided, assistant Jay John said, "in the first five seconds of Saturday's practice."

And for the first time this season, Olson went with Edgerson instead of Michael Wright in the last 10 minutes. Edgerson was more than just a spiritual leader, he was a one-man fortress, his don't-give-an-inch attitude contagious as he played 18 minutes, the most he has played since early December.

Plus, Olson believed in Woods when others did not.

"The strong survive," Edgerson said. "That's the only way it could be today."

EDITOR'S NOTE: Arizona routed Michigan State in the Final Four, winning 80-61 to reach the national championship game for only the second time in school history. Once there, the Wildcats lost to Duke 82-72.

RENEE SAUER

Luke Walton wades through a sea of UA fans at McKale Center following a 2002 win over UCLA. The Cats outscored the Bruins 43-13 in the final 13 minutes.

# Poor start becomes
# Game for the Ages

*Sunday, January 20, 2002*

Before hearing became impossible at McKale Center on Saturday, no one was more intense than UA junior manager Jack Murphy, his Irish eyes aflame, standing next to the Wildcats during pre-game layup drills.

Murphy would shout into the ear of one Wildcat after another, sort of like Bundini Brown psyching up Muhammad Ali before a big fight.

"This is our house!" he bellowed at Rick Anderson 10 minutes before tip-off. "They can't beat us here! You've got to attack 'em!"

But whatever Murph was selling, the Wildcats weren't buying. Almost unaccountably, the Wildcats were flat for the annual Game of the Year in Tucson, one that two hours later would become a Game for the Ages.

"You cannot come out thinking of the past," Lute Olson would say, citing his young team for getting caught up in Thursday's rousing victory over USC. "We were in serious, serious trouble."

Serious trouble is a 21-point deficit against Oregon State.

But "serious, serious" trouble is a 73-53 deficit against UCLA, 13 minutes on the clock. Better teams than the 2002 Bruins have played at McKale, but none has played better than UCLA for the first 27 minutes.

"We're supposed to be the team that scares other teams," UA junior Luke Walton said. He wouldn't say it, no one would, but the Wildcats were more than scared. They were impressed.

UCLA was good. Seriously, seriously good.

It wouldn't take a run to beat the Bruins. It would take a space launch.

And so, in the final 13 minutes at McKale, Arizona went into orbit. There has never been anything like it in Lute Olson's 19 seasons at the UA. Search the record books, review the videotapes, interview witnesses, you cannot top the UA's 96-86 victory in the category of Great Escapes.

"Chills went down my back," said Walton.

Olson, not given to hyperbole, gave the weekend sweep over USC and UCLA the ultimate definition.

459

"These (games) have to be as good as any we've ever had here," he said.

No one spoke up or disagreed.

At this time and place, given the personnel losses absorbed by Arizona and the strength of opposition, the coach is dead-on correct. Sweeping the Trojans and Bruins had become commonplace at Arizona — the Wildcats have done so 13 times under Olson — but on Saturday, freshmen played 45 percent of Arizona's minutes.

For the first time in memory, a split would have been acceptable.

"Maybe you figure in the back of your mind that you can come back from 20 down against Oregon State," said assistant coach Jim Rosborough. "But from 20 down against UCLA?"

This wasn't some cosmic interference or random fluke. I mean, Arizona wiped out UCLA's 20-point lead in THREE minutes. You get hot periodically. This wasn't getting hot. This was storming the fort and taking no prisoners.

It was as if adrenaline was on sale at the concession stands, and everybody but UCLA had some.

Those in Los Angeles will cry that UCLA coach Steve Lavin lost it; that he had no answer to Olson's implementation of a three-guard defensive press that unalterably changed the game and gave Arizona a chance to rally.

Lavin gets no respect as a coaching tactician, and justifiably so, but he was fighting a few intangibles. One was the McKale crowd, which rose to the occasion and remained energized early in the second half when UCLA actually expanded its 15-point halftime lead.

"This is the loudest place in the country," said UCLA senior Matt Barnes, who has been at some of the country's most ear-piercing basketball arenas. "It was a great atmosphere and home-court advantage."

The game turned when UCLA relaxed at the precise time Arizona turned up its tempo to blur-speed. Jason Gardner, Salim Stoudamire — anybody else recommend Stoudamire as the leading contender for Pac-10 Freshman of the Year? — and Will Bynum so rattled UCLA's ball-handlers that the Bruins played the final 13 minutes in a state of panic.

Oh, Arizona hasn't seen the last of UCLA yet. It still must play at Pauley Pavilion next month, and a third game, at the Pac-10 tournament in L.A., is likely. UCLA will get better. It still has the look of a Final Four contender.

All of that was meaningless Saturday.

The UA's victory was a down payment on its future. Most of the analysts project the Wildcats to return as a monster team next year and certainly in 2004. Saturday's comeback accelerated those projections.

This resourceful young team continues to find a way to win when all seems lost. It's not much of a stretch to see how Arizona's 13-4 record could be much worse. The message seems to be: Don't underestimate this club.

"There was a lot of enjoyment out there," Gardner said. "It was a great win."

This is one time the adjective "great" merits use.

EDITOR'S NOTE: The youth-laden Wildcats tied for second in the Pac-10's regular-season standings, then promptly won the conference tournament to reach the 20-win plateau for the 15th straight season. Victories over UC-Santa Barbara and Wyoming put Arizona in the NCAA tournament's Sweet 16, where it lost to Oklahoma 88-67.

JAMES S. WOOD

From left, UA players Fil Torres, Jason Ranne and Isaiah Fox cheer during the final moments of the Cats' stunning come-from-behind win at Kansas in 2003.

# Wildcats now clearly favored to win it all

*Sunday, January 26, 2003*

*LAWRENCE, Kan.*
Arizona beat Kansas in a game of much greater consequence six years ago. It was a Sweet 16 game in Alabama, and the Wildcats outplayed the best Jayhawks team in 50 years.

Beating Kansas on that night was currency; it paid for the UA's berth in the Final Four and, ultimately, the 1997 national championship.

KU coach Roy Williams wept after the game, crushed, uncertain he would ever so clearly possess the nation's No. 1 team again. It all slipped through his grasp, a 34-1 start, an extraordinary blend of four future NBA players, in 40 minutes.

On the last day of January 1997, Kansas was 21-0. It had won a game 134-73. It went to UConn and won. It pounded UCLA and Cincinnati. It was all instantly diminished on a Friday night in Birmingham, Ala.

Six years later, beaten at home 91-74 by No. 1 Arizona, Williams neither wept nor felt helpless. The Jayhawks have about 50 days to gather themselves and make preparations for the NCAA tournament, which, frankly, Kansas could win as easily as anyone else.

The sense of opportunity this time belongs to Arizona coach Lute Olson, who left historic Allen Fieldhouse on Saturday with much more than a triumph that left him, his team and his town positively aglow.

The Wildcats are now the favorite, plainly so, to win it all. There will be no backing off.

Given the venue and the quality of competition, Arizona surely played its best second half in school history Saturday (regular-season division). Olson's Iowa team beat Georgetown in a near-perfect second half to advance to the 1980 Final Four, and his Arizona teams have rallied to beat highly ranked Stanford, UCLA and Duke teams in the last decade.

But Saturday's comeback stretched the limits of sports belief. Said Olson, who is not prone to exaggeration: "This is the toughest place I've had a team play."

The meek did not inherit this game.

"I've never seen anything like it," said UA center Channing Frye. "It was ridiculous. I've never heard a crowd so loud. Just ridiculous."

Williams defined his team's first-half performance as "sensational." Sensational? That's not quite justice to how well KU played.

Keith Langford scored on an alley-oop 5½ minutes before halftime. Kansas led 44-24. The joyful reaction at Allen Fieldhouse wasn't a roar; it was more like thunder.

It wasn't difficult to read the grim faces on Arizona's bench.

"Hey, at halftime, maybe we can sneak out the back door and get out of town."

During a timeout, in the bedlam, facing embarrassment, Olson and his assistant coaches knew they had to change strategies. Kansas had positively exploited Arizona's man-defense, turning the first 20 minutes into a layup drill. (How does 65 percent shooting sound?)

"We put Salim (Stoudamire) at the top of our 1-3-1 defense, something we hadn't worked on longer than three minutes all year," said associate head coach Jim Rosborough. "We needed to get some longer arms on the wings. Rick Anderson and Luke Walton. We had to stabilize things and not let the (deficit) get any greater. I'm telling you, it looked bleak, didn't it?"

With Stoudamire at the top of the defense, and Jason Gardner running the baseline against players a foot taller, the game subtly began to change. Kansas' shooters no longer got uncontested shots. By stopping KU on the perimeter, Arizona also took away the Jayhawks' inside game.

The Pac-10's decades-old rap of being soft did not apply Saturday.

Olson defined his team's comeback with two words: toughness, togetherness.

"It was one of the greatest games I've ever been involved in," said Rosborough, a Division I coach for 28 years. "We adjusted almost by the seat of our pants. We haven't used that zone defense for about five years."

It's one thing to beat Kansas in Lawrence in a buzzer finish. It's another to outscore the Jayhawks 67-30 in a 25½-minute finish. It requires depth, which Arizona has in abundance over the thin Jayhawks. And it requires extraordinary talent, which the UA has more so, perhaps, than at any time in school history.

Stoudamire and Gardner were superb, which is hardly big news. Gardner has been the best Big Game player in college basketball over the last four seasons. Stoudamire ached for 13 months to redeem his 2-for-19 shooting performance in last season's home loss to Kansas.

Saturday's best news? Olson said that he and Williams have agreed to continue the series, on a home-and-home basis, "immediately."

"It's a win-win situation, even if we had lost," Olson said. "You have to play in that Big Game feel, in this kind of environment, and you have to play against great teams."

Arizona is not yet a great team. But on Saturday, it took a mighty step toward becoming one.

EDITOR'S NOTE: Arizona finished the regular season 25-3 as Pac-10 champions and the No. 1-ranked team in America. The Wildcats were given a No. 1 seed in the West Region of the NCAA tournament. After winning their first three games, the Cats were faced with a rematch against Kansas in the Elite Eight in Anaheim, Calif. Kansas won 78-75 to reach the Final Four, and the UA ended its season 28-4.

KELLY PRESNELL

Arizona's Jawann McClellan is consoled by Illinois' Luther Head, whose team's furious rally in the final minutes led to the UA's ouster in the Elite Eight in 2005.

# Several ways to feel, but not sorry

*Sunday, March 27, 2005*

*ROSEMONT, Ill.*

The door to Arizona's locker room opened after a 10-minute cry and out came Channing Frye, in tears, followed by Salim Stoudamire, his eyes red and puffy.

Lute Olson was third. He hugged his wife, Christine, and softly said "sorry." He followed Frye and Stoudamire down a flight of stairs, the season over.

Sorry? No need to be sorry for a 30-win season and an epic game against No. 1 Illinois. Maybe "sad" would've fit better. Maybe "stunned."

Someone asked Frye if he was stunned by Illinois' rally from a 15-point deficit in the final four minutes of regulation and a chaotic 90-89 overtime victory.

He nodded, never looking up.

"We can't be unstunned," he said. "The game's over and we can't do anything about it. There's no more McKale Center. There's no more Bear Down. I'm sorry I disappointed the fans."

There's that nasty word again. Sorry.

Arizona shouldn't be sorry about winning a Pac-10 championship, knocking out second-seeded Oklahoma State in the Sweet 16 and, for about 38 minutes Saturday night, playing like a potential national champion.

But the Wildcats and their fans should indeed be sad, stunned and shocked by the terrible way it all unraveled in a blur of mistakes and panic. Arizona was engulfed by one of the great rallies in college basketball history, a historic comeback by what looks to be a team of destiny.

"It just seemed like we were dying," said Illinois coach Bruce Weber.

Arizona lost, but nobody died. That's the good news. In a basketball context, the Wildcats have probably never had more reason to grieve. Oh, perhaps there was more sorrow at the 1989 Sweet 16, a last-shot loss to UNLV, when the Wildcats were No. 1 and Sean Elliott sobbed for 10 minutes at the end of his college career.

But this one will hurt for years, a decade or more.

"We'll look at the end of the game for a long time from a coaching standpoint," said Olson. "There are a number of things that are going to cause a lot of sleepless nights for everyone."

In the litter of broken hearts in the UA dressing room, the most sobering fact was that Illinois played superb defense in the last 11.8 seconds of Arizona's season. Olson and his staff eschewed a plan that would put the final play in Stoudamire's hands. Given the way the game had evolved, with Frye and Hassan Adams making a cumulative 20 of 27 shots, a nightmare matchup for the Illinois defense, it made sense to punch a Final Four ticket with Adams and Frye, with Stoudamire as a decoy.

"It was designed for Hassan to take it to the basket, dribble into the lane and either shoot, get fouled or pass to Channing," Stoudamire said. "But Deron Williams did a great job of cutting it off."

After all the misplays in the final four minutes of regulation, Arizona could've erased it all in the final 11.8 seconds.

Adams was covered, Frye was boxed out, and Stoudamire wasn't in the play.

"It just slipped away," said Adams, who probably played his best — and final — college game. "Salim was covered."

Until the final play of Arizona's season, Salim was never covered when the Wildcats absolutely, positively needed to win a game. But Illinois (36-1) isn't UCLA, which left Stoudamire free for a game-winning try. And Illinois, with the crowd roaring its approval, isn't Arizona State, which allowed Stoudamire to get deep into the paint from where he hit a jumper to win the Pac-10 title.

And Illinois isn't Oklahoma State, which ended its season by allowing Stoudamire to dribble and shoot at the worst possible time.

"I don't know what happened," said Frye. "We had a mental breakdown, but I don't want to make excuses. Illinois played great when it had to, but I feel like crap now. It's like running a marathon and not going the last mile."

UA fans will have the next six months (and probably the next six years) to chew on the Wildcats' failure to close out the Illini. They had played a perfect game. Their defensive quickness, size and execution were dazzling. Adams and Frye were fabulous. Olson's decision to play a small lineup, inserting Jawann McClellan for Ivan Radenovic, was genius. Mustafa Shakur was outstanding.

But in the end, it came down to Stoudamire's 2-for-13 shooting performance, the exact number that Steve Kerr shot at the 1988 Final Four, a monumentally bad moment to play the worst game of his career.

And thus, history repeated. The two best shooters in school history went out 2 for 13, tears everywhere, lamenting what could have been.

"This is extremely hard for me," Olson said, "but it's harder for the kids because I've been there before. My disappointment is for them, not for me."

Either way, Arizona's season has ended in the most painful way possible. Feel free to have a good cry for the next six months.

# From the first stanza, Cats' effort far from well-versed

Sunday, January 28, 2007

*The outlook wasn't brilliant for the Tucson five that day.*
*The score stood 43 to 25 with but one half more to play.*
*Then from 14,000 throats there arose a lusty yell.*
*It rambled through the rafters, rattled through McKale.*
*It echoed off the Tar Heels and recoiled through Zona's Zoo.*
*For Arizona, mighty Arizona, was turning Carolina blue.*
*And then Mustafa missed another trey, and Ivan did the same.*
*A pall-like silence quickly fell upon the patrons at the game.*
*Oh, once Cat fans were eager, for this North Carolina date.*
*But there is no joy in Tucson, for the Wildcats lost by 28.*

If you are a North Carolina fan, Saturday's 92-64 victory over Arizona was poetry.

The Tar Heels were so overpowering they made the Wildcats appear:

Helpless.

Hopeless.

Hapless.

If you are an Arizona fan, you probably wish Ernest Lawrence Thayer, author of "Casey at the Bat," had some eligibility left.

Ernest has been dead for 67 years, but, c'mon, even a corpse could stick one three-pointer in 23 attempts.

All but lifeless themselves, the Wildcats played the worst home game of the Lute Olson era. They were all the things they have rarely been on that hallowed floor: intimidated, skittish, out of control, looking for a place to hide.

Olson was dumbfounded.

"It's like, 'Whose team is this?' " he asked, rhetorically. "We looked like a team that was trying to do everything wrong."

The Tar Heels had 12 dunks and 21 layups. Four times they intercepted UA inbounds passes after making a basket. It looked easy.

They put on a clinic of toughness, beating the Wildcats with screens, box-outs, pushes and shoves. North Carolina was always hitting the accelerator, relentless, a team of interchangeable parts setting a

470

pace that wore the Wildcats flat.

"After the first four minutes," said Jawann McClellan, "I was tired."

Said Ivan Radenovic: "I can't explain it. Maybe I was tired."

Olson agreed that UNC was the best visiting team he has seen at McKale. "Ever," he added.

It was shocking as much as it was unprecedented.

In all of Olson's Arizona years, his teams had never failed to strike back. They lost 90-80 to the best team in Oregon history in 2002, but, playing without Luke Walton that night, they still pushed the Ducks to the end.

They lost 71-61 here to UCLA's 1995 national champions, but they battled to the buzzer.

On Saturday? It was a surrender.

"In a day's time, I think our team will forget about it," UA freshman Chase Budinger said.

Alas, it probably won't be that simple. How do you forget 40 minutes of horror? Saturday's game is more likely to be a scar on the UA's psyche for the rest of the season. Being humbled is one thing. Being embarrassed is another.

The Wildcats were hopeful they would run into the Tar Heel club that lost its focus two weeks ago in a stunning loss to Virginia Tech, a game in which it trailed by more than 20 points. They were hopeful the loss of 6-9 super freshman Brandan Wright, ill with a stomach problem Saturday, would shake UNC's soul.

None of that happened; the Tar Heels are deeper than the Hoover Dam.

"From our film study, you can see that something changed after that Virginia Tech game," said associate head coach Jim Rosborough. "The next two games they were just brutal; they absolutely went after people with a killer instinct.

"They just barrel into you, play after play. They don't have those lulls that have hurt us so much. It's, boom, they're there, right in your face. They have the killer instinct that we lack."

From Jan. 14 to Jan. 20, Arizona suspected it had played against, and been torched by, the two leading point guards in college hoops. Oregon's Aaron Brooks and UCLA's Darren Collison dazzled the Wildcats with speed, clutch shooting and leadership.

But neither Collison nor Brooks played as well as UNC freshman Ty Lawson did Saturday. Holy smokes. Did you see him blow past anyone and everyone who attempted to guard him? He outscored every Arizona player on the floor, and, more importantly, passed for eight assists, stole the ball from Mustafa Shakur four times and had just one turnover.

And Lawson didn't even get tired. The Heels are so deep he played a scant 30 minutes.

Olson didn't predict that the Tar Heels are going to breeze to another national championship, but he did use "very" three times when he described UNC as "very, very, very good.

"They're the team at the top of the heap," he said. "Everyone tries to get where they are."

Had UA played its best game, shooting 50 percent instead of 34, cutting turnovers from 20 to 10 — and being fortunate enough to keep Marcus Williams healthy and on the court for 35 minutes, not 20 — it probably still couldn't have beaten the Tar Heels.

North Carolina belongs to a higher league — the one the Wildcats vacated Saturday afternoon.

EDITOR'S NOTE: Arizona went 6-3 the rest of the way in the 2006-07 regular season, but the Wildcats stumbled thereafter. They were routed by Oregon in the first round of the Pac-10 tournament, then quickly exited the NCAA tournament with a first-round loss to Purdue. It was the last game Lute Olson ever coached, although it took 19 months for the UA's distinguished coach to officially retire.

# No splitting hairs,
# these Wildcats are 'rewarding'

*Friday, February 13, 2009*

OK, nobody shave. Nobody tempt the basketball gods. This replacement-team-makes-good story has crossed the line and become more than just some unexpected fun.

Ladies and gentlemen, start your dreams. And why not?

Nobody wants to hear about the UCLA-ASU-Washington gantlet that awaits the Wildcats. Not a word about Jordan Hill's aching ankles. The UA is deep into February and all is well.

Who says the Wildcats can't beat UCLA on Saturday? Or the Sun Devils in Tempe after that?

I'm not going to be the one to tell them this rise to glory has its limits.

Here's how much this has caught on: On Thursday night, 14,728 people paid to enter McKale Center. It was the third-largest crowd in McKale history. This is such fun that the school could probably sell 25,000 tickets for Saturday's UCLA game.

"In many ways, this is one of our most rewarding wins," UA interim head coach Russ Pennell said.

You cannot doubt Pennell — his credibility is off the charts — but there is some confusion; in the last two months there have been so many "rewarding wins" that you have difficulty keeping them in order.

Kansas. Yes.

Gonzaga. Certainly.

Washington. Fabulous.

The comeback against Houston? Superb.

But Thursday's rally to beat USC 83-76 was as charming as any, and, perhaps, as unlikely.

"I said this the other day to someone, 'Chemistry is the hardest thing to find in sports, but when you find it, you can do some great things,'" said Pennell.

Beating USC isn't a great thing; the Trojans are neither ranked nor widely feared. But in the context of this fractured Arizona basketball program — and the way the Wildcats won Thursday — go ahead, use "great."

The Wildcats essentially won without a third of the Big Three;

473

Hill's ankles were so sore that he could barely move. But who says they have to have a Big Three to win?

They won Thursday with the Big Two, Nic Wise and Chase Budinger combining for 52 points. Wise was so good down the stretch that, in his honor, it wouldn't be wrong to say The Little One Shall Lead Them.

At least he did on Thursday. His three-pointer with 43.9 seconds remaining broke a tie at 76 and, for all purposes, won a game that seconds earlier Arizona seemed sure to lose.

How did a team that was 11-8 and on life support as recently as Jan. 24 find happiness?

Pennell said: "No. 1, we work harder. We hustle more."

Budinger said: "We're just a totally better team."

A lot of that is on Budinger, who has never played better. In this six-game winning streak he has scored, in order, 15, 25, 19, 17, 25 and 25.

Budinger has become a tough sonofagun just in time. He has become an emotional leader.

"First of all, it was a very physical game," he said. "When that tends to happen, your emotions come out. It was one of those up-and-down-type games. For us, we just use the crowd. The crowd erupted, and we just used that to our advantage.

"I feel our team is more confident down the stretch of games now."

On the game's first possession, before the adrenaline had begun to flow, Hill put his size 15 Nike in the wrong space at the wrong time.

It was the space in which USC's Taj Gibson planted his oversize sneaker a split second later, pinning Hill's left foot to the ground. As Hill started to maneuver for position under Arizona's basket, his left leg was trapped. His ankle momentarily buckled.

Only Hill noticed.

By halftime he could barely move his left ankle. USC had rallied, trailing just 41-38, and Hill had one rebound and three free throws. Here's how out of character that was: Hill is averaging 18.3 points and 11.3 rebounds. He is the first Pac-10 player to average a double-double this decade, and the first at Arizona since Larry Demic in 1978-79.

When the Trojans extended their lead to 58-50, Arizona had one chance. Hill had to forget the pain and play hard.

"You could just tell on the way he was running, by his facial expressions that he was hurting pretty bad," Budinger said. "He competed for us. He manned up tonight, especially in the second half and played like a beast. He was our defensive key. He got a lot of rebounds and blocked a lot of shots."

Said Pennell: "We kept asking for more in the second half, and Jordan gave it."

Hill finished with 12 points and five rebounds, far below his averages, but he kept a lot of loose balls alive under the basket during Arizona's rally. Incredibly, he played 39 minutes. A good guess is that he won't be able to walk much today, and perhaps, be limited Saturday against the Bruins.

The beauty about college sports is that, suddenly, out of nowhere, Saturday's game is meaningful on a national scale to both teams.

"You have to be careful or winning can become a poison," Pennell said with a tone of caution. "We made a lot of mistakes in the game tonight, and those are mistakes that we have to correct.

"And you've got the No. 6 team in the country coming in here off a loss. That should get your attention. We won't be overconfident."

And nobody will be clean-shaven, either.

EDITOR'S NOTE: Arizona beat UCLA, but its winning streak ended in its next game, at Arizona State. That began a four-game losing skid. Despite a 1-5 finish to the Pac-10 season, the Wildcats garnered a berth in the NCAA tournament for the 25th consecutive year. Their selection to the Big Dance despite a 19-13 record created a minor controversy, but the Cats proved their worth by beating Utah and Cleveland State to advance to the Sweet 16. There, they were trounced by Louisville 103-64 – the worst loss in the UA's tournament history. After the season, Chase Budinger and Jordan Hill left school early to play in the NBA. Russ Pennell was hired as the new head coach at Grand Canyon University, a Division II school in Phoenix.

# INDEX

Made in the USA
Charleston, SC
03 December 2009